Business in an Information Economy

DAVID GRAF, Ph.D

Professor and Chairperson
Department of Business Systems and Analysis
Northern Illinois University
Dekalb, Illinois

OLIVE D. CHURCH, Ph.D

Professor of Business and Economic Education
Department of Vocational Education
University of Wyoming
Laramie, Wyoming

THOMAS B. DUFF, Ph.D

Professor and Head
Department of Finance and Information Sciences
University of Minnesota
Duluth, Minnesota

GREGG DIVISION
McGRAW-HILL PUBLISHING COMPANY

New York   Atlanta   Dallas   St. Louis   San Francisco
Auckland   Bogotá   Caracas   Hamburg   Lisbon
London   Madrid   Mexico   Milan   Montreal   New Delhi
Paris   San Juan   São Paulo   Singapore
Sydney   Tokyo   Toronto

Sponsoring Editor: Larry Wexler
Editing Supervisor: Melonie Parnes
Design and Art Supervisor: Caryl Valerie Spinka
Production Supervisor: Catherine Bokman

Text Designer: Nancy Sugihara
Cover Designer: PLK
Cover photograph: COMSTOCK, Inc.

Library of Congress Cataloging-in-Publication Data

Graf, David.
  Business in an information economy.

  Includes index.
  1. Business.   2. Management.   I. Church, Olive D.,
date.   II. Duff, Thomas.   III. Title.
HF5351.G655   1990   650   88-32584

ISBN 0-07-010900-1

  2 3 4 5 6 7 8 9 0   VH VH   8 9 6 5 4 3 2 1 0 9

ISBN 0-07-010900-1

Contents

iii

Preface

Enrollments in postsecondary schools of business are at an all-time high. Business degrees are considered desirable by men and women alike. Standards for admission to business colleges are often competitively based—and competitive standards are maintained even after students are admitted to the school of their choice. Other students graduate from high school, gain work experience, and form their own businesses. Their background in basic business principles may be woefully weak. This lack of formal business education adds one more time constraint to the hectic process of getting their businesses off the ground.

Students of business and young entrepreneurs often lament the fact that they had not selected a business course in high school. Worse, they might have elected a business course in high school if they could have found one with a strong business administration base. Many high schools have Business Principles, Business Management, Business Analysis, or similar courses, but teachers have had difficulty finding an appropriate text. *Business in an Information Economy* has been written to fill a void—the need for a text that incorporates economic and technology concepts within an established base of business administration principles to help prepare students to study, work, and interact with the business community.

This textbook and its supplements (teacher's course guide and key, student activity guide, and test booklet) are part of a program designed to provide factual business and economic information to help students reach responsible adulthood. The academic content is relevant and suitably rigorous. But the program does more than pass on relevant information about business and economic subjects. The selective use of information briefs, technology features, text illustrations, end-of-chapter and end-of-unit textbook exercises, and study guide materials, provides the motivation to students so that they can become involved in American business and economic activities. The content and activities of the program will be a decided plus as students begin to cope with life and work in our complex information-driven economy.

Objectives of the Program

The primary purpose of the program is to provide students with a realistic view of American business within our economic system. Business in an Information Economy takes a careful look at the ownership of businesses of all sizes. All the functional areas of business—management, finance and accounting, marketing, human resources, production of goods and services, and information systems—are examined. Each functional area is placed in an economic and technological context, thereby giving students a well-rounded portrait of contemporary business. The social and legal environment of business (taxation, regulation, and ethical considerations) as well as the global dimensions of business operations are examined in order to provide as complete a picture as possible within the framework of a one- or two-term course.

The second purpose of Business in an Information Economy is to present the business side of decision making. Business decision making necessarily includes:

- Analytical skills
- Communication skills
- Computer and technology skills
- Human relations skills
- Problem-solving skills
- Resource management skills

These decisions-making skills address business problems as opposed to consumer problems. Students learn what it takes to make a business successful, what economic questions face all businesses, how best to organize a business, how a business manages its finances, what techniques businesses use to market products and services, and how businesses manage their most important resources—people, materials, and information.

The third purpose of the program is to address the need to develop critical thinking skills. Critical thinking skills are necessary to convert data into useful information so that individuals and organizations can make goal-oriented decisions. These same skills are also needed to separate facts from opinion, truth from partial truth, and emotion from rational thinking. Such skills are particularly vital to business decision makers because they are exposed to a seemingly constant flood of contradictory data in this era of rapid communication.

In this program, students develop critical thinking skills as they participate in activities that also build comprehension, interpretation, reading, and communication skills. For example, each chapter includes case material for student analysis and interpretation and other end-of-chapter exercises that enable students to demonstrate critical thinking by reporting—and communicating orally or in writing—findings from interviews, observations in the business community, outside readings, and research.

Organization of the Text

Business in an Information Economy is divided into seven units. Unit 1, Business in America, provides an exciting overview of "why the business of America is business." The first chapter introduces students to the different classifications of business enterprises, the importance of entrepreneurship, and the role of small business ownership. A stimulating review of business history follows, adding a distinctive color and perspective to today's business environment. Students learn how and why our economy has become information-based.

Unit 2, The Economic Environment of Business, includes an extensive discussion of the basic economic concepts, principles, and practices that move our market system. The dimension of a global economy enhances the more traditional "rules of the game."

Unit 3, Organization and Management of Business, provides a starting point for the examination of the functional areas of business. A discussion of business structures, a description of the social and legal environment of business, and an explanation of the role that management plays in all business enterprises prepare the student for a more detailed look at the functional areas of business which follows.

Units 4 to 7 delve into the specifics of business operations. Chapters 9 to 20 introduce and provide practical advice on finance, accounting, risk management and insurance, marketing, human resources management, production and operations, and information systems. Each chapter provides basic terminology, incorporates real-life examples, and concludes with exercises and case material reflecting the kinds of problems businesspeople face. The last chapter, "Careers in an Information Economy," brings matters down to a more personal level by focusing student attention on career opportunities in business and the need to begin preparing now—academically and otherwise—for that day when they become full and active participants in the business community or the labor market.

Special Features of the Text

Each unit is introduced through a strong visual image and unit objectives. A discussion of the unit theme sets the stage for the chapters that follow. A *mock newspaper or magazine article,* based on real-life business sources, opens each chapter and is designed to capture the reader's attention. The situation or concepts introduced in the article are then expanded in the case study at the end of that chapter. The case study concludes with questions that require students to utilize analytical, interpretative, decision-making, and other skills. Similarly, an end-of-unit reading, case study, or project provides a capstone to each of the text's seven units.

In each chapter *feedback questions or short situations* are interspersed among short reading segments. These questions, which are set off by blue rules, are designed to pique the students' interest and help them develop self-analytical skills as they advance through the chapters. They are also intended to help students deal with business situations within the affective domain of learning—that is, they often incorporate difficult business decisions and choices which have no clear right or wrong answer. In such cases, one's values and attitudes may affect the decisions or choices that one makes. These questions help students recognize the values and attitudes that might shape their own business viewpoint and have an impact on their own decision making.

Information Briefs (or Career Briefs in Chapter 20) are liberally interwoven into the side margins of the text. These briefs have been structured to clarify content, provide real-life examples of the concepts and practices described in each chapter, and introduce business media to students. They have been written in a compact newspaper style for easy reading.

The discussion of the information economy would be incomplete without highlighting the role of technology. Thus, each chapter includes a *Technology Feature* (Technology in an Information Economy) to illustrate how technology—computers, compact disks, cellular telephones, and the like—are changing the way business and work are conducted today.

End-of-Chapter and End-of-Unit Activities

Each chapter and each unit concludes with exercises that enable students to demonstrate learning in various ways and at different levels. The answers to *Select Terms to Know* and *Review Questions* are found directly in the text material. Fundamentally, they help students demonstrate learning at the recall level.

The *Select Terms to Know* exercise is intended to help students build a strong business vocabulary. Defined terms are highlighted in boldface type throughout the text. Students may cull the definitions from these boldfaced terms or refer to the *Glossary/Index* at the back of the text, which has definitions of over 350 key terms.

Thought and Discussion Questions go beyond the recall and comprehension level to the application and problem-solving level. *Projects* are in-class or out-of-class activities designed to reinforce critical thinking skills. Most of these activities can be completed by students individually. However, in some situations students are required to work together in small teams or groups. In either case, the Projects can serve as useful tools for bringing "business action" into the classroom.

The *Case Study* at the end of every chapter develops student learning at the highest level—analysis and decision making. Each case is crafted from a realistic business situation. Most of the case study questions relate specifically to the subject matter in a particular chapter and ask students to make business judgments and decisions based on informed analysis.

A culminating activity, a *Unit Reading, Case Study,* or *Project,* concludes each unit. These activities enable students to tie together the learning derived in each chapter of a given unit, the business and economic fundamentals accumulated throughout the course, and practical experiences.

Course Supplements

The supplemental *Study Guide* is a natural extension of the textbook. Terms and review questions have been turned into helpful objective review questions. Projects and cases found in the text provide the opportunity for the highest levels of learning. The study guide continues and expands this theme with all *new* activities, projects, and cases. The *Test Booklet* has been carefully constructed to measure learning outcomes. Each question is drawn from the text with care and attention to testing principles and business content.

The *Teacher's Manual and Key* has been written to guide the teacher in orchestrating the entire *Business in an Information Economy* program. It presents the rationale for a new Business Principles and Management course based on content that (1) realistically portrays contemporary business and (2) is relevant to the needs of today's students. The goals and philosophy for this course are presented. Specific course outlines and sample lesson plans are also included. General and specific teaching ideas are outlined for the course and for each chapter. Most important, the philosophy, background, and answers behind each of the projects, situations, and cases are provided as practical aids for the relatively new as well as the experienced teacher.

"Open for Business" Videotape Program

A special educational version of *Open for Business,* a videotape program developed by Maryland InTec (Maryland Instructional Television) is available through Gregg/McGraw-Hill and can be used to complement *Business in an Information Economy.* The video program, which is accompanied by a student manual and a teacher's manual, can be used most effectively by teachers who want to reinforce or expand upon concepts in the text relating to small business ownership and entrepreneurship.

Dr. David Graf
Dr. Olive D. Church
Dr. Thomas B. Duff

Acknowledgments

Reviewers

The authors wish to give special thanks to the following individuals who reviewed the manuscript and offered many constructive suggestions for improvement.

- Laurie K. Collier, Director, Vocational and Business Education, Newport News Public Schools, Newport, Virginia.
- Dr. Gary O. Hall, Chairperson and Instructor, Business Education, Tempe High School, Tempe, Arizona.
- Louise Petraglia, Acting Chairperson of Curriculum and Teaching Department, Hofstra University, Hempstead, New York; formerly Director, Business Education and Work Experience, Mineola High School, Mineola, New York.

Advisory Board, National Conference on Basic Business

The inspiration and many of the ideas for this program came from the National Conference on Basic Business held by the Gregg Division in August 1985. The Conference brought together nationally recognized leaders in business education to chart a new direction for Basic Business, Business Principles, Business Management, and other related courses for the 1990s.

Business in an Information Economy was an outgrowth of the Conference's recommendations. For helping to shape the philosophy, pedagogy, and core content of this program, the authors express their deep gratitude to the following individuals who served as members of the Advisory Board of the National Conference:

- Lois Anderson, Utah State Business Education/Technology Specialist, Utah State Office of Education, Salt Lake City, Utah
- Dr. Kenneth W. Brown, Chairperson, Department of Business Technology, University of Houston, Houston, Texas
- Dr. Michael G. Curran, Jr., Manager of Vocational Programs Bureau, State Department of Education; Trenton, New Jersey
- Clara-Lea Gaston, Adviser, Vocational Business Education, Bureau of Vocational and Adult Education, State Department of Education, Harrisburg, Pennsylvania

- Ann Masters, Administrator of Vocation Programs, Nebraska Department of Education, Lincoln, Nebraska
- Dr. James L. Morrison, Professor of Consumer Economics and Vocational Education, College of Human Resources, University of Delaware, Newark, Delaware
- Professor Gary Seiler, Business Administration Department, College of St. Catherine, St. Paul, Minnesota
- Dr. Margaret M. Beilkee, Project Director, Business and Marketing Education, Oregon State University, Corvallis, Oregon
- Sandra Yelverton, State Specialist, Business Education, State Department of Education, Montgomery, Alabama

Colleagues and Family

The authors also want to thank those colleagues who proofread the manuscript with a critical eye and made meaningful comments and suggestions. Finally, the authors want to pay special tribute to their spouses and families. They gave up time that otherwise might have been spent together with us, thereby enabling us to participate in this worthwhile enterprise. In a very real and personal sense, their sacrifice and continuing encouragement made it all possible.

Photo Credits

© Bettmann Archive: 5. © Pattie McConville, Image Bank: 10. Courtesy of Egghead Discount Software: 16. Courtesy of IBM Corp.: 20. © Bettman Archive: 31. © Robert Frerck, Oddyssey Productions: 35. © Greg Davis, The Stock Market: 46. © George Bellerose, Stock Boston: 54 (top right). © Brett Froomer, Image Bank: 54 (middle left). © Gabe Palmer, The Stock Market: 54 (bottom left). © Cameramann International Ltd.: 54 (top left). Courtesy of The Southland Corp.: 54 (bottom right). Courtesy of Sperry: 56. © Van Bucher, Photo Researchers: 71 (top left). © Peter Menzel, Stock Boston: 71 (top right). © Ed Kashi Photographer: 80. © James R. Holland, Stock Boston: 100. © 97 Mug Shots, The Stock Market: 116. Courtesy of Olive Church: 123. © Michael L. Abramson, Woodfin Camp: 131. © Gamma-Liaison: 144. © Craig Hammell, The Stock Market: 147. © Richard Hackett Photography: 166. © Brownie Harris, The Stock Market: 171. © Robert Frerck, Oddyssey Productions: 186. © Cameramann International Ltd.: 193 (top left). Courtesy of General Motors: 193 (top right). © Richard Hackett Photography: 197. © Peter Menzel, Stock Boston: 219. © James Wilson, Woodfin Camp: 222. © Cary Wolinsky, Stock Boston: 241 (bottom left). © Mark Antman, Stock Boston: 241 (bottom right). © Dan McCoy, Rainbow: 246. Courtesy of American Dairy Farmers National Dairy Board: 260. Courtesy of NYNEX: 268. © Jules Allen Photography: 275. © Spencer Grant, Photo Researchers: 276. Courtesy of Ford Motor Company: 285. Courtesy of Bobbin International: 286. Courtesy of The Wiz: 289. Courtesy of AT&T, GE, Dupont, Mr. Goodwrench: 303. Courtesy of Spiegel: 304. © 1987 Reebok International Ltd.: 309. © Will Faller Photography: 316. Courtesy of NYNEX: 333. © Gabe Palmer, The Stock Market: 334. © Gary Gladstone, The Image Bank: 340. © Bettye Lane, Photo Researchers: 345. © Hank Morgan, Rainbow: 352. Courtesy of Eastern Airlines: 355. Courtesy of Era Real Estate: 366. Courtesy of National Technology University in Ft. Collins: 373. © Michael Hayman, Photo Researchers: 377. © Tom Hugh, Photo Researchers: 389. © The Image Bank: 392. © Jules Allen Photography: 418.

U N I T 1

Business in America

Information has always been important to business. Business people need timely and relevant information as a basis for making sound business decisions. With the very rapid communication systems that exist today for conveying information, we call this "an information age."

Before the invention of the telegraph and telephone that helped to introduce the industrial age, communication systems were linked to, and hindered by, the speed of transportation systems. It took days, weeks, and sometimes even months, for vital business information to reach its destination. Today, however, modern communications and transportation systems and high tech equipment, such as the computer, make it possible to transmit business information at high speeds from almost anywhere 24 hours a day. Those who can use and apply this information wisely may well become the business winners of our information age.

UNIT OBJECTIVES

1. Identify the major classifications and types of business enterprises.
2. Describe the contributions that business makes to society.
3. Assess the role of profit, risk, and planning in business.
4. Identify the traits and attributes associated with entrepreneurs, and give examples of business winners and losers.
5. Trace the nation's historical progress toward an information economy.

CHAPTER 1

Business Winners

Big Dreams

Steve Jobs and his buddy, Steve Wosniak, sold their calculator and a VW Bug to get the money they needed to start their business. Working on a dining room table and in a garage, these two men in their early twenties dreamed of introducing a small desktop machine to the market.

Their machine launched the microcomputer industry and helped usher in today's information age. Their machine was named after the Northwestern orchard product Jobs had picked as a teenager—the apple. Thus the Apple Computer company was born.

Later, still an enterprising individual and risk taker, Jobs helped introduce another computer to the market. It was called the Pixar. (You will find out more about the Pixar in a later chapter.)

Study this chapter to learn more about the nature of American business and why people like Jobs and Wosniak are considered business winners. Use the information in this chapter to help you answer the questions in the end-of-chapter case study, "Making Business Dreams a Reality."

Just about everywhere we look, in town and beyond, we can find businesses. Without leaving our homes, we can find evidence of business, of commerce and trade, of goods and services. The food we eat, the clothes we wear, and most items we use or see—such as on TV commercials—are products that some business produced or distributed and sold.

The television set is a product. The entertainment TV provides and the information that comes to us through that broadcast medium are services. Thus TV itself is a business. Country-western, soul, Latino, and rock singers are in business. The professional football player is in business. Nearly all business-people strive to succeed, that is win.

In this chapter you'll learn about business, owners and their enterprises, and what it takes to win in business.

WHAT IS BUSINESS?

Calvin Coolidge, one-time President of the United States, said this about America and business: "The business of America is business!"

Characteristics of a Business

In the United States, **business** is the operation of an enterprise that:

- Satisfies human needs and wants by providing goods or services
- Operates for the purpose of making a profit
- Uses private money and resources, or capital, to pay for the costs of getting started and continuing to operate

Satisfying Human Needs and Wants. All people have basic needs and social and psychological wants. We *need* shelter, food, clothing, and, in today's modern world, transportation. But most of us *want* more. A single, cheap, warm coat satisfies a basic need. But a half-dozen fashionable coats, one for each activity, satisfies both a psychological and a social want. Psychologically, your ego is satisfied in knowing you can have lots of things. Keeping up with one's friends is important to many people, too, which satisfies a social want.

Businesses Provide Goods and Services. **Goods** are physical objects that satisfy people's needs or wants. Examples are the basics of food, clothes, and vehicles or luxuries like stereos and records. **Services** are tasks that people have others do for them because they satisfy needs or wants businesses provide. Examples are preparing and selling hamburgers at fast-food restaurants, altering clothes, repairing vehicles and stereos, singing professionally, and playing football commercially.

Businesses satisfy human needs and wants when they identify what these are and then offer for sale those goods and services that customers will buy. **Customers** can be individual consumers, other businesses, or government and other organizations who buy goods and services.

Making a Profit. In business, **profit** is the amount of money left from income earned by selling goods and services after paying for all costs and expenses. Profit is what the businessperson gets as payment for satisfying consumer needs and wants. Profit, to businesses and their owners and stockholders, is like the wages employees get for working.

▼ How would you feel about working 40 hours a week for someone, week after week, without getting paid? How would you feel as a business owner if you worked long and hard without earning a profit?

Using Private Capital. In business and accounting terms **capital** includes money and other resources, including land and assets that can be used to raise money. Some people go into business for themselves. Many individuals and firms invest their capital in other businesses by buying shares of ownership, called **stocks.** In countries that don't operate by the private enterprise system, private capital is usually unavailable. Capital resources in other systems come mainly from the government.

WHAT BUSINESS CONTRIBUTES TO SOCIETY

Collectively, all the workers and all the business owners and investors and their families make up society. Individual growth contributes to social and economic growth. The major contributions that business makes to society in a private enterprise economy are a means of exchange; utility of form, place, time, and possession; economic wealth; employment; and certain individual and business freedoms.

The Contribution of Exchange

At one time people exchanged goods and services directly without the use of money. (This is called barter, and will be discussed in greater detail in Chapter 3.) Today, however, money is the principal medium used to facilitate the exchange of goods and services.

In our society business allows for the exchange of goods and services at many different levels. To illustrate this point, let's suppose that you want a new pair of jeans. If you have no money, you could shovel snow off your neighbor's walks for a price. Then you could purchase the jeans from a retailer, exchanging the money you earned for the jeans. The retailer might then exchange the money received from the sale of the

Figure 1-1. In colonial America, *bartering*—the direct exchange of goods and services without money—was commonplace. Here colonists are shown bartering with the Indians. Today business uses other means, mainly money, for business exchanges.

jeans with a wholesaler who distributes the jeans. The wholesaler, in turn, could then exchange the money received from the retailer for a new batch of jeans produced by the jeans manufacturer. Finally, the jeans manufacturer might exchange the money for cotton and other raw products that go into making the jeans.

We obtain food, shelter, clothing, and the means of communication and transportation through the buying and selling process. These activities demonstrate a major contribution business makes to society—it provides a method and a means of exchanging needed goods and services.

The Contribution of Utility

To be useful, goods and services have to be in the form needed and available at the right place and time. **Utility** means to be made useful.

Utility of form means that goods need to be in the right form to be useful. You want to buy a pair of finished jeans, not the raw cotton. **Utility of place** means that goods and services are available to you *where* you need them. If you want the jeans for tonight's party, you can go to a local store. **Utility of time** means getting goods and services *when* you need them. For tonight's party, you can't wait for a pair of jeans to be custom-made for you, or even wait for delivery from a telephone order. **Utility of possession** is an arrangement for the transfer of ownership or title to goods or services. It also involves giving consumers the ability to own or possess goods or services by, for example, extending them credit to make a purchase.

Resources must be made useful to satisfy our needs and wants. One of the major contributions business makes in our society is to provide various forms of utility.

The Contribution of Economic Wealth

To some people, wealth means having a lot of money. To others, wealth includes money and all the things that can be purchased with money. Thus wealth includes goods, services, and recreation, that money can buy, as well as savings and money itself. Many people want to buy more goods and services. Or they want, the security of having a good savings plan to see them through hard times and to help support them in retirement.

The more goods and services that are produced for people who want and need them, the faster the economy grows. Thus another contribution business makes to the society is to generate and increase wealth.

The Contribution of Employment

People need money to pay for their homes, cars, food, and other items. People earn money by working at a job, by running businesses and employing workers, and by getting interest on savings, etc. By providing gainful employment for millions, business helps people obtain needed earnings.

The Contribution of Certain Freedoms

The freedoms that Americans enjoy are possible because of the private enterprise economic system under which we live. Through the taxes individuals and businesses pay, we're free to:

- Go to public school.
- Train for the jobs of our choice.
- Go after any job, and also to quit—to try elsewhere, or start our own business.
- Live or relocate wherever we wish or at any level we can afford.

- Buy whatever goods and services, and in whatever quantity, that our incomes will permit.
- Save money by depositing it in banks.
- Invest our savings in other people's businesses, for example, by buying shares of stock, or ownership, in corporations. We then expect these corporations to make money for us and pay us **dividends,** which are part of the profits a corporation makes and divides among its stockholders.

We're generally free to open any type of business, anywhere. We can try to raise money from friends and bankers to go into business. We're free to introduce new goods and services to the market and to withdraw old ones. We're also free to fail and then start anew or to go work for someone else. As individuals in a democratic society, we have the right to make all these decisions based on our abilities and earnings.

▼ How would you feel if, as a young adult, you couldn't make any of the above decisions? How would you feel if the government made all these decisions for you?

CLASSIFYING BUSINESSES

Organizations are divided into two major categories: public and nonprofit enterprises and private profit making enterprises. In the private sector, U.S. businesses can be classified by type and by size.

Public and Nonprofit Enterprises

Government agencies at the city, county, state, and federal level are included in the public sector, and so are public schools. The **public sector** includes agencies and organizations whose operating funds come from taxes collected from individual and business taxpayers. One out of five employees in the United States work in the public sector.

Nonprofit organizations get their operating funds from memberships, contributions, and endowments (gifts). Examples are museums, symphonies, private schools, churches, unions, and business, professional, and trade associations.

For-Profit Enterprises—The Private Sector

Enterprises that are in business to make a profit are said to be in the **private sector.** Both public- and private-sector organi-

Information Brief 1-1

Jobs Mean Education

True, business generates many jobs, but a lack of education can doom you to a lifetime of low pay or unemployment. That may sound preachy, but a study of 20 million 16- to 24-year olds found this to be so.

This study stated that those [with less than a high school diploma or a college education] "must scramble for good jobs in a sea of part-time, low-paying, limited-future opportunities" in our highly competitive technological society.

To reinforce this point the study noted that from 1973 to 1986 alone, families headed by 20- to 24-year olds who lacked a good education saw their incomes decline 27.4%. That was equal to the drop in personal income for those who lived through the Great Depression of the 1930s!

Source: The Commission on Youth and American's Future, "The Forgotten Half: Pathways to Success for Youth and Young Families," November 1988.

zations can be classified or put into groups in several different ways.

Classifying Businesses and Organizations

An **industry** is a group of businesses that operate in a similar fashion to provide the same type of goods and services. The **standard industrial classification (SIC)** is a federal system that assigns numbers to each business and classifies businesses and industries into 10 major divisions (see Table 1-1). Another common way to refer to several different types of business as being similar is to put them into these classifications: extraction, production, distribution, communications and utilities, construction, and services.

Extraction means to extract (get) something off of or from under the land or sea. Thus both agricultural and mining activities come under this classification. Agriculture covers farming, ranching, dairies, and fishing and timbering activities. Mining

TABLE 1-1 Standard Industrial Classification System (SIC)
Major Classification Divisions*
A. Agriculture, forestry, and fisheries
B. Mining
C. Contract construction
D. Manufacturing
E. Transportation, communication, electric, gas, and sanitary services
F. Wholesale and retail trade
G. Finace, insurance, and real estate
H. Services (hotels, amusements, auto repairs, medical, legal, and educational)
I. Government
J. Nonclassifiable Establishments

* Each major division is further broken down into subclassifications indicated by numbers, for example, 2521 for manufacturing of wooden office furniture. There are 99 major groups in all, with Manufacturing having nearly 450 individual (or four-digit) classifications.
Source: Standard Industrial Classification Manual, Executive Office of the President, Office of Management and the Budget, U.S. Government Printing Office, 1972.

involves getting natural resources out of the ground, such as coal, copper, and diamonds. Extracted materials are raw materials.

Production covers processing and manufacturing. Food processors change the form of raw agricultural products. For example, they make flour out of wheat. They produce leather from the hides of cattle. Sawmills make lumber out of timber. Manufacturers make steel out of these raw materials: iron, carbon, manganese, chromium, nickel, copper, tungsten, cobalt, and silica from sand. Petroleum firms produce natural gas, crude oil for asphalting highways, plastic, and many other derivatives.

Other processors and manufacturers turn the above products into new forms of goods. They make bread out of flour and shoes out of leather. They use lumber to make wood products like furniture. Manufacturers use silica to make glass and concrete. They use steel and plastic and many other products to produce cars, appliances, electronic gadgets, and components that go into still other goods.

Distribution includes both retail and wholesale trade. Also included are the business activities that get raw materials, products, and finished goods from one place to another. Thus shipping (transportation) firms help distribute goods. Warehouses store goods in between all the shipping activities. Advertisers and marketers who let customers know what goods are available help distribute goods. People who sell raw materials and unfinished goods and finished products help distribute goods. Retailers and salesclerks also help distribute merchandise.

Communications cover the print and broadcast media, such as newspapers, magazines, book publishing, and TV and radio stations.

Utilities provide customers with natural gas, water and sewage disposal, electricity, and telephone lines to help us operate homes and businesses.

Construction covers the activities and trades that build things, such as bridges, buildings, and highways. Related work includes carpentry, electricity, plumbing, roofing and siding, asphalting, tiling, decorating, and so on.

Services involve many types of businesses. Subcategories of the service classification are professional, business and financial, hospitality and recreation, personal, and public. (Public and nonprofit services have already been described.)

Professional services include health and medical and anything that requires its operators to pass tests and get licensing.

Business and financial services include banks, insurance and real estate firms, stock market brokerages, credit unions, and tax and accounting services. Also included are firms that provide the processing, retrieval, and storage of information.

Hospitality and recreation services include hotels, motels, restaurants, and every sort of leisure-time and recreation service. Personal services include beauty and barber shops, dry cleaners and laundries, numerous repair services, housecleaning, personal shoppers, baby-sitting, and day-care centers.

Using SIC Information. Businesspeople refer to the SIC to find their type of business. Information is often gathered by government and private sources and classified by SIC categories. Businesspeople can therefore locate information about such things as production, sales, employment, and financial data in a particular industry. This information helps businesses to compete with other similar businesses and to check their own profit and growth rates to see if they're on the winning track.

Figure 1-2. Of the 14 million businesses in the United States, 99 percent are small. They must do many of the same things as larger businesses, but with fewer resources.

BUSINESS SIZES: MOST ARE SMALL

The U.S. Congress, in its 1982 Report to the President, stated that a small business employs fewer than 500 workers. However, most small businesses actually employ fewer than 100, with the largest majority employing from 1 to 20 workers. Generally, firms that employ from 100 to 1000 workers are considered midsize. And firms with over 1000 workers are considered large.

The Role of Small Business

Many new and different jobs are created in small businesses. People who work for small firms get to participate in nearly every business function. Small firms have a lot of flexibility. They can change faster than bigger ones. New inventions produced in a small business often have a chance of reaching the market faster, because there are fewer procedures and people to go through to get approval for creative decisions. However, small firms have fewer resources and less money than bigger ones. (See Figure 1-2.)

The Characteristics of Small Business

Of the 14 million U.S. businesses, 99 percent are small. Some of the things usually true about a small business are listed below:

- It's small relative to other firms in its industry.
- It's independently owned by one or a few people (rather than by hundreds of thousands of stockholders, as in a large corporation).
- It usually operates in a single local area.
- Its owners usually run and manage the firm themselves.

Even some of the very largest and most famous of businesses once began as small enterprises. (See Information Briefs 1-2 and 1-3, for examples.) But businesses do not become either large or famous unless they succeed. These successful businesses and their equally successful owners and employees are economic winners within our private enterprise system.

Information Brief
1-2

Some Big Companies That Started Small

Frank L. Carney, founder of Pizza Hut International, paid his way through college by making and selling pizzas from one small Wichita, Kansas, outlet.

Experimenting with bicycles in his barn, Henry Ford started the auto industry.

Naomi Sims, one-time model, gathered snips of hair from her friends' heads. Three years after introducing her wig collection for black women, her firm was grossing over $5 million annually in sales.

Sources: Ron Christy and Billy M. Jones, *The Complete Information Bank for Entrepreneurs and Small Business Managers,* Wichita State University: The Center for Entrepreneurship and Small Business Management, 1982; and Bena Kay and Frances Ruffin, "How to Make a Million Before You're 34," *Redbook,* May 1977, pp. 60–64.

Information Brief
1-3

Winners and Losers, Young and Old

At age 19, Debbie Fields began selling chocolate-chip cookies from a tiny 325-square-foot shop. Within four years she owned a chain of stores, Mrs. Fields Cookies. A few years later she had 500 stores, bringing in revenues of $90 million annually. (See also the "Technology in an Information Economy" feature in Chapter 6 for additional information about the successful operation of Mrs. Fields Cookies.)

Not every entrepreneur wins the first time, however. Colonel Sanders failed repeatedly, with one business after another. Finally, he decided to market his recipe. When he was past the age of 70, his Kentucky Fried Chicken became famous, and he had, at last, become a business winner.

Sources: "Business Profiles—Entrepreneurs," PBS, July 21, 1987; and Fran Weinstein, "How To Become an Entrepreneur," *Working Woman,* 1977, pp. 14–15.

WHAT IS AN ENTREPRENEUR?

People who start and own firms are called entrepreneurs. Webster's dictionary defines **entrepreneur** as "one who organizes, manages, and assumes the risk of a business or enterprise." **Risk** is a hazard, the chance of loss, damage, or injury.

Characteristics of Winning Entrepreneurs

Entrepreneurs like to be in charge, to plan and make decisions. Among a number of physical and emotional traits, they characteristically have energy, courage, and self-confidence. (See Information Brief 1-4.) They generally deal with lots of people. They also have the ability to take calculated risks.

Being in Charge—Planning. Entrepreneurs like to make decisions and be in charge. Successful entrepreneurs are flexible. As one business winner put it: "Plan! Work out your direction, but be spontaneous enough to respond to the reality of any situation. Creative planning and creative *un*planning are both essential." The ability to unplan is a mark of flexibility—the ability to change quickly to handle unforeseen problems.

Being in Charge—Making Decisions. Owning a business can be lonely. If you were the sole owner, you'd make your own decisions. Win or lose, you'd be the one to suffer the consequences. But when your firm wins, so do you.

"To be a winner in business," says Sandra Brown, president of a multimillion-dollar firm, "you have to want to win. When problems come home to roost, they come home to you."

Physical and Emotional Traits. Says one winning business owner: "You need energy and courage, and the ability to make yourself happy." Business winners believe in their ability to accomplish something. That's self-confidence. They also usually have a lot of physical stamina. Leeann Chin, a Minneapolis woman whose carryout food business grosses over $5 million a year, put it this way: "I can do the work of three people. I'm not afraid to work 20 hours a day. If you don't have that attitude, you shouldn't be in business."

Dealing With People. Every day businesspeople talk to customers, employees, suppliers, bankers, advertisers, and the like. Entrepreneurs sell goods and services, make employee assignments, negotiate loans with bankers, and describe what they want to advertisers. They persuade some people to do some things, and they also have to compromise with people. All these things require using language effectively—in writing, in person, and over the phone.

Taking Calculated Risks. Managing a business involves taking risks. Successful businesspeople take calculated risks, however, not careless ones. That means that unlike blind gambling, smart entrepreneurs gather and study data and then make complete and careful plans before committing themselves. This commitment includes investing money. But entrepreneurs also commit themselves to investing every bit of time and energy they can possibly muster. Since every risk cannot be forecast, however, businesspeople also try to prepare for the unexpected.

Why Do People Start Their Own Businesses?

Some specific early-life experiences sometimes motivate people to prove themselves through entrepreneurship. Another motivation is a keen desire for independence. Entrepreneurs sometimes start their own businesses because they want to get rich through their own efforts. Many entrepreneurs, though, want to do something worthwhile with their lives.

Early Experiences. Successful entrepreneurs often had positive role models when they were young, such as a family member who is (or once was) successful in business. Other winners, however, say they had a poor relationship with parents who either ignored them or were coldly demanding. These business winners were motivated to prove themselves to their fathers or mothers or to overcome their deprived childhoods by being supersuccessful as adults.

A lot of business winners report having had work experience. Many of them were part-time or temporary entrepreneurs in their youth. They made and sold crafts. They delivered papers, shoveled walks, mowed lawns, or provided services such as minor repairs, baby-sitting, and the like.

Independence. The drive for independence is related to the take-charge trait that characterizes many entrepreneurs. As Naomi Sims, the founder of a wig collection for black women, said, "I am mistress of my own destiny!" (See Information Brief 1-2.)

Information Brief 1-5

Rich American

At a time when most retailers were targeting big cities to capture sales from well-to-do urban shoppers, Sam Moore Walton headed for the country. He saw opportunity for success in the small towns and cities of rural America. Starting in 1962 with a single discount store in Rodgers, Arkansas, Walton built Wal-Mart Stores into a chain of 900 outlets in 22 states. Walton became the richest man in America.

Source: "Who Owns Corporate America," *U.S. News and World Report,* July 21, 1986, p. 37.

Win, lose, or draw (barely survive), apparently independence and control are worth plenty to some entrepreneurs.

Desire for Riches. Of the 410,000 millionaires in the United States, at least 75 percent are over 50 years old. Most millionaires, say researchers, got rich by starting their own businesses and working, on average, 12 hours a day for 30 years. But sometimes people make it big at a very young age. (See Information Briefs 1-3 and 1-5.)

Meeting Humanitarian Needs. In addition to money (from profits), some businesspeople look for an opportunity to meet humanitarian needs. For example, they seek to help others, to overcome poverty and injustice. They're concerned about senior citizens, the handicapped, the environment, and many other social needs. (See Information Brief 1-6.)

WHAT IT TAKES TO WIN IN BUSINESS

Of the more than 600,000 new businesses that start up each year, about half disappear within five years. The rate at which businesses are failing has also been climbing. Winning businesses are owned by winners who also hire winning people.

Winners Versus Losers

Experts have tried to list the key factors that separate business winners from losers. They cite the following as the principal reasons why some people win at business and others experience business failure.

Business Winners. Winners have the following abilities and talents in common:

- The ability to manage money.
- The ability to be creative, to plan and still be flexible.
- The ability to correctly identify the market (customers).
- An ability to locate a business so it has access to the market.
- An ability to project a good image for the firm.
- An ability to develop an effective marketing and advertising plan.
- A talent for getting productivity out of employees.
- An ability to control the quality of products and services.

Business Losers. Businesses that fail usually do so for one or more of the following reasons:

- They are poorly located.
- They were operated by owners who lacked managerial competence.
- They seldom introduced new or improved products to the market.
- They had emphasized quality at the expense of pricing and competition. That is, quality products were either priced so high that their customers wouldn't buy or priced so low that their companies couldn't make a profit.

Misconceptions About Entrepreneurship Can Lead to Business Failure. Some would-be entrepreneurs, inexperienced in the ways that business needs to operate to win, go into business with little if any planning. Other business innocents suppose that having a technical skill in the product or line is all they need to be winners.

Technical Versus Business Skills. Depending on the type of business, technical skills can be important. Expert mechanic skills are needed to open an auto repair shop, and word processing skills are needed for a word processing service. Having a broad business background is even more important, though. Academic disciplines associated with winning in business include finance, accounting, business law, communications, economics, information systems, management, marketing, office procedures, and human relations.

Intrapreneurs. A study conducted in Texas and the Rocky Mountains found that entrepreneurs who hire employees look for the intrapreneurial type. An **intrapreneur,** according to this study, is a person who works for someone else but who thinks and acts like an entrepreneur. Thus intrapreneurs are enterprising people who manage their jobs and responsibilities as if they were the owners. They look for ways to save the company money or to help it earn more. They are productive and innovative. They care and show it.

Helping a Business Be a Winner

People who would win in business develop strengths and skills that help their business or the firm that employs them. They

---

Information Brief
1-6

Humanitarian Goals in Business

It's not often that companies cheer the news that a competitor has beaten them to market with a hot new product. But that's what happened when an important new vaccine was announced.

The product is a vaccine against hepatitis B, a virus that causes an incurable and sometimes fatal liver disease. It strikes about 200,000 new victims every year in the United States. Merck, a pharmaceutical giant based in New Jersey, and Chiron, a small California biotechnology firm, got approval from the U.S. Food and Drug Administration to produce their vaccine. They market it commercially.

Source: Janice Castro, Linda Kramer, and Dick Thompson, "A Breakthrough for Biotech," *Time,* August 4, 1986, p. 52.

The World's Fair of Software

A 3-day software vendors' exhibition in Chicago drew over 50,000 customers. The "World's Fair of Software" was sponsored by Egghead Discount Software, a retailing chain based in Bothell, Washington.

Software stores have come on-line around the country. Unlike their more stodgy competitors, these store chains use marketing flash. They offer big price discounts and locate in suburban shopping malls. K mart's, Waldenbooks, and B. Dalton Bookseller are examples.

Dallas-based Babbage's Inc. also has software stores in malls—just like traditional retailers. Says the Dallas company's chairperson, "We put the product in an environment the customer is familiar with. Next to the shoe store they've been shopping in for years."

Victor Alhadeff, founder and president of Egghead, says he became interested in the business in the mid-1980s. He was searching for programs to run his son's computer. Mr. Alhadeff said that the independent-owned software stores in his area didn't show any pizzazz in selling products. He concluded that a market existed for stores offering a wide selection of programs at cut-rate prices.

Egghead's stores are arranged like bookstores. Hundreds of software titles are separated by category. For instance, they're arranged by entertainment or by the type of computer hardware they'll run on. Customers can try out the merchandise and get help from salesclerks who must learn new programs every week.

More than half of Egghead's sales, however, are generated by salespeople who work out of the stores' backrooms. They sell directly to business customers, offering volume discounts from the stores' retail prices.

Source: Hank Gilman, "Learning a New Pitch: Software Retailers Adopt Mainstream Marketing Techniques," *Wall Street Journal,* September 30, 1987, p. 39.

understand business. For example, they understand competition, profit, the need for owners to get a return on investment, the relationship of profit and risk, and the need for getting business information.

Competition in a Private Enterprise Economy. Competition in the marketplace helps to determine what goods and services are produced. Like football teams competing for touchdowns and basketball teams competing for baskets, businesses compete for customers. Firms that win beat their competition. Winning strategies include offering higher quality, fair prices, special services, or being unique in some other way. They thereby seek to attract sufficient customers to ensure consistent sales.

Profit as a Scorecard of Winning Businesses. Few people would be interested in athletic competitions if there were no scores. When you watch two football teams compete, you want to know who's winning, who's losing. The running score helps you track the progress of the game. Business is no different. The profit (or loss) figure is the score that tells business owners whether they're winning or losing in business.

Imagine, for example, that you owned a wardrobe shop. Put yourself in the owner's place and think about all the money that has to go out to keep your business operating. Even during the days and weeks when you have few customers, you still have to pay the rent and the utilities. You need to pay your employees their wages. To get customers, you have to continue advertising and paying for this expense. And you better pay for insurance to protect yourself and your establishment. You need to pay the wholesale prices to get inventory in stock, or you'll have nothing to sell when customers do show up. There might be transportation and shipping expenses, supplies to purchase, and miscellaneous and unforeseen expenses. You also have to pay the government taxes owed. (See Table 1-2.)

After everything has been paid, you'll be counting on some money for yourself. If owners can't earn a livelihood from their businesses, they usually have to close their firms' doors, lay off their employees, and go to work for others to earn a living.

▼ How would you feel if, after paying for and managing all of the above, you made no money? How would you feel if your business was a loser?

Owners' Return on Investment. Not all people who have money invest it by going into business for themselves. Instead, they invest their money in a savings plan or in existing businesses. Owners expect to earn a return on the investment of their time and energy, and the risks they take, as well as on their money.

TABLE 1-2 Revenue Less Operating Expenses and Taxes Equal Profit*

LAKEVIEW WARDROBE SHOP
Profit or Loss
(for 3-month period)

Revenues

Women's clothing.	$25,000.00	
Children's clothing	15,000.00	
Men's clothing.	7,500.00	
Accessories, misc..	2,500.00	
Total revenues.	$50,000.00	100%
Less cost of buying/selling goods above	25,000.00	50%
Profit (before deducting expenses/taxes, etc.).	$25,000.00	50%

Operating Expenses

Wages.	$10,000.00	
Payroll taxes/benefits	1,775.00	
Rent.	1,500.00	
Utilities/telephone	1,225.00	
Advertising.	2,225.00	
Insurance.	100.00	
Professional fees	400.00	
Packaging and delivery	500.00	
Miscellaneous	2,275.00	
Total expenses	20,000.00	40%
Profit before taxes	5,000.00	10%
Less taxes	2,000.00	4%
Net profit/loss (for 3 months) on sales.	$ 3,000.00	6%

* In the case of Lakeview Wardrobe, net profit amounted to 6 percent after all costs, including operating expenses and taxes, were deducted from sales revenues. People sometimes confuse sales revenue with profit. However, they are not the same.

To understand this principle, let's look at a purely monetary investment. Suppose you had $10,000 saved. If you put this money into a top-dollar savings plan, you might expect to earn from 6 to over 10 percent annually, or $600 to $1000 or more each year (divided by 12 months = $50 to $83 or more per month). Add another zero to your investment ($100,000) and also to the return on the investment and your money would be earning from $6000 to $10,000 or more in annual earnings. Such dividends would be yours without putting in a single hour of work time and energy. Conversely, when owners put their time and energy as well as their savings into a business, they need to earn a return on the investment of their effort. If a business does not generate this return, it will keep losing, and the owner will usually have to quit.

The Relationship of Risk and Profit. The more a business has at risk, the more likelihood there is of making either a profit or a loss. Suppose you invested $1500 to buy a snowblower and pay expenses. With a snowy winter and plenty of business, you might take in $2000 and thus clear $500 in profits. With a dry winter and no customers, however, you risk losing your $1500 investment. Instead, suppose you bought a truck with a snowplow attached to the front. Total costs might run to $15,000. You would have invested more money (put more of your money at risk). But in a snowy winter you could earn $20,000 in revenues and thus clear $5000 in profits. But you could still risk facing a dry winter. If so, you have more at risk.

Getting Business Information

Entrepreneurs who win don't use a crystal ball to predict whether their dreams of a business will succeed. They plan, organize, and test their plans before deciding to invest their money, time, and energy. They take business courses and read trade and industry publications. They talk to and get help from other entrepreneurs and from business consultants. They get and pay for expert advice. This advice comes from bankers, accountants, lawyers, and other business consultants. They gather data and interpret and analyze information, using computers and other modern business tools.

Financial Information. Wise businesspeople know that to win they have to get the money it takes to start a business and keep it running until it has a good sales record. Sales have to be sufficient to provide a healthy cash flow—as much or more money coming in as is going out. Bankers can give advice, whether they authorize a loan or make other recommendations for how to get financial backing.

Information Brief 1-7

A Winning Investor

As a teenager Reginald Lewis dreamed of becoming a professional athlete, but an untimely shoulder injury stopped him. However, it did not stop him from striving for success in other areas. After high school and college, he obtained a degree from Harvard Law School. Next, he went to work for a New York law firm. Then, starting in 1983 he became a full-time investor.

How well did Lewis do? In July 1987 he made news headlines by selling McCall Pattern Co. for $63 million, earning 90 times the investment he had made in 1984. Just 37 days later, Lewis' name was in the headlines again. His company, the TLC Group, agreed to buy the foreign food operations of the Beatrice Corporation for $985 million.

Successes mounted, and by 1988 TLC became the top-ranked black-owned business in the U.S.

Source: Adapted from "The Best of 1987," *Business Week,* January 11, 1988, p. 153.

Figure 1-3. Today, more than ever, business success depends on an entrepreneur's ability to use information effectively. Modern business tools, such as the computer, can help entrepreneurs interpret and analyze information.

Accounting Information. Knowledgeable businesspeople know they need to keep a careful accounting of every financial transaction. Accountants help new entrepreneurs set up the accounting records, and they also provide continuing information to company bookkeepers.

Legal Information. Lawyers alert owners to government regulations, to tax paying requirements, and to what steps to take to avoid getting sued. Businesspeople who want to organize their companies as partnerships or corporations especially need legal help. When organizing, partners usually get a lawyer to prepare a contract, called a partnership agreement. Corporations often rely on lawyers to get a state-granted charter.

Risk-Management Information. Among the business consultants contacted are insurance representatives. Owners need to be sure they protect their businesses and themselves against natural disasters, crime, and so on. Owners also need to protect their businesses from liability for injuries done to others in the course of doing business.

"The Business of America Is Business!"

Most winning businesses start with a plan. A single person with a great idea might start the ball rolling. He or she sells the idea to others. Once a business is operational, any "intrepreneurial" type of employee can come up with other great ideas. Together, these entrepreneurs and intrapreneurs are willing to work long and hard to turn dreams into reality.

Many people are losers, to be sure. But, like Colonel Sanders, many of them keep on trying until they too become winners. Business winners, however, never really stop trying. They learn from their mistakes and failures. Moreover, they stick to it in bad times, thrive on challenge, overcome difficulties, and by so doing rejoice in the business victories that await them.

Select Terms to Know

business	intrapreneur	stocks
capital	private sector	utility
customers	profit	utility of form
dividend	public sector	utility of place
entrepreneur	risk(s)	utility of possession
goods	services	utility of time
industry	standard industrial classification (SIC)	wealth

Review Questions

1. Give one or more examples of the contributions that business makes to society.

2. Describe some differences between public and nonprofit organizations and businesses in the private sector.

3. Describe the role and characteristics of small business.

4. Describe and give examples of entrepreneurial characteristics and of entrepreneurial motivations.

5. Describe and give examples of some differences that separate winners from losers, as cited by experts in business.

6. What do winning entrepreneurs and intrapreneurs understand about business—for example, competition, profit, business risks, and the owners' return on investment?

7. What types of information do businesspeople get to help them avoid taking unnecessary risks? Where do they go to get this information, and how do they use it?

8. What information did you get from the information briefs about winning and losing the game of business? About risks and planning?

Thought and Discussion Questions

1. What evidence of business and business products and services do you see when you look around the schoolroom, your home, and the community?

2. Compare a winning business with a winning athletic team; a losing business with a losing team. Why would you want to help a business win?

3. If you owned your own business, what personal needs would you seek to satisfy, and why?

For example, which of the following would interest you most and least: money, independence, getting to be in charge, humanitarian goals, or something else?

4. If you owned your own business, in which SIC would you like to be? What size of firm? What goods or services would you offer? Why?

5. If you were to seek a job working for someone else, how could you convince the employer that you're the intrapreneurial type?

Projects

1. You and a friend each have $10,000 to invest in stock. You buy 165 shares of Computer Company A, which pays a $3 annual dividend per share. Your friend buys 128 shares of Computer Company B, which pays a $3.25 annual dividend. How much money do each of you get, annually, from dividends? If paid quarterly, what do each of you get from dividends? In your opinion, which stock (Company A or Company B) is better? Why?

2. In a library obtain a copy of *Business Week* magazine's annual listing of the 1000 largest companies in the United States or a copy of *Fortune* magazine's annual listing of the 500 largest industrial companies.

   a. Make a list of the companies with the five highest profit percentages compared with sales.
   b. Make a list of the companies with the five lowest profit percentages compared with sales.

   c. Based on your lists, do you think there is a relationship between a company's degree of profitability and a company's success or failure in business? To what extent do you think a company's success or failure is related to its ability to satisfy customer needs?

3. Arrange to interview someone in business, preferably a family member, neighbor, or close friend. Record your findings about the following:

   a. What personal needs the entrepreneur sought to satisfy by going into business—make money, use talents and skills, be independent, be in charge, a desire to provide humanitarian needs, and so on.
   b. What information the entrepreneur gets, and from where, to help plan, make decisions, meet the competition, and minimize risks.
   c. What recommendations the entrepreneur has for someone interested in going into business—as an entrepreneur or an intrapreneur.

Case Study: Making Business Dreams a Reality

Steven Jobs and Stephen Wozniak decided to form a company to market their personal computer (PC). They raised $1300 from the sale of Jobs' Volkswagen and Wozniak's scientific calculator and opened a makeshift production line in Jobs' garage. Then they shared their dreams and plans with A. C. Markkula. When Markkula offered $250,000, plus his expertise (experience and information), Jobs and Wozniak made him an equal partner. Markkula then got a loan from the Bank of America. Later, to get more capital to run the business, the company sold stock to anyone interested in investing.

In the 1978 business plan, the 2-year-old Apple Computer company's entrepreneurs forecast $100 million in sales by the end of 1979. Apple reached its goal and went on to post a 43,154 percent gain over a five-year period: from $774,000 sales in 1977 to $334,783,000 by 1981.

Soon many other brands and models of personal computers were introduced to the market. Some of these competitors went bankrupt or quit. They were losers in the computer marketplace. Once International Business Machines (IBM) entered the market with its PC, however, Apple started getting plenty of competition.

By age 26, Steve Jobs alone held over 7 million shares of the corporation—worth nearly $200 million. But all was not roses. Competition from the outside, and conflicts and problems from the inside, soon caused Jobs to leave the company he'd founded.

Sources: Phillip Elmer-DeWitt and Charles Pelton, "Computers," *Time,* September 1, 1986; Robert A. Mamis, "Born To Grow," *Inc.,* May 1982; and Alexander L. Taylor, III, "Striking It Rich," *Time,* February 15, 1982.

---

1. Based on the opening article and the above case, would you say Jobs and Wosniak were true entrepreneurs? Why?

2. On the basis of the chapter's opening article and the above case, express your opinion about starting a business alone versus with others; that is, you might start with partners or you might sell shares of ownership or stocks in your business. How would each of the following influence your choice of one of these options?

   a. Sharing both profits and risks

   b. Getting and sharing expertise and information

   c. Getting investment money

CHAPTER 2

Growth of the American Economy

A Modern Clark Kent

As production manager Marc Silag drove down the busy California highway, he spotted a roadside phone booth. Very quickly, Silag jumped out of the car and disappeared Clark Kent style into the booth—toting his laptop computer. Instead of changing into a red cape and boots, Silag hooked his computer to the telephone, using a portable acoustic coupler. This is Silag's way of going to the office, and it's even faster than flying. In the end-of-chapter case study, "Electronic Mail—Offices on the Run," you can see how some executives are able to "carry their offices with them" in today's information economy.

Study this chapter to trace our nation's 300-year growth toward an information economy and to help you answer the questions in the end-of-chapter case study.

In the early 1800s the business of America was farming. In this *agricultural economy*, farming families not only raised crops and livestock to meet their own needs, but they deliberately produced more than they needed. By selling surplus crops and livestock, they could obtain enough money to buy farming tools and supplies and other necessities. The success of a farm was largely based on the family's ability to develop a crop that would provide them with enough income both to buy the necessities and expand the farm.

Unlike animals, humans don't merely accept the planet as it is. We keep making changes, trying to better ourselves and make life easier. Nature challenges, humans respond.

Today we are in an era that can be described as the *information economy*. Business managers send written documents to people in other cities, states, and countries with the push of a button. You can use a computer and a telephone to find just about any of the information you might need for an important project. The success of a business today is largely based on its ability to obtain accurate, up-to-date information quickly and to use it efficiently.

Our economy did not move directly from an agricultural economy to the current information economy. America's economic growth and change extends over roughly three centuries (300 years)! It involves the lives of millions of people. This process of economic growth and change has been a gradual one and is likely to continue into the future.

In this chapter you will learn about the four basic economic eras that have developed as people have reacted to the challenges presented to them. You will also learn about some of the responsibilities of business entrepreneurs during each of these eras.

THE FOUR ERAS OF OUR ECONOMY

There have been four distinct eras in the American economy: agricultural, industrial, service, and information. An **agricultural economy** is present when the majority of the income in a society is earned from the production and sale of goods that come from the land—plants, animals, trees, and the like. From the time of the first settlers, farming was an important influence in early America. By the beginning of the nineteenth century, our country had a strong agricultural economy. Then, about 1890, we witnessed a period of rapid industrial expansion that evolved into the beginning of an era recognized as an industrial economy. An **industrial economy** is present when a majority of the income in a society is earned from the manufacturing and sale of factory-made products. Clothing, tables, chairs, automobiles, and bicycles are a few examples of factory-made products. Industry was the main emphasis of our economy for more than half a century.

In the middle of the twentieth century, consumers began to demand more services than were available in the past. They wanted more restaurants, hotels, airline travel, luxury vacations, entertainment, and a variety of other services. Businesses also demanded more services to assist them in becoming more productive. Some of the services sought after by business were management consultants, accounting services, and payroll services. In response to both consumer and business demand, our economy shifted its emphasis from the production of products to the production of services, and thus began the service economy. A **service economy** is present when the majority of the income in a society is earned from the production and sale of services.

In the early 1980s our economy shifted its emphasis once again. Although the demand for services is still growing, our society has shown a strong desire for instant access to accurate information. Businesses and an increasing number of consumers began demanding the ability to acquire specific information instantly. They also wanted to transmit information just as rapidly through telephone lines with the aid of computers. These demands called for the development of more effective communication systems. This caused the latest shift in our economy to our current information economy. An **information economy** is present when the majority of income-earning activities in a society depend on the use of accurate, up-to-date information.

A PROCESS OF GRADUAL CHANGE

As our economy has moved from one era to the next, an interesting transition has occurred. For some time each of the new economic eras has grown and developed while the era before it was still in progress. There was no abrupt change from one era to the next. In fact, historians and economists may not even agree on the dates when each era began and ended.

Ultimately, each new economic era has supplemented the prior era instead of entirely replacing it. Farm machinery such as gasoline tractors and harvesters that were developed during the industrial era helped American farmers to produce crops more efficiently. Services introduced during the service era gave industry valuable new choices and approaches in the way they produced goods. A business could decide to hire an employment service instead of having its own personnel department, for example, or it could use the services of an outside accounting firm instead of employing its own full-time accountant. Technology introduced during the information era gave service businesses the ability to receive and transmit up-to-the-minute information quickly and easily. Airlines can, for example, accept reservations for the same flight at locations throughout the country. Because all these locations are connected to the same computer, reservation clerks know instantly when the flight is full.

As our economy has entered each new era, the emphasis has shifted, but the overall result generally has been beneficial. At this time our country has successful agricultural businesses, industries, service businesses, and businesses that depend mainly on information. To illustrate the development of our economic system, we will look closer at each of the economic eras.

THE AGRICULTURAL ECONOMY

When the first U.S. census was taken in 1790, the population was about four million. At that time, 95 percent of the population was made up of farmers living in the eastern states.

The First American Entrepreneurs

People must eat. And because these early farmers needed cash for necessities (salt, iron, guns, farm implements, kitchen utensils, rum, and the like), they produced surplus crops. In many ways, these early farmers were the first American entrepreneurs. By improving their farms—draining wet meadows, buying neighboring farms, building barns—they were able to fill their pastures with more animals and plant more crops. By producing surpluses of their crops, they repaid debts and expanded their farms.

Agricultural Legislation

A major piece of legislation, the Homestead Act of 1862, encouraged settlers to move west and settle undeveloped publically owned land. The Act granted 160-acre farms to anyone who lived on them for five years and developed them for farming. As an alternative, settlers could buy the land for $1.25 an acre.

In the same year, 1862, Congress passed the Morrill Act which granted states large plots of land to sell. The proceeds from these sales were used to found colleges of agriculture and mechanical arts.

Similar grants were made by Congress during the period from 1817 to 1871 to promote the building of railroads and canals. The Erie Canal, which ran for a distance of 364 miles through the state of New York to Lake Erie, was the most extensive internal waterway. The eventual reason for the failure

Information Brief 2-1

Cheap Farm Labor

The agricultural economy was not built entirely by entrepreneurs. The vastness of the lands to be farmed caused some entrepreneurs to seek cheap sources of farm labor. In early times, especially in the south, they turned to slave labor.

The practice of slavery became established within a generation after the first black Africans were brought to Virginia in 1619. Most slaves were assigned to field and household work, but others were taught trades. Still later their owners rented the services of slaves to others. Skilled black artisans thus competed with and were considered a threat by some freeholders (laborers who worked for wages). As a result, many freeholders migrated westward, along with others who sought land and agricultural or business opportunities. Later, of course, slavery was banned by law.

Source: Willena Stanford, "History of Blacks in Vocational Education," unpublished doctoral dissertation, University of Wyoming, 1984.

of the slower canal system was the introduction of the faster railroad. The first transcontinental railroad was completed in the late 1860s, linking the eastern half of the United States to the Great Plains with the first modern transportation system.

Rapid Expansion

In the period between 1862 and 1900, about 500,000 families acquired land under the Homestead Act. The railroad provided these homesteaders with a very efficient means of transporting their crops to buyers in distant locations.

Much of the land acquired by homesteaders was in the Great Plains states (North Dakota in the north, south through Texas). Water is needed to grow successful crops. Unfortunately, the rainfall in this area is light and undependable. As a result, crop yields were lower than the farmers' expectations and needs. Farmers in the Great Plains area learned that wheat and ranching is well suited to dry lands. Successful wheat farming and ranching enabled them to produce surpluses nearly every year. This is still true today. Soon the Great Plains became one of the world's major wheat and cattle producing regions.

When telegraph lines were installed along the railroad rights of way in the late 1800s, a fast new method of communication was established for the agricultural entrepreneurs. This communication link enabled them to create new markets across the nation and in other countries. Farmers and ranchers were able to offer crops for sale by telegraphing their offers to prospective buyers. When buyers telegraphed acceptance, the goods were shipped by rail.

Thus by the late 1800s the first American entrepreneurs knew more than just how to produce crops and raise animals. They were experienced in communicating with prospective buyers. They could negotiate fair prices for their products, sell them within our country and overseas, transport and store their products, make a profit, and expand their businesses.

▼ Despite declining numbers today, the first American entrepreneurs remain the most productive farmers and ranchers in the world. They produce enough food to feed our nation and the people of many other nations. How would you feel if they weren't as efficient and productive? Would this affect the way you and your family live? If so, how?

THE INDUSTRIAL ECONOMY

The industrial revolution in Europe, which began during the late 1700s and early 1800s, had been developing in the United States since the first settlers arrived. In colonial times, besides gristmills, shipyards, and sawmills, there began to emerge brick and tile yards, potteries, and the glass industry. About a third of Britain's ships were being built in America at the time the colonies declared their independence in 1776.

Another strong industry in the colonies was iron manufacturing. Iron was the only plentiful mineral obtained in the colonies. During the first half of the nineteenth century, British iron manufacturing innovations that were introduced into the United States made the industry more productive. A few American companies were even able to export iron to Great Britain.

Gradual Growth of Industry

In the colonial period, three stages of manufacturing existed side by side: the cottage industry (another name for household manufacturing), the domestic system, and the factory system. These early businesses were an important factor in our change from an agricultural to an industrial economy.

Cottage industries were those operated from the home. Working out of their own homes as entrepreneurs, people also produced and sold workshop crafts. They were actively involved in spinning and weaving, blacksmithing and silver-smithing, soap making, and so on. Instead of specializing, each person did many things.

In the domestic system, homeworkers were employed by other entrepreneurs. As late as 1820, two-thirds of the textiles used in American homes were made by American workers under this system.

Under the **factory system,** people went to work in factories, just as they do today. Lumbermills, gristmills, glass and paper factories, and textile and leather factories were springing up all over. By 1775, the American colonies had more blast furnaces and forges than England and Wales combined.

As the transportation system in the United States improved, more and more families were able to buy goods manufactured a distance from home. By the early 1830s industrialization was increasing more rapidly in the eastern United States, while the western areas of the country remained more agricultural.

Information Brief 2-2

The Gospel of Wealth

Powerful businesspeople—called the "captains of industry"—became heroes to some and villains to others during the industrial era. They dominated all the key industries. Andrew Carnegie became the president of our nation's largest steel company. John D. Rockefeller amassed a fortune in oil and founded the Standard Oil Company. James J. Hill, with Edward Harriman, controlled many of the nation's largest railroads. James Duke was dominant in the tobacco industry, Philip Armour in meat-packing, and Charles Pillsbury in flour milling. These business leaders generally believed in the "gospel of wealth." Summing up this idea, Andrew Carnegie declared, "Not evil, but good, has come to the race by the accumulation of wealth by those who had the ability and energy to produce it." For example, many jobs are created for workers, investment opportunities for stockholders, and new products for consumers, when companies have a chance to grow.

Iron manufactured in Pennsylvania was used for agricultural tools, railroad track, and building materials. This industry was so strong that U.S. ironmakers were able to compete with those in Great Britain in the international market.

Although manufacturing was growing steadily during the middle of the nineteenth century, it accounted for less than a fifth of all U.S. production in 1840. We were still an agricultural economy.

The Change From an Agricultural to an Industrial Economy

By 1870, industry was advancing faster than agriculture. The census of 1890 reported that manufacturing output was greater in dollar value than farm output. And by the mid-1890s the United States was considered a leading industrial power among the nations of the world. By 1900, the annual value of industrial goods was more than twice that of farm products.

As the emphasis of our economy shifted from agricultural to industrial, the farmer realized some important side benefits. Gasoline tractors, plows, cultivators, reapers, and harvesters are all examples of agricultural implements that reduce the time and work required to cultivate the soil, harvest crops, and raise animals.

Exploitation of Labor

As the emphasis shifted toward industry and away from agriculture, employers became eager to make money, often at the expense of their employees. Becoming an industrial employee, or a source of labor for the manufacturers and other employers, may not sound so bad because that's what many people do now. But in those days there was no minimum wage law. No laws regulated how many hours per day or week people worked or working conditions.

There were no child-labor laws, and thus the children of the working class often began their work experience at the tender ages of 6 or 7. In 1880, about a million boys and girls between the ages of 10 and 15 were employed in the nation's factories. By 1910, that number had grown to nearly two million. Twenty percent of all the nation's children were employed, and they made up 5.2 percent of the work force.

Women were also exploited in the early factories. The number of women who were employed increased rapidly after 1880.

Figure 2-1. During the early industrial revolution, child laborers worked long hours at very low wages, oftentimes under very poor working conditions. Later, child labor laws were passed to regulate child labor and curb the worst abuses.

These women worked in the lowest-paid fields—often cotton-textile manufacture—and had little opportunity to advance. It is generally recognized that they added more to the value of the products they produced than they received in salary.

▼ How would you feel if instead of going to school you had to work 12 hours a day, 6 days a week at very low wages? Suppose you couldn't keep a nickel from your labor. You had to help support your family with what little you did earn. How would you feel about this situation? What would you do?

Employee Protections

The unacceptable working conditions during the industrial era led to the establishment of labor unions. Because workers achieved very little by complaining individually about poor working conditions, they were forced to band together. By withholding their services, they could seriously affect production and force factories to close. This, naturally, affected the profits of the owners.

The first national labor union was the Knights of Labor. It made its greatest impact in the 1880s. In 1881, the American Federation of Labor (AFL) was formed. The AFL organized only skilled workers. In the mid-1930s, the Congress of Industrial Organizations (CIO) was formed to organize unskilled workers. In 1955 the two organizations joined forces and became the AFL-CIO. The goal of these unions and other smaller ones is to increase the power of their members (the workers) to obtain better wages, improved hours and working conditions, protection from discrimination by employers, and job security.

Unfair Practices Toward Business

Labor was not the only victim of those who were eager to make money. Sometimes businesses were the victims too. During the early part of the industrial era there were few laws to protect a business from the unfair practices of other businesses.

A few big businesses, for example, formed trusts. A **trust** is any business combination that limits or eliminates competition. These trusts gave participating companies a chance to control vast sums of wealth, resources, and economic power. Sometimes these trusts would result in monopolies. A **monopoly** is a market where there is only one buyer or seller of the resource, good, or service being exchanged. Trusts and monopolies dominated the steel, oil, and railroading industries until industrial legislation was passed to protect labor and business against certain abuses. (See Table 2-1.)

The Industrial Era in the Twentieth Century

An improved transportation system in the form of superhighways and an efficient network of railroads has helped industries to do business nationwide and often (with the aid of cargo ships) worldwide. As industry grew, more and more farmworkers came to the towns to get jobs.

Factories installed faster machines which required fewer workers. As a result, some jobs became unnecessary. However, as production increased and new products were developed, workers were usually able to find other jobs in new industries.

Industry continues to be very important today. Some of our largest industries, in fact, were not in existence 50 years ago. The manufacturing of such things as televisions, VCRs, computers, and microwave ovens could not have been anticipated in the early years of the industrial era.

TABLE 2-1 Major Industrial Legislation	
Year Enacted	**Name and Purpose of Act**
1887	*Interstate Commerce Act.* Created a commission to regulate rates and services of companies providing interstate transportation of passengers or freight.
1890	*Sherman Antitrust Act.* Outlawed contracts, combinations, and conspiracies that served to restrain trade.
1914	*Clayton Antitrust Act.* Outlawed anticompetitive sales contracts and price cutting to force competitors out of business. Gave limited protection to labor unions.
1935	*National Labor Relations Act (Wagner Act).* Provided the legal foundation for the rights of unions and workers.
1964	*Civil Rights Act, Title VII.* (See EEO Act of 1972).
1972	*Equal Employment Opportunity Act* (EEO Act, amendment to the 1964 act). Prohibited discrimination in any avenue of employment on the basis of race, color, sex, religion, and national origin. The Equal Employment Opportunity Commission (EEOC) seeks to enforce the provisions of the act.

The Entrepreneur of the Industrial Era

Throughout the industrial era, entrepreneurs were involved with a variety of important decision-making tasks. They identified products that meet the needs of a portion of the population (either consumers or businesses). They dealt with those people who could supply them with the raw materials to manufacture their products. They developed the most efficient possible technology for producing their products. They hired, trained, and bargained with employees concerning working conditions and wages. They set prices, communicated with potential customers, and arranged sales transactions (often nationwide or internationally).

These entrepreneurs dealt with the challenges of transporting and storing their products. They became efficient in dealing with the effects of competition and in working within the limits established by legislation. To acquire the funds they needed to operate, some entrepreneurs sold shares of stock (an ownership interest) in their businesses. When they were successful, these companies realized a profit. After sharing the profit with stockholders, entrepreneurs often used some of the money to expand and upgrade the business.

The activities of industrial entrepreneurs today are very similar to those during the industrial era. However, the resources available to today's entrepreneurs include a wide range of business services (a result of the service economy) and the access to instant information (due to the information economy).

THE SERVICE ECONOMY

In the middle of the twentieth century, our economy again shifted its emphasis—from an industrial economy to a service economy. Service industries are business firms, government agencies, and nonprofit organizations that produce services rather than manufactured goods or agricultural products. Services are intangible activities. This means that, like watching movies or going bowling, there's no product to own.

The Change From an Industrial to a Service Economy

The first services to gain the attention of a great number of people were consumer services. In fact, some economists trace the introduction of the service economy to the popularity of the fast-food restaurant.

In 1940, Richard and Maurice (Mac) McDonald of San Bernadino, California opened a drive-in restaurant. Typical of drive-ins of the decade, carhops served customers who pulled their cars into the parking lot. In December 1948, the brothers decided to dismiss the carhops and pare down the menu to nine standardized, inexpensive items and speed up the serving process. By 1952, they were capable of serving a customer a hamburger, beverage, french fries, and ice cream in only 20 seconds. Their fast-food restaurant was such a success with area residents that they decided to sell franchises of their "McDonald self-service system" by the fall of 1952. The first licensed McDonald's franchise was established in 1955. In other words, the McDonald brothers decided to sell the rights to use their fast-food system, and their name, to other people interested in starting a successful restaurant business like theirs.

The success of the fast-food business created by the McDonald brothers led to the development of competing franchises like Burger King, Burger Chef, and Hardee's.

Figure 2-2. The first McDonald's. Some experts believe that the success of McDonald's fast-food business helped to usher in the era of the service economy in the United States.

The success of McDonald's was also the start of a trend toward the demand for services by both consumers and businesses. Contributing to this demand was the fact that the public had more leisure time available and a little more money to spend. Most people were working 40 hours a week at higher wages than in the past. They had enough time and money to demand more services in the form of hotel and motel rooms, vacation trips, entertainment, restaurant meals, and so forth. Another factor that contributed to the popularity of services was the fact that the new products created by more advanced technology required more servicing to keep them in good running condition. As computers, calculators, stereos, televisions and a variety of similarly complex products were developed, service jobs were created too.

The Entrepreneurs of the Service Era

Service entrepreneurs make decisions that are unique to providing services. They plan services that satisfy specific needs and wants. Unlike the process of producing a product, the planned service may have to be flexible to meet varied customer needs. Service entrepreneurs usually are also adept at setting prices.

The Change From the Service Economy to the Information Economy

The demand for services has grown since the 1950s. It is estimated that by the beginning of the 1980s consumers were spending about half their income on services.

Now, though, we have moved to an information economy. Information has been important since the first colonial farm. The farmer had to know how much to plant, how much the fields would yield, how much this yield would bring at market, and so on. The farmer kept track of this information by penning entries into a journal.

Although the term "information economy" is an unfamiliar one, the struggle to deal with information more efficiently has gone on since the late nineteenth century. The first computer was developed by Dr. Herman Hollerith back in 1890 to help with the processing of census figures. Called a census machine, Hollerith's invention speeded the processing of the census information from ten years to less than three.

The next major development in computer technology happened during World War II when the Electronic Numerical Integrator and Calculator (ENIAC) was invented. It was so large that it took up several rooms. By 1954, the first business computer was introduced. Between 1954 and the mid-1970s, computers were made more compact, more versatile, and less expensive. A tiny chip called a microprocessor is the basis of most of today's computers. This chip, which is no larger than a shirt button, can perform a million calculations in one second.

THE INFORMATION ECONOMY

Regardless of their size, all businesses manage various kinds of information. **Information** is the orderly and useful arrangement of **data,** or facts, so that they are accurate, timely, complete, and concise. To create information, people start with data, which then are classified and organized in a meaningful way.

If you own a garden store, the fact that you sold 155 bags of grass seed today is of little value to you until you combine that fact with other facts. If you know that you paid $2 a bag and sold them for $4, the fact that you sold 155 bags becomes more useful. If you know that yesterday you sold 62 bags of grass seed and the day before yesterday you sold 76, the fact that you sold 155 bags today becomes even more useful.

The success of businesses during the information economy depends on how efficiently they are able to manage the information that is important to them. If all this information is on paper, the task of managing it becomes a very difficult one. For this reason, the computer has become very closely tied with the success of businesses in today's information economy.

Technological advances in both computers and communication systems have enabled businesses (and an increasing number of consumers) to obtain the information that is important to them more quickly and easily. Those businesses that have access to important information more quickly than other businesses have a definite advantage in the marketplace.

The Information Processing Cycle

To handle information effectively, most businesses process it through the **information processing cycle** which is a series of stages, or steps, that make information usable to the business. These steps consist of input, processing, output, distribution, and storage and retrieval.

Input is receiving the information in the form of facts. The cost of grass seed, the selling price, the number of bags sold, and the expenses involved in selling them are all forms of input for the garden supply store. **Processing** is the sorting, calculating, and arranging of facts. It could be adding the selling price of all the grass seed sold, subtracting this figure from the total cost of the grass seed, and then subtracting the expenses of selling. **Output** is the producing of the information in a readable, usable form. For the garden supply store, it could be a profit and loss statement. **Distribution** is making sure that the output is communicated to the people who need it. The profit and loss statement is most valuable to the owner or manager of the garden supply store. **Storage and retrieval** is being able to file the input data or output and get it again whenever it is needed. If the profit and loss statement is lost in a pile of papers on someone's desk, it will be of no use to the owner of the garden supply store.

Managing Information With the Computer

Computers can help businesses manage the enormous quantity of information that they have to deal with. Five different types of computer programs are of particular help to businesses: word processing, database, spreadsheet, graphics, and electronic communications. We will briefly discuss the purpose of each one, then take a closer look at electronic communications in the information economy, commercial data banks, and the skills needed by employees and others in the information economy.

Word processing is an efficient way of putting words on paper. Using it, you can create a document and correct it before

Information Brief 2-3

Computer Tools

Word processing and graphics are two valuable tools for managing information with a computer. They can be used together to create effective reports. Word processing is an efficient way of putting words on paper. Mistakes can easily be corrected or words changed anywhere in a document without having to redo the whole thing. This can save hours of work compared to retyping. You can save what you've created and recall it on the computer whenever you want to work with the document. Graphics is a picture showing the relationship between numbers. For example, instead of telling people about something that involves the numbers 1435, 2453, 8764, and 845, you can show them a simple pie graph that represents these numbers as pie-shaped wedges. Computer programs can automatically create a variety of useful graphs.

you print it. You can store the document electronically and retrieve it whenever you want. You can change the document and save both versions, the original and your changed version.

A **database** is an electronic filing system for facts and figures. You can store both alphabetical information and numbers and ask the computer to organize them for you. You can arrange them alphabetically or numerically. You can also ask the computer to find only certain names or numbers for you.

A **spreadsheet** is a computerized version of an accountant's working paper with horizontal rows and vertical columns of numbers and words. It includes a calculator that automatically adds, subtracts, multiplies, and divides the numbers for you. If you change one or more of the numbers, the spreadsheet recalculates the totals for you automatically.

Graphics is a picture showing the relationship between numbers. Computers can create bar graphs, pie graphs, and line graphs when you feed in the numbers you want graphed.

Electronic communications is the ability to send and receive data or information with the aid of a computer, the telephone, and a modem. A **modem** is an electronic device that converts computer signals into telephone signals (and back again) for sending and receiving information over telephone lines.

Electronic Communications and the Information Economy

In the Pony Express days there was a 25-day lag between mailing a letter in the Midwest and having it read in San Francisco. Now the letter can be received shortly after it has been written.

As the information era progresses, it is becoming apparent that electronic communications is the key to success. Entrepreneurs who can send and receive information electronically will have access to specific pieces of information when and where they need it. With the help of electronic communications they can be in constant touch with people in other locations. To **telecommute** means to use computers and telephone equipment to work at home instead of at the office. Telecommuters, like Marc Silag in the introduction to this chapter, do not work in the office. They can work at home or travel on the road. Their employers equip these workers with complete electronic workstations. Armed with a computer and linked to headquarters by a telecommunication system, they receive assignments at their terminals. They process data and then transmit work

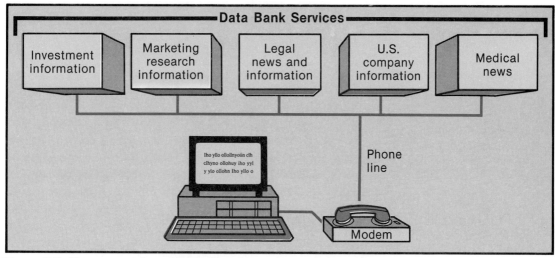

Figure 2-3. You can retrieve information from any number of data bank services available today. To retrieve such information, entrepreneurs need to acquire skills for working with a variety of information handling equipment and services.

through the same network. Occasionally they physically commute to the workplace for instructions, evaluation of performance, and personal interaction with others.

Another concept closely tied with telecommuting is teleconferencing. A **teleconference** is a meeting or conference among people at different locations electronically linked by audio and/or visual connections. Despite the comparative efficiency of today's transportation system, it costs money and takes time and energy to travel. Many of today's busy businesspeople appreciate the opportunity of "getting together" without having to leave their offices.

Electronic communications has also led to an increased use of data banks. These are collections of data on specific subjects, such as investments, that a person or firm may access electronically for a fee. However, to use data banks and other information technologies means learning new ways of doing business.

The Need for Trained Information Workers

Many unskilled and skilled labor jobs are disappearing. Automation, robotics, and competition from foreign markets dictate that both labor and management people must be more productive and develop entrepreneurial attitudes and work habits.

Heroes of Desktop Publishing

Married to his work, Paul Brainerd is one of two heroes of the desktop publishing (DTP) software industry. (**Desktop publishing** is a computer-driven system that allows a user to create professional looking documents with illustrated matter such as graphics. These documents are created by a desktop computer, special computer programs—so-called software—and a printer.) The other hero is John E. Warnock. Despite the profits each of their businesses have made, both entrepreneurs seem more motivated by the challenges of their industry than by the financial rewards.

Steve Jobs, Apple Computer's former chairperson, said this about John Warnock: "His motivation is to revolutionize the whole printing industry." Through their work with Apple, the desktop publishing pioneers formed a strong business friendship, even though they are now competitors. A native of Utah, Warnock majored in computer science and is a computer graphics whiz. Raised in Oregon, Brainerd has a master's degree in journalism.

John Warnock got the entrepreneurial urge in 1982 after Xerox decided not to commercialize his research in interactive graphics. He and a colleague started a company named Adobe to make graphics workstations for the printing industry. But Adobe's emphasis shifted when Steve Jobs heard about Warnock's work. Jobs needed software to make Apple's LaserWriter crank out fancy reports. Apple invested $1.5 million to fund the de-velopment of a software package called Postscript.

Back in the Midwest, Paul Brainerd was production manager for the *Minneapolis Star & Tribune* in the late 1970s. He left that job to move out west, where he managed Atex, Inc., a computer supplier. Then Eastman Kodak Company bought the Redmond, Washington, company and shut Atex down. Out of a job, but afire with ideas, Brainerd persuaded four Atex engineers to help him start a company they called Aldus.

At first, Brainerd's idea was to develop a program to prepare newspaper ads on microcomputers. But when he got a Macintosh (manufactured by Apple Computer), Paul switched directions. Now he wanted to develop a software package that would enable Mac owners to make high-quality documents for printing on a laser printer.

Paul Brainerd figures that desktop publishing might never have gotten off the ground if the two entrepreneurs had not met—through Steve Jobs. Brainerd claims he's more of a businessperson, whereas John Warnock is a technologist. But the two DTP heroes shared a dream and an appreciation for good design. With Jobs as one of their few allies, Brainerd and Warnock agreed that their most important joint effort was persuading Apple to promote desktop publishing.

Paul Brainerd's Aldus company produces the DTP software program called

(continued)

Technology Feature *(continued)*

PageMaker. And John Warnock's Adobe company produces the DTP program called Postscript.

To deflect concern that Adobe might be at great risk because it was a one-product company, in the late 1980s War-nock came up with Adobe Illustrator. This software package is designed for graphic artists. Meanwhile, Brainerd's people started looking for ideas to broaden the product base of Aldus as well.

Source: Katherine M. Hafner, "How Two Pioneers Brought Publishing to the Desktop," *Business Week*, October 5, 1987, pp. 61–62.

It is estimated that 75 percent of the jobs available throughout the information era will be in the information technology area. A vast pool of skilled technological labor is needed to process the data and create information for the information economy.

The Entrepreneur in the Information Economy

Business entrepreneurs in the information economy must obtain many new skills that were not needed in prior economic eras. They will be involved in making important decisions about the most efficient way to access, handle, and communicate information. In addition to the skills that were needed by entrepreneurs in earlier eras, they will learn how to use computers, modems, on-line data banks, and a variety of information handling equipment and services that were not previously available. They will have to acquire technical knowledge that was not needed prior to this era.

The development of the American economy has been an interesting one, from agriculture to the current information age. This era will not, however, be the last. The economy will continue to evolve into eras that we cannot, at this time, predict. Entrepreneurs knowledgeable about the options open to them in the information era and skilled enough to take advantage of these options will be best equipped to move into the economic eras of the future.

Select Terms to Know

agricultural economy	factory system	information processing cycle	teleconference
database	graphics	service economy	trust
domestic system	industrial ecoomy	spreadsheet	word processing
electronic communications	information economy	telecommunicate	

Review Questions

1. What four economic eras has our country experienced in its 300-plus-year history? Give some examples of the economic activities that dominated in each era.

2. How has each economic era supplemented and built upon the era before it?

3. Why are farmers considered "the first American entrepreneurs"? By the late 1800s, what entrepreneurial skills and abilities did they use?

4. How did the Morrill Act and Homestead Act assist in the economic growth and expansion of our country?

5. Explain the difference between cottage industries and the factory system.

6. How were labor and some businesses exploited during the early industrial era?

7. What landmark industrial legislation was passed to protect workers and business from unfair practices?

8. What talents and abilities did the entrepreneurs of the industrial era exhibit?

9. Distinguish between data and information and identify the steps of the information processing cycle.

10. What are some skills and talents that entrepreneurs and workers need for success in today's information economy?

Thought and Discussion Questions

1. In your opinion, what was the single-most important contribution, talent, or skill of each of the following: (*a*) agricultural entrepreneurs, (*b*) industrial entrepreneurs, (*c*) service entrepreneurs, and (*d*) information entrepreneurs.

2. Ever since the agricultural era the number of farms and farmers has been declining. Do you think it is the responsibility of the government to help maintain farming as a way of life? Explain your answer.

3. Do you think the United States would be the major world power it is today without the achievements of the industrial entrepreneurs? Explain your views.

4. Do you think that workers should have the right to form and join unions? Do you think that people in business should have the right to stop workers from joining unions? Fully explain your answer.

5. Compare modern telecommuters with the people of yesteryear who worked in cottage industries. How are they alike? How are they different?

Projects

1. Research at a library to find out the total population and the number of farm and factory workers in our country in the years 1800, 1850, 1900, 1950, and today (latest available figures). Determine the percentage of the population that was engaged in farming and factory work in each of these years. Report the results in table or graph form to your class. Based on the figures, what conclusions can you reach about farming and industrial activity during different eras in American history? Assume that you had a graphics computer program. In what ways might it help you to show the relationship between farm and factory employment at different points in American history? How might the program save you time in carrying out this project?

2. Select one group—women or a minority, such as blacks, American Indians, Hispanics. Research to find out how the group fared in business and society during one of the four economic eras described in the chapter. Share the results with your class.

3. Research in greater depth to find out the working conditions of children in the early industrial era. Then imagine yourself as a child laborer. Write a letter to a lawmaker describing your working conditions and stating what, if any,

actions you want the lawmaker to take to help improve your conditions.

4. During the industrial era some workers and businesses were exploited by businesspeople eager to make vast sums of money. Some called these businesspeople "captains of industry," and others called them "robber barons." Research to find out why these individuals were given these names. Then prepare a report which explains how one of these individuals amassed a fortune, giving special attention to evidence of business practices that would not be allowed today. Possible individuals to research are Jay Cooke, Andrew Carnegie, Jay Gould, James H. Hill, John D. Rockefeller, J. Pierpont Morgan, Cornelius Vanderbilt, Philip Armour, or Charles Pillsbury.

Case Study: Electronic Mail—Offices on the Run

As a busy production manager in the entertainment field, Marc Silag spends most of his time traveling from one concert to the next. His clients include such celebrities as Paul Simon and Patti LaBelle.

Silag's heavy travel schedule makes it difficult for him to work at a traditional office. But with the help of electronic mail, or e-mail, he can send information to people at his office and other offices by using his computer, a modem, and any telephone. E-mail is a method of electronic communications where information sent is filed on a computer until the recipient is ready to receive it. Each person who uses the system is given an electronic mailbox. Any messages received are filed in the electronic mailbox.

E-mail messages can be sent at any time—24 hours a day. Silag can send his supervisor important information about a future concert when he ends his day at 2:00 a.m. instead of waiting until the next morning. All Silag has to do is dial the phone number of his office's computer system and address his message to his supervisor's mailbox. Then he can go to sleep without worrying about calling the first thing in the morning.

The next morning when his supervisor goes to the office, she can read and act on Silag's message. If there is an answer, Silag can read it when he picks up his e-mail messages.

Source: Adapted from Ina Mayer, "Clark Kent's Biggest Scoop," *OnLine Access Guide*, Winter 1986, p. 13.

1. If e-mail had been available in 1862, how might it have changed the lives of the farmers during the agricultural era?

2. If Marc Silag had lived in 1925 and been a production manager for celebrity Rudy Vallee, how might his job have been different?

3. A new communications system that has recently been introduced will allow you to communicate through radio waves instead of telephone lines. With this system, you can send messages from a specially equipped computer without connecting it to a modem and a telephone. What changes might this new system make in Marc Silag's daily schedule and his method of communicating with his office?

Computers Awash With Data as the Stock Market Explodes

INTRODUCTION

Nearly half the 2000 New York Stock Exchange employees worked on the weekend of October 24 and 25, 1987, following 15-hour days early in the week. Thousands more reported for weekend work at brokerages around the country.

Clerks and brokers from coast to coast worked overtime, processing information to determine who bought what, how much, and from whom. The stock market, as an exchange place, is where floor traders buy and sell shares of stock—ownership in corporations. (You will learn more about this in Chapter 10.) On Monday and Tuesday, October 19 and 20, 1987, over 600 million shares were traded. That, of course, is a lot of information to record and keep track of, even with computers. The following news account recalls the feel and flavor of what happened on October 19 and 20, perhaps the most eventful days in the history of the New York Stock Exchange.

BACKGROUND

New York, October 20, 1987. At 2:53 p.m. a senior Stock Exchange trader fields a call. A buyer wants 613,000 shares of General Electric stock. The trader shouts to the dozen men and women in the packed room, "Somebody find a seller, and fast!" Several other traders spring into action, punching at the white buttons from their 140-button phone consoles. (The red buttons connect them with floor traders at the New York Stock Exchange. Green buttons go to the floors of the American or Midwest Stock Exchanges.) In less than a minute a bearded trader has a seller with 100,000 shares. At 2:55 p.m., another trader hits pay dirt—someone with 513,000 shares to sell. By 3 p.m., seven minutes later, the whole transaction is completed.

As noted previously, trading volume on Monday and Tuesday, October 19 and 20, hit a record 600 million shares sold and bought. Worse, however, was the 508-point drop in the Dow Jones averages (averages of stocks traded in industrials, utilities, and transportation stocks). This record breaking drop in the price of shares resulted in a trillion dollar total loss in stock values for shareholders around the world. Before October 19 was half over, the effect of the plummeting U.S. market was felt on the Tokyo and Hong Kong markets and elsewhere around the globe. The Hong Kong market closed down for a week. In London, all computers were down and nobody could get through to either buy or sell.

Financial and information specialists wondered whether computerized trading was partly to blame for the crash of '87. **Computerized trading**, using computers and telecommunications, means that buy-and-sell orders are preentered into the computer. If the price of a stock is currently going for $30 and you want to buy 10,000 shares at $25, you give your stockbroker the order. The computer is programmed to automatically buy your 10,000 shares when the price drops to $25. But suppose 999,000 other people submit similar orders to either buy or sell shares of stock. With all those computers automatically clicking on, that's a lot of information moving back and forth. And after each buy or sell is completed, somebody has to prepare individual account records and mail them out all over the world.

Sources: John R. Dorfman, Clare Ansberry, and Robert Johnson, "The Crash of '87: Coping on the Day After," *The Wall Street Journal*, October 21, 1987; Gary Weiss and Chris Welles, "Was Program Trading to Blame, and Did the Specialists Do Their Job?" *Business Week*, November 2, 1987; and "Saturday Is Overtime Day for the Stock Market," *Laramie Boomerang*, October 25, 1987.

DISCUSSION QUESTIONS

1. How does this news account demonstrate that we are living in an information economy?

2. How does the news article illustrate some of the pitfalls of living and working in an information economy?

3. In what ways does the news account show that we are living in a world in which what happens to one nation's economy affects the economies of other nations?

4. How does the news story illustrate the importance of risk in our information economy?

5. If you were a clerk or stockbroker with all that information to process, how would you feel about working 15-hour days under stress? Suppose you made a mistake in entering data at the computer that caused somebody to lose a lot of money. How would you feel?

UNIT 2

The Economic Environment of Business

After reading and studying a bit about business and the development of our economy, you may be wondering how business and the economy are related. Why are businesspeople interested in economics and the economy? Why do business organizations iike your local Chamber of Commerce work so hard to improve the local, state, or national economy? Although you have some ideas about it, you might be wondering just what "economics" is. The material presented in the three chapters of this unit will begin to provide you with answers to these questions. The general objective of this unit is to help you become more familiar with and better understand the role of business in our national economy and the global economy.

UNIT OBJECTIVES

1. Describe what economics is and is not.
2. Understand some basic economic principles that guide all economic systems.
3. Compare the features of different economic systems.
4. Describe the role business plays in the unique economic system of the United States.
5. Discuss how the role of business has been changed and expanded in today's global economy.

CHAPTER 3

The Basics of Economics

Bidding Goodbye to the Big Apple

"We're moving!" These words are important ones. And when they come from the head of a huge corporation, they can affect employees, suppliers, customers, and many times entire communities. Peat Marwick (the biggest U.S. accounting firm), J. C. Penney, Mobile Corporation, Trans World Airlines, and Deloitte, Haskins & Sells (the seventh biggest U.S. accounting firm) are all companies that have made the decision to move their national headquarters out of New York City.

Why would a firm decide to move from one city to another? Since this type of decision affects those who work for the firm and their families as well as other business firms and their employees, it is not an easy one to make. How would a firm go about making such an important decision?

Learn how basic principles often play a vital role in these and other major decisions when you read the end-of-chapter case study, "Big City Trade-offs—Choosing Less to Get More."

Businesses make many decisions as they carry on their normal activities. Some of these decisions affect only the business, its workers, and its customers. Other decisions, like the ones being made by the companies moving their headquarters from New York City, affect many more people. They may affect other companies, cities, states, and even nations. Think of how many people would be affected if one of the largest companies in your town or a nearby town decided to move or close down.

Why do businesses make such decisions? How do they make them? You may have heard the expression, "It's all economics." What does this mean? The purpose of this chapter is to help you answer that question. You will learn the meaning of some commonly used terms, see examples of some important economic principles in action, and learn how economics helps us to make decisions.

WHAT IS ECONOMICS?

You started learning about economics long before you entered this course. In fact, by the time you were three or four years old, you already understood two important economic concepts. First, there are a lot of things you would like to have. Second, you can't have everything you want—you have to make choices. If you have a dollar in your hand, you can have either a 98 cent pen or a 98 cent bag of candy. You can't have both.

Businesses have to make choices just as you do. Most businesses would like to have a great many things. Computers, telephone systems, new production equipment, new trucks, new office furniture, a short commuting time for employees— the list of business wants could go on and on. But with limited money to work with, most businesses can have only a small portion of the things that they want.

Just as individuals and businesses have to make choices, so do countries. Countries want a great many things for their citizens, but they can afford only a portion of them. A country may want excellent schools, beautiful parks, an environment that is free from pollution, more social security benefits for senior citizens, no unemployment, no crime, and more medical research. The country may also want to be a leader in the production of industrial machinery, computer systems, and medical equipment. Each country also has important, sometimes difficult, choices to make.

Scarcity—A Basic Economic Problem

How do all these choices relate to economics? Choices are what economics is all about. When you learned that you have to make choices because you can't have everything you want, you learned the most basic of all economic concepts. You learned that there is a condition called scarcity which exists throughout the world. **Scarcity** refers to the general condition of having unlimited wants and limited resources for satisfying these wants. We have many wants, but here we are referring only to **economic wants**, wants which can be satisfied by having a good or service. Similarly, we are referring only to economic resources in this case. **Economic resources** include anything that is used to produce or create goods and services.

This weekend you may want to repair your car, finish a term paper, go to a concert with your friends, paint your bedroom, shop for clothes, and visit with your cousin who lives three

Information Brief
3-1

Over 1000 New Goods Hit the Market in One Month

If you can't find the products you want when you go shopping, just wait a few days.

More than 1000 new food, health, and beauty products were put on the shelves of supermarkets and drugstores in a recent month.

"Consumer needs are changing dramatically, and that creates a lot of opportunity," says David Driscoll of General Foods Corporation's grocery sector.

It creates opportunities for consumers to find just the type of products that satisfy their needs and wants. At the same time it creates money making opportunities for businesses.

In fact, only 1 out of 10 new products introduced by food companies need to be a hit for the company to make money.

Sources: "Business Bulletin," *The Wall Street Journal*, June 11, 1987, p. 1; and "USA Snapshots," *USA Today*, June 22, 1987, p. 1B.

hours from your home. You can't possibly do all these things because you do not have enough of another resource—time. Although it is not normally considered to be an economic resource, time is a resource we often refer to as being limited. Everyone has the same amount of the resource—24 hours each day—but often that isn't enough time for us to do all the things we'd like. The resource is limited relative to our want for it.

What do limited resources have to do with economics? **Economics** is the study of how societies use their limited economic resources to produce, exchange, and consume goods and services to satisfy the economic wants of their members. Societies must make choices as they decide how to use their economic resources. Many of the choices that they make involve deciding which goods and services to produce to satisfy the wants of their members. Since the terms *goods* and *services* have been used several times here (and in previous chapters), let's take a closer look at how economists and businesspeople use them.

Goods and Services—A Way to Satisfy Wants

In Chapter 1 you learned that *goods* are objects that satisfy people's needs and wants. They are tangible things, or things which you can touch and see, taste and smell. Cars, clothes, VCRs, and food are examples of material things people are willing to pay or trade for because they satisfy their wants. In the United States we have many goods, and thousands more hit the market each month. (See Information Brief 3-1.)

Some of the things people want cannot be satisfied by obtaining goods. You may need to have your compact disk player or your 10-speed bicycle fixed, for example. You may need a physical exam before you can participate in a sport, or a haircut or styling before taking a yearbook picture. These are examples of services. You learned in Chapter 1 that *services* are tasks that people have others do for them because they satisfy needs or wants. While goods are physical, or tangible, things, services are intangible. This means that you cannot actually see or touch a service even though you may be able to see and touch the person who provides it or some of the things used in providing it. Repair persons, lawyers, dentists, social workers, police and fire department workers, professional entertainers and athletes, and teachers are all people who provide services for others.

While it is true that most goods and services are bought for money, they cannot be created from money. Other resources are used to produce the goods and services that satisfy our wants. What are these resources and why are they considered to be limited?

▼ Which do you think we produce more of today: goods or services? Do you feel this is what should be happening? Why?

FACTORS OF PRODUCTION

As noted earlier, goods and services are produced or created by using economic resources. Therefore, countries need economic resources if they wish to satisfy the economic wants of their citizens. The economic resources needed to produce goods and services are called the **factors of production.** The factors of production are made up of three different kinds of economic resources: natural resources, human resources, and capital resources.

Natural Resources

The gifts of nature that are used to produce goods and services are called **natural resources.** Natural resources include fertile land, oil and mineral deposits, trees, water, fish, and so on. They are the basic elements which are combined in various ways to create goods. Even synthetics which are so common in modern goods are produced by combining or breaking down natural resources. Nylon, for example, is a synthetic material derived from coal, water, and air.

It is important to realize that some natural resources are only available to be used once. The world's reserves of oil and certain kinds of minerals that are definitely limited are examples of these. Since they cannot be replaced or renewed, they are sometimes referred to as *nonrenewable resources.* As we continue to use up these nonrenewable natural resources, they become increasingly scarce.

Other natural resources renew themselves, or can be renewed through our conscious efforts. Water, trees, and other growing things such as fruit and vegetables are examples. As you might expect, these are sometimes referred to as *renewable resources.* The amount of renewable resources available varies They may be scarce at times and abundant at other times.

The kind and amount of each type of natural resource owned or available to individuals, business firms, or nations is impor-

Information Brief
3-2

Workers Spell Success

How important is the quality of human resources that are available to a company? Experts believe that they can spell the difference between success and failure.

More and more employers are looking for workers with computer literacy who are generalists instead of specialists. They want people who are flexible, creative, and have good communication and people skills. And employers are willing to pay more for quality human resources.

Source: Adapted from Rhea A. Nagle, "The Ideal Job Candidate of the 21st Century," *Journal of Career Planning and Employment,* Summer 1987, pp. 36–40.

tant. The supply of natural resources has a direct effect on the amount and kinds of goods and services that are produced.

▼ Do you feel we are doing enough to preserve the trees and water we have available as renewable natural resources in our country? Why do you feel as you do?

Human Resources

Natural resources used to make goods and services usually need to be processed, combined, or somehow changed to make them useful. These activities do not happen automatically; people perform them. **Human resources** are the people who provide all forms of physical and mental effort involved in the production of goods and services. This includes the technical, administrative, and managerial skills as well as the physical activities normally thought of as labor. It also includes the thinking and research done to develop the methods used to change raw, natural resources into goods and services.

The number, or quantity, of human resources available to a firm or nation is important. The number of hours they are available to work is also important. Most important, however, is the quality of the human resources available. Their health, strength, education, and motivation directly affect the level of production. (See Information Brief 3-2.)

Human resources are also referred to as **labor,** and references are made to a nation's labor force. In the United States, the **labor force** is made up of all the people who are 16 years or older and have jobs or are actively looking for jobs. Table 3-1 shows the number of people in the U.S. labor force during recent years. As the table indicates, the U.S. labor force has been increasing steadily. Likewise, the number of persons actually employed was increasing during the years shown.

Capital Resources

The third factor of production is capital resources. All the buildings, machines, equipment, and tools used to produce goods and services are examples of capital resources. Basically, **capital resources** are items (other than natural resources) that are used to produce goods and services. Capital resources do not satisfy our needs directly. Instead, they help us become

TABLE 3-1 U.S. Labor Force, 1984–1987 (Millions of Persons)				
	1984	**1985**	**1986**	**1987**
Total people who could work*	178.6	180.4	186.8	184.4
Civilian and military labor force	115.8	117.7	120.1	121.5
Civilian labor force	113.4	115.5	117.8	119.2
Nonagricultural employees	101.7	104.0	106.4	108.1
Agricultural employees	3.3	3.2	3.2	3.3
People who choose not to work	62.8	62.9	62.7	63.0
Unemployed persons	8.5	8.3	8.3	7.9

* Noninstitutional population who are 16 years of age or older.
Source: Adapted from *Federal Reserve Bulletin*, vol. 73, no. 6, June 1987, p. A45. Based on data from *Employment and Earnings* (U.S. Department of Labor).

more efficient in the production of goods and services that do satisfy our needs.

A person using a knife or hand peeler can peel and slice potatoes by hand to make french fries. The same person using an electric peeler and an automatic slicer can do the same job many times faster. The electric peeler and automatic slicer are examples of capital resources. They do not directly satisfy anyone's hunger for french fries. If the quality of the french fries is the same, those who buy them will hardly be concerned about the type of capital resources used for their preparation.

The word *capital* is sometimes used to refer only to money. This is common in accounting and financial discussions. Remember, however, that when we are talking about economics, capital resources are all the items (except natural resources) that are used to produce goods and services, including money.

INFORMATION—ANOTHER IMPORTANT RESOURCE

Although it is not considered to be one of the three basic productive resources, information is another important resource which businesses must have to produce goods and services. Why is information important to a business? It is true that you cannot produce goods such as TVs or VCRs from information. However, in some respects information is very similar to an economic good or service. It can be bought and sold, and it can take the tangible form of a printed report. Some firms specialize in putting information together in meaningful and useful ways and then selling it to others. (See the Technology in an Information Economy feature for more about this.)

Figure 3-1. Examples of the factors of production are: *(a)* information, an increasingly important resource; *(b)* fish (natural resources); *(c)* labor and *(d)* management (human resources); and *(e)* a robot (capital resources).

To be successful, a business must have accurate and timely information about such things as the availability, location, and quality of the factors of production it uses. Computers, satellites, and other new communication devices are now widely used in business to provide more and better-quality information.

MAKING CHOICES

You know your resources are limited. You can't have everything you want. Other people, businesses, and even societies have something in common with you. Their resources, the factors of production we just discussed, are also limited. Because economics studies how societies make choices as they use limited resources to meet unlimited needs and wants, it can help us learn how to make choices. Two economic tools that can help us make choices are opportunity costs and trade-offs.

Opportunity Costs

Let's say that you have a chance to go to a concert or a party on Friday night. The concert and the party are scheduled at exactly the same time, so you can't go to both. If you go to the concert, you'll miss the party; if you go to the party, you'll miss the concert. You have to make a choice; you have to give up something. There is a "cost" involved that is not related to money. It is called opportunity cost. **Opportunity cost** is the benefit given up when choosing one alternative over another. The opportunity cost of going to the concert is giving up the enjoyment you would have at the party. The opportunity cost of going to the party is giving up the fun you would have at the concert. You might say it costs you the concert to attend the party, or it costs you the party to attend the concert.

Now let's look at the same type of choices when we are talking about spending money. You have enough money to buy either seat covers for your car or a new jacket. You can't have both. The opportunity cost of buying seat covers is giving up the benefit you would get from the jacket. And the opportunity cost of buying the jacket is the benefit you would get from the seat covers. It is important to keep in mind that you will get the benefits from whichever alternative you choose. You will choose one or the other because you feel the benefits are the greatest from having the jacket or the seat covers.

TECHNOLOGY IN AN INFORMATION ECONOMY

Information at the Touch of a Button

You need to find the names of all the businesses in your area that employ more than 200 people and the names of the top executives. Where will you start your search? At the library? At the chamber of commerce? You probably picture hours of exhausting research.

You may be pleasantly surprised to learn that the information is no farther away than your computer, provided that computer is hooked into an on-line data service.

Sales of information delivered by phone lines is growing at a surprising rate of 23 percent annually in the United States. In fact, the sale of information has become an exciting new computer-related service. The businesses that sell information are a part of the information services industry.

Much of the information that is available is business information such as stock quotes, legal information, and credit checks. You will probably have no trou-ble finding information on the businesses in your local community. All the information related to a specific economic or business area is called a database. And there are now more than 1500 different databases available to computer users who are hooked into on-line data services.

The need for consumer information is growing at even a faster rate than the need for business information. Some authorities estimate that the demand for electronically delivered consumer information is growing by a rate of 60 percent a year.

In response to this growing demand companies are providing an increasing amount of information to home computer users. There are more than 7 million homes in the United States with computers hooked up to modems. If you are in one of these homes, you can do your banking, buy and sell stocks, and communicate with business partners all from the comfort of your home computer keyboard.

What is the future of the information service industry? Before you know it you may be able to receive your mail, go to school, shop, have doctors diagnose your medical conditions, vote in local elections, and participate in town hall meetings from the comfort of your easy chair.

Source: Adapted from Marvin Cetron, *The Future of American Business*, McGraw-Hill, 1985, pp. 95–96 and 167–168.

Every decision we make has an opportunity cost attached to it. If a toy company decides to produce model cars instead of model helicopters on its assembly line, the opportunity cost of producing cars will be the helicopters it didn't produce.

Societies have the same type of choices to make. A particular piece of land can be used for either a library or a hospital. It can't be used for both things at the same time. Therefore, a community must decide if it wants the benefits of a library or a hospital; it must give up one of the two.

Trade-Offs

When you have a difficult choice to make, you can compare the benefits and costs of each alternative by considering the trade-offs. By taking a close look at the benefits and costs, you can "trade them off" until you have the best choice. In economic terms, a **trade-off** is accepting or choosing less of one thing to get more of another.

Let's look at your choice of going to the party or the concert. What are the benefits or advantages of going to the party? You have heard that there will be live music there, and you don't have to pay to get in. You also know that there will be lots of pizzas to eat. But before you decide to go to the party, you have to look at the costs or disadvantages. You have heard the group that is playing at the party, and you are not too fond of their music. You can eat pizza any day and will have lots of time to get together with your friends at other parties.

What about the concert? What do you feel are the benefits and costs of that alternative? Well, you really like the group that is performing, and you have been wanting to go to one of their concerts for a long time. You have a chance to get the tickets, for very good seats. However, the tickets will cost $40, and you have to drive over an hour to attend. You will have to pay for parking. And only one of your friends has any interest in missing the party to go to the concert with you.

From this situation and each choice that you make, you can trade off benefits against costs for each of the alternatives to come to the best decision. For most personal choices such as the one described here, you identify the benefits and costs from your personal point of view. You may consider some other person's opinions, but you make the final choice based on *your* feelings about the costs and benefits. But what about more difficult choices such as how to use a piece of land or how to use limited resources? In these cases there may be many people directly affected by the decision. Who considers the trade-offs and makes the final decisions in these cases? In Chapter 4 we will take a look at the questions each society asks as it decides how to use its limited productive resources and the ways each society considers the trade-offs and makes decisions.

EXCHANGING GOODS AND SERVICES

People in all societies have exchanged goods and services since the beginning of recorded history. Originally they exchanged things directly through a system called **barter,** which is the direct exchange of goods and services without the use of money. Serfs, for example, worked for their lords in exchange for food and a place to live. A property owner may have exchanged five cows and four chickens for a piece of land or some plowing tools and seed. But even in very primitive societies with relatively few goods and services, people came to realize that barter was a cumbersome and inefficient way to exchange goods and services. Therefore, they set up a different method. Instead of exchanging things directly, they "sold" something called a medium of exchange and used that to "buy" what they wanted. The medium of exchange was something that was widely accepted in exchange for goods and services in the society.

Grain, animals, shells, trinkets, and salt, among other things, were used for the medium of exchange over the years. No matter what was used, the principle involved was the same. Instead of direct barter, persons could exchange their labor or other service for a certain amount of the medium of exchange and then exchange the medium of exchange for other goods and services. Although the medium of exchange has changed, this is exactly what happens in our society and almost all the societies of the world today. People are willing to exchange or sell their labor or other productive resources for a certain amount of money—our medium of exchange. And businesses are willing to exchange or sell the goods and services they produce for a certain amount of money.

Markets

During earlier periods of history, a market was a place where buyers and sellers actually met to exchange their goods and services. Farmers came to town and set up stalls to display their produce. Townspeople would then come and buy the produce directly from the farmers. Some communities in the United States still have "farmers' markets" which operate in much the same way today. However, most goods and services are no longer exchanged in this way.

The term market now refers to more than a physical location. Now a **market** is considered to be any system or arrangement that enables buyers and sellers to negotiate prices and exchange goods and services. We buy and sell goods and services through letters, newspapers, telephone, TV, and computer networks as well as personal relationships and face-to-face discussions. Further, the original producer and the final consumer of the good may not deal with one another directly. Instead, there are many people or businesses who perform specialized functions that help move goods from producer to consumer. For example, most farmers sell their vegetables or fruit to wholesalers who package or process the produce and transport it to grocery stores. Consumers then buy the produce from the grocery store. You will learn more about the channels, or paths, that products take as they move from the producer to the consumer when you read Chapter 15.

Markets aren't limited to the exchange of goods. They are also used to exchange labor, services, property, and even money. If you answer a newspaper ad for a part-time job, you are taking advantage of the labor market. The employer is the buyer who needs workers, and you are the seller of your labor to the employer.

Prices

The price of something is usually stated in terms of money. **Prices** are the amounts of money people pay in exchange for a unit of a particular good or service. It is the amount of money the buyer pays to get some good or service and also the amount the seller receives for providing the good or service.

Notice that both the buyer and seller must agree to exchange the good or service at a certain price or there will be no exchange. How is price determined? Reading through the next section will help you answer this often-asked question.

DETERMINING MARKET PRICES—SUPPLY AND DEMAND

How much are you willing to pay for a hamburger? A dollar? Two dollars? Ten dollars? A hundred dollars? "Not a chance!"

Information Brief 3-3

Where's the Fish Machine?

How much do you like fish? Enough to pay for it as prices continue to rise?

In the last five years our demand for fish has risen over 20 percent as a result of healthier eating habits. But fish aren't like carpets or cars. We can't just turn on a machine and produce more. The increased demand has caused flounder, sole, cod, and haddock to be in very short supply. And this short supply leads to higher prices.

Industry officials are concerned that rising prices could lead consumers to switch to other protein sources even though they would prefer to have fish.

Source: Adapted from "Business Bulletin," *The Wall Street Journal,* June 18, 1987.

you might shout when the price is $100. Yet you and all the other people who buy hamburgers actually determine the prices that restaurants charge for them. The system that is used to set prices in our country is referred to as *supply and demand.*

▼ How would you feel if the prices of hamburgers, hot dogs, and fries suddenly shot up to $100 a serving?

What Is Supply?

If you knew you could sell hamburgers for 10 cents each, how many would you be interested in making? What if you could sell them for $1 apiece? How about $10 each? And how many hamburgers would you be willing to make if you could sell them for $100 each?

Supply refers to the quantities of a resource, good, or service that will be offered for sale at various prices during a period of time. Generally producers are willing to make larger quantities of their products available at higher prices. You would probably be willing to make a lot more hamburgers if you could get $100 for each of them than you would if you could get only 10 cents for each one.

What Is Demand?

Demand refers to the quantities of a resource, good, or service that will be purchased at various prices during a period of time. Your desire for a product or service isn't considered demand unless you are *willing and able* to pay for it. You may want a sports car, a diamond watch, and a trip around the world. But if you can't afford to buy these things or can afford them but are not willing to spend your money on them, your wants are not considered demands.

Generally consumers are willing to buy more of an item when the price is lower than they are when the price is higher. You probably would like to buy a lot more hamburgers at 10 cents each than you would at $100 each.

Picturing Supply

To help keep track of supply and demand figures, economists often use tables and graphs to illustrate the quantities of an item that are demanded or supplied at different prices.

Let's switch our attention from hamburgers to felt-tip pens. Table 3-2 shows that the number of black felt-tip marking pens

TABLE 3-2 Supply Schedule for Black Felt-Tip Pens	
Quantity Supplied by Producers (in Millions)	**Price per Pen**
125	$4.50
100	4.00
85	3.50
72	3.00
60	2.50
50	2.00
35	1.50
16	1.00
1	0.50
0	0.25

that producers are willing to supply is 125 million pens at $4.50 and 100 million pens at a price of $4.00. But they are willing to supply only 1 million pens at 50 cents each. And at a price of 25 cents, they are willing to offer no pens for sale because they cost 40 cents a piece to manufacture.

Figure 3-2 shows the same information in picture form. The picture is actually a graph that is called a supply curve. A *supply curve* illustrates the quantity of a good or service that suppliers are willing to provide at various price levels. Notice that the line on the supply curve slopes upward because the quantity supplied increases when price increases.

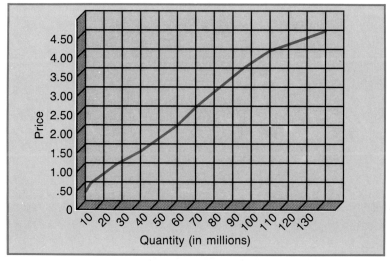

Figure 3-2. Supply curve for black felt tip pens.

TABLE 3-3 Demand Schedule for Black Felt-Tip Pens	
Quantity Demanded by Consumers (in Millions)	Price per Pen
0	$4.50
3	4.00
10	3.50
23	3.00
38	2.50
50	2.00
63	1.50
80	1.00
95	0.50
115	0.25

Picturing Demand

Now let's see how many black felt-tip pens people are willing to buy at different prices. Table 3-3 shows that at a price of 25 cents, people want to buy 115 million felt-tip pens. The number of people interested gradually decreases as the price increases. And at a price of $4.50, nobody is interested in buying any.

A *demand curve,* which illustrates the quantity of a good or service that consumers are willing to buy at various price levels, is shown in Figure 3-3. Notice that the demand curve slopes

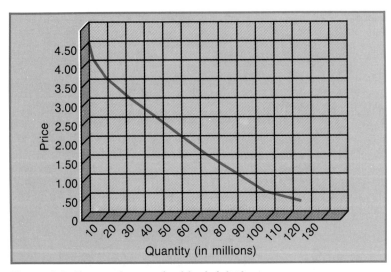

Figure 3-3. Demand curve for black felt tip pens.

downward because the quantity demanded increases as prices decrease.

Putting Supply and Demand Together

Now let's look at supply and demand together. Generally speaking, the quantity of a good or service which will be supplied will tend to rise when the quantity demanded is great and fall when the quantity demanded is low. This means that producers will try to make more of something when they believe consumers want and are able to buy more of it. But if producers find out that fewer people want and are able to buy the good or service, the producers will provide smaller quantities. This general situation is sometimes referred to as the law of supply and demand. It makes a lot of sense because businesses do not want to produce goods and services that no one wants to buy.

Picturing Supply and Demand

How do the demand and supply for our felt-tip pens look when we put information about them together? Table 3-4 shows both the quantity demanded and the quantity supplied at various prices. Can you find the price at which the number of pens producers want to supply equals the number of pens consumers want to buy? The price is $2. At that price, producers want to produce and suppliers want to buy 50 million pens.

TABLE 3-4 Supply and Demand Schedule for Black Felt-Tip Pens		
Quantity Supplied by Producers (in Millions)	**Price per Pen**	**Quantity Demanded by Consumers (in Millions)**
125	$4.50	0
100	4.00	3
85	3.50	10
72	3.00	23
60	2.50	38
50	2.00	50
35	1.50	63
16	1.00	80
1	0.50	95
0	0.25	115

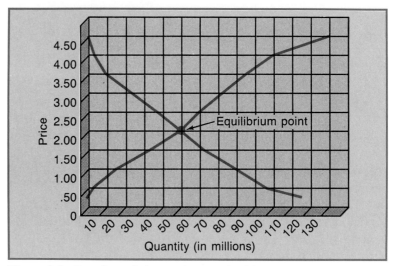

Figure 3-4. Supply and demand curve for black felt tip pens.

Figure 3-4 shows the supply and demand curve together. Notice the place on the graph where the supply and demand curves cross, or intersect. This point is called the *equilibrium point* and identifies the market clearing price, in this case $2. The **market clearing price** is the price at which the quantity supplied and the quantity demanded for a resource, good, or service are equal.

What does all this information mean? It means that at a price of $2 there are enough people who want to make felt-tip pens to produce the number of pens people want to buy. As the price goes up, more people will want to produce the pens or those already producing them will want to make more, but fewer people will want to buy them or those who have already bought them will buy fewer. And as the price goes down just the opposite will occur.

FITTING IT ALL TOGETHER—THE CIRCULAR-FLOW MODEL

As you have seen, economics is the study of choices. You have also seen that price, as determined by supply and demand, has a very important bearing on our choice of goods and services. But how do the choices that you make when you buy jeans, shoes, books, soft drinks, and haircuts become part of the economics of the United States?

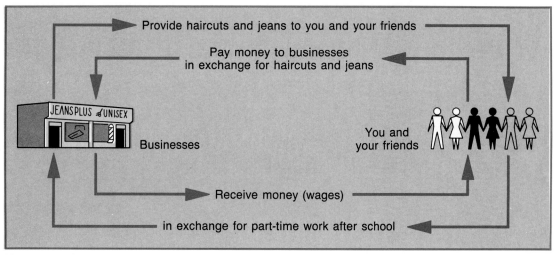

Figure 3-5. Simplified circular flow chart.

Take a look at Figure 3-5. It may help you to understand how your choices affect the U.S. economy. It shows what happens when you buy a pair of jeans and get a haircut. First, the retail store selling the jeans and the hair stylist provide you with a pair of jeans and a haircut. In exchange, you give them money. For the sake of illustration, let's also imagine that these same businesses (the retail store and the hair stylist) hire you and your friends to work part-time after school. In exchange for the labor you provide, unpacking boxes in the stockroom of the retail store and sweeping the floor for the hair stylist, you and your friends receive money from the businesses in the form of wages.

If you think carefully about the figure, you'll realize that goods and services flow *from businesses* to you. You can also see that you provide business with an important factor of production, work or labor. Money flows in the opposite direction *from you* to businesses in the form of payment for goods and services. It continues to flow from businesses back to you in the form of wages for the part-time work.

Now let's look at the circular-flow model in a more complete format (see Figure 3-6). This figure again shows goods and services flowing from producers (businesses) to consumers (you). It shows factors of production flowing from consumers to producers. These include the labor they provide for producers, the land consumers rent to producers, and the capital they provide to producers as investment money.

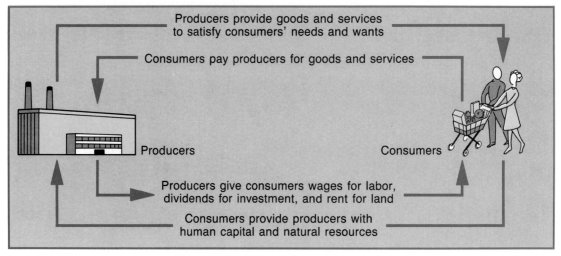

Figure 3-6. Circular flow of goods and services.

The circular-flow chart shows that there is an ongoing relationship between you (and others like you) as consumers and the businesses that serve as producers. It also illustrates that there is a continual exchange of money between consumers and producers. Indeed, it is this continuous exchange that keeps our economy going. By buying goods and services from producers and by engaging in business activities, such as working for, renting to, or investing in business firms, you and others help keep the U.S. economy functioning.

Select Terms to Know

barter	factors of production	natural resources
capital resources	human resources	opportunity cost
demand	labor	prices
economic resources	labor force	scarcity
economic wants	market clearing price	supply
economics	markets	trade-off

Review Questions

1. What are two economic concepts you may have been familiar with before you entered this course?

2. Why do economists say there is a "basic economic problem"?

3. What are the three basic types of factors of production?

4. What is the difference in the way accountants and economists use the word capital?

5. How do capital resources satisfy the wants and needs of consumers?

6. Why is information important to businesses? How is it used in business?

7. How is the price of a good or service determined in the market? Explain your answer.

8. What two specific conditions must be met before demand is created for an economic good or service?

Thought and Discussion Questions

1. Why do you suppose the "basic economic problem" exists? Do you feel people are too greedy or are there just too few resources?

2. Two of the productive resources needed for producing goods and services are natural resources and human resources. Which do you think is more important to have in a nation? Why?

3. What is the opportunity cost for you to complete the assignment you are now working on? What trade-offs did you have to make to work on this?

4. Figure 3-6, the circular-flow model, and some other parts of the chapter indicated that government produces some goods and services in an economy. In what other ways does government participate in economic activities in our economy?

Projects

1. You learned from reading the chapter that the factors of production are the things which are needed to produce goods or services. Think about your favorite chair or sofa at home. What things were needed to produce the chair or sofa? Prepare a list of all the factors of production which would be needed to produce a chair or sofa. When you have completed the list, go back and identify which of the three basic categories of factors of production each of the things you listed falls into.

2. Suppose you suddenly received $25 to use in any way you wished. (Perhaps for your general good behavior or just for being such a nice person!) You may use it all on one activity or item, or you may use it to do more than one thing. Prepare a list of seven alternative uses for the $25. Each combination of things which would cost $25 should be considered as one of the separate alternatives. When you have completed your list of seven alternatives, rank them in order of your preference. Indicate which alternative is your first choice, which your second,

and so on. Write a statement discussing why you selected the alternative you did for your first choice.

    a. What is the opportunity cost involved in your first choice?

    b. What trade-offs did you make in selecting your first choice?

3. The supply and demand schedule for sugar doughnuts at Popular High School during a given period of time is as follows:

At $0.20, suppliers provide 100 and students demand 400

At $0.30, suppliers provide 150 and students demand 350

At $0.40, suppliers provide 200 and students demand 300

At $0.50, suppliers provide 250 and students demand 250

At $0.60, suppliers provide 300 and students demand 200

At $0.70, suppliers provide 350 and students demand 150

At $0.80, suppliers provide 400 and students demand 100

a. Prepare the supply and demand schedule for sugar dougnuts at Popular High School during this time. Use Table 3-4 as the model.

b. As price decreases, what happens to the quantity demanded?

c. As price increases, what happens to the quantity demanded?

d. As price increases, what happens to the quantity supplied?

e. As price decreases, what happens to the quantity supplied?

f. At what price will the quantity of doughnuts that students are willing to buy be equal to the quantity of doughnuts that sellers are willing to supply? What term is used to describe this price?

Case Study: Big City Trade-Offs—Choosing Less to Get More

When Peat Marwick, J. C. Penney, Mobile Oil, Trans World Airlines, and Deloitte, Haskins & Sells decided to move their headquarters from New York City, they didn't make their decisions lightly. These companies are moving to decrease commuting time of employees and to get away from the crime, blight, and high rents of the city. According to *USA Today*, the cities with the most expensive prime downtown office-space costs (based on annual cost per square foot) were midtown Manhattan ($65), Boston ($60), and Washington, D.C. ($42).

To make the move from Manhattan even more attractive, some companies have been offered relatively low-cost office space and other incentives by suburban communities to coax them to move their headquarters.

But what are companies giving up to move out of a city like New York? City officials and real estate people point out that a Manhattan location provides ready access to suppliers, customers, and service. Further, because Manhattan is the heart of one of the world's largest transportation, financial, and communication hubs, it offers many other benefits as well.

Companies also have to keep in mind that a move of any distance will cause employees to make a major decision. When J. C. Penney moved from New York City to Plano, Texas, employees either had to relocate or find another job. Some employees might not have been eager to relocate because this meant they had to leave family and friends. Others have spouses who

might not have wanted to leave their jobs and children who might have had difficulty changing schools. This means that companies such as Penney's have to hire new employees to staff their ranks when they arrive in the new location.

The cost of relocating employees can be a major expense for both the company and the employee. The average cost of relocating an employee in 1987 was estimated to be about $36,250 for a homeowner (up from $34,700 in 1986). For a renter, the cost of relocation was $10,500 (up from $9200 in 1986).

Sources: Adapted from Lee Berton, "Deloitte to Move Its Headquarters From Manhattan," *The Wall Street Journal*, June 18, 1987, p. 18; Elys McLean-Ibrahim, "What Office Space Costs," *USA Today*, June 16, 1987; and Brian Tumulty, "Region's Costs Keeping Transfers Away," *Gannett Westchester Newspapers*, January 28, 1988.

---

1. What are the advantages of living in a city such as New York City? What are the disadvantages of living in a city such as New York City?

2. What are the advantages of relocating to another location from New York City? What are the disadvantages of relocating from New York City?

3. What is the opportunity cost of staying in New York City? Of relocating?

4. What are the trade-offs that a company makes by considering a move from New York City and then deciding not to move? What are the trade-offs in deciding to relocate?

CHAPTER 4

Comparing Economic Systems and Measuring Economic Success

Four Minutes Worth of Milk

How many minutes do you have to work to buy a bottle of milk, a loaf of bread, or a color TV set? You've probably never thought of prices or the cost of goods in terms of how much time you need to work to earn enough to pay for them. One way to compare the standard of living in different countries is to translate the prices of such goods into work time needed to pay for each product in each country. For example, such comparisons can be made for the United States, Great Britain, and the Soviet Union. These comparisons are important when studying these three countries because these three countries have different economic systems.

A liter of milk will cost you 4 minutes of work in Washington, D.C., 6 minutes of work in London, and 20 minutes of work in Moscow. You will learn more about the differences in the prices of common products when you read the end-of-chapter case study, "Comparing Costs—A Study in Time."

Have you ever wondered what it would be like if you and your family lived in some country other than the United States? What are some of the differences that would affect you directly? One of the first things you would probably notice is the price of everyday items such as milk and bread. What are some other differences?

It is fairly common today to hear comparisons between life in our country and other countries in the world. These comparisons are almost certain to mention the amount of freedom and the high standard of living enjoyed by most members of our society compared to those living in other nations. Our way of life is largely shaped by the economic system in our country.

69

In this chapter you will look at the features of different economic systems and learn how they each answer basic economic questions. You will learn about the unique features of our economic system and how the success of an economic system is measured.

BASIC DECISIONS MADE BY ALL ECONOMIC SYSTEMS

As was true for our ancestors, the 5 billion people who inhabit the earth today must deal with the basic economic problem of scarcity. There are not enough productive resources available to produce all the goods and services we desire. Therefore, we must decide how to use the resources that are available. We can make these decisions by determining the trade-offs and opportunity costs of using resources in various ways. But who actually makes these decisions? That depends on the society in which we live.

As societies mature, they develop systems to govern how various activities are to be carried out. All societies, for example, have legal and political systems. All societies also have an economic system. An **economic system** consists of all the institutions, laws, attitudes, and activities which together determine how economic decisions are made in society. The economic system provides a framework for making the tough economic decisions every society faces in trying to satisfy the needs and wants of its people. It helps the society answer three very important economic questions: What to produce? How to produce? For whom to produce?

What to Produce

Every society has to decide how to use its resources to meet the needs of its people. It has to know what to produce and how much to produce. The resources that are used for one purpose cannot be used for something else. For example, land may be used to grow corn or cotton, or for an office building or a manufacturing plant, or for a house, park, or highway. However, it can only be put to one of these uses at a time. Deciding to use it for one purpose means that the opportunity to use the land for another purpose has been given up. As with all choices, there is an opportunity cost involved.

The same principle holds for the use of other factors of production. People can work at making computers, missiles, or

Figure 4-1. The same piece of land can be put to only one use at a time. It cannot be both a shopping center and a playground at the same time. The principle of opportunity cost often comes into play when businesspeople or others decide how to use available economic resources, such as land.

vacuum cleaners, but they can only do one of those at any time. Similarly, machines and equipment used to manufacture military weapons cannot be used to produce clothes, books, or TV sets. Because its members always have unlimited wants and it has limited resources, every society must decide which of the many possible goods and services to produce. Since everything cannot be produced, deciding *what will be* produced is also deciding *what not to* produce, or what to do without.

How to Produce

Who will produce the goods and services that a society has decided on? What equipment or machinery will they use? How many people will work on the project?

The answers to all these questions depend on the resources that a society has available to use. Almost all the goods and many of the services being produced could be made by using some mix of resources that is different from what is now being used. In fact, different societies may produce similar goods by using different combinations of resources.

Let's say that two different countries have each decided to produce clothing. One of these countries is less-developed than the other. It will use hundreds of unskilled laborers with needles and thread. The other country may use fewer people who are trained in the operation of the most-advanced sewing equipment. Both produce the same good, but they use a different mix of productive resources to do so.

Societies also change the way they produce goods and services as they discover or learn new ways to combine productive resources. For example, the development of tne computer during the last 30 years has significantly changed the way goods and services are produced in the world. As we near the beginning of the twenty-first century, it is difficult to imagine producing goods and services without the aid of computer technology in the United States and other developed nations.

For Whom to Produce

Even though each society is not able to produce everything its members want, it does produce many goods and services. How should they be divided among its members? Since there is not enough to satisfy everyone's wants, there must be some way to decide who gets them and who does not.

While the other two basic economic decisions are important, deciding who gets the goods and services produced in a society is probably the one that interests us most. Will everyone get an equal share of goods and services? Why is it that within a society there are some who are able to get lots of goods and services while others get very few? Why do some people get BMWs or Corvettes while others can't get any kind of car?

There are many reasons; however, in most societies you can have as many goods and services as you can buy. Therefore, the amount of income people receive affects how many goods and services they get. This raises many other questions. Should goods and services be provided only for the rich? Should heart transplants and expensive medical services be available only to those who can afford them? Is it true that those who work hardest in a society can get the most goods and services because they have the most income? Different kinds of economic systems decide how to distribute goods and services in different ways.

BASIC KINDS OF ECONOMIC SYSTEMS

Today there are more than 170 independent countries in the world. The societies of these nations have developed a great variety of economic systems. No matter how much they differ, however, each nation faces the same basic economic problem. It is trying to satisfy the unlimited wants of its citizens with the relatively limited productive resources it has available. In trying to accomplish this objective, these societies use many approaches to decide what, how, and for whom to produce.

Although there have been and continue to be many variations in economic systems, there are three basic types: traditional, command, and market. The economic systems in countries throughout the world can be divided into these three types or some mix of these types. Let's look at the ways that each of these systems answer the basic questions of what, how, and for whom to produce.

Traditional Economic Systems

In a **traditional economic system,** decisions about what, how, and for whom to produce are based on custom and tradition. If pictures of these societies were taken over many years, they would seem frozen in time. Not much changes from one generation to the next. In traditional economies, people do the same type of work as their parents and grandparents. The same types of goods and services are produced in the same way they were for many generations. They are also distributed among the people in the same way from one generation to the next. There is little or no provision for change in such societies because most of their methods are based on habit, custom, and religious belief. Although you may consider this to be an inefficient way to make decisions, you may be influenced by custom, habit, and religion in some aspects of your life, too. For example, many Americans eat turkey on Thanksgiving for no reason other than custom.

Today this sounds like a strange way for an economic system to operate. Tradition is not as influential as it once was. However, it is still a major force in some economic systems. The Kwakiutl Indians of Vancouver Island on the west coast of Canada, for example, have a traditional economic system. Other examples can be found in remote parts of Africa. This is not as strange as it may seem because life in these societies is very different from ours. Family units live together longer, and they provide more of the goods and services they need for themselves. As was true in earlier societies, these people are much more self-sufficient and less dependent on trade than members of our more modern societies.

Information Brief
4-1

Drawbacks in Planning

Until recently, when faced with the choice of government planning versus the free market, many Third World countries chose planning.

Now, however, it is becoming clear that government planning of production does not motivate people to be more productive. Communist China found this was so. Under planning, its wheat production was very low. But when the government allowed farmers to freely plant what they wanted, wheat production soared.

Increasingly, nations are finding that the market is the better allocator of what is scarce and what is plentiful. Why? Because, some experts say, information about what people need and want comes much more quickly from the bottom up than from the top down. Planners at the top levels of government are often too far removed from the day-to-day lives of people to respond to their needs and wants quickly or efficiently.

Information Brief
4-2

Soviet Couple Contracts to Raise Cows

Soviet farmer Vasily Ayatayev, 37, and his wife are facing a new challenge. For years they lived on a collective farm and worked for a fixed income.

Now they have formed a two-person contract with the government. It allows them to manage their livestock business (raising 220 calves to milking age) even though the government still owns the collective farm.

The fatter the cows, the more money the couple can make. But if a cow dies, they can be sued by the collective farm.

Most of the milk from their cows goes to the government at controlled prices, but the couple can sell 30 percent of it at farm markets.

Together, the couple makes $1800 a month, which is big money by Soviet standards, but they sometimes work 15 hours a day.

Source: Adapted from Peter Galuszka, "On the Farm, Ma and Pa Ayatayev Are Raising Some Cash Cows," *Business Week*, December 7, 1987, p. 80.

Command Economic Systems

Economic systems influenced by commands, or directives, have been around as long as traditional economies. In a **command economic system** the basic economic decisions of what, how, and for whom to produce are made by a central authority and are obeyed by members of the society. The central authority consists of one person or a small group who have the power to control others in the society. There are two basic types of command systems in the world today, strong and moderate.

Strong Command. If you visit the Soviet Union, the People's Republic of China, East Germany, or Romania, you will be able to see how this type of command system works. These nations, which are described as being communist, all have strong command economies. Such an economy calls for government ownership of both natural and capital resources. This means that the government owns and carefully controls factories, equipment, and land. The leaders of the country, the ruling members of the communist party, are the ones who answer the three important economic questions. As the rulers, they decide what will be produced to meet the goals of their country. In the Soviet Union, national security, defense, and industrial investment are top priorities. The leaders also decide on the types and amounts of consumer goods that will be produced.

When it comes to deciding how goods and services will be produced, the country's leaders carefully study the available resources and decide how to use them. The primary goal of each business is to fulfill the government plan in the most efficient way. By contrast, in the United States the primary goal of most businesses is to make a profit by serving members of our society.

By setting both wages and prices at the level they feel is appropriate, the government leaders or ruling party can also decide who receives the goods and services that business and industry produce. By keeping tight control on the economic system in communist countries, leaders make sure that it works in what "they" feel are the main interests of the country.

Moderate Command. If you visit Sweden, Great Britain, West Germany, or France, you will see how a moderate command economy works. These nations, which are described as socialist, use a more liberal form of command system. Their system calls for government ownership of major industries. This includes railroads and the steel and iron industries. In contrast to the communist countries, socialist countries do provide some opportunities for private ownership.

Laws require government and private business to work together in socialist countries. They work together when government representatives become members of the management committees for private business. They decide what to produce and how to produce it. Some socialist countries are currently stressing the development of high-technology industries.

The government, however, plays the major role in deciding who will receive the goods and services that are produced. All workers are taxed in socialist countries, but people who inherit money and people who earn high salaries are taxed at an extremely high rate, much higher than in the United States. By collecting money through this type of taxation system, the government is able to provide free medical services, lifelong welfare services, and social security benefits to everyone. However, some critics of socialism say that the high rate of taxation discourages successful private businesspeople from increasing productivity or personal earnings. And that, they claim, can harm a nation's economy as a whole.

Market Economic Systems

Countries such as the United States, Japan, Canada, and West Germany have economies referred to as market economies. In a **market economic system** the basic decisions of what, how, and for whom to produce are based on the actions of people and business firms participating in many different markets. A market economy may also be referred to as a capitalist, free enterprise, or private enterprise economy. Many people feel our system is best described as a private enterprise economy.

In our private enterprise system most economic decisions are made by you and your friends and all the other people who buy goods and services. The question of what should be produced is answered in the marketplace. If customers are willing to buy goods and services, then they should be produced. Of course, the government does prohibit the production of some substances such as illegal drugs. You will read more about government restrictions that are designed to protect consumers in a later section of this chapter.

In a private enterprise system the business owners and managers decide how goods and services will be produced. They decide the best way to combine the factors of production—natural, human, and capital resources—to produce goods and services. All businesses try to produce the best-quality goods and services for the lowest cost possible in this system.

In a private enterprise system goods and services are produced for anyone who can buy them. The circular-flow model in Chapter 3 describes how consumers earn money to buy goods and services by providing human, capital, and natural resources that producers can use in the production process. Basically, people must work to earn money if they wish to buy goods and services. If the system is operating as it should, those who do the type of work that contributes to producing the goods and services that society wants will earn income. Some people earn more income than others because they work more hours or because others are willing to pay more for what they do. The more money one has, the more goods and services one can buy.

Mixed Economic Systems

While we talk about traditional, command, and market economic systems, the fact is that none of today's economic systems is based totally on one of these approaches. Modern economies have some element of all three of these influences in them. Therefore, it is probably more accurate to refer to the economies as mixed economies. However, one of the approaches or influences is usually much stronger than the others. Because of this, economic systems are still described as being traditional, command, or market to indicate which of the approaches most influences how the economy functions.

We say that the Soviet Union has a command economy even though there is some tradition and increasingly more market influence in the Soviet economy. In fact, recent Soviet leaders have begun to allow more market activities in their economy. (Information Brief 4-2 gives an example of a privately owned Soviet business.) Similarly, we say that the American economy is a market economy even though there is some command through government regulation.

Figure 4-2 summarizes the major characteristics of traditional, both types of command, and market economic systems.

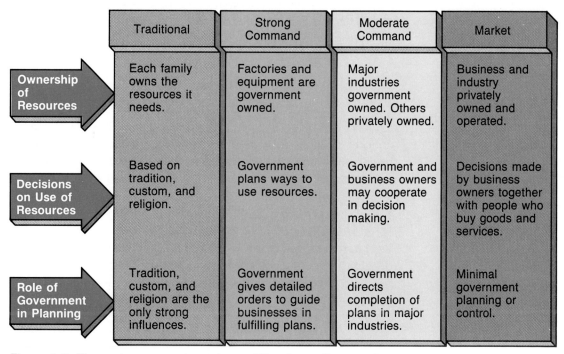

	Traditional	Strong Command	Moderate Command	Market
Ownership of Resources	Each family owns the resources it needs.	Factories and equipment are government owned.	Major industries government owned. Others privately owned.	Business and industry privately owned and operated.
Decisions on Use of Resources	Based on tradition, custom, and religion.	Government plans ways to use resources.	Government and business owners may cooperate in decision making.	Decisions made by business owners together with people who buy goods and services.
Role of Government in Planning	Tradition, custom, and religion are the only strong influences.	Government gives detailed orders to guide businesses in fulfilling plans.	Government directs completion of plans in major industries.	Minimal government planning or control.

Figure 4-2. The major economic systems differ depending on who owns available economic resources, who decides how the economic resources will be used and for what purpose, and the degree of government involvement in economic planning.

HOW DOES THE PRIVATE ENTERPRISE SYSTEM WORK?

Now let's take a closer look at some of the features of the private enterprise system of the United States. These features include private ownership, freedom of choice for both workers and consumers, competition in the marketplace, and limited government involvement.

Private Ownership of Resources

One of the distinctive features of our economic system is that most of the factors of production are owned and controlled by private individuals. Land, minerals, equipment, and buildings are owned by people as individuals or as owners in business firms. In addition, private individuals control and decide how to use their physical and mental skills, which are referred to as human resources. Of course, government units do own some land which is used for things such as roads, parks, and military bases; they also own buildings and equipment. However, individuals and business firms own and decide how to use most of the factors of production available in our society.

Freedom of Choice

Owning resources is of little value if you can't use them as you choose. Two basic features of our economy which give owners freedom to choose how to use the resources they own are referred to as free enterprise and consumer sovereignty.

Free Enterprise. One of the things Americans value most is the freedom they have to decide how they will earn a living. If you are motivated and willing to work hard enough, you can do almost anything you wish to earn income. This is what is meant by **free enterprise.** People are free to use their resources—labor, natural resources, and capital resources—in any type of legal enterprise or undertaking they wish.

You might start a business of your own or work in just about any type of job you want. If you think you are talented and want to be a professional singer, actor, or athlete, you are welcome to audition and try to become one. For some professions, such as doctor, attorney, beautician, certified public accountant, and public school teacher, you may have to become certified by fulfilling a series of requirements or passing examinations. If you are willing to work hard and have the ability, you are welcome to try.

If you wish, you may also use your resources to start a business of your own. As you learned in Chapter 1, persons who own and run their own businesses are called entrepreneurs. More specifically, entrepreneurs are people who invest their own money, energy, time, and management skills in a business in hopes of making a profit. Because entrepreneurs own and operate their own businesses, they accept more financial risk than those who work for others. However, they are also freer to do whatever they want with their business as long as they comply with the laws that regulate business activity in this country. There is *some* regulation in a mixed economy, as you will see in a later section of this chapter.

Consumer Sovereignty. In our economy, consumers create demand for goods or services by being willing and able to buy them. As you learned in Chapter 3, if there is enough demand to indicate that it would be profitable to do so, some-one or some group will likely supply the good or service desired.

Some people say consumers in a market economy are casting dollar "votes" for the production of certain goods or services when they buy them. These dollar votes by consumers play an important role in deciding what will be produced. Unless consumers continue to buy a product or service, it will not continue to be produced. So the consumer in our economy is sometimes thought of as a king or queen of the marketplace.

Because they have so much power, kings and queens are referred to as sovereigns. In our economy, we have **consumer sovereignty,** which means that consumers play a major role in deciding what will be produced in the economy by their purchases of goods and services. If you purchase a set of Bestmark felt-tip pens instead of a set of Speedy felt-tip pens, you have "voted" for Bestmark pens. If thousands of consumers select Bestmark instead of Speedy, the demand for Speedy may fall so low that it will no longer be produced.

▼ Do you agree that consumers have more power than producers in deciding what goods and services get produced in our economy? Why do you feel as you do about this?

Competitive Markets

When we are talking about our economy the word competition is used to describe the rivalry existing in a market for types of goods and services. A **competitive market** is one in which there are so many buyers and sellers of the resource, good, or service being exchanged that no one is large enough to influence the price. There are competitive markets for the exchange of natural, human, and capital resources as well as for the exchange of goods and services in our economy. This is one of its key features. We support competitive markets because we feel producers will generally provide better-quality goods and services at lower prices if there is competition.

Another advantage of competition is the number of products available. There are so many products that each consumer can take his or her choice. If you don't like Hershey bars, for example, you can buy Mars, 3 Musketeers, Snickers, Nestles, or any one of a number of other candy bars.

The number of buyers and sellers varies in the different

markets. When there are large numbers of buyers and sellers, none of them can individually control enough of demand or supply to noticeably affect the market price. The markets for agricultural products such as wheat, corn, and milk are examples. No one producer in this type of market has much more "economic power" than anyone else. As the number of buyers or sellers decreases, it is easier for one producer or a small group of producers to gain enough control to exert economic power. When there are a small number of either buyers or sellers, the market is described as being less competitive. For example, there are only a few producers of steel, aluminum, and cars. Therefore, each producer such as GM, Chrysler, and Ford has much more economic power than one dairy farmer.

The number of buyers or sellers and thus their economic power is also affected by how easy it is to enter or leave a market. If it is difficult to enter the market for any reason, there will be fewer buyers or sellers and, therefore, less competition.

It is much more difficult to enter the market as a radio manufacturer, for example, than as a gardener. The capital resources required to produce radios cost a great deal more than a lawn mower and a selection of good-quality garden tools.

Some utilities such as electricity, water, and natural gas are available from only one producer in a community. If you want

Figure 4-3. In a competitive market there is often a large number of sellers of a good or service. Because buyers can choose among competing sellers, consumers usually play a key role in determining which businesses succeed or fail in a market economy.

electricity in Minneapolis, for example, you must buy it from Northern States Power. No one else can provide it for you. Northern States Power, like many other utility companies, has a monopoly. A monopoly, you will recall, is a market where there is only one buyer or seller of the resource, good, or service being exchanged. The monopoly markets in our economy are carefully monitored by government, or a unit of government is actually the supplier. One of our largest government monopolies for many years was the postal service. Now, as noted in Information Brief 4-3 and in the Technology in an Information Economy feature, there is competition for delivering packages and mail.

Limited Government Involvement

In a pure market economic system, the government would pose very few restrictions on business. In our mixed economic system, however, the government does regulate many economic activities. Without government controls, legal monopolies such as natural gas and electric companies could take advantage of their customers. In contrast, government takes steps to prevent monopolies in other areas so that the private enterprise system can operate with as much competition as possible. Further, the government also restricts competing firms from getting together and agreeing on the prices they will charge for similar products.

A very important area of government regulation involves protecting the rights of consumers. As it protects consumers, the government is involved in almost every type of business. It inspects meats and poultry and requires that they be graded accurately. It requires that food and drugs be labeled accurately. The government also inspects restaurants to ensure that the food is safe to eat and the premises are clean. These are just a few of the many consumer protections the government provides. It has been pointed out that each of these consumer protections restricts business in some ways. There is a trade-off involved here.

Some Americans feel that government has become too involved in regulating economic activities. They argue that there are so many agencies regulating so many things that our economic freedoms are being reduced by *too much* government involvement. Others feel just the opposite. They argue that wealthy families, big businesses, labor unions, professional associations, and some institutions have gained too much eco-

Information Brief 4-3

Picking a Postal Service

Some people are unhappy with the U.S. Postal Service. Therefore, you may be deciding which company will deliver your first-class mail someday.

The Postal Service is a government-operated monopoly. Some people say private firms should be allowed to compete in delivering letters as they currently do in delivering packages and overnight mail. They believe that like all monopolies this government-operated one offers poor service at high prices.

However, supporters of the current system say only a tiny percentage of mail is lost or delayed, and the cost is reasonable. They believe competition would destroy the tradition of nationwide mail delivery set up in the Constitution. They argue that private firms would not be able to guarantee mail service at uniform rates to everybody, everywhere, which they say is a necessity in our democratic society.

Source: "The Debate: Delivering the Mail," Opinion Section, *USA Today*, June 16, 1987, p. 12A.

Making a Federal Case out of Delivery

When your package absolutely, positively must be there tomorrow, you've got it made. Federal Express has the latest technology that should guarantee you delivery. More than 99 percent of its letters and packages arrive on time. To make things even better, they have competition. UPS and several other overnight carriers are hot on their heels, using determination and hard work to make up for the technology that they don't yet have. UPS claims that it now delivers 99.5 percent of its packages on time.

Even the U.S. Postal Service, which once had a legal monopoly over all mail deliveries, now finds itself in competition with Federal Express and other private carriers. The government Postal Service and the private carriers engage in competition in many areas. One of the most important involves the application of technology. The basis of competition here is which carrier can use modern technology most efficiently and effectively for the benefit of the customer.

What can Federal's technology do for a customer? For starters the company's mainframe computer in Memphis knows where every package is at all times. Let's track a typical Federal delivery to illustrate how this works.

A Federal courier arrives at *The Wall Street Journal* office at 7:10 on a Wednesday evening to pick up an important package that must be at a radio station near Orlando, Florida, the following morning. A member of the *Journal* staff has already completed the Federal Express airbill and attached it to the package. The upper right corner of the airbill has a special bar code that represents our airbill number. The courier checks the address on the package and leafs through a book that translates zip codes into Federal's own coding system. She writes the code SFB on the package and hurries to her van.

Once inside the van our courier hits a button and a small computer terminal lights up. It lists her stops and flashes several special requests from the dispatch center in Manhattan. By 7:30 our courier has met another van and transferred our package (together with 55 others) into a van headed for the sorting station in lower Manhattan.

At the sorting station cargo handlers wear headsets that are attached to special wands. A wand is passed over the bar code on each package at the sorting station. As cargo handlers scan each package, they listen for a beep to indicate that the computer in Memphis knows where the package is.

Next, our package is trucked to Newark, New Jersey, where it is loaded into the belly of one of Federal's new Boeing 727s. Cargo handlers again scan the airbill and listen for a beep. By 1:24 a.m. the package is in Memphis, where 3000 workers sort 880,000 packages each night from 11 p.m. to 3 a.m. at the national hub. The location has an amazing 65 miles of conveyor belts and chutes.

At the Memphis hub, workers sort the paperwork by hand and type our destination code into a computer before they

(continued)

TECHNOLOGY FEATURE *(continued)*

send our package along the belt. A computer determines how many seconds it will take for our package to reach the mouth of the chute, where a mechanical arm shoots out and directs it to the right region of the country. The package is sorted again for the proper city and loaded onto another plane. Cargo handlers are careful to scan the package with their wands as it is loaded onto the plane.

At 3:30 a.m. our package is headed to Orlando, where it arrives at 5:54 a.m. A large container carrying our package is rolled onto a truck and sent to a sorting center in Longwood, Florida, and scanned again. At 7:35 a driver plucks the package from a conveyor belt and rushes it to a van full of other packages and envelopes. By 8:10 the driver pulls away from the sorting center and begins deliveries. By 9:30 a.m. our package has arrived at the radio station near Orlando thanks to an interesting combination of human and technological efforts.

Source: Adapted from Larry Reibstein, "Federal Express Faces Challenges to Its Grip on Overnight Delivery," *The Wall Street Journal*, January 8, 1988, p. 1.

nomic power. This has decreased the amount of competition in many markets for resources, goods, and services. Government needs to do something to decrease the economic power of these giants. This group feels that our economic freedoms are being reduced by *too little* government involvement.

Regardless of how you feel about the level of government involvement, there is much less of it in our economy than in other economic systems. This is why others who study our economic system feel it is a free or market economy.

MEASURING ECONOMIC ACTIVITY

Now that you know basically how the economy works, let's look at ways to judge how it is performing. Remember that the overall objective of an economy is to produce goods and services that satisfy our needs and wants.

To determine how well the economy is achieving this objective, we can look at the level of activity in some of the sectors or areas of the economy. We will look at three measures of economic activity: general economic indicators, business indicators, and productivity.

General Economic Indicators

There are many ways to measure the performance of the economy as a whole. One of the most popular ways is to look at

Information Brief 4-4

Which Economic Indicators Count?

Enough is enough! There are just too many economic indicators! "Which ones really count?"

A group of economists and the 12 Federal Reserve Bank presidents were recently asked that question. Their nearly unanimous response was that they all count, but how much depends on the current situation.

They agreed that the quarterly GNP figure, adjusted for inflation, is the best overall measure of economic activities. The Labor Department's monthly employment report is the best monthly gauge of how the economy is doing. And the monthly CPI best reflects changes in prices or inflation, according to these folks who should know.

Source: Adapted from Connie McGeorge, "Economic Indicators: Which Ones Count?" *The Region*, published by the Federal Reserve Bank of Minneapolis, December 1987, pp. 5–7.

figures for general economic indicators. These indicators are used by businesses, government leaders, and economists. In fact, they are used so much that the government has set up special units such as the Commerce Department and Bureau of Labor Statistics to collect and analyze data needed to prepare and report these indicators each month or quarter. Although there are several general indicators, we will look at only three: gross national product, employment, and inflation. (See Information Brief 4-4.)

Gross National Product. Goods and services that satisfy our needs and wants are the final output of an economy. They are the results of all the economic activity in the country. One way of telling how well an economy is performing is to determine how many goods and services it produces for a certain period of time. This is done by collecting sales data to calculate the total value of all the goods and services produced. The result is called the **gross national product,** commonly referred to as the **GNP,** which is the total of all prices paid for all the goods and services purchased by those who consume them in a year.

The GNP includes the prices paid for food, clothing, cough syrup, skating lessons, football, bicycles, and all the other goods and services consumed. GNP figures include only the prices of goods and services paid by the final consumer. Prices paid for materials used in the production process are not counted; only the price of the final good or service is used. For example, the prices of tires, steering wheels, carburetors, engines, mirrors, and windshields that are used in producing cars are not counted separately. Only the price the final user pays for the car is included.

The GNP is the most frequently used measure of all economic activity. There are some things to keep in mind about the GNP. First, it is reported as the "market value," or price, at which goods and services were bought. But prices are always changing. If you paid $1.89 for a gallon of milk two years ago and $2.19 today for the same gallon of milk, the level of goods sold (1 gallon of milk) remains the same even though the price has gone up. The amount included for 100 gallons of milk would be $219 now, but only $189 two years ago. To keep price changes like these from affecting the GNP figure, those who collect price data for determining the GNP use something called *constant-dollar* figures. The constant-dollar figures show the GNP in figures that have been adjusted to compensate for price changes. Notice in Table 4-1 that the difference between the 1980 and 1987 GNP figure in "current," or actual, dollars is much greater than the difference reported in constant dollars. The constant-dollar figures show the value of the total of goods and services produced each year in 1982 prices. This gives a more accurate picture of what has happened to the GNP because the effect of price increases from 1980 to 1987 has been eliminated. When the GNP is reported in constant dollars, the figures are referred to as the *real GNP.*

A second thing to keep in mind when you look at GNP figures is that the GNP is not very meaningful by itself. Although the GNP for two nations may be similar, their population may be quite different. The **per capita GNP** is a nation's GNP figure divided by its population. Knowing the per capita GNP for two nations is much more meaningful than just knowing the GNP. For example, the GNP of Libya and the United Arab Emirates (UAR) was the same during a recent year, $25 billion. With just this information, you might think the economies performed at about the same level. However, you could make a better judgment if you know how many people had to share the GNP. If you know the population of each nation, you can calculate the per capita GNP and make a more meaningful comparison. Since Libya's population was about 3.75 million and the UAR's about 1.3 million, the per capita GNPs were roughly $6600 and $19,200, respectively. There were almost three times as many

TABLE 4-1 GNP in Current and Constant (1982) Dollars		
	Gross National Product (GNP)	
Year	**In Current Dollars (Billions)**	**In Constant (1982) Dollars (Billions)**
1970	$1,016	$2,416
1975	$1,598	$2,695
1980	$2,732	$3,187
1981	$3,053	$3,249
1982	$3,166	$3,166
1983	$3,406	$3,279
1984	$3,765	$3,490
1985	$4,010	$3,608
1986	$4,235	$3,713
1987	$4,489	$3,821

Source: U.S. Bureau of Economic Analysis, *The National Income and Product Accounts of the United States* and *Survey of Current Business,* May 1988.

Information Brief 4-5

Checking Your Basket

Are items in your "market basket" typical of the items that the average consumer buys today? That's what the government asked when they looked at the so-called market basket of goods and services which makes up the consumer price index.

To update the market basket, the government surveyed 40,000 households from 1982 to 1984. Compared to the last survey in 1978, these households used more poultry and less red meat, sugar, and fatty foods. They spent less on auto repairs but more for entertainment. And health care costs decreased because more people were covered by insurance.

Starting in 1987, the CPI figures began to reflect the costs of this new, more-accurate market basket of goods and services.

Source: Adapted from "More Poultry, Less Pastry," *Time,* March 9, 1987, p. 65.

goods and services produced for each person in the UAR—quite a difference!

Employment. Another important general economic indicator is the number of people who are employed during a given period of time. The Bureau of Labor Statistics gathers data related to employment and unemployment in our economy each month. Its findings are then published very early in the next month. When the findings are released, the news media usually report and emphasize the rate of unemployment. Those who are most interested in this data believe the employment figures are more important than unemployment figures.

Business and government leaders are interested in how many new jobs the economy creates during a period of time, because this is one indicator of economic growth. They are also interested in the total number of people employed in various sectors of the economy—goods-producing, service, public, and private. Changes in these totals reveal which sectors of the economy are growing and which ones are not.

Inflation. Business and government leaders also consider the inflation rate to be an important general indicator. **Inflation** is the general increase in prices in an economy. Government units gather information about prices in our economy and publish it as price indexes from which the rate of change can be determined. A **price index** measures changes in prices using the price for a given year as the base price. The base price is set at 100, and the other prices are reported as a percentage of the base price. This is similar to the technique for converting GNP values and is done for exactly the same reason. Changing the actual prices to index numbers makes it easier to compare them in meaningful ways.

The *consumer price index*, or *CPI,* is the most widely watched and used measure of inflation in our economy. The CPI reports changes in the price of a "market basket of goods and services" purchased by the average consumer. (See Information Brief 4-5.) Table 4-2 shows the U.S. CPI and the annual percent of change from the previous year for the 1980s. The base period for the CPI is shown as 1967. This just means that the figures have all been converted to 1967 prices so that they can be compared.

As is true for all indicators, it is important to compare the changes in the rate of inflation over a period of time. This

TABLE 4-2 U.S. Consumer Price Index for the 1980s (1967 = 100)		
Year	Index	Change From Previous Year, %
1980	246.8	+ 13.5
1981	273.3	+ 10.7
1982	288.6	+ 5.6
1983	298.4	+ 3.4
1984	311.1	+ 4.3
1985	322.2	+ 3.6
1986	328.4	+ 1.9
1987	345.3*	+ 5.1

* Estimated.
Source: Bureau of Labor Statistics, U.S. Department of Labor.

allows you to determine whether there is a trend of increasing or decreasing inflation.

▼ Based on the figures reported in Table 4-2, do you feel we have controlled inflation in our economy during the 1980s? Why do you feel as you do?

Business Indicators

Although general economic indicators provide some information about business activity, business leaders want accurate, current information about business activity. This information will help them make better business decisions. Business indicators provide this type of information.

Various units of the government collect and report information for business indicators. One of the most valuable services provided for business by the federal government is called the *index of leading indicators*. This index gives data for 11 economic indicators. People feel that these figures usually signal what might happen in the economy six months or so later. The individual measures in this index represent broad categories of activity. Two of these indicators, average weekly hours of employment in manufacturing and new applications for unemployment, report valuable employment trends. If the overall index is up or down for three straight months, people feel it signals an upturn or downturn in the economy as a whole.

Many private business firms and professional associations also collect and report this type of information. They sell the information to others in the form of periodic reports. For example, some business papers and journals purchased by business and government leaders present information on business indicators. The private businesses gather their data from many different sources. They may provide production indicators by reporting information on the number of automobiles and trucks and the amount of paper and lumber which have been produced. Or they may report information on financial indicators such as stock prices, business failures, and the money supply. Some of them also report prices on basic commodities such as gold, copper, wheat, and cotton.

Information for current periods can be compared with that from previous periods to get an idea of how well an area is performing and whether activity is increasing or decreasing. Many business decisions are based on trends in the general business indicators.

Productivity

In recent years there has been a great deal of discussion among our business and government leaders about productivity. Because it is of concern to such people, productivity has also been the topic of many stories in the news media. It is evident from some of the discussion that not everyone who talks about it knows how productivity is defined in an economic sense. **Productivity** is the amount of output (goods and services) produced per unit of input (natural, human, and capital resources) used. It is a measure of the efficiency of production.

Almost everyone is interested in increasing productivity in our economy. Increases in productivity help reduce the basic problem of scarcity. Notice they *reduce* the problem, they do not eliminate it. As productivity has been defined, there are two basic ways to increase it. First, more goods and services can be produced with the same amount of resources. Second, the same amount of goods and services can be produced with fewer resources. Of course, productivity could also be increased by using a combination of these two basic approaches.

Businesses are interested in increasing their productivity because doing so will increase their profits. However, it is common to measure or refer to productivity only in terms of the labor involved. This assumes the only way to increase productivity is to have people produce more during the same amount of time. It is important to keep in mind that all the inputs to a production process are part of the productivity measure. The costs and quality of both natural and capital resources affect productivity just as human resources do. In fact, the increasing use of technology in many different production activities in recent years has been the major source of increased productivity in our economy.

Select Terms to Know

command economic system	gross national product (GNP)	price index
competitive market	inflation	productivity
consumer sovereignty	market economic system	traditional economic system
economic system	monopoly	
free enterprise	per capita GNP	

Review Questions

1. What are the three basic questions every society must answer about the use of its available factors of production?

2. Explain what is meant when it is said that: "By deciding what to produce, a nation is also deciding what to do without."

3. What are the three basic types of economic systems? Briefly describe each of them.

4. Why is it most accurate to describe today's economies as being mixed economies?

5. What are the three major features of our economic system, and why are they important parts of our system?

6. Why do people say that we have "free" enterprise in the American economy?

7. Why do people say that we have consumer "sovereignty" in the American economy?

8. Why do people say we have "limited" government involvement in our economy?

9. What are two basic ways to increase productivity?

Thought and Discussion Questions

1. "The most important question to be answered by an economic system is the distribution question. Who gets the goods and services that are produced?" Do you agree or disagree with this statement? Why?

2. Although Americans feel our market-type economy is the best, very few other nations have an economy as heavily market-influenced as

ours. In fact most countries have some type of command economy. Why do you think this true? Why haven't more countries changed their economy to be like ours since it is generally agreed that ours has been very successful?

3. Some people say that we do not *really* have "free" enterprise in our economy. Do you consider yourself free to prepare for a career and earn a living in any way you wish in our economy? Why do you feel as you do? Do you agree that this is part of free enterprise? Why?

4.   Besides the postal service which was discussed in Information Brief 4-3, there are a number of other markets in which there is only one supplier of a service. Name two monopolies in your community. Why do you think these noncompetitive markets were set up, and why are they allowed to operate this way? Why do you think these producers are the only ones allowed to provide the service or goods they do?

Projects

1.   The Consumer Price Index (CPI) was discussed in this chapter, and Table 4-2 reported the CPI figures for 1980 to 1987. Since the CPI is the most widely watched and used measure of inflation, you should find out as much as you can about it. Go to the library and find out where you can get additional information about the CPI. Then answer the following questions about the CPI:

   a.   What agency or group gathers the information and calculates the CPI?
   b.   How often is the CPI figure updated and a new one published?
   c.   What specific goods and services are used to determine the CPI? What goods and services are included in the "market basket"?
   d.   What was the CPI figure for each of the years since 1987, and what was the rate of change from the previous year?
   e.   What is the most current CPI figure you can find? When was the figure published?

After searching out the answers to these and other questions you might have about the CPI and how it is calculated, do you feel the CPI is an accurate, representative measure of the overall price of consumer goods and services in our economy? Why or why not?

2.   The outline of a table shown below is designed to help you collect data to compare the economic performance of different nations. Prepare an outline similar to this one on a sheet of paper and fill in the data for each nation. Use the most current edition of the *Statistical Abstract of the United States, The World Almanac and Book of Facts*, or some other reference book to find the data. Indicate the publication date of the reference you use. When you have completed the table, summarize your findings.

3.   Use the GNP data provided in Table 4-1 to answer the following questions. You will need to calculate the percentage of change between figures from different years. Do you know how to do this? Check with your teacher if you are not sure how to do this.

Comparing the Performance of Different Economies							
	GNP	Popu-lation	Per Capita GNP	Percent Change in Consumer Prices	Life Expectancy at Birth (in Years)	Education Percent of Population Literate	No. of Phones per 1000
United Kingdom							
United States							
Soviet Union (U.S.S.R.)							

a. What was the amount of change and the percentage change in GNP as reported in current dollars from 1970 to 1987?

b. What was the amount of change and the percentage change in GNP as reported in constant 1982 dollars from 1970 to 1987?

c. What was the amount of change and the percentage change in GNP as reported in current dollars from 1975 to 1980?

d. What was the amount of change and the percentage change in GNP as reported in constant 1982 dollars from 1975 to 1980?

e. Check in a reference such as the ones listed in project 2 above and find the GNP figure as reported in current dollars for the years since 1987. What is the amount and percentage of change from the previous year for each of the years you found?

Case Study: Comparing Costs—A Study of Time

If you lived in Moscow or in London, you would find that the prices of goods and services are different than they are in the United States. Because of the differences in money in the three countries, the best way to compare prices is in terms of work time. *Work time* is the number of minutes, hours, or months of work it would take you to buy goods and services if you received the take-home pay of an average industrial worker.

Table 4-3 compares the cost of some common goods and services in Washington, D.C., Moscow, and London. Use the table to help you answer the questions that follow.

TABLE 4-3 Comparison of Work Time* Costs for Various Commodities in Three Countries

Commodity	Washington	Moscow	London
Milk (1 liter)	4 min	20 min	6 min
White bread (1 kilogram)	6 min	17 min	11 min
Sirloin steak (1 kilogram)	83 min	195 min	123 min
Frankfurters (1 kilogram)	30 min	145 min	70 min
Vanilla ice cream (1 liter)	13 min	107 min	11 min
Eggs (10)	5 min	50 min	10 min
Potatoes (1 kilogram)	9 min	11 min	3 min
Apples, eating (1 kilogram)	18 min	28 min	14 min
Butter (1 kilogram)	40 min	195 min	38 min
Cola (liter)	7 min	58 min	5 min
Medium-sized car	9 mo	84 mo	15 mo
Bicycle (men's cheapest)	17 h	49 h	23 h
Jeans	4 h	56 h	5 h
Refrigerator (cheapest)	44 h	102 h	30 h
Color TV (61-centimeter screen)	30 h	669 h	75 h
Suburban movie (best seat)	40 min	28 min	52 min
Toothpaste (75 grams)	6 min	22 min	7 min
Deodorant (200-milliliter spray can)	18 min	139 min	17 min

* Time abbreviations are min = minutes, h = hours, mo = months.
Source: Adapted from *"What's the Difference?"* an educational poster prepared by the National Federation of Independent Business, San Mateo, CA, copyright © 1987.

1.   How much total work time would it cost you to buy all of the following items in Washington, London, and Moscow: milk, bread, eggs, apples, butter, and cola?

2.   Can you find any items in the table that are less expensive in Moscow than they are in both Washington and London? If so, what items?

3.   Can you find any items in the table that are less expensive in London than they are in Washington and Moscow? If so, what items?

4.   From the information in the table, make a general statement about the prices in our country compared with those in the Soviet Union and Great Britain.

5.   What type of economic system is there in the United States? The Soviet Union? Great Britain? Based on the work time table, make a general statement about the standard of living in the United States compared to the Soviet Union and Great Britain.

6.   If you had 120 minutes of work time to spend on anything that you wanted, how would you spend it in Washington? Moscow? London? Explain your choices.

CHAPTER 5

Business in a Global Economy

Increasing Trade With Our Close Friend Canada

The President of the United States received a standing ovation (in 1988) when he finished addressing the 386-member Canadian Parliament in Ottawa. The applause was in reaction to his promise to do all he could to convince the U.S. Congress it should approve a proposal to increase trade between the two countries.

By the late 1980s the total value of the trade between the two nations had reached about $150 billion each year. This amounted to roughly 20 percent of our total foreign trade and made Canada our largest trading partner. Similarly, the United States clearly was—*and still is*—Canada's leading trading partner. Over 75 percent of Canada's total exports (goods and services it sells to foreign countries) comes to the United States each year.

Even though the exchange of goods and services between the countries was very active, some barriers and restrictions to trade still existed. To encourage even more trade, the president addressed the Parliament in support of a new trade agreement. The goal of the agreement was the elimination of all restrictions to trade between the two nations over a ten year period.

While the Parliament "cheered" the president's address, some trade experts in both countries "booed." Some in the United States felt that Canada would definitely get the better end of the deal if this trade agreement were signed. And, interestingly, some in Canada felt that the United States would benefit more. Learn more about this controversy when you read the end-of-chapter case study, "Weighing the Wisdom of Free Trade With Canada."

If you take a quick check of some of your clothes or the electronic appliances in your home or at school, you will almost certainly turn up one item which was made in another country. Likewise, a search of the phone book yellow pages or a shopping mall in any large city will usually turn up at least one store that specializes in goods produced in other countries.

We rely on goods from Canada and a great many other countries as an important part of our daily lives. You may write with a Bic pen made in France, wear Reeboks made in the Philippines, eat bananas grown in Latin America, use paper products from Canada, and watch a Panasonic TV made in Japan. Similarly, people in other countries may use IBM computers, fly in Boeing aircraft, drive Caterpillar tractors, and wear clothing fashioned out of Du Pont fabrics that are all made in the United States.

Although nations of the world have always traded with one another, there has been a dramatic increase in international trading since the end of World War II in 1945. Currently more nations than ever before are involved in trading both goods and services. Because international trade is so important to the world today, we say there is a global economy.

Why do nations trade goods and services? What are the different types of international trade? What are some of the barriers to such trade? As you read this chapter you will find the answers to these and other questions.

HOW DID THE GLOBAL ECOMOMY DEVELOP?

As you may recall from your study of world history, one of the reasons why countries financed explorers was their hope that they would find new products and new countries with which to trade. These countries are sometimes referred to as "trading partners." Marco Polo's expeditions to China and the other areas of the Far East were responsible for the beginning of trade between Europe and that area. Others sailed the seas in search of new trade and ended up discovering new territories. Today, nations still send representatives to other parts of the world to discover trade possibilities. Although these representatives do not discover new lands, they continue to look for new trading partners.

Three general developments during the twentieth century have made it easier for nations to conduct international trade:

- The ships, planes, and pipelines of today enable businesses to transport large quantities of natural resources and finished goods rapidly and safely.

- Communications technology has made it possible for the businesses in over 170 nations of the world to communicate with each other in a matter of seconds or minutes.

- Political agreements specifically designed to increase world trade have been signed and honored.

Because of these developments, virtually every country is able to carry out at least some international trade today. Why do countries trade with each other? The next section will provide some answers to that question.

▼ It has been said that the general developments of the twentieth century have made the nations of the world "equal" trading partners. Do you feel that all nations are equal trading partners? Why do you agree or disagree with this statement?

WHY DOES INTERNATIONAL TRADE OCCUR?

International trade occurs for exactly the same reason that two individuals might trade things between each other. Both parties believe that they will benefit or acquire some advantage from making the trade. The exchange of goods and services among different nations in the world is discussed in terms of exports and imports. **Exports** are goods and services that are sold to foreign countries. **Imports** are goods and services that are bought from foreign countries. Nations support importing and exporting because they believe that these activities will benefit their citizens.

As you can see from Figure 5-1, the United States both exports and imports a variety of different products. Notice that busi-

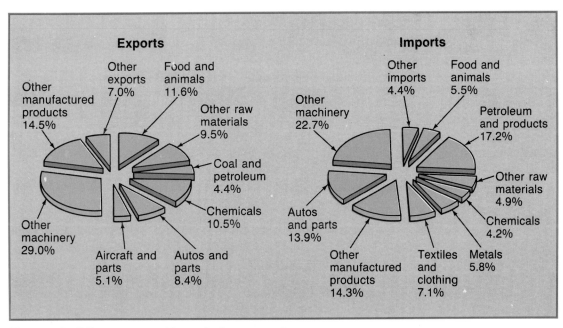

Figure 5-1. U.S. exports and imports for a recent year.

nesses in our country import more autos and auto parts than they export. Notice also that we export more machinery than we import. We import textiles and clothing, while we export airplanes and aircraft parts.

Where do some of our imported products come from? Figure 5-2 takes a closer look at six different types of imported products: fruits and vegetables, coffee, finished iron and steel products, paper products, petroleum products, and clothing. From

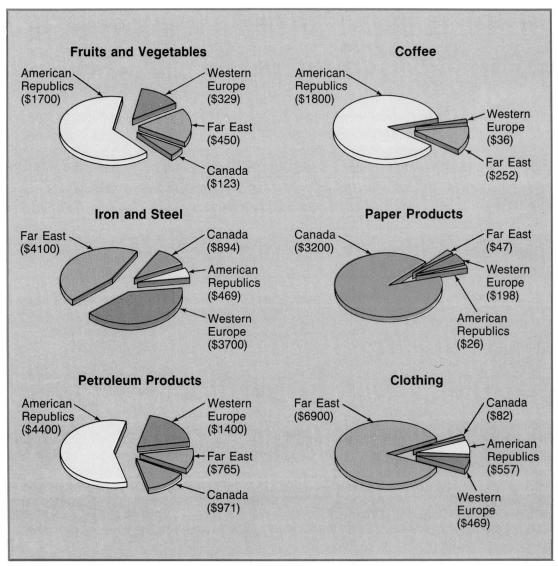

Figure 5-2. U.S. imports for one year in millions of dollars from four different areas. (*Source:* created from information supplied by Jack R. Fraenkel et al., *Civics Government and Citizenship,* Allyn & Bacon, Newton, Massachusetts, © 1986, p. 482.)

the six pie charts in the figure, you can see the amount of each of these products that we import from four different areas of the world—Western Europe, the Far East, Canada, and the American Republics (Central and South America countries). Of course, we import products from other areas, such as Africa. Notice that we get the vast majority of our coffee, fruits and vegetables, and petroleum products from the American Republics. We get most of our clothing from the Far East and our paper products from Canada. Iron and steel products come primarily from Western Europe and the Far East.

To understand why countries specialize in producing and exporting certain goods and services, we need to understand the economic concepts of absolute advantage and comparative advantage.

Absolute Advantage

Natural, human, and capital resources are not distributed evenly around the world or within a country. Some nations can produce things which cannot be produced in other areas. In turn, they need things that are produced in other nations but that they cannot produce themselves. Let's look at two states within our own nation as an example. South Dakota has a lot of land which is ideal for growing wheat, corn, and other farm products but has a rather small population. Connecticut, on the other hand, has very little land area but has a relatively large population of skilled workers and is located in an industrial region. In this case, South Dakota can raise farm products more efficiently than Connecticut, and Connecticut can produce industrial goods more efficiently than South Dakota. If it was necessary, South Dakota could produce industrial goods and Connecticut could raise farm products. However, the cost of these activities would be very high.

The same type of comparison can be made between two countries. For example, the tiny country of Kuwait specializes in producing oil because it has an abundance of this natural resource. Columbia, on the other hand, has the climate, soil, and type of labor needed to produce coffee.

When one nation or region can produce a good or service less expensively than another, we say that it has an **absolute advantage**. The businesses within a nation generally specialize in producing as much as possible of the good or service for which they have an absolute advantage. They then trade part of their output for goods or services which can be produced more efficiently by other nations. Both nations benefit when each produces things for which they have an absolute advantage.

The principle of absolute advantage explains why it is profitable for very dissimilar countries to trade goods and services. We could not enjoy coffee, chocolate, bananas, and similar items if we did not trade with the South American, Latin American, and African nations. Likewise, most of them would not have the machinery they use to produce these products if they did not trade with the United States and other industrialized nations.

Some world trade occurs because nations have an absolute advantage in producing certain goods and services. But the majority of world trade takes place between nations that could produce the same products or services equally as efficiently. When this is the case, we look at the theory of comparative advantage to see why nations specialize in producing certain products or services.

Comparative Advantage

It may be easiest to think about comparative advantage from an individual standpoint to begin with. Assume you are considered to be the best carpenter and also the best auto mechanic in your community—you are indeed a talented person! You discover that you can work as a carpenter for $9 per hour or as a mechanic for $5 per hour. Even though you are the best mechanic in your area, it is not a good idea for you to work for only $5 an hour. If you did, you would give up the opportunity to work at $9 per hour as a carpenter. In economic terms, your opportunity cost is the additional $4 per hour that you would give up. Therefore, you will be better off if you work as a carpenter.

When one nation can produce several goods or services more efficiently than another nation but has a greater advantage in producing one rather than others, we say that the nation has a **comparative advantage**. In other words, a nation will produce only those items that it can make less expensively than others, and it will not produce those items that it can buy more cheaply elsewhere.

Although we can grow nearly all the food we want to eat here in the United States, we import items like coffee, processed foods like tuna fish, fresh produce like broccoli, and even apple juice. This is so mainly because human resources (labor) are much less expensive in other countries. We have no comparative advantage because we cannot produce these items less expensively than we can import them. However, in the case of apple juice, we can bottle it less expensively here. As a result, we buy it after the apples have been picked and the juice has been processed because other countries have a comparative advantage in these areas. Then we bottle and pack it into shipping boxes here in our mechanized plants. We have the comparative advantage when we use our automated assembly processes.

HOW DO U.S. COMPANIES CONDUCT INTERNATIONAL TRADE?

International trade is conducted in a variety of ways by U.S. companies. One of the first things they must do is decide whether the company should be based solely in the United States, solely in a foreign country, or set up in some combination of these two. The next section describes some of the alternatives for conducting international trade as a U.S.-based or as a foreign-based firm. It also describes an important trend in international trading referred to as offshore manufacturing.

U.S.-Based Methods

A firm that is located in the United States can conduct international trade and continue to be based here during its trading activities. Exporting, foreign licensing, marketing agreements, and joint ownership are some of the methods which such a company can use.

Exporting. Exporting allows companies a great deal of flexibility. Some businesses sell their goods to local buyers who, in turn, sell them to overseas buyers. Others participate more directly in exporting by selling directly to overseas importers. Firms of all sizes participate in exporting. In fact, 60 percent of all American firms engaged in exporting have fewer than 100 employees. Some smaller firms find that they can sell surplus products to overseas importers. Others find that they reduce the costs of each product when they produce more goods, and so they benefit in two ways. First, they sell more products because of the international trade. And second, they make more profit on each unit they sell in the United States.

Licensing. Many firms enter into licensing agreements with companies in other countries. Under these agreements a U.S. firm permits a firm in another country to manufacture one of the U.S. products there. Coca-Cola, Pepsi-Cola, and McDonald's, for example, have entered into licensing agreements. This means that foreign firms can use the trademarks, patents, and technical processes of the U.S. firm granting the license. In return for these rights, the foreign firm pays the U.S. firms a fee or portion of the revenues. Licensing allows companies in the United States to take some advantage of overseas markets without investing a lot of money. There is no need to build manufacturing facilities or learn how to market the product in a foreign country. They can also avoid the high tariffs (or taxes) that they might otherwise pay if the product were produced in the United States and exported to the foreign country. (We will look more closely at tariffs later in the chapter.) However, licensing does have a few disadvantages. The licensing company has little control over the development and sale of the actual product. For example, McDonald's recently granted a foreigner the license to operate a McDonald's restaurant in Paris. However, the company was so unhappy with the cleanliness of the restaurant that it soon considered taking away the license.

Marketing Agreements. A firm can also participate in international trade by setting up marketing agreements for its products in other countries. When a company chooses this option, the production facilities remain in the home country.

Figure 5-3. Many U.S. businesses, such as Dairy Queen, are popular overseas. Some companies rely on licensing agreements that allow businesspeople to sell the company's goods or services in foreign countries.

Then the company sets up marketing operations in countries where it wants to sell its product or contracts with a company that already specializes in marketing there. In some cases this type of arrangement gives the manufacturing company more control than it would have with a licensing agreement.

Joint Ownership. Sometimes a company will form a partnership with a foreign company or with the government in a foreign country. This arrangement may come about because the country doesn't allow foreigners to hold controlling interests in companies there. Neither Mexico nor Japan allow business firms that are controlled by owners in foreign countries. However, both allow joint ownership arrangements. When there is joint ownership, the foreign co-owners often specialize in knowledge of local conditions. They may also help by providing capital resources (such as buildings, machinery, and trucks) and sharing the risk of business operations.

Foreign-Based Trading Methods

When companies are definitely committed to international trade, they may decide to manufacture and sell their own products in foreign countries. General Electric, for example, owns and operates plants in Brazil. The electrical appliances and locomotive engines produced there are sold worldwide.

When a company owns and operates production and marketing facilities in several countries, it can be referred to as a **multinational company.** Exxon, Mobil, Texaco, and Ford are four of the largest multinational companies. When companies are multinational, they can organize their production so that different countries specialize in different product lines. This may allow them to cut down on transportation costs by locating their manufacturing facilities near both the raw material they need and the people or companies that will buy their products.

Offshore Manufacturing

In his book, *The Future of American Business*, Marvin Cetron* gives an example of a very interesting trend in international trading. He explains, "If you test-drive a Nissan, Honda, or Volkswagen, you'll probably be behind the wheel of a Japanese- or German-engineered car that may have been assembled by American workers at a plant in North Carolina, Ohio, or Ten-

* Marvin Cetron, *The Future of American Business*, McGraw-Hill, 1987, p. xxv.

Source: Adapted from Christopher J. Chipello, "Foreign Rivals Imperil U.S. Firms' Leadership in the Service Sector," *The Wall Street Journal* March 21, 1988, p. 1.

Information Brief 5-1

Selling Service at a Bargain

They are accurate, experienced data-entry workers and they only charge 20 cents an hour for entering detailed information into computer terminals! Where are they? China! And many of our U.S. businesses have found them!

Offshore work isn't limited to manufacturing. Computer technology and lower wages have made it attractive for some U.S. companies to send their service work offshore.

According to experienced buyers of offshore services, language isn't a problem. Chinese keypunch operators concentrate on keying in letters that appear on each page rather than reading the words. Generally, the result , is very accurate. Of course, some people object to offshore work because it takes job opportunities away from Americans.

nessee, from a mix of imported and U.S.-made parts that provide work for other Americans."

Today it is often difficult to determine what country has manufactured a product because countries often share the work. The name for this type of arrangement is offshore manufacturing. When a company engages in **offshore manufacturing,** it arranges for a foreign company to produce some parts or do some parts of the manufacturing for it at a foreign location. Usually a company will engage in offshore manufacturing when it can obtain special skills or processes in the other country that aren't available in its own country. Another popular reason for doing offshore manufacturing is to take advantage of the lower labor costs in other countries.

When you drive a Nissan, Honda, or Volkswagen, you are driving a product that may be the result of offshore manufacturing done in the United States. Foreign automobile manufacturers have contracted to have part of their assembly process completed in our country.

Offshore manufacturing is not limited to the manufacturing of products. As you will see in Information Brief 5-1, some U.S. companies are sending service work offshore because of the dramatic difference in the cost of labor.

▼ How do you feel about offshore manufacturing? Do you think U.S. companies should be allowed to do offshore manufacturing? Why or why not?

HOW IS INTERNATIONAL TRADE FINANCED?

Very little of the exchange of goods and services within a nation or between two nations is on a barter basis. Although we speak and read about international "trade," almost all exports and imports are actually exchanged for payment rather than for other goods and services.

When a trade is made, the price of the good or service is stated in terms of the money used in the producer's country. There are no problems when people of the same nation trade. Each party clearly understands the price and knows the type of currency that will be used for payment. However, when the buyers and sellers are from different nations, problems arise. There will usually be at least two different types of money, or currency, to consider. In France they use francs, in Great Britain they use pounds sterling, and we use dollars in the United States. Those involved in international trade want to know the price and usually want to make or receive payment in their nation's currency.

Foreign Exchange and Exchange Rates

Those involved in international trade and finance must know the value of the currency of all the different nations they deal with. However, they always measure prices and discuss the level of activity in terms of their own currency. To do this, there must be a way to compare and convert the value of the many different currencies in the world.

In international trade, all foreign currencies are called **foreign exchange.** The Mexican peso, the British pound, the Japanese yen, and even the Canadian dollar are all foreign exchange for Americans. When the cost of a good or service is stated in pesos or pounds, most Americans find it hard to decide whether the price is reasonable. They need to convert the price to U.S. dollars. To do this, they must know the exchange rate between the two currencies involved. The **foreign exchange rate** is the number of units of a nation's currency that the nation must pay to get one unit of another country's currency. You might say that the foreign exchange rate is the price a nation must pay to get a unit of a foreign currency. For instance, one U.S. dollar might buy 1.2735 Canadian dollars on a certain day. The exchange rate for all currencies changes daily. Check the financial section of most daily newspapers, and you should find a list of foreign exchange rates for various currencies.

Americans, of course, are most concerned with the value of the U.S. dollar compared to other currencies. At one time the foreign exchange rates or prices of currencies were set by agreements between and among nations. Now the value of currencies is determined in the same way prices are determined in a market economy, by supply and demand. As you can see from Information Brief 5-2 on page 104, those involved in international trade are interested in trends in the value of the dollar and other currencies.

The market for currencies is made up of a group of special financial institutions throughout the world. They include large banks in the world's financial centers, private brokers, government central banks, and international agencies such as the International Monetary Fund. Payment for imports and exports are often made through these institutions because they spe-

Information Brief 5-2

The Falling Dollar: Good News For Some

By the beginning of the year in 1988, the value of the dollar had fallen 40 percent from its peak in early 1985—and U.S. exporters were happy. Up to then the dollar had been fairly strong in relation to other currencies.

Businesses that engage in international trade must watch the value of the dollar and other world currencies very carefully. A large decline in the value of the dollar, for example, means that exported goods are less expensive for foreigners to buy in the world market.

Because of the large decline in the value of the dollar, the overall exports of the United States grew by 15 percent in 1987. Some industries did considerably better than the average. The export of electrical machinery, for instance, increased by nearly 30 percent.

Source: Vivian Brownstein, "Crawling out of the Tunnel," *Fortune,* December 21, 1987, pp. 43–44.

cialize in dealing in many different currencies. For example, a U.S. business firm would pay U.S. dollars for toys imported from Korea to such an institution. The institution would then pay the Korean exporter in won, Korea's currency. For its services, the institution charges a fee based on the amount of money it handles.

Because the exchange rates for all currencies are constantly changing, international trade can become quite complicated. Suppose an American supermarket chain buys some cheese from a Norwegian company for 200,000 kroner (Norway's currency). If the exchange rate that day is 6.42 kroner to the dollar, the U.S. supermarket chain needs to exchange $31,152 in kroner to make the purchase. But if the krone falls to 6.0 kroner to the dollar, it will cost the supermarket chain $33,333 to get the same number of kroner to buy the same amount of cheese.

▼ Do you feel foreign exchange rates should be determined by supply and demand so they change each day? Why do you feel as you do? If you do not favor the supply and demand approach, how do you think such rates should be set?

Balance of Trade and Balance of Payments

Nations are interested in how well they are doing in international trade. To determine this, they need to know how much they export and import over a period of time. We'll look at two common measures of international trade: balance of trade and balance of payments.

A nation's **balance of trade** is the difference between the total value of its exports and the total value of its imports for a period of time. If the amount received for exports is greater than that paid out for imports, the nation has a favorable balance of trade, or a **trade surplus.** If the reverse is true and the amount paid for imports exceeds the amount for exports, there is an unfavorable balance of trade. This is called a **trade deficit.**

A nation's balance of trade closely affects its balance of payments. A nation's **balance of payments** is the difference between the total amount paid to all foreign countries and the total amount received from all foreign countries over a period of time. This figure is slightly different from the balance of trade because it includes other factors such as international loans and spending by tourists.

For more than 10 years, our balance of trade and balance of payments have been unfavorable. One major reason for this imbalance is the foreign exchange rate you just read about. For the most part, the U.S. dollar has been worth much more than the money of other countries. As a result, we could buy a lot of foreign products at bargain prices, but people from other countries couldn't afford to buy our products.

One way that all nations, including the United States, control the balance of trade is by restricting international trade. In the next section we will look at some ways countries try to do this.

▼ Do you think it is important for a country to have a favorable balance of trade and a positive balance of payments? Why?

HOW DO NATIONS RESTRICT INTERNATIONAL TRADE?

All nations of the world have policies related to exports and imports. However, nations generally do not restrict exports because they usually bring money into the country. The major exception to this is that some nations do not export military goods and technology to some other nations. Imports require payment to other nations and compete with goods and services produced within a nation. Competition from imported goods should benefit consumers by providing them more choice, better quality, and lower prices. However, when consumers buy imported goods rather than similar goods produced at home, economic activity is being increased abroad rather than at home. Some nations restrict imports to prevent foreign competition and to increase economic activity at home rather than abroad.

Tariffs and Quotas

Knowing how nations restrict international trade may be as important as knowing why they do so. To protect certain industries and businesses in their economies, all nations put some restrictions on imports. Putting tariffs and quotas on goods or services are two of the most common actions. A **tariff** is a tax placed on imported goods. As is true of all taxes, a tariff is paid to the government and raises the price of an item. The increased price makes the item less attractive to consumers. A **quota** is a limit on the quantity of a specific type of good that can be imported. A major problem with using tariffs and quotas is trying to decide exactly what imports to tax and limit and how much the tax or limit should be. In addition, if Nation A puts a tariff or quota on imports from Nation B, Nation B will likely take similar action against imports from Nation A.

Trade restrictions such as tariffs and quotas are established primarily to help the growth of industries within the country that imposes them. They help each country to handle the competition from imported goods. For example, as U.S. industries feel that they are threatened by imports, more and more have asked the federal government to protect them by establishing trade barriers and setting up quotas.

In addition to tariffs and quotas, nations control international trade in other, less obvious ways. Some of these controls also protect consumers who buy imported goods. Governments may, for example, require that imported goods be clearly labeled as imports in some way. This involves additional cost to the manufacturer and may mean that some consumers won't purchase the goods because they are foreign-made. They may also require that detailed tests and inspections be conducted on foreign goods. The ingredients of food products and the fiber contents of clothing may have to be spelled out in a label.

▼ Do you feel the United States should restrict the importing of goods by using tariffs or quotas? Why should or shouldn't we use these measures?

Other Trade Barriers

Some barriers to trade are set up specifically to discourage importers. The French government requires that all imports of Japanese video recorders pass through the same understaffed customs office. The Australian government insists that margarine be pink in color. And the Egyptian government insists that the dubbing of voices on all foreign films that are brought into that country be done in Egypt. These types of protective measures add to the cost and time of getting goods into a nation. They may eventually discourage exporters from trying to get their products into a foreign nation.

Embargoes

Finally, the ultimate trade restriction, an embargo, may be used. An **embargo** prohibits trade in certain goods or services or with certain nations. An embargo may be put on imports or exports and is often done more for political than trade reasons. For example, the United States put an embargo on the export of grain to the Soviet Union in 1980 because the Soviets had invaded Afghanistan.

HOW DO NATIONS ENCOURAGE INTERNATIONAL TRADE?

Governments don't always restrict international trade. Sometimes they encourage it. Both political agreements and free-trade zones aid the growth of international trade.

Political Agreements

In 1947, the United States and 22 other nations signed the General Agreement on Tariffs and Trade (GATT). Those countries that signed agreed that they would not discriminate in trading with any of the other signers of the agreement. This meant that all 23 of the countries would negotiate one set of terms for exchanging goods and services among them. This was quite different from the earlier trade agreements. Before GATT, a nation had separate agreements with each of its trade partners, and each agreement might be different. Currently, over 75 countries have signed the GATT and are covered by the same trade agreement. This has been a very positive influence in increasing the amount of international trade since 1947.

Since the signing of GATT, there have been meetings in 1962, 1979, and again in 1982 to strengthen and extend the GATT agreements. But the initial agreement in 1947 is noted as the most important of the agreements.

Free-Trade Zones

Another effort to encourage international trade has been the establishment of free-trade zones. A **free-trade zone** is a designated area within a country where foreign goods can be assembled, processed, or stored free of tariffs until they are moved out of the zone into another area of the country. There are several hundred free-trade zones throughout the world.

CULTURAL BARRIERS TO WORLD TRADE

Some barriers to international trade are the result of cultural differences rather than tariffs, quotas, or embargoes. Differ-

Information Brief
5-3

Translating Is Big Business

A computer company doing business internationally was not amused when it saw "software" translated as "underwear" in its ads. Businesses in the United States are coming to realize the value of doing business in a client's native tongue. But they have become aware, after mistakes like the one above, that a translation must be precise.

As U.S. businesses try to work in their customers' or clients' languages, American translation services are booming. Already they are a $20 billion-a-year industry.

Today, much of the translation work is done by computers. Although computers initially were used for translations in the 1970s, only recently have they been able to deal with such nuances as the difference between "software" and "underwear."

Sources: Diane Wagner, "The Importance of Universal Understanding," *Republic Magazine*, March, 1986, pp. 23–27; and Victoria Pope, "A Tower of Babble," *The Wall Street Journal*, June 12, 1987, pp. 30–31D.

ences in languages, customs, and political climate all contribute to these cultural differences.

Language

Companies may encounter problems when they deal with language differences. When U.S. brand names and advertising are translated into other languages, they sometimes come out in unexpected ways.

"Nova" is a name that we associate with a compact car made by Chevrolet. The company was surprised to find that the name translates in Spanish to mean "It doesn't go." The Pepsi slogan "Come Alive With Pepsi" means "coming alive from the grave" when it is translated into German. In Indonesia, the term "software" that is used for computer programs translates into "underwear," or "computer junk." And the Ford truck called "Fiera" translates in Spanish to mean "ugly old woman."

Problems translating slogans and product names aren't the only language difficulties companies face when dealing with international trade. They often have difficulty finding managers who speak more than one language well. Having managers who understand both the language and customs of a country with which it is trading helps a company to avoid problems.

Customs

Social expectations, values, and attitudes are different in many countries. In Japan, for example, the decision process involved in negotiating a business deal is deliberately slow and complex. On the other hand, American businesspeople are used to making fast deals under the pressure of deadlines. In dealing with their Japanese counterparts, Americans can become frustrated by the slower pace of negotiations. Further, if a U.S. business wants to sell an American product which requires an instruction manual in Japan, the manual might interfere with the sale. Why? Because the Japanese take offense at the cold, impersonal tone of many of our instruction manuals. They are used to a friendlier, more personal tone. And, as American businesses have found, Japanese consumers expect to find goods packaged in clean, unmarked, undamaged containers when they arrive at their final destination.

Customs can influence business dealings all over the world, not just in Japan. For example, German and Dutch businesspeople often take their wives or husbands with them on business trips, but this activity is almost unheard of in Asia. In Moslem countries it is considered a cause for embarassment for a businessperson (or others) to show affection in public— even toward a spouse. In some countries it is illegal to show public affection because physical contact is considered a strictly private matter. In the Soviet Union, however, businesspeople, including men, often greet one another with an embrace.

As you can see, if those involved don't do their "homework" before doing business in another country, it would be easy to make a mistake that would violate the local customs.

▼ Suppose you worked for an American company which sent you overseas to complete a major business deal in a foreign country. How would you feel if you lost the deal because you made an embarrassing social mistake because you didn't know the local customs? How could you prevent this from happening?

Political Climate

Nations have basic disagreements about how leaders should be selected, how governments should operate, and how the economic and other social systems should function. These types of disagreements are sometimes referred to as political disagreements. They also serve as barriers to developing a friendly, cooperative relationship among people from different nations. And when there is no friendly and cooperative relationship, international trade becomes more difficult.

In all countries a foreign company must learn how to operate with the government's approval. But this may be more difficult in communist nations such as the Soviet Union and the Peoples Republic of China. There, the foreign company often has to form a partnership with the host government before it can operate legally. In other countries the government controls the operations so closely that companies may be required to give up their secret formulas in order to be able to do business. When the government in India asked Coca-Cola to do this, the company decided to discontinue operations rather than pass on their secret formula for Coke.

There is always some risk in carrying out trade with other nations. However, the degree of risk increases as the level of intensity of basic political differences between nations increases. Basically this means that the more unfriendly Nation X

Establishing Worldwide Communications Systems

A clerk at a Honda dealership in New York can order new inventory by using a computer terminal that communicates with 10 regional U.S. warehouses. These warehouses are tied to Honda's U.S. headquarters in Gardena, California, as well as the world headquarters in Tokyo.

American President Cos., a worldwide shipper, uses a complex network of satellite and land-based communication links to keep track of its cargo movements throughout Asia and North America. Customers who want to know the whereabouts of a shipment can call a toll-free number, and a digitized voice-response system will give the location in 10 seconds.

A stockbroker in Chicago can use Merrill Lynch's trading system to take a client's order by phone and instantly buy 1000 shares of British Petroleum Co. on the London Stock Exchange.

All the above are examples of worldwide communications systems. Today such communications systems are creating an opportunity for people throughout the world to conduct trade on a direct basis. Interpreters and other go-betweens are no longer needed.

As a result of worldwide communication systems, multinational companies are beginning to focus on a larger, worldwide market.

In much of the world, however, sophisticated communications systems have not been developed. Worldwide communication systems can be set up by private companies, but usually they rely on existing phone lines or satellite networks. These are regulated by individual countries.

Some countries are fearful that an electronic communication system would increase competition. They are afraid that local or national companies will not be able to compete against large multinational companies. If the country's own businesses become less competitive and begin to lose money, they may have to reduce their work force, resulting in increased unemployment.

In some cases, countries have established restrictive regulations that act as barriers to setting up an international communication system. For example, when Texas Instruments (TI) wanted to build a base for satellite transmission in Bangalore, India, it took two years to get approval from seven different regulatory agencies. It also took a major compromise to avoid government construction of the facility, which would have taken five years. TI built it in two. But it turned over operating control to India.

Until now, numerous protests of such rules by Washington have had little effect. But something new is happening. Some countries are discovering that by opening themselves to worldwide communication systems and eliminating communications roadblocks, they are not losing sales but are, instead, gaining new investments from the international community.

Source: John Keller, "A Scramble for Global Networks," *Business Week*, March 21, 1988, pp. 140–148.

is toward Nation Y, the greater the risk for anyone from Nation X who is visiting Nation Y to conduct business. For this reason, business firms and governments worry about the safety of employees and officials who are sent to certain foreign nations to conduct business. There have even been isolated instances of terrorism and kidnapping that have been directed against U.S. companies operating abroad.

Nationalization is another serious problem that businesses must face in the global economy. **Nationalization** is the takeover of foreign companies by the government of a nation in which the business is located. Between 1970 and 1974, $1.2 billion worth of American property and investments were taken over by the governments in 34 different countries. Sometimes companies can appeal and reach a cash settlement. Anaconda Co. received $47.5 million in cash for its copper mines in Chile when the government took them over. The government could have forced Anaconda to leave the country with nothing, but the company was able to reach a settlement through the legal system. Unfortunately, not all companies are as fortunate as Anaconda. It is important to remember that companies participating in international trade are at the mercy of the country where they have chosen to do business.

Despite the problems associated with cultural and political barriers to trade, more and more businesses are enjoying the benefits of the global economy. Experts in international business recommend that companies learn as much as they can about the countries where they plan to do business. The information they gather may help them to avoid problems caused by language and custom differences. Political problems are a little more difficult to predict. However, governments sometimes warn prospective businesses that they are politically unstable. Some Latin American countries now tell foreign companies that they may have to be prepared for some form of government takeover within the next 10 to 15 years. As a result of this warning, many companies are selecting joint ownership and licensing as their methods of international trade there. Both these methods may provide a foreign company with some protection against nationalization.

Select Terms to Know

absolute advantage	balance of trade	embargo	foreign exchange
balance of payments	comparative advantage	exports	foreign exchange rate
			free-trade zone

imports
multinational company
nationalization

offshore manufacturing
quota
tariff

trade deficit
trade surplus

Review Questions

1. What are some reasons why the amount and type of international trade has increased during the twentieth century?

2. Why do the nations of the world trade with each other?

3. Explain what is meant by the principle of absolute advantage and give an example to illustrate it.

4. Explain what is meant by the principle of comparative advantage and give an example to illustrate it.

5. What are four methods of international trade which can be used by U.S. firms that wish to be located in this country? How do these methods differ from those used by multinational companies?

6. What are some reasons why U.S. firms engage in offshore manufacturing?

7. Why is the foreign exchange rate sometimes referred to as the "price" of a foreign currency?

8. How are the values of currencies determined today?

9. What are some reasons why nations put restrictions on imports of some foreign goods?

10. How does the GATT differ from trade agreements which existed before 1947?

Thought and Discussion Questions

1. Some of the citizens of our country feel that we should not trade with the Soviet Union, China, or any other nation generally recognized as being in the communist group of nations. They feel any trade with these nations is helping "our enemy." Do you agree or disagree with this viewpoint? Why?

2. Read Information Brief 5-1 again. How do you think the practice of U.S. firms using offshore services will affect our economy?

3. Which do you think causes more problems in conducting open, friendly international trade between and among nations: language, customs, or political climate? Why?

4. Do you think the United States should restrict imports of goods from other nations?

    a. If you answered "No," discuss why you think we should allow completely free trade in our country when other countries do not allow all our goods to be imported freely for their citizens to buy.

    b. If you answered "Yes," identify two goods that you think we should restrict importing in some way and discuss why you think we should restrict imports of them.

Projects

1. Go to the library and find a recent reference book which has information on U.S. international transactions. Find and record the figures for each of the following for 1981, 1983, 1985,

1987, and the most current year available:

a. Total merchandise exports
b. Total merchandise imports
c. Balance of trade (on the current account)
d. Balance of trade with West Germany
e. Balance of trade with Japan
f. Balance of trade with Canada

Write a brief narrative commentary describing the trends in the figures you found and expressing your feelings about what is happening to our international trade activities.

2. Check the daily newspaper or any other source of foreign exchange rates for the next 10 days. Report changes in the foreign exchange rate for any four of the following currencies for each of the 10 days: British pound, Canadian dollar, French franc, Israeli shekel, Japanese yen,

Mexican peso, South Korean won, and West German deutsche mark.

Write a narrative identifying the most important points of your findings. For example, discuss why you feel value remained stable or why any major changes occurred in any of the rates during the 10 days you watched them. (Assume that major changes are increases or decreases of 10 percent or more)

3. Read at least three articles on the balance of trade and/or balance of payments from current issues of your local newspaper, *The Wall Street Journal, Time, Newsweek, Business Week*, or some other business publication. Identify the author (if one is listed) and the other source information for each of the three articles. Then summarize the information provided in the articles in a 1½- to 2-page written report.

Case Study: Weighing the Wisdom of Free Trade With Canada

The United States and Canada have been moving toward the complete elimination of all tariffs when goods and services are traded between businesses in the two countries. This will benefit the Canadian wood products, minerals, and automobile industries which are big exporters to the United States. It will also provide some small benefit to the U.S. heavy machinery and appliance industries which provide a large percentage of the total U.S. exports to Canada.

Based on the data available, however, it appears that this agreement will benefit the Canadians much more than it will the Americans. For example, while Canada sends about 78 percent of its total exports to the United States, the United States only sends about 25 percent of its total exports to Canada. Further, the overall affect on the GNP is estimated to be about 5 percent for Canada but less than 1 percent for the United States. The fact that the agreement seems to provide much greater benefits for Canada than it does for the United States raises some questions.

1. Given the information provided in the case, do you agree that the trade agreement is much more important to the Canadians than it is to the Americans? Why do you agree or disagree?

2. The U.S. steel industry is one group which is not supportive of this agreement. Which other U.S. industries are likely to oppose this agreement? Which U.S. industries would be most likely to support the agreement?

3. In view of the fact that the 1986 U.S. balance of trade showed a deficit of about $150 billion, why do you suppose the President of the United States was so supportive of this trade agreement which would almost certainly increase the balance of trade deficit with Canada in 1987 and beyond?

4. Do you feel that we should now begin to pursue a similar trade agreement with our second largest trading partner, Japan? Why or why not? Do you think it is possible to make a similar type of agreement with Japan? Why or why not?

The International Marketplace

GLOBALIZATION, COMPETITION, AND MERGERMANIA

A recent survey of top business managers identified their two greatest challenges—the globalization of business and increased competition. For most firms these two challenges go hand in hand. Individual business firms must make difficult decisions to remain competitive. Large corporations that produced a wide variety of goods and services have been forced to concentrate on one or two operations which they do best. This action often results in closing unprofitable plants.

Another result of increased competition has been the trend toward business mergers. (Some have called this trend "mergermania.") While there is a danger of concentrating the production of goods and services in the hands of too few firms, mergers that simply create large firms seldom work. If the new firm, which is the result of combining the operations of the two firms, does not promote economic efficiency and innovation, a new innovator is likely to move in to compete. Nor is a business firm immune from competition simply because it is large. At one time General Motors was thought to be big enough to take over the automobile industry in the United States. Today they are on the defensive from Ford, Chrysler, and Japanese companies.

Business firms have also been forced to turn their attention to a global marketplace. Two of Germany's biggest automobile makers are wholly owned American companies: Ford of Cologne and General Motors of Russelsheim, which makes the Opel. Jobs are both created and lost through international competition. Our country has largely moved away from production of turbine engines, clothing, zinc, sewing machines, and women's shoes. Instead, we have moved strongly toward development of computers, semiconductors, biotechnology, and scientific instruments.

GOVERNMENTS AND "INDUSTRIAL POLICY"

Another important factor in the international marketplace is the role government plays. When the politicians, economists, and public policy makers within each country talk about the economy, they often refer to their country's "industrial policy." Simply put, industrial policy has to do with how much or how little government interacts with business and industry. In adopting an industrial policy, the governments of the world are faced with a very difficult decision: *Should traditional and less efficient business firms be sacrificed to promote efficiency and technological modernization, even if this means the loss of jobs?*

The decision becomes especially knotty where matters of trade are concerned. Free trade with other nations often means that jobs will be eliminated in one industry when goods are imported, while other jobs will be gained when a nation's exports in another industry increase.

Evidence abounds that the governments of the world are facing this difficult decision and, in some cases, changing their industrial policies in light of it. For example, the Soviet Union and Communist China have begun to change their industrial policy by opening the door to a more competitive environment. Capitalistic concepts such as price competition and profits are beginning to creep into the Soviet and Chinese vocabulary. Many socialist nations, such as Great Britain, are shifting away from government ownership of large industries to private ownership to try and make such industries more efficient. Some African governments are offering higher prices to farmers to increase farm production. And the U.S. Congress continues to debate whether free trade or protection of its basic industries will make our nation's economy more efficient and competitive.

THE GLOBAL MARKETPLACE AND THE AMERICAN CONSUMER

As you discovered in this unit, in the United States consumers drive the marketplace. The American consumer is well aware of our unfavorable balance of trade with our international competitors. Almost every month the media, our nation's investment community, and government economists analyze the latest trade figures—usually a trade deficit. Our society has always wanted the latest and most innovative products and services. Generally this has meant that we look for "the latest and the best" no matter who produces it—whether Americans or foreigners. However, jobs are created or lost through shifts in supply and demand, through changes in fashion, and improved technology in the production of goods and services. That, in turn, has major implications for our domestic economy and the global economy.

SITUATIONS FOR ANALYSIS

Below you will find a description of several situations. These situations are based on events or circumstances that have actually occurred. The incidents occurred for some, but not all, of the reasons mentioned in the above reading. Your task is to analyze the economic implications and the possible reasons for the business decisions and/or government policies that were adopted.

You may outline your answer or write it in paragraph form. Use this reading and the chapters in Unit 2 to help you analyze and respond to each situation.

1. A large U.S. tire company sells its aerospace and appliance divisions. It also borrows large amounts of money to modernize some of its plants but it is forced to close several unprofitable plants.

2. An American government agency that oversees medical drugs moves very slowly in approving new drugs. In the meantime, a European firm is given approval to market the drug by its government.

3. A socialist country decides that its highest priority is to maintain jobs for its people. This means that the country will continue to concentrate on maintaining an agricultural economy.

4. A highly industrialized country has a shortage of land for housing. In fact, even a small house, 90 minutes from one's place of employment may cost up to $1 million. Due to government policies, 3 percent of the nation's land is used for housing and 15 percent of the land is reserved for farming. Farm products cost consumers of this country twice as much as they do in the United States.

UNIT 3

Ownership and Management of Business

Business organizations are part of a larger processing system that converts resources into goods and services. Businesses acquire labor, equipment, raw materials, and capital as inputs, or resources, that go into this system. Businesses then take the resources and convert them into outputs—end products or services that have value to their users. Managers are the ones who help organize the entire processing system. If a business is to thrive in this processing system, it must be organized and managed to the best advantage. The general objective of this unit is to help you understand how businesses are organized and managed.

UNIT OBJECTIVES

1. Describe the legal forms of private business ownership.
2. Understand the framework of government regulation of business.
3. Contrast viewpoints regarding the social responsibilities of business.
4. Describe how businesses organize themselves internally.
5. Identify the functions of managers and relate them to the process of management.

CHAPTER 6

Business Structures

Keeping Baseballs Popping in Pittsburgh

In 1985 the Pittsburgh Pirates baseball team had the worst record in the major leagues. They finished dead last in the National League's Eastern Division, 43½ games behind St. Louis. But even more important to the owners of the team, they lost $10 million.

In fact, the Galbreath family, the principal owner of the team, had been losing money on the Pirates since 1976. By 1985 they were understandably very eager to sell. The other owner, Warner Communications, had bought a minority interest in 1983, hoping to put the Pirates on a pay-cable television system in Pittsburgh. But the cable system folded after one season. Now, they, too, were ready to sell the team.

Other investors were interested in the Pirates, but they wanted to move the team to another city. Pittsburgh, however, wanted to keep the Pirates.

Learn how the city, using a special form of business ownership, sought to keep the Pirates in Pittsburgh. Study this chapter to learn about the different types of business structures and to help you answer the questions in the end-of-chapter case study, "Pittsburgh Plays Hardball."

Every day in the United States over 1300 new firms, on average, open their doors to do business, or more than a half-million per year.

Most businesses start small. The majority are owned by one person only, which is a sole proprietorship. One reason for this is that many people have dreams of being their own boss, of being independent, and of running things their own way. (See also Chapter 1.) Maybe you are or will someday be one of these people. If so, you might choose to go into business in any one of several ways. This chapter covers the business structures of a sole proprietorship, partnership, corporation, franchise, and cooperative.

COMMON BUSINESS STRUCTURES

The American society fosters independence. Entrepreneurs often have an independent, courageous personality. This type of person likes to open and run his or her own business—"be the boss." A one-person business owner is called a **sole proprietor.** The owner of a sole proprietorship has legal title and exclusive right to his or her profits and assets (real and personal property).

When two or more people start a business, they are partners, and their business is legally structured as a **partnership.** A partnership involves two or more partners. They hold joint interest in an enterprise and share the profits and risks of the business.

A **corporation** is a legal body or association created by state law authorizing a group of people to carry on an enterprise. The enterprise is granted certain legal powers, rights, and responsibilities by state law.

Two other business structures are the franchise and the cooperative. Neither of these structures have as long a history as the other three, but franchises are growing in number and popularity.

About 70 percent of total U.S. businesses are sole proprietorships. Their combined revenues, however, comprise only about 5.6 percent of the total; their profits about 20 percent. The majority of sole proprietorships are small. The partnership is the least common business structure. It comprises only about 10 percent of the total, with revenues representing little more than 4 percent.

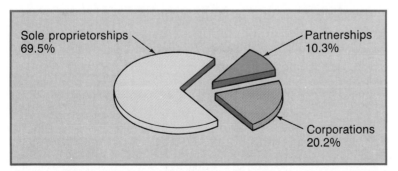

Sole proprietorships 69.5%

Partnerships 10.3%

Corporations 20.2%

Figure 6-1. Percent of U.S. businesses organized as sole proprietorships, partnerships, and corporations. Franchises are included among the sole proprietorship, partnership, and corporation totals.

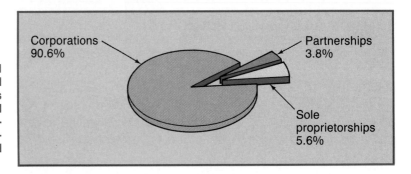

Figure 6-2. Percent of total sales revenues generated by each type of business organization in the United States. Franchises are included among the sole proprietor, partnership, and corporation totals.

Only about 20 percent of U.S. businesses are structured as corporations. (See Figure 6-1.) But because many of these are large, they produce over 90 percent of the nation's total business revenues and two-thirds of the profits. (See Figure 6-2.) Corporations also tend to dominate many key industries.

SOLE PROPRIETORSHIP

The total revenues from sole proprietorships represent a small percentage of the total. But their combined impact on the economy is significant in other ways. For example, over 50 percent of all inventions and innovations come from entrepreneurs and their employees who own and/or work in sole proprietorships.

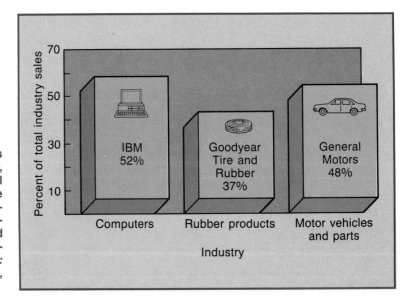

Figure 6-3. Corporations such as IBM, Goodyear, and General Motors still dominate their respective industries. Recently, however, IBM and General Motors have lost some ground to both domestic and foreign competitors. (*Source:* "Fortune 500 List," *Fortune,* April 27, 1987.)

Characteristics

Legally, a sole proprietorship consists of one person, the owner. The sole owner receives all the profits, suffers all the losses, and assumes all the legal responsibilities. The entrepreneur and the enterprise are one under the law. One legal implication is the concept of **unlimited liability**. This means that a company's owner is personally liable for its debts or losses. If the company experiences financial difficulties, not only the firm's assets but also the owner's personal assets are subject to sale.

With this legal structure, there is little formality and few legal restrictions. For example, to operate as a sole proprietor new business owners need only get a tax number from the Internal Revenue Service (IRS). However, self-employed people with no employees can use their Social Security number to identify the business as a proprietorship. Some businesses, such as food and beauty or barber shop enterprises, need to get a license from the local or state government to operate. That's because they involve products and services that can affect customers' health and safety.

Advantages and Disadvantages

There are both advantages and disadvantages to the sole proprietorship.

Advantages. Making one's own business decisions can be fast and lead to flexibility because there's nobody else to confer with. Keeping all the profits that the business generates is another advantage.

Many people like the freedom, independence, and flexibility of the sole proprietorship. They can make fast decisions, keep the profits, and work as hard as they wish, depending on their goals.

▼ How would you feel about getting to make all business decisions and being able to keep all profits from the business?

Disadvantages. Lacking either sufficient talents or money to operate the business effectively is a disadvantage of the sole proprietorship. The statement, "It can be very lonely at the top," applies here. Also, one person alone might not have enough money to get started or be able to get a bank loan. Loans are often needed to provide enough capital to start a business and keep it operating until it makes a profit. The capital referred to here is money or other purchasing power.

Sole owners are responsible in full for any business debts that exceed the total investment. This liability extends to all of a proprietor's assets, including house and car. Proprietors are liable for such things as physical loss or personal injury to others. (This risk, however, can be reduced by getting insurance coverage.)

Still another disadvantage is that, because of illness or death of the proprietor, the enterprise's financial ability can be hampered, or it might require termination. But this potential disadvantage can be overcome if family members become active in the business and are positioned to take over in the event of illness or death of the proprietor. (See Information Brief 6-1 for a discussion of some of the problems facing a family-owned business.)

Some of the advantages and disadvantages of a sole proprietorship are outlined later in Table 6-2 on page 129.

Types of Businesses Suited to Sole Proprietorships

Any small or local business that deals with either goods or services can be structured as a sole proprietorship. Two criteria are (1) a lot of capital is not needed, and (2) the owner, along with employees, can effectively manage the enterprise.

Many small retail stores and service firms operate as sole proprietorships, including beauty and barber shops, repair shops, cafes, small motels, carpenters, and electricians.

PARTNERSHIPS

Partnerships are less common than sole proprietorships. Partnerships produce only about 4 percent of total U.S. business revenues.

Characteristics

The Uniform Partnership Act defines a partnership as "an association of two or more persons to carry on as co-owners of a business for profit." Like the sole proprietorship, partners

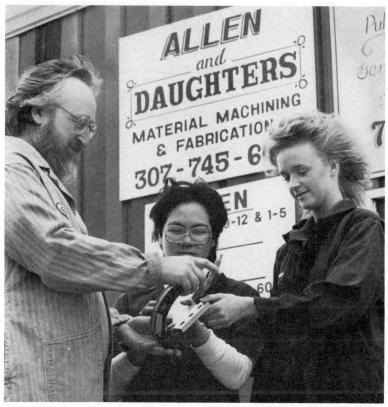

Figure 6-4. Owning and operating a family-owned business remains a cherished dream to many Americans. Many family-owned businesses are organized as proprietorships.

usually have unlimited liability. The partners have co-ownership of the assets. They usually share in the management and profits. They hold **mutual agency**—which means that each partner may act legally for one another or for the partnership as a whole.

There are several kinds of partners. They differ in the degree to which they participate in the affairs of the partnership, whether their relationship to the partnership is known to the public, and the degree of liability they have for the partnership's debts. (See Table 6-1.)

Two types of partners prevail. A **general partner** takes an active part in the management of the firm and is publicly known as a partner. A general partner has unlimited liability for the firm's debts. A **limited partner** usually does not play a direct day-to-day role in the management of the partnership. Although his or her involvement is known to the public, the liability of a limited partner is *limited* to his or her investment in the firm.

TABLE 6-1 Types of Partners			
Kind of Partner	Participation in the Business	Relationship to the Public	Degree of Liability
General	Active	Known	Unlimited
Secret	Active	Unknown	Unlimited
Silent	Not active	Known	Unlimited
Dormant	Not active	Unknown	Unlimited
Limited (or special)	Not active	Known	Limited

The Partnership Agreement. Although not specifically required by the Uniform Partnership Act, for the protection of all partners it is best to draw up written Articles of Partnership.

These articles outline the contribution each partner will bring to the business, whether financial, material, or managerial. It generally describes the roles the partners will play in the business relationship. Some typical topics of clauses in a partnership agreement are:

Name of the business, purpose, domicile (location and address of the business)

Duration of the partnership agreement—beginning and ending dates

Character of partners—general, silent, etc.

Contributions by partners—financial or otherwise

Business expenses—how they will be handled

Authority—each partner's authority within the firm

How disputes between partners will be settled

How the partnership's books and records will be kept

Division of profits and losses

The rights of partners to draw salaries—amounts, conditions, etc.

What happens if a partner dies, such as dissolution of the partnership

Information Brief 6-2 makes it clear that the partnership relationship can be a difficult one. A carefully drafted partnership agreement can help avoid some of these difficulties.

Advantages and Disadvantages

There are both advantages and disadvantages of the partnership.

Advantages. Partners can often raise more capital than the sole proprietor. Partners can bring different skills to the business. Partners are usually motivated to apply their best abilities because they share in the profits. The partnership also has more freedom from government control and special taxation than corporations.

Disadvantages. Each of the partners is an owner in the business and is subject to certain legal responsibilities. Each usually has unlimited liability, much the same as a sole proprietor. One partner can be held personally liable for the actions of the other partner(s). Suppose you and Alice Gomez are partners in a shoe store. Alice makes several bad purchases, which result in a financial loss. If Alice does not have enough money to pay for the loss, you are legally responsible for paying the debts Alice has arranged for the firm. A partnership is also subject to unlimited liability for personal injuries.

The elimination of any partner automatically dissolves the partnership. The business can continue to operate only if the remaining partner(s) seeks to create a new partnership or restructures the firm as a sole proprietorship. Whether by death or personal desire to get out, the remaining partner(s) sometimes has difficulty in raising the capital to buy out the partner who leaves or to buy out the estate of one who dies.

These advantages and disadvantages, among others, are outlined in Table 6-2 on page 129.

▼ How would you feel if you had to sell your car, stereo, and other belongings in order to raise the cash to pay the business debts incurred by your partner? What if you didn't know about those debts and wouldn't have agreed to them in the first place?

Types of Businesses Suited for Partnership

Firms that sell different goods and services are suited to the partnership structure, as are those where different talents are required. An accounting and consulting service needs people who are good with figures and financial analysis. Sometimes this type of person prefers working alone with data. Yet, to get

---

Information Brief 6-2

Avoiding Partnership Problems

A partnership is like a marriage, and dissolving it can be as messy as a divorce. After her own partnership failure, Gloria Gilbert Mayer, the owner of a restaurant in St. Paul, Minnesota, formulated some principles that could prevent problems in partnerships: (1) Thoroughly investigate your partner. Find out any negatives before you commit yourself to the partnership. (2) Know your own strengths and weaknesses. Discuss them with your partner. (3) Mention the unmentionables. Any secrets that could affect the partnership should be openly discussed. (4) Share and discuss the potential for loss equally. (5) Plan a regular schedule of meetings and stick to it. (6) Before you begin, ask an experienced lawyer to draw up a clear and binding method for settling disputes.

Source: Adapted from Gloria Gilbert Mayer, "The Ten Principles of Partnership," *Working Woman,* November 1984, pp. 77–78.

VALDEZ, KLEIN, AND O'BRIEN

CIVIL AND CRIMINAL LAW PRACTICE

Over 90 Years Combined Experience

A LAW PARTNERSHIP SERVING THE PUBLIC & THE PROFESSION

FREE INITIAL CONSULTATION

24 HOUR TELEPHONE SERVICE

555-2626

108 MAIN STREET, HIGHTSTOWN, NJ 08520

Figure 6-5. Many professional businesses, such as law offices, are organized as partnerships. A partnership gives professionals an opportunity to pool their resources, experience, and expertise.

clients, and to work with them in person, the outgoing-type personality does best. So two types of personalities might do well in this type of partnership—a back room type and a public relations type.

Businesses that are open long hours or whose owners are on 24-hour call are usually suited to the partnership form. Thus this business structure is often chosen by these types of firms: doctors' offices and medical clinics, law offices, gasoline stations, and restaurants.

Also generally well-suited to the partnership structure are small manufacturing firms or any other type of enterprise where considerable capital is required to get started and keep operating. If very substantial amounts of capital are needed, however, the corporate structure might be better.

CORPORATIONS

Compared to sole proprietorships and partnerships, corporations are small in number. But many are large in size. A firm does not have to be large to incorporate, however. Anybody can decide to structure his or her business as a corporation.

Corporations play an important role in the economy. They employ millions of people. They provide consumers with many needed goods and services.

Characteristics

The best-known definition of a corporation is that written by Chief Justice Marshall of the U.S. Supreme Court in 1819. He said that a corporation is "an artificial being, invisible, intangible, and existing only in contemplation of law." See Information Brief 6-3 for the most-admired corporation in the United States.

A corporation is a legal creation of the state government. Corporations that do business in more than one state must comply with the federal laws regarding interstate commerce and with state laws. To form a corporation, the corporate officers, who are referred to as **the board of directors,** begin by taking subscriptions to stock or getting people to buy stock once the corporation is official. Stock is the share in the ownership of a corporation held by each stockholder. Stockholders are people who own stocks, or shares of ownership, of a corporation.

The stockbroker buys and sells stocks according to regulations. The stock dividend is a form of payment, usually money, and/or additional shares in the same corporation from the company's profits. The dividend is so called because it represents a share of the profits that is divided among the stockholder members of a corporation.

To operate, the corporation needs approval (in the form of a charter) from the secretary of state's office in all states in which the corporation will do business. This approval comes in the form of a **corporate charter.** This charter is a written document that specifies rights granted by a government to a group of individuals whose purpose is to form a corporation.

The charter, sometimes called a **Certificate of Incorporation,** is granted on the basis of these criteria:

- The name of the proposed corporation is satisfactory.
- The certificate contains all necessary information and has been properly executed.
- Nothing in the corporation's proposed activities violates state law or public policy.

Steps Toward Incorporating

Guidance from an attorney ensures that:

- The articles of incorporation and the bylaws are tailored to the needs of the business enterprise.
- Tax obligations are understood.

- The enterprise will be in compliance with state, local, and federal laws affecting the corporation in the location(s) where the corporation decides to do business.

To obtain the Certificate of Incorporation, owners state:

1. The corporate name, address, and names and addresses of the proposed board of directors.
2. The purpose for which the corporation is formed.
3. The length of time the corporation will operate.
4. The maximum amount and type of stock to be issued.
5. The capital required at the time of incorporation.
6. The rights, if any, to be granted to the stockholders and the restrictions, if any, on stock transfers.
7. The provisions for regulation of corporate internal affairs.

After getting the Certificate of Incorporation, the new corporation must hold a meeting of officers and stockholders to establish and accept the bylaws. These **bylaws** establish the company's internal rules and regulations and also cover state and federal laws so that the corporation will be sure to comply with these laws and tax plans.

Advantages and Disadvantages

There are both advantages and disadvantages to the corporate form.

Advantages. Corporations have a separate legal existence, and ownership is readily transferable. In case of illness, death, or other loss of an officer, the corporation continues to exist and do business. The company thus has stability and relative permanence.

Capital can be acquired by issuing stocks and bonds. A bond is an interest bearing certificate issued by a government or business that promises to pay the holder a specified sum on a specified date. It is a common means of raising a large amount of funds. Securing long-term financing from lending institutions is easier than with sole proprietorships or even partnerships. The corporation can take advantage of company assets and also of stockholders' and officers' personal assets.

The incorporators can retain control because when they delegate authority it is to hired managers. The corporation can also draw on the skills of more than one individual.

TABLE 6-2 Different Forms of Business Ownership: Advantages and Disadvantages		
Ownership	**Advantages**	**Disadvantages**
Sole Proprietorship	1. Ease of business setup, operation, and closing. 2. Owner receives all profits. 3. Owner can determine appropriate level of effort, depending on business goals. 4. Lower tax rate.	1. Owner has unlimited liability. 2. Business's ability to raise capital is dependent on owner. 3. Owner's sickness or death can mean the end of the business.
Partnership	1. Relatively easy to set up, operate, and dissolve. 2. Partners share the profits. 3. Greater diversity of operating skills. 4. Increased ability to raise capital. 5. Relatively free from government control. 6. Better tax rate than corporations.	1. Partners have unlimited liability. 2. Possible conflicts between partners. 3. Partnership must be restructured or dissolved when a partner leaves.
Corporation	1. Separate legal existence. 2. Liability of investors limited to their shares of stock. 3. Stability and permanence. 4. Ability to acquire large amounts of capital. 5. Ease of getting financing. 6. Professional management.	1. Complex and expensive to set up, operate, and go out of business. 2. Subject to extensive government regulations and legal restrictions. 3. Corporation is taxed at a higher rate.

Disadvantages. Business activities are limited by the charter and by various laws, although some states do permit very broad charters. The corporation is subject to extensive government regulations and must provide numerous reports to local, state, and federal agencies. State and attorneys' fees are necessary in getting started and continuing operations.

These advantages and disadvantages, among others, are outlined in Table 6-2.

Types of Businesses Suited for Incorporation

Any type of business and any business owners can decide to incorporate. Corporations usually are formed, however, when two basic conditions prevail:

● ● ● ●

Information Brief
6-4

_____

Risky Business

_____

Corporations must take
risks to grow. Ask Bill
Davilla, President and
Chief Operating Officer
of Vons Groceries, a
subsidiary of the $3.2
billion Pons Compa-
nies, Inc.

Under Davilla, Pons
recently started Tian-
guis, a chain of His-
panic grocery stores in
Southern California.
Each store requires a
$10 to $12 million in-
vestment. Two stores
are now in operation
and four more are
planned.

At Tianguis stores
the signs, advertise-
ments, and personnel
are bilingual.

The stores are a re-
sponse to the large
Hispanic population in
southern California.
They have been very
successful, but Bill
Davilla has his own ex-
planation of Vons' suc-
cess: "I try to inject my
own experience."

Source: Aileen Schlef, "Bill Davilla: Back to the Future," *Hispanic,* July, 1988, pp. 25–27.

● A business needs lots of capital to get started and keep operating. (See Information Brief 6-4, for an example.)

● The future of the business appears uncertain, and the business owners are loathe to put their personal assets at risk.

Capital requirements are a major reason why the corporate form of business predominates among manufacturing firms, airlines, construction firms, and large-scale real estate developers. Efforts to minimize risks are a major reason why oil exploration and mining ventures and manufacturers and distributors of faddish or trendy products tend to choose the corporate business form.

FRANCHISES

The International Franchise Association defines a **franchise** as "a continuing relationship between the franchiser and the franchisee. The franchiser supplies its knowledge, image, success, and manufacturing and marketing techniques to the franchisee for a consideration."

A legal term, consideration usually means money, but not always. Consideration can also be an agreement to do or not do something, or to exchange services or products instead of money. Thus a franchise is a legal agreement giving others a right or license to market a company's goods or services in a particular territory.

The **franchiser** is the company that gives the franchise rights to the franchisee. The **franchisee** is the recipient of these rights, usually an entrepreneur. Usually the franchisee has previous business experience. The franchisee(s) can decide to organize the franchise as a sole proprietorship, a partnership, or a corporation.

Characteristics

The franchiser may be a manufacturer, a wholesaler, or a service company. The franchisee gets permission to use the company's name; plus help in starting, advertising, and managing the company. When franchisees buy a franchise, they buy the trade name of an already proven product or service and the right to do business. The franchisee, in turn, agrees to follow specific marketing and operating procedures.

Advantages and Disadvantages

There are both advantages and disadvantages to the franchise.

Advantages. The failure rate for franchises is somewhat lower than that of independent businesses. New owners avoid the risky first steps of starting their own businesses, since the franchise idea already has been conceived, developed, and refined. Since the guidelines for management have often been created from A to Z, new owners can benefit from both the mistakes and the successes of others. Banks are usually more amenable to making loans for such well-planned ventures as a franchise, which is another advantage.

Franchisers often help their franchisees select a location, and will supervise construction and stage the opening promotion. Franchisers sometimes train their franchisees to follow standard procedures, help to hire employees, to buy at discount rates, and to establish and administer financial records.

Disadvantages. Any of the above can prove to be disadvantages as well as advantages, however, since many entrepreneurs go into business because of the freedom they anticipate. These types of persons want to make their own mistakes and develop the new business's standards, procedures, controls, and decisions.

Figure 6-6. Franchisers often train new franchisees and their managers and employees to follow standard procedures that ensure uniformity among different franchise operations. Here managers and employees receive training at McDonald's Hamburger University.

Making Dough by the Hour

In 1977, Debbi Fields had a unique way of running her cookie store. She set *hourly* sales goals. Today, Mrs. Fields Cookies Inc., with nearly 500 stores in 37 states and earning nearly $90 million a year, is still run the same way that Debbi Fields ran her first store—with hourly sales and baking goals. Although Mrs. Fields cookies may be delicious, this phenomenal growth is due to, of all things, a computer system that has helped create a very special type of business organization.

Unlike many fast-food stores, Mrs. Fields Cookies has not franchised. Each of the stores is owned by the company. Despite its size, Mrs. Fields Cookies has an unusual amount of direct, day-to-day control of its stores because of its computer system.

For example, on a typical day a store manager turns on the store's computer and calls up a program that gives the day's sales projections based on sales from a year earlier. The computer asks the manager some questions: What day of the week is it? What type of day: a normal day, sale day, school day, holiday, other?

Based on the manager's responses, the computer reports: Here's what you'll have to do today, hour by hour, product by product, to meet your sales projectons. It tells the manager how many customers are needed each hour and how much each customer should buy. It tells how many batches of dough to mix and when to mix them to meet the demand and to minimize leftovers.

During the day cash registers automatically feed data into the computer, which revises the hourly projections. The computer can make suggestions. It even recognizes when the store is having a bad day and automatically reduces sales projections and baking estimates. It might even suggest that the manager give away free samples to increase sales. It could suggest that the sales staff ask customers if they have tried a particular type of cookie.

The computer system ensures that, without realizing it, each store manager is running the store in pretty much the same way that Debbi Fields ran her original store.

Stores can also communicate with Debbi Fields through the computer. A manager can type a message to Debbi on the computer and she has it by the next morning. She promises an answer within 48 hours. There is also a computerized phone-message system, which allows employees to hear messages from Mrs. Fields and to phone her with urgent messages.

Mrs. Fields Cookies is able to control its operations and reach every employee in a way that would have been unthinkable even a few years ago. With computers, the company has been able to project Debbi Fields' vision of the perfect cookie store to over 2000 employees nationwide.

Source: Adapted from Tom Richman, "Mrs. Fields Secret Ingredient," *INC*, October 1987, pp. 65–72.

Also, the franchiser might require of the franchisee a specified amount of capital, which can be quite large in some cases; for example, to open a McDonald's or a Holiday Inn. (To raise the large sums of capital needed, some franchisees structure their businesses, legally, as partnerships.)

Types of Businesses Suited for Franchise

Early franchise arrangements involved automobile dealerships and gasoline stations, and soft drink companies like Coca-Cola. Auto dealerships and gas stations once accounted for about 50 percent of retail franchise sales.

Many retail stores, restaurants and fast-food places, and service firms are franchises. Walk through any big shopping mall in the United States and around the world and you'll find familiar names. The last few decades have seen the growth of many franchises, including those that provide fast foods, entertainment and recreation, and personal and business services. By the late 1980s McDonald's was opening a new franchise every 15 hours somewhere in the world.

Types of Franchise Relationships. There are four common types of franchises involving relationships between franchiser and franchisee; namely:

- Manufacturers and wholesalers
- Wholesalers and retailers
- Manufacturers and retailers
- The brand-name-based relationship, which also covers certain services

1. The relationship between manufacturers and wholesalers is illustrated by soft drink companies and breweries. Because it is difficult for the manufacturer to produce the entire finished product, it franchises the recipes and special ingredients (such as the syrup to produce Coca-Cola) to the franchisee. The franchisee assembles and bottles the products and distributes them to retailers.

2. The relationship between wholesalers and retailers works like this. The wholesaler, as the franchiser, is able to buy in volume from manufacturers at a discount and can in turn pass the resulting savings on to the franchised retail outlets that market its products. Examples include such automotive product lines as Western Auto Supply and Goodyear.

● ● ● ●

Information Brief
6-5

A CO-OP with Something to Crow About

Gold Kist Inc. is a farmers' cooperative that acts like a big business. Or, more appropriately, Gold Kist is a big business that happens to be a farmers' cooperative. With sales of $1.2 billion, Gold Kist is a chicken, farm supplies, and grain co-op in Atlanta. It's been forced to act like a big business to compete against large national companies like Frank Perdue.

Gold Kist supplies the chicks and feed and dictates the chicken-tending rules to its farmers. Over a seven-week cycle, each farmer raises an average of 30,000 chickens. Gold Kist picks up the grown chickens. The farmer is paid for the chickens by the pound. When the co-op makes money, farmers get a fraction of the profit in cash and the rest in shares in the co-op.

Source: David Henry, "Capitalist in the Henhouse," *Forbes,* January 26, 1987, p. 37.

3. The relationship between manufacturers and retailers has the manufacturer as franchiser supplying the retailer as franchisee with the entire stock, a complete product line. Naturalizer shoe stores and Midas Muffler shops are examples. The franchisee has very little decision making authority over the products offered.

4. The fourth franchise relationship is based on brand name. Popular brand-based franchises in the food and refreshment industry are known for their recipes and/or specific menus. Kentucky Fried Chicken and Baskin-Robbins are examples of franchises that provide recipes and menus. Other popular franchises include motels such as Holiday Inn and Ramada Inn, and auto rental firms such as Hertz and Budget Rent-a-Car. Many services are offered by such popular franchises.

▼ How would you feel if you were a new franchisee who could rely on the assistance and training of a nationally known and respected franchise?

COOPERATIVES

Far less numerous or well-known is the cooperative, which is similar to a corporation. A **cooperative** is an organization, owned collectively by its members, for the production or marketing of goods or services. The purpose of a cooperative is to provide its members with cost-and-profit benefits not available elsewhere. Usually cooperatives are relatively small, but some are quite large. (See Information Brief 6-5.)

Characteristics

People sometimes form a cooperative in which production, marketing, or purchasing activities and facilities are jointly owned. Cooperatives are operated mainly to provide a service to members rather than to make a profit. In a cooperative, any profits generated are usually distributed among members as a rebate or dividend. Another use of profits is to maintain and expand facilities and offerings.

Members of a cooperative, like stockholders in a corporation, usually join a cooperative by buying shares of stock. They appoint officers to run the enterprise. A cooperative must also get a charter from the state in which it is organized. Some types of cooperatives must get authorization from the federal government.

Types of Businesses Suited to a Cooperative

The agricultural economy has the longest tradition in cooperatives. Cotton gins, silos, and other food-processing firms are often organized as cooperatives. Besides processing grains, they offer many other products and services, including gasoline and oil, feed and equipment parts, and even insurance. Farmers and ranchers, through their cooperatives, work together to get better prices for products.

Practically every type of industry and many large corporations also have credit unions, which is another type of cooperative. Employees use credit unions much like they do banks. They deposit and withdraw money in checking accounts and savings accounts and seek loans. Many health insurance plans are formed as cooperatives.

Retailers with small stores often form cooperatives to enable them to buy larger quantities than each store could do alone, and thus they get discount rates on the prices they pay. Consumers also join food and other merchandise and service cooperatives so they can get better prices while also getting dividends if and when available.

▼ How would you feel if you were a farmer raising cotton who had to buy a very expensive cotton gin that would be used only occasionally throughout the year? Can you see why farmers might form cooperatives?

CHOOSING A BUSINESS STRUCTURE

People choose one type of business structure over another based on the type of business, the need for capital and expertise, and personal preference. New and emerging businesses, the economy, and the needs of the marketplace can all produce changes. When changes suggest that another structure is better-suited to the needs of the business, the owner(s) can revise the structure accordingly.

Select Terms to Know

board of directors	corporation	limited partner
bylaws	franchise	mutual agency
Certificate of Incorporation	franchisee	partnership
cooperative	franchiser	sole proprietor
corporate charter	general partner	unlimited liability

Review Questions

1. Which business structure has the most businesses in the United States? Which one has the fewest?

2. Compare some advantages and disadvantages of the sole proprietorship.

3. Name some advantages and disadvantages of the partnership.

4. Describe some advantages and disadvantages of the corporation.

5. Compare the three forms of business structures, namely, sole proprietorship, partnership, and corporation. See Table 6-2.

6. Name some advantages and disadvantages of the franchise.

7. Describe the cooperative. Compare it with the corporation.

8. What businesses are suited to sole proprietorship? Why?

9. What businesses are suited to the partnership? Why?

10. What businesses are suited to the corporation. Why?

Thought and Discussion Questions

1. If the majority of U.S. businesses are sole proprietorships, why does such a large share of sales come from corporations?

2. Why should a partnership agreement be prepared? What items are typically covered, and why?

3. Suppose that you and a friend are partners in a T-shirt shop. Discuss the possible effects each of the following could have on your shop: (a) your partner dies, (b) you and your partner disagree and he or she quits, (c) a new partner is added.

4. As an entrepreneur, which path to business ownership appeals to you most now, the franchise or the independent business? Why?

5. Some people "make their money work for them" by investing their funds in starting a business. Other people invest their money in buying stock; they are stockholders. They actually own a share of the company they invest in. Assume that you inherit, first, $10,000; then $100,000. Given your current knowledge and personal preferences, which of these two investment options appeal to you? Why?

Projects

1. Dorn Kowalak invested $50,000 and Pan-Ching Tun invested $25,000 in their partnership, a computer training service. Last year their net profit after taxes was $22,000. They have agreed to spend $11,000 on expanding the size of the store. They share profits and losses in proportion to their investment. What amount should each receive of the profit remaining after the store's expansion?

2. Tonequa, Inc.'s board of directors decided to distribute $68,050 as dividends to its stockholders, who hold 22,503 shares of stock. How much money, per share, will be distributed in the form of dividends? Suppose you own 287 shares. What amount of dividends should you get?

3. Find an entrepreneur to interview. Check with somebody you know first—a relative, neighbor, or family friend—who might be a sole proprietor, partner, franchisee, or a corporate or cooperative officer. Find out the firm's business structure. Ask the owner(s) why he or she chose the particular form. Ask about advantages and disadvantages, and compare your findings with those listed in the chapter, that is, in Table 6-2.

4. Find out the procedures and licenses needed to start a business in your community. You might interview a lawyer, visit the county courthouse, or check with people in the chamber of commerce. Discuss a specific type of business, such as a fast-food firm, a beauty or barber shop, a repair shop, or a product-sales booth in a flea market or shopping mall.

5. Identify a type of business you might be interested in starting. For example, think about your skills, talents, and interests in relation to products or services that consumers in your community might need and want. Consider whether one or more friends might also be interested in joining you in starting this business.

a. List your skills, talents, and interests.

b. Identify one or more businesses you'd like to run.

c. List the skills, talents, and interests of a friend.

d. Decide whether you would prefer to open a sole proprietorship or a partnership. Discuss the reasons for making the above decisions.

Case Study: Pittsburgh Plays Hardball

Pittsburgh's problem with the unprofitable Pittsburgh Pirates baseball team whose owners wanted to sell the team (described in the chapter opener) was really a matter of civic pride. Pittsburgh simply did not want to see its baseball team go to another city.

So some of Pittsburgh's leading citizens, including the mayor, came up with an interesting solution to the city's problem. They asked the largest corporations in the Pittsburgh area to contribute $2 million each to form a *limited partnership* called Pittsburgh Baseball. In a lim-

ited partnership, most of the partners are granted limited liability, meaning that they cannot lose more than the amount they invested in the business. Limited partners are also not allowed to take an active part in managing the business. The main advantage of this type of partnership is that it allows a partnership to acquire capital from investors who will not be involved in running the business.

Eight corporations invested $2 million and became limited partners in Pittsburgh Baseball. They were Alcoa, Mellon Bank, National Intergroup, PNC Financial Corp., PPG Industries, Ryan Homes, U.S. Steel, and Westinghouse Electric.

As you learned in this chapter, stock in a corporation is a share in the ownership of that corporation. This means that someone who owns stock in any of these eight corporations is, in an indirect way, a part-owner of the Pittsburgh Pirates. The corporations are all large. Between them they have nearly half a million shareholders. In this sense, the Pirates have more stockholders than any company in the United States except AT&T and its regional spinoffs, General Motors, Exxon, IBM, General Electric, and GTE.

When shareholders learned that their corporation had become a part-owner of the unprofitable Pittsburgh Pirates, they may not have been pleased. However, each of the corporations was large enough that its maximum loss ($2 million) would amount to no more than about 3 cents per share. There was always the chance, of course, that the Pirates could earn a profit. But the most important aspect of the partnership was that the corporations had helped the city retain its civic pride. Besides, in 1991, if the Pittsburgh fans don't come to the games and the Pirates remain unprofitable, the investors are allowed to sell the team even if the buyer wants to take it to another city.

Source: Adapted from Allan Dodds Frank, "How to Play Ball in Pittsburgh," *Forbes,* February 24, 1986, pp. 42–43.

1. Why was a limited partnership an attractive form of ownership for the corporations owning Pittsburgh Baseball?

2. In your opinion, is it a good idea for a corporation to help the community in which it is located? (*Hint:* Consider how a corporation is formed. How do you think the people of Pittsburgh would have felt if the corporations centered in their city had been unwilling to help?)

3. If you were a stockholder in one of the corporations forming Pittsburgh Baseball, how would you feel about this limited partnership (particularly if the Pirates continued to lose money)?

CHAPTER 7

The Social and Legal Environment of Business

Big Business Spending "Big Bucks" to Improve Its Image

Americans are fed up with white-collar crime. This was the conclusion drawn from a poll conducted by a major news magazine. Sixty-two percent agreed with the view that crime committed by businesses is a growing problem which shows a decline in ethical conduct. Another major poll showed that baby boomers, a large and influential group of people in the 30- to 44-year-old age range, favor stricter environmental controls of business.

Business firms are spending sums as never before to polish their images and ward off regulation by government. For example, Waste Management Inc., in cooperation with a major university and two governmental agencies, is sponsoring ads that point out its high regard for the environment.

Corporations are spending hundreds of millions of dollars each year on image advertising. Often this advertising relates to matters of public policy. Firms such as W. R. Grace & Co. and Mobile Oil have sought to increase their prestige through media advertising about issues such as taxation, productivity, and the hiring of the hard-core unemployed. The ads portray their sponsors as concerned and socially responsible citizens.

Study this chapter to learn more about the social, legal, and ethical environment in which business operates. Also, use the contents to help you answer the questions in the end-of-chapter case study, "PREFAX Acts to Improve Its Ethical Standards."

Apex Inc. established a chemical plant along the banks of Lake Michigan in 1905. Unchecked, for almost 70 years Apex dumped millions of tons of chemical pollutants into Lake Michigan. Then in the mid-1970s citizens of the area near the plant noticed that thousands of dead fish had washed ashore near the plant. Beaches near the plant had to be closed due to chemical pollution. The TV and other media gave the public a daily dosage of news about the firm's misdeeds. Then came the governmental investigations which accused the firm of being one of the lake's major polluters. Angered, some citizens formed groups to protest Apex's actions. Some called for the permanent shutdown of the plant. Eventually Apex was fined $25 million under antipollution laws. That fine nearly caused Apex to file for bankruptcy.

Today, however, Apex is a changed company. It has installed water treatment facilities to remove pollutants from any chemical wastes before they are discharged into the lake. Apex has taken an active part in cleaning up the lake. It even allows its chemical engineers to advise other local companies about the best ways of combating water pollution. The nearby lake waters have almost been restored to their former natural health and beauty, and many citizens now credit Apex for this achievement.

True story? No, but in many ways the story mirrors developments that actually occurred in recent American business history. In this chapter you will learn about these developments. You will also learn how business is interwoven into the fabric of our social and legal system.

THE SOCIAL RESPONSIBILITY OF BUSINESS

About the time the imaginary Apex Inc. was founded there was little public concern about the social responsibility of business. As long as businesses such as Apex created jobs and income, most people felt that business could simply overlook social problems. Many considered it the job of government or charitable organizations, not business, to deal with social problems. Today, however, business social responsibility is a major concern to many. Is there a cause for such concern? Some experts believe there is. They cite some disturbing evidence. From 1972 to 1982, 115 of America's largest corporations were convicted of at least one major crime or paid civil penalties for serious misbehavior. Further, a recent poll by *U.S. News and World Report* and the Roper Organization showed a general feeling that dishonesty was prevalent in most of American life, including business. More than half those polled felt that people were less honest today than they were 10 years ago.

Whether the poll truly reflects reality is almost beside the point, some say. The image or perception that dishonesty is a problem is a reality which business must deal with. In times past, when public mistrust of business existed, the government has often stepped in to take policing or corrective regulatory action. Such regulation has generally had a profound effect on business operations.

Phases of Social Responsibility

Since the turn of the twentieth century, views about business social responsibility have undergone considerable change. Experts have identified at least three major phases or waves of change.

Phase 1. Starting in the late 1800s and early 1900s, the main goal of society was to promote the creation of railroads, factories, and mines. Business was considered to be acting in a socially responsible manner if it advanced that goal. This push for rapid industrial growth largely ignored issues such as the conditions of workers, the rights of minorities and women, the environment, health and safety in the workplace, and similar social problems. Economic self-interest was the principal concern of business rather than solving social problems.

Phase 2. After the stock market crash of 1929 and during the great depresson of the 1930s, society became concerned that the average citizen and small business had been victimized by big business. Laws were enacted to protect small business and investors. As a result, greater control of the banking system and protection of mom-and-pop small businesses from large corporations became commonplace. Laws were also passed to protect workers in organizing labor unions.

Phase 3. From 1960 to the present day society has become increasingly concerned about the social responsibility of business in new areas. Major changes occurred in the 1960s and 1970s that still have a profound impact on business operations. Ralph Nader's crusade against unsafe cars, concern about air and water pollution, the push for equal employment opportunity for minorities and women, and concern for health and safety in the workplace are now areas of interest for most businesses.

Today we seem to be experiencing yet a new phase of social concern. As the *U.S. News and World Report* and Roper poll show, there is rising public concern about the ethical behavior of businesses, including that of corporate executives and employees. Today many people are as interested in the ethical conduct of a firm as they are about its economic performance.

Differing Views About Social Responsibility

But how far should business go in trying to address the public's growing concern about social responsibility? Even today there isn't complete agreement about this. Indeed, there is much debate about the issue that seems to involve differences about two related matters:

- Should social responsibility be a factor in the decision making process of a firm?
- Should social goals be woven directly into the business goals of a firm?

The Broad View of Social Responsibility. On one side are those who hold a broad view of business social responsibility. They believe that social responsibility should be a major factor in business decision making and that social goals should be a part of a firm's overall business goals. They argue that social responsibility is in the self-interest of business and a necessary ingredient of modern business life. Some of their supporting arguments are outlined in Table 7-1.

The Restrictive View of Social Responsibility. On the other side are those who take a more restrictive view of business social responsibility. They argue that the business goals of a firm are essentially economic in nature. According to this view, creating jobs, satisfying customer needs, and earning profits for the owners of the business are the essential goals of any business firm. They believe that paying too much attention to social goals will only divert a firm's attention away from these critical goals. Table 7-2 lists some arguments for this viewpoint.

▼ Suppose you ran a small business in a medium-sized town. A committee of local citizens pays a call on you and suggests that you should become more involved in the community by investing in some much-needed social projects. How would you feel about this? Would you take a broad or restrictive view of your firm's social responsibilities? What would you do?

Business Self-Regulation

The issue of business social responsibility will be debated for years to come. Meanwhile, in the wake of growing public con-

TABLE 7-1 Broad View of Business Social Responsibility

1. Business has no choice but to include social goals in its overall business goals. If business does not include social goals as part of its objectives, the public will press for legislation requiring it to do so.
2. No real conflict exists between a firm's goal of making profits and its duty to act in a socially responsible way. Business can set as its goal the achievement of rising profits over a longer period of time and thus accommodate social goals. Besides, no concrete proof exists that social activities are really harmful to a firm's profits over any extended period of time.
3. The public would look more favorably upon business if it became more socially responsive. In fact, it might even be possible for a firm to turn social problems into business opportunities and realize benefits itself. For example, business support for education may not only help society but also provide business with a better-educated work force. (See also Information Brief 7-1 on page 141.)
4. Business is in a better position than government to help society solve its social problems. Collectively, business has greater managerial talent, technical resources, and financial strength at its disposal to help solve these problems than the government.
5. Business has a positive duty to help solve social problems. It is only through the social, political, and economic strength of our free society that business has an opportunity to grow and prosper. To the extent business helps our society solve its problems, it strengthens the very society that enables it to survive and prosper.

TABLE 7-2 Restrictive View of Business Social Responsibility

1. There is no real way to include social goals in the overall business goals of a firm. Moreover, it is impossible to really measure business progress in achieving social goals. The reason? There is no clear definition or public consensus about which social goals business should even address.
2. The large corporation is actually owned by its shareholders. A business manager has no right to factor social goals into business decisions that may not be in the economic self-interest of the actual owners.
3. If business gets too involved in the social and political arena, it will become more and more powerful. This action could actually diminish the role of government and the average citizen.
4. Business has little or no experience in solving social problems. It would be a waste of its time, energy, and resources to even try.
5. The business firm plays a major role in allocating resources in our economic system. Its role is to create jobs, produce goods and services, generate profits and wealth, and allocate scarce economic resources. It would be inappropriate and inefficient if social concerns were mixed in with these purely economic goals.

Information Brief 7-2

How Some Companies Are Dealing With the Ethics Issue

Here's a selective list of what some companies are doing in regard to the ethics issue:

1. General Mills has guidelines for dealing with vendors and customers. It seeks recruits who share the company's ethical values.

2. Johnson & Johnson has adopted a set of ethical standards which it calls the company's "Credo." The company monitors compliance with periodic companywide surveys.

3. At Xerox, the company has developed handbooks and policy statements that stress integrity. The company orients employees and managers regarding values and policies.

Source: Adapted from John A. Byrne, "Businesses Are Signing Up for Ethics 101," *Business Week,* January 15, 1988, p. 56.

cern and clamor about business ethics and social responsibility, some businesses have learned to fend for themselves. Some use public relations advertising to show that they are responsible citizens of the community. Some firms show their concern by actively contributing to worthy causes, such as the United Way. Others have joined industrywide organizations to lobby for business views and interests.

Some firms, either individually or in combination, have tried to put their own houses in order. Some firms have adopted strong codes of ethics. These are statements setting forth the ethical and moral considerations that should guide managers and employees in their business dealings. (See Information Brief 7-2.) Still others belong to industrywide associations that have taken on the job of policing business practices within certain industries. For example, some belong to Better Business Bureaus or to industrywide panels that help resolve consumer complaints. Table 7-3 provides a sampling of the industrial associations engaged in self-policing or regulatory activities.

Still some people believe that self-regulation is too much like letting the fox guard the chickens. They believe that laws and governmental regulations still are needed to protect society from possible business misconduct. In our country today, however, we do not rely on one method to protect society from

Figure 7-1. Many businesses demonstrate their social responsibility by supporting worthy causes. For example, some well-known companies supported "Hands Across America," a fundraising effort to help the less fortunate.

TABLE 7-3 Select Associations Engaged in Business Self-Regulation	
Name of Industry Association	**Regulated Product or Service**
American Movers Conference	Moving companies
Carpet and Rug Institute	Floor coverings
Direct Selling Association	Mail-order companies and door-to door sales
Homeowners Warranty Program	New homes (home warranties)
Manufactured Homes Institute	Mobile homes
National Automobile Dealers Association	New automobiles

potential business misbehavior. Instead we rely on a mixture of elements, including business self-regulation, government regulation, legislation, and the good conscience and ethical standards of people in the business community itself.

▼ Imagine you own a firm that belongs to an organization that regulates businesses within your industry. The panel rules in favor of a consumer who has filed a complaint against your business. Would you obey the ruling? Why or why not?

BUSINESS LAW

Our legal system recognizes two basic types of law: crimes and torts. **Crimes** are considered so evil that they are considered wrongs against society and the state as well as against the victim. **Torts** are civil wrongs, wrongs done to individuals rather than to society as a whole. Crimes and torts represent society's definition of unacceptable conduct. This conduct is related to ethics. **Ethics** go beyond crimes and torts and represent the moral principles or values that motivate individual or group behavior. Punishment for crimes and torts are specifically assigned by society. However, there is no universal point of view about what constitutes ethical conduct.

There is also a specific body of law that governs commercial, or business, relationships. In this section you will learn about business torts and this specific body of commercial law.

▼ You are the purchasing agent for a large business. One of the persons from whom you buy materials has offered you an

Information Brief 7-3

New Drug Poses Nightmare

Oraflex was the miracle drug of 1982. Introduced by Eli Lilly, the drug was taken by arthritis sufferers to relieve pain and inflammation.

After only 30 days on the U.S. market, 500,000 people were taking the drug. Then disaster set in. In Britain, where the drug had been on the market for two years, people began having dangerous side effects. These included internal bleeding and kidney and liver problems.

Lilly instantly pulled the drug from the market. Was it soon enough? Lawyers for more than 200 people who said they or their relatives were injured by the drug began looking for negligence on the company's part. More than seven cases have been settled, with $500,000 the largest amount awarded.

Source: "The Miracle Drug That Became a Nightmare for Eli Lilly," *Business Week*, April 30, 1984, p. 104.

all-expenses-paid trip to Mexico for the holidays. How would you feel about this offer? Should you accept the gift? Explain your answer.

Torts Affecting Business

The law of torts contains three broad areas: negligence, intentional torts, and torts based on strict liability. All three areas apply to business firms and their employees. Under tort law an employee owes the same care to business clients as he or she does to them as individuals or as private citizens. Also, a business firm is generally responsible for wrongful or illegal acts of its employees.

Negligence. **Negligence** is defined as the failure to exercise the degree of care that a reasonable person would have exercised under the same or similar conditions or circumstances. In business situations, negligence arises when no care or a lower degree of care was taken to protect a person or property of another party than is legally required. To prove negligence, a complaining party must show that (1) a legal duty of care was owed him or her, (2) the other party failed to exercise the degree of care required under the cirsumstances, and (3) the complaining party suffered damages due to this lack of care. For example, failure by an auto repair shop to test the safety of newly installed brakes could result in a lawsuit claiming negligence due to lack of care. Flaws in workmanship, inattention to detail in providing services, and failure to anticipate the safety needs of customers are other typical situations where claims of negligence often arise. (See Information Brief 7-3 for an illustrative example.)

Intentional Torts. Negligence generally involves the accidental or unintentional actions that cause damage or injury to the property or person of others. By contrast, **intentional torts** are actions committed deliberately outside established guidelines of business conduct. Assault, battery, and trespass are the most common of intentional torts. In business practice, however, this tort occurs most often when a firm wrongfully interferes with another firm's legal relationship with a third party. (See Information Brief 7-4 for an example.)

Strict Liability. The most controversial tort law in today's marketplace involves strict liability. Under the doctrine of strict

Figure 7-2. Failure by an automobile repair shop to test the safety of newly installed automobile equipment could result in lawsuits based on claims of negligence.

tort liability, a business firm or individual may be liable for damages even though it exercised reasonable care in a given situation. Under the concept of **strict liability** a person or firm may be sued and penalized for damages, even if it was not directly at fault for causing injury to others.

Commercial Law

The body of law that applies directly to business conduct is known as commercial law, or simply as **business law.** These laws deal with business matters such as contracts, the sale of property, the transport and storage of property, agency, and employment.

Contracts. Each day businesspeople enter into contracts of one form or another. Some of these may be written contracts. At other times, the contract is oral, arising from the spoken agreement of the parties. Still on other occasions the actions of the parties, if they imply an agreement, can result in a contract. What, then, is a contract?

A **contract** is a promise or set of promises in which two or more parties (or firms) agree to act or not act in a certain way. Over the years courts have determined that a valid and enforceable contract should contain the following elements:

1. *Offer and acceptance.* An agreement includes an offer by one party and acceptance by another party.

2. *Legal capacity of the parties.* The agreement must be made by parties who are considered legally able to make contracts. That means that they must be of legal age and legally sane.

3. *Voluntary agreement.* The contract must be made in a voluntary manner by all parties.

4. *Legality of purpose.* The purpose of the agreement must be legal. A contract to fix prices would be invalid because it was made for an illegal purpose.

5. *Exchange of value.* The parties to a contract must exchange something of value (money, property, a promise of work, or the like.) This exchange of value is referred to as the consideration that binds an agreement.

6. *Proper legal form.* The contract must be prepared in the legal form required by law. For example, contracts involving real estate must be in writing.

The law involving contracts is complex. Businesspeople, especially managers, face the decision of how detailed to make a contract, the length of time a contract should stay in force, and the actions to be taken if a contract is broken. Because of the complex nature of the law of contracts, businesspeople usually consult lawyers before making decisions such as these.

The Sale of Property. Each day business is involved in countless numbers of transactions involving the sale or transfer of property. One type of property is **real property,** which consists of land or things with a long-term attachment to land such as buildings or uncut timber. **Personal property,** on the other hand, includes movable things such as automobiles, machinery, and furniture. Property ownership is valued and protected in the United States. An important aspect of protecting property ownership is defining the terms and procedures by which control passes from one owner to another. Real property may be transferred by deed or lease. A **deed** actually transfers ownership to a new owner. A **lease** gives temporary, partial control of real property. Extensive and complex legal guidelines and traditions surround the writing and interpretation of these agreements.

Ownership of personal property is transferred by sale. Even a simple sales transaction requires considerable legal definition and regulation.

Transportation and Storage of Property. When an owner gives up goods to others for safekeeping, a **bailment** is created. The owner of the goods is the **bailor**, and the one who takes possession of the goods is the **bailee.** Common carriers that transport goods for others illustrate the relationship between a bailor and bailee. A **common carrier** is a public transporter of goods such as a truck line, railroad, airline, or bus company. The common carrier, as a bailee, owes a standard of care to the bailor in keeping the transported possessions safe. A similar bailment is created when a firm stores its property in a public warehouse. The warehouse, as a bailee, owes a duty to the firm as bailor to keep the stored property safe.

Agency and Employment Law. Nearly all business transactions are carried out through agents or by employees. An **agent** is a person or company authorized by a company to carry out business and enter into agreements with other parties on behalf of the authorizing person or company. The authorizing person or company is called the **principal.** This relationship exists when employees of a company—executives, purchasing agents, sales representatives, and others—act on behalf of a company. An agent may also be an outside third party especially skilled in handling certain kinds of business. Lawyers often act as agents, particularly in negotiating contracts for others. The principal is also responsible for the contracts made by an agent with third parties in behalf of the principal.

Closely related to the law of agency is the law of employment. This now includes a whole collection of laws, regulations, and court decisions. These laws and regulations govern matters such as minimum wages and maximum hours, overtime pay, child labor, equal employment opportunity, and health and safety in the workplace.

Trademarks, Copyrights, and Patents. The reputation of a company and the good name of its products and services are among a firm's most valuable possessions. So, too, are the creative ideas and inventions developed by its personnel. The law gives special protection to these possessions through trademarks, patents, and copyrights. A **trademark** is a symbol, word, name, device, or any combination of these adopted and used by a business firm to identify its products from those sold by other firms. Names such as ANACIN, DieHard, and Rainbow are trademarks. A **trade name** is the name used to identify the firm, whether it is classified as single ownership, a partnership, or corporation. Honda Motor, Chrysler, Federal Express, and Nynex are trade names. The Patent and Trademark Office issues trademarks for 20 years. However, they may be renewed as long as they are used in commerce.

Copyrights protect published and unpublished original work for the author's lifetime plus 50 years. Copyrights are especially important to book publishing companies, motion picture studios, and record companies. A copyright can also be obtained for computer software, which are treated in the same way as literary works.

A **patent** is a grant issued by the U.S. Patent and Trademark Office. The patent gives the inventor or discoverer of a new and useful work, manufacturing technique, or useful improvement of these categories the exclusive right to them for a period of 17 years. Approximately 77,000 patents were issued in 1986.

Holders of trademarks and patents may sue individuals or firms that infringe on them. The owner of a trademark may sue to protect a monetary interest in a product or to keep customers from being misled by a copycat trademark. (See, for example, the case study at the end of Chapter 13, where this became an issue for perfume manufacturers.) Patents actually create a limited and exclusive right to make and sell a product. Other patents are sold or a license is given to produce a patent item.

The Uniform Commercial Code (UCC)

The National Conference of Commissioners on Uniform State Laws and the American Law Institute sponsored the Uniform Commercial Code (UCC) in 1952. By 1968 every state except Louisiana had adopted the UCC in its entirety. Louisiana has adopted some but not all parts of the UCC. The **Uniform Commercial Code** is a model law or guide for the states to follow in passing their own business laws. Many states have enacted parts of the UCC into law. Many businesses today are involved in transactions that cut across the state lines. Think of the confusion and complexity that would result if each state had a totally different way of handling and processing business transactions. One of the great advantages of the UCC is that it helps avoid this confusion by making state business laws more nearly uniform (hence, its title, the Uniform Commercial Code.)

The UCC is not the last word in business law, however. If you owned or managed a business, your firm would be subject

The Gray Side of Technology

Computer software has become the key to making many important business decisions today. These computer programs have provided an easy and efficient means of writing, filing, calculating, and representing information to organizations large and small. The industry that creates and sells the software has grown to a billion dollar market with millions of Americans employed. Computers, the machines that run on the software, have become the focus of a new generation of high-tech employees. The computer and its software have produced what some describe as the computer revolution.

Unfortunately this phenomenon has produced a new class of criminals, new corporate policies toward computer use, and a new debate about ethics. New terms have evolved as well. A "hacker" infiltrates computer systems to tamper with payroll systems, student grades, or other confidential data. "Electronic theft" is a term used when employees "steal" computer time to conduct personal business or manipulate numbers for fraudulent purposes. A "software pirate" illegally copies copyrighted software.

Computer crime is normally classified into five general areas:

1. Financial crime is the taking of funds by an employee, often through the diversion of funds from the firm to the employee.

2. Theft of property is the actual theft of computers or software from the organization.

3. Information crime has the employee stealing important data and using it for personal gain. Mailing lists owned by the business are often the prime target of this crime.

4. Vandalism is the physical damage to computers and related equipment such as printers or the alteration or destruction of data in order to deliberately hurt the organization.

5. Theft of service or computer time happens when the employee uses the company computer for personal use during working hours.

The concept of computer crime would seem to be well-defined. Many states have proposed or passed legislation making many computer practices illegal. The truth is that the issue of computer crime is not clear-cut. A telling statistic was uncovered by the Data Processing Management Association in a recent study of the nation's 1000 largest businesses. They found that only 2 percent of computer crime or computer abuse was ever reported to legal authorities. Further, they found that 98 percent of crimes and abuses were conducted from within the firm by its employees. They found that computer crimes often go unreported within organizations. They concluded that many crimes go unreported because there is no clear definition of crime versus ethical behavior.

Nowhere is this distinction argued more heatedly than in the area of software piracy. Although unauthorized copy-

(continued)

Technology Feature *(continued)*

ing of software is an infringement of copyright laws, it has been estimated that for every software package sold one is copied illegally. This problem amounts to more than a billion dollars in lost sales by the computer industry.

The computer ethics–computer crime issue is far from resolved. Questions such as "can intangible property be stolen?" and "what does the ethics issue do to

employer-employee relations?" must still be answered.

Sources: Manuel Schriffres, "The Struggle to Thwart Software Pirates," *U.S. News and World Report,* March 25, 1985; J. J. Buck Bloombecker, "New Federal Law Bolsters Computer Security Efforts," *Computerworld,* October 27, 1986; Jay Bloombecker, "Lobbying for Protection," *Computerworld,* August 4, 1986; Jay Bloombecker, "Can Software Makers Win the War Against Piracy?", *Business Week,* April 30, 1984; Elizabeth Ranney, "As the Computer Industry Grows, So Do Related Crimes, Study Says," *Infoworld,* March 10, 1986; Nancy Finn and Peter Finn, "Don't Rely on the Law to Stop Computer Crime," *Computerworld,* December 17, 1984.

to numerous other federal, state, and local laws and regulations. That would make it necessary for you to check, sometimes frequently, that your business dealings were proper and legal.

GOVERNMENT ROLES

Government and business are closely tied in many ways. Our federal Constitution sets up the basic structure of central government and its relationship with state governments. The Constitution provides lawful and peaceful means for bringing about social change. Its effect on business (commerce) is felt in many ways; two important ways, (1) the regulation of the economy and (2) economic planning, have been discussed in Chapters 3, 4 and 5. In other interactions with business, government may be described as a promotor of business, buyer and seller of goods and services, and guarantor of business.

Promotor of Business

The government offers business a wide variety of tax breaks and other aids to promote business. The government has paid subsidies to many industry groups including agriculture, airlines, and the housing industry. A subsidy is a government grant, usually of money, to a private person or company. Closely related to subsidies are the tax breaks given to individuals and business firms to stimulate spending for certain goods and services. Toyota was granted $125 million in government aid to build a new auto assembly plant in Kentucky. Illinois offered more than $150 million to Mitsubishi in assistance to build a plant in Illinois—a cost of $50,000 for each of the 2900 jobs that have been created.

▼ You operate a small motel in a ski area. One day you learn that the government is helping a developer to build a large hotel just down the road from you. The local community is very excited about the proposed new business because it will bring more jobs to the community. What is your reaction?

Buyer and Seller of Goods and Services

A large part of the nation's output of goods and services is produced for the government. This also means that a large share of the nation's income is claimed by the government in order to pay for it. (See Information Brief 7-5.) In numerical terms the federal government takes in about 19 percent of its revenues from taxes and accounts for about 24 percent of all spending in our economy. About two-thirds of total government spending is for the outright purchase of good and services. Many industries depend on government purchases for their very existence. For example, 29 companies are poised to bid on the $8 billion to build the NASA space station by 1994.

Business Owner

The government is also a major business owner. Although it directly controls relatively few of the factors of production in our economic system, government is a major player in many sectors of our economy. The federal and local governments generate nearly 20 percent of the electric power used by consumers and business. Government is also in the railroad business (Amtrak), health business, insurance business, and postal business. The business activities of the government have a great influence on our economy.

Guarantor of Business

The Lockheed Corporation, a major defense contractor, faced economic ruin in the late 1960s and early 1970s. They had tried to focus their business on the private sector by introducing a new plane. The engine was to have been built by Rolls-Royce, a British firm. Technological problems at Rolls-Royce meant delays in filling orders at Lockheed. In 1970 the company had a net loss after taxes of $86.3 million. Since the risk for banks was too great to support the failing firm, it turned to the federal

---

Information Brief 7-5

Space Station Profits

At least 29 firms are ready to bid on the proposed $8 billion space station that would be launched and manned by 1994.

The most expensive segment, the structural framework, is estimated to cost $3.7 billion. Two pressurized modules where the crew will live and work will cost $2.5 billion. The station's power generation, management, and distributon will cost $1 billion to build.

The elements of the space station will result in a major bidding war between companies such as Boeing, McDonnell Douglas, GE, and TRW.

Source: High Technology, August 1987, p. 11.

government. After much debate by Congress, the loans Lockheed needed were guaranteed by the government. Chrysler faced a similar financing situation. In 1979 it suffered a loss of $800 million. Again, Congress was asked for help in saving the firm and the 360,000 jobs at stake. Chrysler was granted $1.5 billion in loan guarantees.

The situation at both firms had a happy ending. Today they are productive and profitable. The debate continues, however, regarding the wisdom of government intervention in the financial affairs of private industry.

GOVERNMENT REGULATION

Regulation encompasses both social and economic aspects of the business environment. Government regulation in the United States is as old as the Constitution, which gave Congress the right to regulate interstate commerce. The first regulatory agency, the Interstate Commerce Commission (ICC), was established in 1887.

REGULATIONS PROMOTING BUSINESS COMPETITION

The term **antitrust** has evolved to mean virtually any anticompetitive business practice which abuses economic power. Antitrust legislation was passed because many economic abuses were committed by large corporations and combinations of firms in the mid-nineteenth century.

Three major laws govern antitrust regulation. The Sherman Act of 1890 forbids contracts, combinations, or conspiracies "in restraint of trade or commerce." A more modern term for combination is a merger. A **merger** occurs when one company buys another firm to form one larger, combined company. The act is applicable only to interstate or foreign commerce. **Intrastate activities,** commerce within a state, are left to state and local governments to regulate. The Sherman Act makes it possible for a guilty firm or individual to be liable for civil and criminal penalties. The criminal penalties for individual violators are up to three years in prison, with fines up to $100,000, or both. If a corporation is criminally convicted, it can be fined up to $1 million.

The Clayton Act of 1914 was passed to attack unfair economic practices not covered in the Sherman Act. For example, the law and later refinements to the law made it illegal to:

1. Charge one buyer more than another for the same product unless the cost of making the product was different or the product was to be sold in varying quantities.

2. Cut prices in one location (in the case of a chain operation) to force small stores out of business in that area.

The Federal Trade Commission Act of 1914 created the Federal Trade Commission (FTC). The act allowed the federal government to attack practices which diminished competition. The FTC Act is best known for its prohibition of false or misleading advertising and untrue claims about the quality or performance of a product or service.

Antitrust laws tend to be enforced more or less depending on the attitudes of society and the presidential administration. In the 1980s the enforcement of the laws was eased and the number of large mergers increased.

ADMINISTRATIVE LAW AND REGULATION

The part of our legal system dealing with the control and regulation of businesses and individuals is known as **administrative law.** Administrative law is recognized as existing outside the regular judicial system. This form of law is enforced through government administrative agencies created to oversee administrative laws. Administrative agencies make rules regulating commerce and have judicial powers to hear cases under their jurisdiction. Most federal administrative agencies have been created by Congress, which can undo their creation at any time. This action is rarely taken, however.

Figure 7-3 outlines the general procedure for enforcing an administrative regulation. A complaint may be brought by the agency, a business firm, or an individual. The agency, through its appointed commissioners, rules on the infraction. The firm accused of violating the regulation may appeal to an agency's administrative law judge. If the decision goes against the firm, it may appeal the action through the regular judicial system.

Broadly speaking, administrative agencies provide two types of regulation: (1) industry regulation and (2) social regulation.

Industry Regulation

Industry regulation began with the creation of the ICC. The ICC is an example of a traditional economic regulatory agency with responsibility over a specific industry—interstate trans-

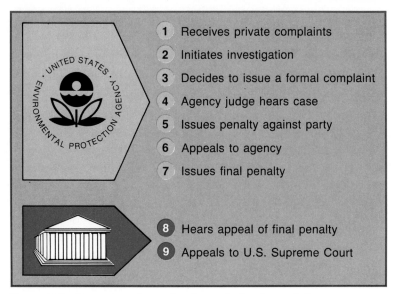

1 Receives private complaints

2 Initiates investigation

3 Decides to issue a formal complaint

4 Agency judge hears case

5 Issues penalty against party

6 Appeals to agency

7 Issues final penalty

8 Hears appeal of final penalty

9 Appeals to U.S. Supreme Court

Figure 7-3. Procedure for enforcing a federal regulation.

portation. Other industry-specific agencies are the (1) Federal Communications Commission (FCC, 1934) and (2) Civil Aeronautics Board (CAB, 1930). These agencies do not exhaust the entire field of industry regulation. They are merely intended to provide examples of agencies that are industry-specific in nature. They have also been chosen to show the extent that industrywide agencies have moved toward deregulation.

Interstate Commerce Commission (ICC). The ICC has changed its regulations dramatically. Beginning in 1980 new trucking firms were able to enter the field as long as they could prove they were fit, willing, and able. Prior to this time, new firms had to prove they offered the public service it did not already have. Collective rate making was also eliminated. Rates could now be competitive. Deregulation has also made it possible for railroads to abandon unprofitable routes.

Federal Communications Commission (FCC). The FCC was given the authority to regulate the complex broadcasting and telecommunications industries. Included in its jurisdiction are telephone companies, telegraph carriers, private microwave carriers, and satellite carriers. The forced breakup of the Bell Telephone System in 1984 has been the most significant deregulatory activity undertaken by the FCC.

Civil Aeronautics Board (CAB). The CAB was established to regulate the airline industry. Probably the most dramatic of the deregulation activities of the 1980s was the elimination of the CAB as an administrative agency. While safety regulation is still the responsibility of the federal government, many of the former regulations have been abandoned. The allocation of airline routes and the price charged for tickets is now the responsibility of the air carriers, not the federal government.

Social Regulation

A new wave of regulation swept the business community in the 1960s and 1970s. New agencies were created that reflected the change in social values and concerns of society. In contrast to industry regulation, social regulation extends across the great bulk of the private sector. Industry regulation set up agencies which had jurisdication over the transportation industry or the communication industry. Social regulatory agencies have jurisdiction over the health and safety of employees or protection of the environment regardless of industry.

We will examine several of these social agencies: (1) Occupational Safety and Health Administration (OSHA, 1970), (2) Environmental Protection Agency (EPA, 1970), and (3) Equal Employment Opportunity Commission (EEOC, 1964). Again, these three agencies are representative of the agencies whose duties are to carry out social regulation.

Occupational Safety and Health Administration (OSHA). The workplace exposes workers to many kinds of safety and health hazards. There are an estimated 100,000 work-related deaths each year. OSHA is an agency that works to "assure so far as possible that every working man and woman in the nation has safe and healthful working conditions and to preserve our human resources." OSHA took over the function of setting work safety standards and inspection of workplaces from state governments, which formerly carried out this activity. The agency has the power to levy fines for offenders. In 1987, for example, OSHA proposed a record $2.59 million fine against IBP Inc., the nation's largest meat-packing company, on charges that it failed to report more than 1000 job-related injuries and illnesses over a two-year period. The company responded by saying that they would contest the proposed fine by using the procedure outlined in Figure 7-3.

Environmental Protection Agency (EPA). Pollution laws began with the first major law, the 1955 Air Pollution Control Act. This was followed by the Clean Air Act of 1963, the Motor Vehicle Air Pollution Control Act of 1965, and the Air Quality Act of 1967. In the 1970s an air pollution crisis in New York City and oil well explosions off the California coast resulted in the Clean Air Act of 1970 and the Clean Water Act of 1972. The EPA was created to coordinate and enforce all these governmental efforts in the environmental area.

▼ The state legislature has just passed a law that requires your city to build a garbage incinerator rather than continue using a sanitary landfill. You have bought a new house and are paying as much as you can possibly afford. The new garbage treatment will require increases in your taxes. How would you feel about this?

Equal Employment Opportunity Commission (EEOC). The EEOC was created by the Civil Rights Act of 1964. The EEOC is charged to promote equal opportunities for individuals to work. The agency performs a variety of functions. It issues regulations and guidelines based upon the agency's intrepretation of the Civil Rights Act of 1964. It has broad powers to investigate discrimination charges and to have them resolved voluntarily or through force of law.

The EEOC has seen its responsibilities broadened to include enforcement against age discrimination (between ages 40 and 69), handicapped discrimination, and Vietnam Era Veterans discrimination. The Equal Pay Act of 1963 also placed acts of wage discrimination because of worker's sex under the EEOC. In 1978 the Pregnancy Discrimination Act became part of EEOC enforcement. This act prohibited discrimination in hiring or retaining pregnant women. It also allowed women to be reinstated with retained retirement benefits after their return to work.

TAXATION

Most, but not all, businesses are subject to some form of industrial or social regulation. However, virtually all businesses are subject to the government's tax regulating powers. Except for nonprofit charitable and religious organizations, taxes are imposed on *all* business enterprises.

The most important source of revenue for the federal government is a tax on personal and corporate incomes. An **income tax** is a regular payment made to the government. The amount paid is based on how much an individual earns from employment and investments. **Corporate taxes** are also an income tax based on the profits remaining after all business costs have been paid.

State and local governments impose a variety of revenue generating taxes on businesses. Some have sales taxes. A **sales tax** is determined by the value of the products or services being bought. **Property taxes** are paid at regular intervals, their amount being based on the valuation of real or personal property. Property tax rates vary by state and locality.

Payroll taxes are deducted from regular payments for salaries and wages. The most important of these is the social security tax, shared by the employer and employee. The proceeds are used partly to maintain a retirement and disability fund for American workers. Excise taxes are an example of a regulatory or restrictive tax. **Excise taxes** are collected from manufacturers, or sometimes retailer sellers, on certain kinds of goods. One use of such taxes is to provide revenue for special purposes. Excise taxes on motor vehicles, for instance, help pay for highway construction. Excise taxes may also be imposed in an effort to discourage use of certain goods. This is part of the reason for excise taxes on tobacco products and alcoholic beverages.*

The law of taxation is very complex. For that reason many firms rely on specialized professionals in finance or accounting to help them deal with the ins and outs of the tax code. The law of taxation also changes from time to time. In 1986, for example, the U.S. Congress passed a sweeping overhaul of the federal tax laws which greatly affected individuals and businesses. Keeping abreast of changes in the tax code and its effects on business operations is an important responsibility of a business owner or manager, or those hired to carry out this task.

BUSINESS REGULATION: A PERSPECTIVE

Taxes and other forms of regulation have a profound influence on the environment of business. For example, taxes may in-

---

*Information about taxation derived, in part, from Lester R. Bittel, Ronald S. Burke, and Charles P. Bilbrey, *Business in Action*, Third Edition, McGraw-Hill Book Company, 1988.

Information Brief 7-7

Where Regulation Backfired

The sea otter, a furry creature, nearly became extinct in the eighteenth and nineteenth centuries. Since then they have multiplied along the California coast mainly because federal regulations have given them a protected species status.

These regulations, while successful, have now become an economic problem to the fishing industry. The otter consumes about 25 percent of its body weight (50 to 60 pounds) in clams, abalone, sea urchins, and other marine life. These fish form the livelihood of many fisheries along the coast and they are now endangered—an unforeseen and negative effect of regulations designed to protect the sea otter, once an endangered species itself.

Source: Robert Lindsey, "Appetites of Man and Sea Otter May Prove Fatal to Plan to Save Species," *The New York Times,* July 21, 1987.

crease the costs of doing business or they may be used to discourage foreign competition.

Regulation in other areas also has an impact on the way business is done. Mandatory testing of products, for instance, may slow the introduction of new products on the market. Complying with the raft of antipollution laws and regulations may prove costly, causing a firm to forego investment in other needed areas. Regulation may increase or decrease the cost of doing business with the same industry at the same time. The paperwork alone required to show compliance with regulations may prove very costly and burdensome.

Most experts agree that firms cannot ignore the impact of regulations, whether they like them or not. Regulations affect business operations in just too many ways. In a much larger sense, too, business is wedded to its social, legal, and regulatory environment. Firms which adapt well to factors in these environments, regulatory or otherwise, usually overcome adversity and succeed; those that do not may fail. According to most experts, the business owner and manager has a positive duty to ensure that a firm does not become a victim of the latter fate.

Select Terms to Know

administrative law	crimes	personal property
agent	deed	principal
bailee	ethics	real property
bailment	excise tax	strict liability
bailor	income tax	tort
business law	intentional torts	trademark
contract	lease	trade name
copyright	negligence	Uniform Commercial Code (UCC)
corporate tax	patent	

Review Questions

1. Why should social responsibility be included as a goal of the business firm?

2. What are the reasons given for not including social responsibility as a goal of the business firm?

3. What is the difference between a crime and a tort? Why is a breach of ethics not considered a crime or a tort?

4. Classify the three forms of torts which affect business.

5. What elements must be present in order for a contract to be complete?

6. What is the difference between real and personal property? What is the document that represents ownership or possession of real property? How is personal property transferred from one person to another?

7. How many years is each effective: trademark, copyright, and patent?

8. What is the main advantage of the Uniform Commercial Code?

9. Discuss the ways business and government are tied together in our economy.

10. List the three antitrust laws that monitor business competition. Briefly discuss the role of each.

11. Explain the difference between industry regulation and social regulation.

12. What is the difference between a sales tax and a property or restrictive tax?

Thought and Discussion Questions

1. What are some regulatory considerations the personnel manager of a firm must consider? The plant manager? The marketing manager?

2. Why is the subject of strict liability so controversial with the business community? Why is it so costly?

3. What types of business are commonly owned by local government? State government? Federal government?

4. Why does the enforcement and interpretation of antitrust laws differ from one presidential administration to another?

5. Do you think government should increase or lessen its regulation of business? Defend your answer.

Projects

1. A wide variety of economic and social situations are handled by many federal administrative agencies. For each of the real-life business situations below, name the agency responsible for the action and discuss the possible advantages and disadvantages of each action.
  a. Moved toward market pricing of telephone service by shifting costs from long-distance to local users.
  b. A policy statement in 1984 reduced the amount of evidence required for some advertising claims and put more burden on the consumer for determining the merits of an ad.
  c. Under the guidelines, all air pollution from all sources from a given industrial plant, or from different polluters over a countrywide area, will be regarded as being enclosed in a giant "bubble" and polluters will be allowed to balance their emissions against those of nearby plants.

  d. Employees could take an unpaid maternity leave of up to 18 weeks and would be given the same job or an equivalent one when returning to work.

2. Find a code of ethics set forth by a business firm, organization, or professional group. How do the items listed in the code differ from tort law?

3. Make a list of trademarks and trade names for a particular industry. Try to find those of as many competitors as possible. Do you think that the trademarks and trade names have a measurable value to the firms?

4. Prepare a list of government agencies other than those described in the chapter. Describe their responsibilities and whether they are state or federal agencies.

Case Study: PREFAX Tries to Improve Its Ethical Standards

PREFAX Corporation management has become aware of the public opinion about ethics and dishonesty in business and private life. Corporate management hired a polling firm to ask the public how they felt about employee honesty, ethical standards in business, and the social responsibility of business. They were surprised to find the public had very strong feelings on these subjects. It seems that their poll showed that the public felt that most employees took company property home for personal use. Business executives were perceived as only "average" in their ethical standards. The poll also revealed that most felt that business had a social responsibility toward the community.

As a result of the poll, PREFAX managers were called together to plan a strategy to improve the public perception of the firm. The strategy session resulted in the following plan:

- Hire a public relations firm to develop an advertising program to improve the image of the firm.

- Write a code of ethics that will be applied to business transactions with the public and other firms.

- Require all employees to attend a series of programs to stress a high standard of ethics.

Sources: Anne B. Fisher, "Spiffing Up the Corporate Image," *Fortune,* July 21, 1986; Suzanna McBee, "Morality," *U.S. News and World Report,* December 9, 1985; Alan Murray, "New Book Rates Consumer Firms on Social Issues," *The Wall Street Journal,* January 16, 1987.

1. Do you think the corporate strategy will enhance the image of the firm?

2. Do you think that the shareholders will benefit monetarily if the campaign succeeds? Can the plan be justified to the stockholders?

3. How do you think that the success or failure of the campaign can be measured?

4. How do you feel the employees will react to the plan? What techniques could be used to make the program succeed with employees?

CHAPTER 8

The Role of Management in Business

What Happens When Everybody Is the Boss?

Imagine owning the company you work for. Sound like a dream? Well, over 10 million workers at 7000 companies in the United States do exactly that! They work for companies that have set up programs that give workers direct ownership of their own company's stock. The workers have actually become the owners of their companies. In fact, experts predict that more than 25 percent of all U.S. workers will own part or all of their companies by the year 2000.

This type of program may sound appealing, but it also presents difficult problems for the workers. While they must be able to understand the viewpoint of management, they also must face the day-to-day reality of their work as an employee.

Learn how some employees have dealt with their new management role when you read the end-of-chapter case study, "Who's the Boss?". Study the chapter to learn more about the critical role of managers in business and to help you answer the questions in the end-of-chapter case study.

Sonia Cortez is the director of producton of a firm that manufactures and sells laptop computers. Today her calendar of activities looks like this:

9 a.m.   Evaluate this month's total of computers produced by her department. Begin drafting a plan to meet next month's production schedule.

10 a.m.   Interview an individual to fill an opening on her staff.

11 a.m.   Decide what outside company will be awarded a $200,000 contract to supply the firm with microchips. Sonia and her staff have reviewed pro-

	posals from five different companies over the last month.
12 noon	Lunch with the company president to obtain more information about the president's directive that the firm introduce a new and more-advanced laptop computer within two years.
1 p.m.	Delegate a top-priority project to Bill Cohen, Sonia's assistant, to complete by next Tuesday.
2 p.m.	Lead a staff meeting to identify the sources of some current production-line problems.
3 p.m.	Draft a memo to her staff informing them about the company's new employee profit sharing plan.
4 p.m.	Begin developing a step-by-step organization plan to obtain the resources and staff needed to produce the new laptop computer.
7 p.m.	Attend a meeting at a local college with the company president to announce the establishment of a company-sponsored scholarship program in computer science.

At other firms managers may perform different activities than Sonia does. Nevertheless, Sonia's activities generally typify what managers do. To workers, they are generally considered the "bosses," the ones who supervise the work.

In this chapter you will learn more about the roles and functions of managers like Sonia. You will also learn how managers make decisions that affect their businesses.

THE LURE OF MANAGEMENT

What is management? In reality everyone is a manager. Look at it this way. You are in charge of managing your activities, time, and money. You have short-term goals and it is hoped some long-term goals. Most of your activities and goals require you to work with or rely on others, just as they rely on you. The manager in business generally is involved in the same type of activities. A formal definition of **management** is the process of achieving organizational goals by working with people and other resources.

Today management is one of the most popular career fields in business. One proof of this can be seen at private business schools, colleges, and universities where management courses are usually filled with large numbers of students. In industry, too, management training courses tend to be quite popular.

Why do people like Sonia Cortez want to become managers? If you talk to managers you find that the answers will vary. Some people like the idea of being at the center of important decisions for their firms. Sonia Cortez, for example, is working on a plan to produce the next new laptop computer for her company. Other people like the power and prestige that come from being the boss, the "take charge" person in an organization. There are often financial rewards and fringe benefits that come with being a manager. Although they may work long and hard hours, managers are often among the better paid people within their firms.

▼ You have been working at a fast-food restaurant for the past year. Your boss asks whether you would be willing to supervise the entire staff during the busy lunch hour. How would you feel about such an offer?

ROLES PLAYED BY MANAGERS

One way to study what management is all about is to look at the roles managers play in business. Actually, managers have many roles in an organization. They are leaders, disciplinarians, coaches, spokespersons, and negotiators. Overall, the roles played by a manager can be divided into three categories: interpersonal, informational, and decision making roles.

Interpersonal Roles

Every manager must become involved with people. People skills are often referred to as human relations skills. Managers find themselves in a wide variety of interpersonal roles.

1. As a host, the manager may be required to entertain clients or to speak to groups of visitors. In such cases, the manager represents the company to the outside world.

2. Managers must work with employees to improve their performance and to encourage their growth. Managers often are called on to resolve employee conflicts. Managers are not always directly involved with every problem or conflict, but a manager's influence often has a widespread effect. For

example, a particular method of motivating or rewarding employees may be carried out by a supervisor using a technique or policy established by a higher-level manager.

3. Many managers also act as the link between the people inside the business and the community. Managers may represent the business at United Way and Chamber of Commerce meetings or they may serve on the board of directors of the local YWCA or boy's club.

Informational Roles

Managers must pay attention to the events and forces that affect their businesses. It is also important that they share this information. Managers are the information centers for their organizations. No organization can afford to act in a vacuum.

1. Managers must keep abreast of news and information that could affect their organization. They attend many meetings inside and outside of the firm. Naturally some of what is heard amounts to gossip rather than important information. The manager's job is to screen and use what is most useful.

2. Once a manager finds some useful information, it must be distributed to others in the business. Some information is secret and can only be shared with certain people. Other information could benefit everyone in the business. Man-

Figure 8-1. To carry out their information roles, managers typically attend meetings with persons both inside and outside their organization.

agers must determine the appropriate method of distributing the information. For example, will it be by a memo, a telephone call, electronic mail, or a newsletter?

3. Managers are often called upon to provide information about the business to the public. Managers of B. F. Goodrich announced that they were pulling out of the tire business. William Hewlett and David Packard, of the Hewlett-Packard company, announced that they would locate part of their operation in Boise, Idaho. Of course, managers don't usually provide such newsworthy information. On a day-to-day basis, investors, suppliers, and customers must be kept informed of business activities. Figure 8-2 shows some of the "publics" to whom the manager provides information.

Decision Making Roles

Managers are most importantly decision makers. Information alone is not useful. Managers use information to make decisions. Decisions can sometimes be dramatic—for example, Lee

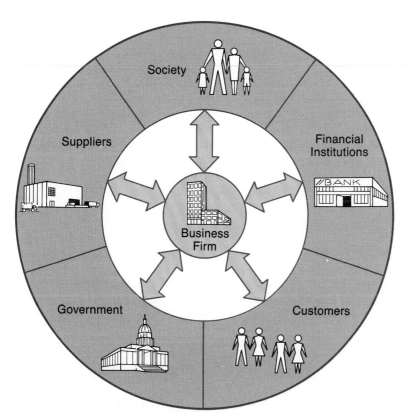

Figure 8-2. Business information publics. Business firms and their managers usually provide information to many parties, such as suppliers, governments, customers, financial institutions, and society in general. A good manager also makes it a point to receive information from these and other "publics" that might affect his or her firm.

Information Brief 8-1

"Managers Aren't Paid to Be Right"

In April, 1985, Coca-Cola Co. introduced a "new Coke." They said they would no longer sell traditional Coke.

In taste tests new Coke beat both Pepsi and traditional Coke. But there was a problem. American consumers were outraged that Coke was being changed. They didn't buy the new Coke.

Roberto Crispulo Goizueta, Coca-Cola's President and Chief Operating Officer, had to make a difficult decision. He brought back traditional Coke as "Coca-Cola Classic" in July, three months after introducing new Coke. Explaining his decision, he said that managers aren't paid to be right; they are paid to produce results.

Source: Nancy Giges, "Adman of the Year: Coca Cola's Roberto Goizueta Engineers Startling Comeback," *Advertising Age,* December 29, 1986, pp. 1, 26–27.

Iacocca's decision to have Chrysler spend $1.4 billion to buy American Motors. Usually, a manager's decisions are more routine. Adding a 15-minute morning break for employees does not have much news value, but it is important to the workers.

A manager must accept the responsibility to make a decision when handling crises such as equipment failures, scheduling delays, and labor strikes. A decision regarding disagreements among workers and arguments between workers and their supervisors requires patience and wisdom on the part of a manager.

On a daily basis managers are responsible for deciding who is assigned to do what and when. Managers organize and schedule the flow of work for a business.

As you can see, managers are involved in a combination of roles. Each manager must determine how much emphasis to place on each specific type of role.

▼ How would you feel if you were called on to represent your company's views on national television?

LEVELS OF MANAGEMENT

In every organization there are levels of management. Most organizations have three primary levels of managers: top-level

TABLE 8-1 A Manager's Many Roles

Interpersonal roles:
  Hosts clients
  Leads and coaches employees
  Acts as contact to other businesses
  Provides link to individuals in the community

Informational roles:
  Keeps abreast of professional and business news
  Informs employees about changes in company policy
  Provides reports to upper management
  Describes company's position on public issues

Decision making roles:
  Responsible for budgets and schedules
  Handles employees grievances
  Hires, promotes, and discharges employees
  Deals with crises

managers (sometimes referred to as executive managers), middle managers, and first-line or supervisory managers. The chief operating officer of AT&T heads a firm with more than 300,000 employees. The marketing director at Tandy Corporation, a middle-management position, is responsible for a sales force of 1500. A supervisor at General Motor's Saturn plant will supervise 90 workers per shift.

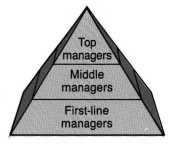

Figure 8-3. The three primary levels of management.

Top-Level Managers

Top-level managers occupy the highest positions in the organization. They have to take a long-range view and have broad responsibility for the operation of the business. The top-level managers are mainly responsible for setting and meeting the goals and objectives of the organization. They often are able to do this by creating an atmosphere that allows the managers reporting to them to achieve their greatest results. For example, James Garfield, the chief executive officer (CEO) of Sonia Cortez's company, likes to delegate a great deal of authority to the heads of the corporate branches such as Sonia. He also likes to be surrounded by the best and smartest managers—he finds it stimulating. Some other top-management titles are chief operation officer (COO) and president.

Middle-Level Managers

Middle-level managers are responsible for carrying out the assignments and directives of top-level management. They also serve as the go-between for lower levels of management. They must take both a long- and short-range view of the organizational goals. Mainly they act as interpreters who are able to see the broad plans of the firm and can turn them into operating policies and programs that can be implemented by supervisors and employees. These duties include finding and allocating the funds needed to carry out plans. They also keep track, through reports, of the general progress of long-range plans. Because they are between the top-level and first-line managers, they have special pressures put upon them. Sonia Cortez, as the director of production in her company, is a middle-level manager.

Some firms have made it a policy to share financial data and goals with middle managers. One such small firm found that employees are much more enthusiastic about their work when they can see the results of their efforts. Each month, the owner of the firm holds a meeting with all the managers to show them how much money is needed in the next month for the company to grow. Middle managers know both the good news and bad news and can direct the employees accordingly. They also know how employees fit into the scheme of things.

Middle-level managers have to be flexible, skilled in working with others, and adaptable to changing work conditions. They must also be creative. A store manager in Michigan put a battery under a box and put a light on it in 1962 and K-Mart's "blue-light special" was born.

Some titles for typical middle-level management positions include plant manager, accounting department head, and personnel director. There are often many different levels of middle managers in a company. For example, at one time in the 1970s, the Dana Corporation had 14 different levels of middle managers. Now there are only four. This reduction reflects a trend recently in American companies to reduce the number of middle-management levels.

First-Line Managers

First-line managers have the responsibility to carry out the directives of their managers. Progressive firms such as Maytag and Ford Motor Company rely heavily on first-line managers and their workers for new ideas. Maytag estimates that 20 percent of the productivity gains has come from worker ideas. First-line managers are hired to see that the immediate goals and objectives of the organization are carried out by the other employees under their supervision. For this reason first-line managers are also referred to as supervisory managers or supervisors. Another important function of the supervisor is the careful monitoring of the use of resources. This means a careful watch on inventories and supplies as well as their efficient use. They usually are concerned with short-term operations. The supervisor must be able to communicate well with employees and middle management. Typical titles for first-line managers include supervisor, project manager, and team leader. Four production supervisors report to Sonia Cortez. Each is responsible for a "production team" of about 10 employees working on a specific part of the production process.

Common Features of All Levels

All managers, regardless of level, can be expected to:

1. *Put in long hours.* Working 50 or more hours in a week is

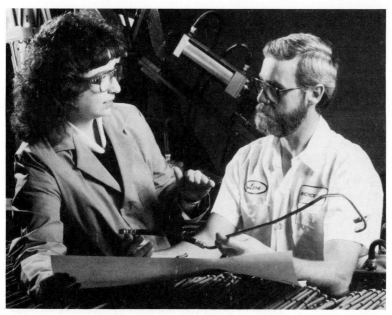

Figure 8-4. Front-line supervisors manage at the first-level of an organization, where hands-on production or service work is carried out. They usually have a great deal of involvement in directing the workforce toward achieving the organization's immediate goals.

typical. Some top-level executives work 80 to 90 hours per week, seven days a week, and go many years without vacation. Typically, the higher up the managerial pyramid, the more work and longer hours a manager is expected to put in. Long hours are especially common for the owner-manager of a small business.

2. *Vary their activities.* All managers are faced with constant interruptions of their work. They often have many different tasks to perform at the same time. As the number of tasks increases, the amount of time they can spend on any one task decreases the higher an individual climbs the managerial pyramid. Managers have to learn to manage their time. They must do what is most important and filter out less-important requests on their time (see Information Brief 8-2.)

3. *Perform under pressure.* The typical workday of a manager involves solving many different small problems and crises crammed into a short time. For example, a first-line manager might organize the work schedule, solve a production problem, provide feedback to an employee, and train employees

Information Brief 8-2

Time Management for CEOs

Chief executive officers (CEOs) of large corporations must learn how to manage their time. There are simply not enough hours in a day to meet all the demands placed on them.

Secretaries and staff assistants are important to CEOs. They help executives plan ahead and can screen people who want to meet with the CEO.

Formal agendas, written notes, and well-planned meetings with employees are tools for time management. A CEO can't afford to waste any precious time. They often have to work on planes, in hotel rooms, and even in cars just to keep up with the work load.

Source: Ford S. Worthy, "How CEOs Manage Their Time," *Fortune,* January 18, 1988, pp. 88–97.

in a new process all in the same day. There are still meetings to attend, letters to write, and professional reading to do.

4. *Communicate.* Managers use many different channels to communicate. They use the telephone, electronic mail, in-person conversation, individual and group meetings, tele-conferences, written reports, and memos to distribute and receive information.

5. *Have human relation skills.* Interacting with others takes up the majority of an average manager's time. Most of this time is spent meeting and working with subordinates, the manager's immediate superiors, or peers. People who don't like to work with others may not be effective managers over the long run.

▼ How would you feel if you were a first-line manager and you were asked to do something that you know could be done in a better way? Do you think the number of layers of management would make a difference to you?

FUNCTIONS OF MANAGEMENT

What a manager does is also called a management function. There are four basic management functions: planning, organizing (including staffing), directing (including leading), and controlling.

Planning

Management begins with planning. An organization must have objectives and plans for meeting those objectives before anything else can occur. Since the purpose of management is to achieve organizational objectives, the most important function of management is planning. In the case of Sonia Cortez, she was asked to develop a new laptop computer. To achieve this goal, she had to develop a plan. There are two types of plans: (1) long-term, or strategic, plans and (2) short-term, or tactical, plans.

  Long-Term Planning. The purpose of long-term, or **strategic, planning** is to (1) determine the major objectives of an organization, (2) adopt courses of action to achieve these objectives, and (3) ensure there are adequate resources available to achieve them. Strategic plans have a major impact on the organization because they develop the business's basic objectives. All the resources of the business are focused on these objectives to achieve success.

Sears Roebuck and Company's decision to become a broad-based financial organization as well as the top general retailer in the nation was the main objective of their long-term plan. This meant that a customer could purchase insurance, shares of stock, a computer, and clothing all under one roof. Strategic planning is the primary responsibility of top-level managers.

Short-Term Planning. The purpose of short-term, or **tactical planning** is to develop those objectives which must be met to meet long-term strategic plans. Every strategic plan needs shorter-term goals that are accomplished in the process of accomplishing the desired long-term objectives. Tactical plans are developed by middle-level managers and usually carried out by first-line managers. Adjusting prices to respond to an excess supply of goods would represent a tactical plan.

Changes occur every day in the availability of resources, amounts of money available, customer demands, and technology. Managers of every level must respond to these changes and revise the plans of their organization.

Organizing

Organizing involves obtaining and coordinating resources so that a business's objectives can be accomplished. Managers deal

---

TABLE 8-2 Examples of Planning

Long-term (strategic) planning:
  Expanding business by selling a new product
  Acquiring a related business
  Entering a new business
  Entering a new market
  Using a new manufacturing process

Short-term (tactical) planning:
  Setting quarterly and annual budgets
  Discounting the price of unsold goods to meet sales quotas
  Establishing policy of working overtime if there is a backlog
    in production
  Cutting expenses to avoid going over budget

with every type of resource: natural, capital, and human. This means that the organizing function includes recruiting and training people to fill positions in the organization. (You'll learn more about this aspect of management in Chapters 16 and 17.)

A manager typically breaks down an organization's plans into specific tasks to be performed. Then the manager evaluates what resources are necessary to perform the tasks. If the resources are available within the company, the manager will make sure that they are allocated to the task when they are needed. If the resources are not available, the manager must locate and obtain the necessary resources before they are needed by the organization. Imagine what would happen to an auto manufacturer, for example, if tires were not available for cars as they were being assembled. Production would soon come to a screeching halt.

At the beginning of the chapter we saw Sonia Cortez drawing up an organization plan to obtain the resources necessary to produce the new laptop computer her company plans to manufacture. Sonia will need additional staff (human resources), some raw materials for the computer's casing (natural resources), new equipment, a production line, and a budget (capital resources).

Organizing by Department

Resources are often assigned to specific units, or departments, in an organization. This process is referred to as **departmentalization.** These units are responsible for coordinating the use of their assigned resources. Departments in an organization can be organized by function, product, customer, geographic location, manufacturing process, or any other way that makes sense to top-level managers. Some of the ways of organizing resources by departments are discussed below.

Function. This method of organizing a department involves putting together all the similar tasks needed to perform a particular activity. Common functional departments include sales, production, finance, and research and development. Sonia Cortez managed the production department, a functional department, in her company.

Product. Using this method, all the operations related to similar products or services are put into one department. General Motors has a separate department or division for each brand of car that it manufactures. At Sonia Cortez's company, they could have a department for laptop computers and another for desktop computers.

Geographic Location. This method of departmentalization places all operations related to one geographic area into a separate department. Sonia Cortez's company, for example, has four domestic sales departments: eastern, midwestern, southern, and western.

Customer. In this method of organization, all operations related to one particular type of customer are placed in a separate department. A company that produces goods and services for consumers, wholesalers, and industrial firms may have a separate department for each.

Many businesses use a combination of these methods to accomplish their objectives efficiently. For example, a business could first organize by function to form a sales department. Then they could organize the sales department by customer, forming a consumer and an industrial department. They could then organize the industrial department by geographic location. It is not unusual for an organization to change its structure from time to time to carry out its strategic plan.

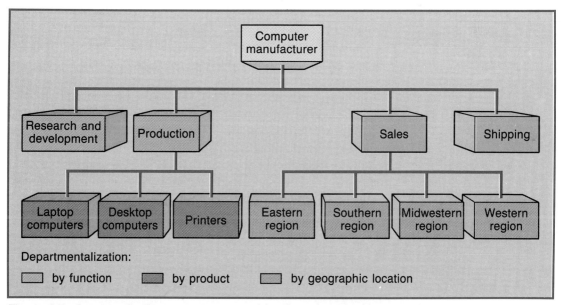

Figure 8-5. An organization may use a combination of methods to departmentalize. Here the departments of a computer manufacturer are organized by function, product, and geographic location.

Organizing by Responsibility

In an organization, responsibility is the obligation an employee has to do the task that is assigned to him or to her. In some systems of management, employees have some freedom to identify the tasks for which they will be responsible. In other companies, employees' tasks are very clearly specified by their manager.

Authority is the right to determine work assignments and to require other employees to perform those assignments. In an organization, authority is delegated to middle managers from the top levels of management. These managers, in turn, delegate their authority to lower-level managers who delegate it to the workers. This is called **line authority.** It can be traced in a line from the top of an organization to the bottom. An organization based on line authority is referred to as a **line organization.**

Many large businesses use a **line-and-staff organization,** which adds specialists to a line organization. The role of these specialists is advisory. While they give advice and assistance to the line operations, they do not have any formal power over them. Most organizations rely on staff employees for legal advice, employee training, and other services.

Figure 8-6 illustrates a small portion of a line-and-staff organization. The president has line authority over the national sales manager. The national sales manager has line authority over the regional sales managers. There are also field managers within each region who report to the regional sales managers. The marketing research specialist and the telemarketing specialist have an advisory relationship to the national and regional sales managers.

Authority may also be granted to a group of employees who have been appointed to a committee. Committee authority is usually too slow when immediate action is necessary. A committee process does have the advantage of getting personnel involved. Another form of committee is the project team. Employees are drawn from various departments to work together on a specific project. Each participant lends support in a special way, depending upon expertise. This structure has been used in the development of space shuttles and missions.

Directing

Directing is the process of influencing, guiding, and leading subordinates to carry out an organization's activities. Directing

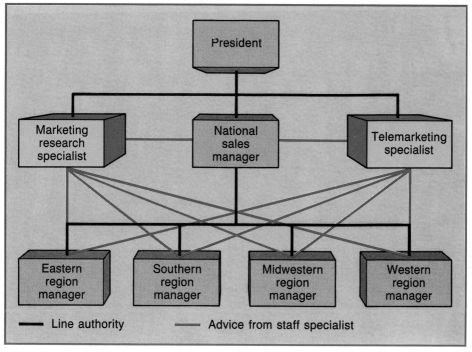

Figure 8-6. A portion of a typical line and staff organization.

is the most widely recognized function of management. It is particularly important at the first-line, or supervisory, level of management.

Managers often say that "people are our greatest asset." By this they mean that a company's human resources, its employees, are what truly distinguish the excellent performance of one company from the mediocre performance of another. A manager's approach to directing subordinates should focus on their value. It should not view workers simply in terms of their output, problems, and costs. A manager must recognize a subordinate's human potential. One aspect of directing is that a manager must build employee responsibility and achievement into a job. To fully realize their potential, workers need and want the demand, the discipline, and the incentive of responsibility. You'll learn about other aspects of directing a business's "greatest asset" in Chapter 17.

Controlling

The final and most overlooked managerial function is **controlling** or evaluating work performance. Controlling is tied to the planning function. Once objectives have been set, man-

Information Brief
8-3

Workstyle Management

Today, some compa-
nies have a unique ap-
proach to manage-
ment. It's called
workstyle management.
Workstyle starts with
the assumption that
employees will always
act in the best interest
of the company if they
have the information,
tools, and opportunity
to do so.
   Companies with a
workstyle approach to
management focus on
increasing communica-
tion, respect, and their
team spirit. They often
share the most-sensi-
tive information with
employees. They tend
to discourage hierarchy
and titles. (See the
Technology Feature on
the next page for a
specific example of this
approach to manage-
ment.)

Source: Gene Stone and Bo Bur-
lingham, "Workstyle," *Inc*, January
1986, pp. 45–54.

agement checks to see that plans are being carried out. If necessary, adjustments must be made to ensure organizational success. The controlling process can be carried out in a systematic way.

First, a manager must set goals or standards for performance. The best standards are those stated in specific measurable teams. Sonia Cortez, from the opening of the chapter, may have set a goal of producing 3000 computers a month.

A manager must monitor performance. How else is a manager to know if a goal is being accomplished? Sonia Cortez has asked her production-line managers to keep a count of how many computers are manufactured on an hourly basis. She is aware that short periods of time when the production line is slowed down or stopped can mean the difference between making her monthly goal and missing it. She meets with her production-line managers on a weekly basis so she can evaluate where the production department stands in relation to her goal.

Actual performance is compared to performance standards. Because performance is so carefully monitored, Sonia and her production crew quickly know if they are "on target."

A manager must determine why the actual results differ from the performance standards. When the standards aren't being met, Sonia must determine the reasons why. She can't correct the problem if she doesn't know what the problem is. Her production-line managers often help her determine the exact nature of the problem and make suggestions for fixing it.

Finally, a manager takes corrective action. If the standards are too high, perhaps they should be lowered. If the standards are reasonable and the cause of the problem is known, steps should be taken to correct the problem. If Sonia discovers that she does not have the workers necessary to produce 3000 computers a month she can (1) reduce her goals, (2) hire additional human resources, or (3) install new equipment that would make her existing work force more productive.

▼ Which management function (planning, organizing, directing, or controlling) would be the most difficult for you to do? Which would be the easiest for you to do?

DECISION MAKING SKILLS

Decisions are made at all managerial levels and within all managerial functions. Decision making is the most important

A Team Management Style

Technology is changing the workplace. Nowhere is this more apparent than in the assembly process of an automobile manufacturer. A computer-controlled hoist lifts the painted body of a car onto a working platform. An elevator, controlled by another computer, then lifts the platform to an upper floor of the factory. There the body passes through an assembly area while the assembly of the chassis begins on the ground floor. Finally, the computer retrieves the completed body from the top floor and joins it with the chassis.

Each day more than 800 cars are produced at the Honda of America plant of Marysville, Ohio. The plant employs approximately 2500 workers, but it makes extensive use of computer-controlled manufacturing and robots. In one process, a car body passes through 40 robot welders where the metal is fused in 2200 spots. This part of the assembly requires only four workers who keep track of the computers controlling the process.

The increased use of computers and robots has required some new management techniques. At the Volvo plant in Kalmar, Sweden, each phase of the auto assembly is accomplished through the use of work teams of about 20 people. They are supervised by managers who have been promoted from the shop floor. All major decisions at the plant must be approved by a joint committee representing both labor and management.

In the Honda of America plant of Marysville, Ohio, the "we" philosophy is more common than the "us versus them" attitude found in many automakers. Honda employees refer to themselves as "associates." Workers are trained in more than one job. There are no executive parking lots, offices, or dining rooms. Management and labor work together. The effect has been low absenteeism and high morale.

The Volvo and Honda examples are not purely American in their origins. A new plant soon will be, however. General Motor's new Saturn facility in Tennessee is designed to stress the newest technology and management techniques. Saturn's workers will be full partners with management. Union representatives will also sit in all planning and operating committees. There will be fewer layers of management. Work will be done in small work teams with plenty of variety for everyone. Ultimately, technology is causing a new management style that focuses more on the needs of the individual worker.

Sources: Marilyn Edid, "How Power Will be Balanced on Saturn's Shop Floor," *Business Week*, August 5, 1985, pp. 65–66; Aaron Bernstein and Wendy Zellner, "Detroit vs. the UAW: At Odds Over Teamwork," *Business Week*, August 24, 1987, pp. 54–55; John Merwin, "A Tale of Two Worlds," *Forbes*, June 16, 1986, pp. 101–106; Otis Port, "The Push for Quality," *Business Week*, June 8, 1987, pp. 130–135; Steve Lohr, "Making Cars the Volvo Way," *The New York Times*, June 23, 1987, pp. 1, 23.

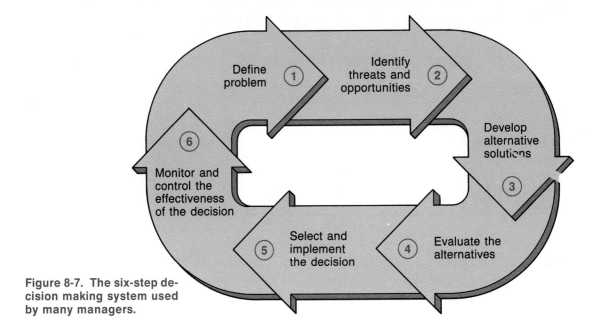

Figure 8-7. The six-step decision making system used by many managers.

task any manager has. Most managers make decisions in a systematic way similar to that shown in Figure 8-7.

The decision making process begins with defining the problem. For example, a chain of take-out chicken stores has no central communication system. No store manager knows what the other managers are doing. The problem here is a lack of some form of centralized communication system.

In the second step of the process, management looks at the problem within the industry and the economy. The threat of not having a centralized communication system is that other chains that already have them are more cost-efficient. The opportunity presented by a centralized communication system would be to take advantage of centralized purchasing and advertising. This would make the chain competitive with other chains.

There are various types of centralized communication systems. The chain's management will investigate each type of system that has some promise. The evaluation of alternatives includes the cost of the system compared to the savings that it could produce.

Finally, the best system is chosen and installed. But the process is not over. Once the system is up and running, management must determine if its assumptions are correct, if the system really does produce the savings they expected. (Remember, this is the management function of controlling.) If the system does not work as it is expected, the decision process begins again with a definition of the problem.

▼ Do you feel that you are a good decision maker based on the process outlined in Figure 8-7?

MANAGEMENT, TECHNOLOGY, AND CHANGE

Every 10 years, the total amount of existing technical knowledge doubles. Managers must be aware of the ways that technology will affect their companies and how they do their jobs. They cannot expect that things will not change. A manager has the responsibility of introducing change into the organization. Often, workers view change with suspicion. They fear that they will lose their jobs to a robot. Or, they worry that the company will depend on a computer to measure their worth.

While managers must be aware of the technical developments that could be economically useful for their companies, they cannot lose sight of the human problems associated with technology. Managers must deal with the problems that result from technology: unemployment, job changes, and employees whose skills have become outmoded, to name but a few.

▼ How would you feel if the skills you had relied on for 25 years to earn a living had become outmoded and you had to learn a completely new set of skills?

Select Terms to Know

authority	long-term planning	short-term planning
departmentalization	management	strategic planning
directing	management functions	tactical planning
first-line manager	middle-level manager	top-level manager
line-and-staff organization	organizing	
line authority	responsibility	

Review Questions

1. Explain how you are a manager in your daily life.

2. Briefly describe the three roles of management in business.

3. How do the duties of top-level, middle-level, and first-level managers differ?

4. What are the common features of management regardless of organizational level?

5. Provide an example of each of the four functions of management. Be sure to include a sentence or two of description of each.

6. What is the difference between strategic planning and tactical planning?

7. How would you describe the difference between a line organization and a line-and-staff organization?

8. Describe how controlling work performance affects the planning function.

9. Describe the decision making process in solving problems.

Thought and Discussion Questions

1. Do you agree with managers who say "people are a business's most important asset?" Explain your answer.

2. Think of yourself as the manager of your life. Describe a strategic plan for yourself. List several tactical plans you are using to achieve your strategic plan.

3. Use Figure 8-2 to develop answers to the following questions:

   a. Give an example of how a change in society's values may affect people's perception of a company and the sales of a product.
   b. Provide an example of how government information could have an impact on the business.
   c. How does a financial institution's perceptions regarding a business affect the business?
   d. What influences do suppliers and customers have on the way a firm does business?

4. Mr. King is the chief executive officer of the Daniels Company. Mr. Lopez, Mr. Jackson, and Mrs. Lin are vice presidents in charge of finance, marketing, and production reporting to Mr. King. There are three divisions producing goods in the firm, each with a general manager. There are three departments within each division. Each department is divided into areas with a supervisor for each.

   a. How many levels of management does the firm have?
   b. Sketch a chart of the firm and label each level as top management, middle management, or first-level management.
   c. From the description of the firm, would you think that it uses a line or a line-and-staff organization? Explain your answer.

5. What kinds of pressures do you suppose first-line managers might have? How do you think they differ from the pressures of upper-level managers?

Projects

1. Locate an annual report of a large company. Describe how the firm is organized through departments. In your report provide:

   a. The name of the firm.
   b. The activity of the firm.
   c. A description of the company's organization (whether it is by function, product, geographic location, or customer).
   d. Does it appear that the company uses more than one type of departmental organizaton? If so, which combination do they use?
   e. Why do you think the company chose this type of organization?

2. Interview the manager of a business. As part of the interview, find out what duties are performed during a typical day. In your report be sure to include:

a. The type of manager: top-level, middle-level, first-line.

b. Where does the person fit into the company management?

c. Is the firm a corporation, partnership, or sole proprietor firm?

d. Describe the general duties of the individual.

e. Provide an hour-by-hour description of what this person does.

f. After talking to the manager, what types of characteristics seem the most important?

g. Compare your results with the rest of the class.

3. As a class project, study the structure of your school district's management system. Begin with the school board level and end with the employee groups necessary to operate the school: teachers, maintenance personnel, office staff, etc. Divide the class into groups, each studying a separate aspect of the school. Some outcomes of the project may include:

a. The development of a hierarchy chart of the district.

b. Examples of the management function within the system—planning, organizing, directing, and controlling.

c. Examples of strategic and tactical planning.

Case Study: Who's the Boss?

There are advantages and disadvantages when workers become the owners of their companies (as described in the chapter opener).

You can see some of the advantages of worker ownership at W. L. Gore & Associates Inc., located near Newark, Delaware, a plant that manufactures electrical cables. There, the 3000 U.S. workers own 10 percent of the company. Workers at Gore are not even called "employees." They're called "associates" because the founder and chairperson, Wilbert L. Gore, dislikes the "boss-employee relationship." The company contributes 15 percent of each person's annual pay to the plan and reinvests the rest of its earnings in the business. This has allowed some workers with 15 years of service to have accumulated over $100,000 worth of stock.

The atmosphere at Gore is informal, family-like. Associates rely on their own initiative. Close supervision is rarely needed. As one associate said, "We manage ourselves here. If you waste time, you're only wasting your own money." Most importantly, the company is doing very well. It's growing at an excellent 25 percent annual rate.

Contrast the glowing picture at Gore with the situation at Dan River, Inc., a textile manufacturer in Danville, Virginia. Although the workers own 70 percent of the company, they don't feel that they have a voice in its management. The problem, they feel, is that control of the company still rests with Dan River's officers and directors. The employee's stock is managed by a bank which votes as it is directed by a management-controlled committee.

The result is that Dan River management has closed four plants since 1983, sold another, and laid off about 1000 hourly workers. Workers have input into decisions only through an old suggestion box system. The company does not disclose its earnings, sales, or stock valuations to employees.

In fact, many experts feel that employee-owned companies are likely to have problems. Hyatt Clark Industries, an employee-owned company in Clark, New Jersey, is typical. The majority of Hyatt's board wanted to buy new machinery with the company's profits, but the union wanted to distribute the money to the workers. No resolution could be reached.

Perhaps Lewis B. Anderson, a vice president of the United Food & Commercial Workers, was correct when he said, "There is no way workers on a meaningful basis can be managers and workers. The interests of each group eventually clash."

Source: John Hoerr with Gelvin Stevenson and James R. Norman, "ESOPs: Revolution or Ripoff?," *Business Week*, April 15, 1985, pp. 94–98, 102, 106, 108.

1. What are some of the advantages of a worker-owned company?

2. What are some of the disadvantages of a worker-owned company?

3. If you were a long-term employee in a worker-owned company with a large amount of stock and the company was faced with the decision of laying off some employees or reporting a loss (probably causing the value of stocks to decline), what would you advise? Would you have a different position if you were a short-term employee with a family to support and very little stock in the company?

4. Do you believe that it is possible to be both a manager and a worker? Or, as Lewis Anderson said, do you think that the interests of each group will eventually clash?

A Look at Future Trends That Affect Managers

Every 10 years the nation turns its attention to the new decade. What will the 1990 decade hold for American business?

As business managers study the trends into the 1990s, their findings have strong implications for those of us who study business. As each of the trends is discussed, think of each of them in light of making the management decisions discussed in Unit 3.

THE OUTLOOK FOR MANUFACTURING

The number of persons employed in manufacturing jobs will decline, but the total output of these business firms will increase. The number of jobs will decrease mainly because firms are becoming more automated. The service sector will continue to grow and hire more employees. The increase in output will occur because firms are becoming more flexible in what they produce and how quickly they are prepared to make changes.

OUR POPULATION WILL AGE

By the year 2000 we will have 34 million Americans who will be 65 years of age or older. The number of new employees entering into the labor force will decrease each year from now to the year 2000.

CONTINUED GROWTH IN HIGH TECHNOLOGY

Growth in technology will take place on several important fronts. In the health and agricultural fields, processes and discoveries will create new products and substances. In agriculture, plants will be developed which are more resistant to pests and poor weather. In human health, substances will be produced that will combat cancer and regulate high blood pressure.

Computers will continue as a major force behind business advances. Computer processing will become faster with some computers understanding thousands of words spoken into them. Lasers and robots will become a more dominant part of business manufacture and operation.

BUSINESS FIRMS WILL BECOME LEANER

The 1980s saw the beginning of the trend toward a "leaner and meaner" business organization. This trend includes an emphasis on greater productivity by employees, strong customer service, and lower costs of doing business. For the 1990s this often means reducing the management work force to increase the company's profits. Many people also believe that the smaller firm will have a better chance of success through its flexibility to change.

These four trends do not represent the entire list of future trends, but they are representative of the variety of forces impacting business.

DISCUSSION QUESTIONS

1. If the number of service-oriented business firms increases, what forms of ownership will they likely take?

2. If the population data is correct, what impact will it have on American business?

3. What are the educational, career, and legal implications of a high-tech workplace?

4. How should management respond to those employees remaining after a cutback?

Financial Management

Every business firm needs strong financial management. When a business is starting up, it will need funds to begin operations. If the business is to remain healthy in a changing environment, it must have adequate funds to finance its short-term and long-term needs. If the firm is successful, it may decide to expand operations in the future. Funds will be needed for this purpose, too. If the business should try to borrow money or attract investment capital for expansion, the lenders or investors will require detailed financial information about the firm. The financial manager must help the firm obtain the financing needed to start, maintain, or expand operations. He or she must also collect, analyze, and interpret financial information for those who use it both inside and outside the firm. Unit 4 will introduce you to the vital role that financial management plays in American business today.

UNIT OBJECTIVES

1. Understand why accounting systems and financial planning are important to business.
2. Learn how businesses interact with financial institutions and markets.
3. Explain the various options available to help finance a firm's short-term and long-term funding needs.
4. Describe the various tools, including insurance, used by businesses to help manage risk.

CHAPTER 9

Accounting and Financial Planning

To Plan Or Not Plan?—Aye, That Is the Question!

Size is no guarantee of success in business. Companies that once stood tall—International Harvester, W. T. Grant, Anaconda Copper, and Kaiser Steel—have now disappeared. One school of thought takes the view that firms go from infancy to adolescence and finally to old age. Another school points to firms such as Chrysler and Penn Central to show that business success is a series of ups and downs.

Most accountants and financial consultants favor developing and maintaining a business plan especially for start-up firms. The business plan defines the goals and objectives the start-up firm will pursue and helps project income and expenses of a firm. Or does it? Many successful firms such as Hewlett-Packard, Federal Express, and Compaq either cannot locate their original business plans or have strayed markedly from them.

According to one school of thought, starting a business, taking advantage of opportunities for growth, and maintaining a successful business are not based on predictable formulas or plans. According to this school, successful financial managers must use many tools, and even intuition, to work their magic.

Study this chapter to learn more about the role of accounting and financial planning in business. Use the contents to help you answer the questions in the end-of-chapter case study, "The Davises Consider a Business Plan."

Accounting and financial planning are two areas of the utmost importance in business. Accounting is so important that it is sometimes known as the language of business. Regardless of how large or how small a business may be, accounting plays an important role in determining the present financial status and the future financial plans of the business.

Accounting and financial planning go hand in hand. **Accounting** is a system of principles and concepts used to record, classify, process, summarize, and interpret the financial data of business. Accountants prepare financial data, analyze it, then interpret it to plan for the financial future of the business. The accounting data may be compared with data from other firms within the same industry or with the business community in general to determine the financial status of the business and to plan for the future. Financial decisions affect many groups including owners, managers, employees, and, in many cases, society itself. In this chapter we will examine the role of the financial manager, discuss basic accounting principles and concepts, and present and analyze financial statements. We will conclude with an overview of planning for future operations.

THE ROLE OF THE FINANCIAL MANAGER

Whether the business is small or large, there is normally one person responsible for the financial management of that business. In a sole proprietorship it may be the owner, in a medium-size business it may be an accountant, and in a large corporation it may be a vice president. Figure 9-1 illustrates the position of the financial manager within a typical large firm. You will notice that the financial manager normally reports directly to the president. Reporting to the financial manager are the treasurer and

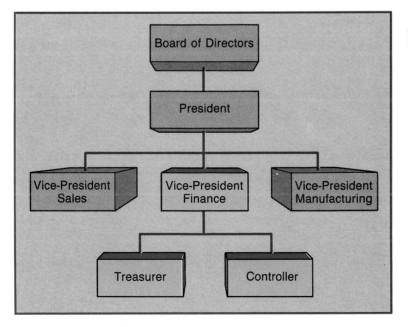

Figure 9-1. Position of the financial manager in a typical large firm.

the controller. The **treasurer** is responsible for managing the firm's cash and investments, for planning the financial base of the firm, and for raising capital the firm needs in order to grow. The **controller** is the chief accountant who is normally responsible for the tax department, for determining the cost of producing goods and services, and for the financial accounting of the firm. In smaller businesses one individual (normally the owner) may be responsible for all these activities.

The major responsibilities of the financial manager are:

1. To make sure the business can meet its financial obligations (payments).
2. To obtain the money needed to meet the business's financial goals through investment of company funds or other means.
3. To plan and forecast costs, technological changes, financial market conditions, and profits of the business.
4. To estimate risks and plan for the insurance needs of the business and its employees. (This role will be discussed in Chapter 11.)

Meeting the Business's Financial Obligations

One of the most important responsibilities of the financial manager is to make certain the business is able to meet its financial obligations and payments. To accomplish this, the financial manager must analyze both the sources of the business's funds and the uses of those funds. Each use of funds must be accompanied by a source of funds. Figure 9-2 illustrates the most common sources and uses of funds in a typical business. The left side of the illustration shows funds from the sale of goods and services, funds supplied by owners, and funds borrowed from outside sources. Management must decide how these funds are to be used. For example, should the business purchase new equipment, purchase additional inventory, pay operating expenses, or spend for other uses deemed necessary?

One of the most important uses of funds is to purchase the resources a business needs to produce goods and services used to make a profit. These resources are commonly known as assets. **Assets** may be defined as anything of monetary value a business owns. Assets include such things as cash, merchandise to sell, equipment, buildings, land, trademarks, and patents. All firms have limited assets; therefore, they must be able to expand these assets in order to grow. One method used to expand

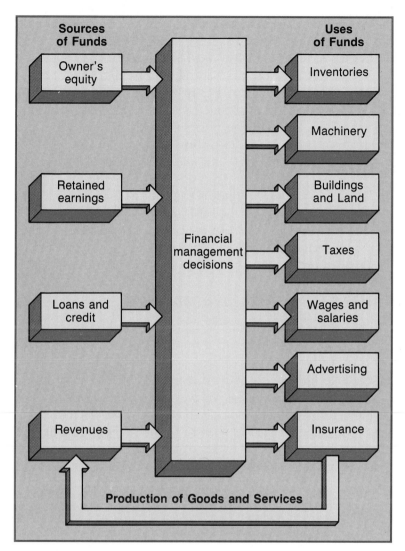

Figure 9-2. Common sources and uses of funds in a typical business.

their assets is by borrowing funds from outside sources. By using cash and by borrowing, a firm is able to purchase more assets, thus generating more income. The use of borrowed money to purchase assets which in turn are used to make more money is called **leverage.**

Another important use of funds is paying various operating expenses. Operating expenses include such things as salaries, rent payments, utility payments, and other payments needed to operate the business. Some of these expenses are predictable, but many of them are not. Therefore, it is very important that the business has enough cash reserve, as well as a regular cash flow, to pay these expenses. Cash reserve is having cash readily available, and cash flow is the difference between cash received and cash paid out. Naturally, a business would like to receive more cash than it is paying out. Another factor the financial manager must consider is converting assets to cash to pay expenses. The measure of how quickly assets can be converted to cash is referred to as **liquidity.**

At times a business may have idle cash that is not needed to purchase assets or to pay expenses. It is the responsibility of the financial manager to find uses for these funds so that they may produce income for the business. The uses of these funds depend on how soon they are needed to make payments. They may be simply saved in interest-producing bank accounts or they may be invested in various short- or long-term securities.

Knowledge of Financial Markets

The exchange of goods and services for money is an everyday business occurrence. However, another type of exchange does not involve the exchange of ordinary goods and services. Businesses, like individuals and governments, often engage in the creation of, or transfer of, financial securities. Financial securities are instruments sold by business to obtain money for operations. They consist of shares of ownership in the business or of credit instruments sold to others. The most common types of financial securities are stocks and bonds. Stocks represent ownership, whereas bonds represent debt. Financial securities are purchased at financial markets such as the New York Exchange. (Financial securities and markets are discussed in greater length in Chapter 10.)

Use of Financial Forecasts

The financial manager participates in the planning and control functions of business. As you learned in Chapter 8, planning is the setting of objectives for the business and choosing the best methods to accomplish them. Controlling is the process that determines whether the objectives are being met and making corrections when they stray off course. A forecast is a blueprint used by a business to help set its objectives. Good forecasts result from (1) accurately reading conditions in the environment outside the company (external forecasts) and (2) gauging the impact of developments within the company (internal fore-

Figure 9-3. Examples of financial securities—stocks, (shown on the left) and a bond (shown on the right).

casts), as these might affect future operations. A forecast can alter a company's business plans in major ways. For example, a forecast showed that increasing numbers of women would enter the work force in the 1980s and 1990s. This caused the Singer Company to reduce its dependence on the sewing machine market. Based on forecasts of decreasing bus ridership, the Greyhound Corporation decided to sell the very bus line for which it was named. Today, Greyhound concentrates on other ventures.

External forecasts are of great importance in making decisions. For example, if a business were planning to expand its building site, it might require outside financing. In this situation, forecasts about the condition of the financial markets and the costs of money would be very important. Economic indicators, anticipated technological changes, and even changes in public attitudes are major ingredients of most external business forecasts.

The financial manager is responsible for assuring financial liquidity, knowledge of financial markets, and participating in the financial planning and control of the business. In a small business the finance function may be part of one person's responsibility. In larger businesses, the work may be delegated to many individuals with specialized skills.

ACCOUNTING PROCEDURES

Now that we have discussed the basic responsibilities of a financial manager, let's examine the basic principles which lead to sound business decisions. Accounting is the basis of financial planning in business. For individuals, businesses, governments, and the like to understand and interpret financial data, the financial system must be uniform. Regardless of the size or type of business, uniform accounting principles and concepts have been developed to classify, record, summarize, and interpret financial data.

Accounting is based on three basic elements: assets, liabilities, and owner's equity. Every business must have economic resources in order to operate. As we've seen, these economic resources are known as assets. A business can acquire these economic resources from two main sources. The owner can invest resources in the business or the business may borrow from outside sources. When economic resources are obtained through borrowing, the debts the business owes are called **liabilities,** and when economic resources are invested by the owner, they are termed **equity.** Let's examine each of these elements more closely.

Assets

In every business there are many different kinds of assets. Accountants classify assets into two basic categories: current assets and plant and equipment assets. **Current assets** are assets that can easily be turned into cash or assets that will be used in the normal operations of the business within a year. Current assets include cash, the amounts owed to the firm (receivables), and inventories. Cash is the most liquid of all assets. Cash is defined as any currency, coin, checks, money orders, etc., a business has on hand. Receivables are less liquid than cash but can be converted to cash quickly. Receivables are amounts of money owed to the business. The most common type of receivables are accounts receivable. Accounts receivable is money owed the business by customers. Another type of current asset is inventories. Inventories are the goods or merchandise a business has on hand to sell. The final type of current assets discussed here are termed prepaid expenses. Prepaid expenses are goods and services to be used in the operation of the business. One of the most common examples of a prepaid expense is insurance.

Plant and equipment assets (also known as fixed assets) are assets which are expected to be used by the business for a number of years. Examples of plant and equipment assets are equipment used by the business, buildings, furniture, land, machinery, vehicles, and anything else a business expects to use for a number of years. Although plant and equipment assets are expected to be used for a long period of time, their actual useful life to the business may be limited. This is true for all plant and equipment assets with the exception of land (land always has some useful purpose). As plant and equipment assets are used, they may become obsolete or deteriorate. The portion of the original cost of the plant and equipment asset that is used each year is termed **depreciation.** Therefore the present value of a plant and equipment asset is the original cost minus the amount it has depreciated.

Other types of assets businesses may own are natural resources and intangible assets. Natural resources are assets that are kept in their natural state until they can be changed into useful products. Examples of natural resources are oil, gas, and coal. Intangible assets are those assets that are used in the operation of the business but have no real physical characteristics. Examples of intangible assets are copyrights, patents, and trademarks.

Liabilities

As noted previously, liabilities are debts that a business owes. The one to whom a debt is owed is termed a creditor. Like assets, liabilities are divided into two main categories: current liabilities and long-term liabilities. Current liabilities are those debts which must be paid within a year. The most common type of current liability is accounts payable. Accounts payable are amounts owed for goods and services bought on credit. Long-term liabilities are debts which will be paid over a number of years. One of the most common types of long-term liabilities is a mortgage. A mortgage is a written promise by a borrower to pay a certain sum of money within a certain period of time. This promise is normally guaranteed by some form of property held as security by the creditor.

Owner's Equity

Owner's equity is the financial interest the owner has invested in the business. Depending upon the type of business, the term owner's equity may be replaced by another term to identify the type of business ownership. For example, if the business is a partnership, the term used is partner's equity. And, if the business is a corporation, the term used is stockholder's equity. Owner's equity normally consists of any investment the owner may have in the business plus any profits the business may have earned (less any loss the business may suffer). The amount the owner has invested in the business is termed capital. The profit in a business is more commonly known as the net income and any loss is referred to as the net loss. The net income is determined by comparing the difference between two other items known as revenue and expenses. **Revenue** is the increase in owner's equity caused by the increase in assets from the sale of goods and services. **Expenses** are the cost of the goods and services used to earn revenue in the operation of the business. When revenues are greater than expenses, the result is a net income; when expenses are greater than revenues, the result is a net loss.

The Accounting Equation

The three elements of accounting have a certain relationship that can be expressed in the form of an equation. The **accounting equation** is

$$\text{Assets} = \text{liabilities} + \text{owner's equity}$$

It can be summarized by stating that all assets must equal the total claims against those assets which are the liabilities and owner's equity. Liabilities are the claims of creditors against the assets of a business, whereas owner's equity is the claim of the owner against the assets of the business. Assets always appear on the left side of the equation; liabilities and owner's equity always appear on the right side of the equation. Mathematically the left side of the equation (assets) must always equal the right side (liabilities + owner's equity).

Input of Data Into the Accounting System

The day-to-day operations of a business do not allow the three elements of accounting to remain stagnant. Anytime a financial event occurs, one or more of the elements may change. Financial events affecting the accounting equation are termed transactions. Typical transactions are the sale of goods or services or the paying of a debt. There are certain asset accounts (cash, accounts receivable, equipment, etc.); likewise, there are certain liability and owner's equity accounts. When a transaction takes place, information about it is recorded in at least two accounts in one or more of the elements. For example, if cash is paid for an asset, the amount of cash the business has will decrease but the amount of equipment the business owns will increase. In this example, two accounts are affected by the transaction, but since they are both asset accounts, the total assets remain unchanged. If equipment is purchased on credit, the amount of equipment increases and the amount owed by the business also increases. Here, an asset account (equipment) increases and a liability account (accounts payable) also increases. As a result, total assets and total liabilities both increase. Transactions represent the input data for the accounting system. Transactions are recorded daily as they occur.

▼ You are a manager of a small florist shop. As owner-manager you have also accepted the accounting duties for your firm. You have just been told by a friend that you should buy a computer to keep track of your records. Your friend says the biggest advantage of a computer is that you can get rid of all your paperwork. Do you think this is true? Explain.

Processing Data Through the Accounting System

Once transactions have been recorded, they are then summarized at the end of a certain period of time (a month, quarter, or a year). This time period is termed an accounting period. An accounting period which is a year in length may extend the normal calendar year (January 1 through December 31), or it

Figure 9-4. Financial events that affect the accounting equation are called *transactions.* **Transactions represent the input data for an accounting system, which may be manual, computerized, or a combination of both. Here we see an accounting worker calculating and recording data about such transactions. The data will then be placed in appropriate accounts.**

may extend for any 12-month period. Rather than operating on a calendar-year basis, many businesses choose to operate on a fiscal year. A fiscal year represents any 12-month period. Businesses that operate on a fiscal-year basis normally begin their fiscal year on a date other than January 1. For example, the accounting records for the federal government begin October 1 and extend until September 30 of the next year. Other organizations may operate on a fiscal year beginning July 1 and ending June 30 of the next year.

Output of Data From the Accounting System

At the end of the accounting period the financial manager will summarize the data collected from all transactions recorded during that period. This data is summarized in financial reports, which are considered the output of the accounting system.

This output is used for both internal and external purposes. If it is used for internal purposes, it is analyzed by managers to make decisions which will affect the business in the future. This function of using accounting information to make internal decisions is called **managerial accounting.** Managerial accounting involves budgeting, analyzing costs, and planning for taxes and the future of the business.

Financial information must be gathered by the business for reporting to external organizations. This is known as **financial accounting.** Individuals such as stockholders, employees, and creditors may be interested in the financial condition of the business. Institutions, such as banks, investment companies, governmental agencies, and others, may also be interested. They are able to analyze the financial condition of a business by reviewing many of the financial reports prepared at the end of each accounting period.

The person who designs and oversees the accounting system is the accountant. Large businesses employ their own accountants, whereas small and medium-sized businesses may hire independent accounting firms to handle their financial records. Most businesses use an accounting firm to review their accounting system. This review is called an **audit.** Certified public accountants (CPAs) arte persons who have passed a uniform exam prepared by the American Institute of Certified Public Accountants. These individuals are certified to conduct audits of business records. An accountant not only reviews the accounting records but also examines financial reports and gives opinions concerning their fairness and accuracy.

FINANCIAL STATEMENTS

Financial statements are prepared at the end of each accounting period. These financial statements summarize the accounting data for that period. They may also be used to compare financial data from other accounting periods. The data that is reported on these statements is used by management to make sound decisions for the future. Accurate decision making relies on a knowledge of the financial statements. At the end of the fiscal year businesses prepare an annual report of their activities. The annual report contains a statement by management concerning the present condition and future plans of the business, the various financial statements for the period, and the opinions of the independent auditor. The annual report is sent to all stockholders and is available to anyone who may request it.

It is impossible to describe the many complex processes that make up an accountant's job in these few pages. Therefore, only three important financial statements will be briefly discussed: the balance sheet, the income statement, and the statement of changes in financial position. The **balance sheet** shows the financial condition of the business on a given day and reports the value of all the assets, liabilities, and owner's equity of the business. The **income statement** reports the revenues, the expenses, and also the net income (loss) of the business for the entire accounting period. The **statement of changes in financial position** focuses on the changes in assets and liabilities during an accounting period. It reports the sources and uses of funds in the business. To illustrate these financial statements more clearly, let's review the statements of an imaginary company called the DAVECO Corporation.

▼ You are a stockholder in the ECKO Corporation. The federal government has made it legal for corporations to publish quarterly summary reports to take the place of their annual report. You notice that this shorter report does not contain as much detail as the former annual report—no footnotes, no breakdown of profits by product, etc. What is your reaction as a stockholder? What has probably motivated the company to leave out these details?

The Income Statement

The first financial statement that we will examine is the income statement. The income statement is prepared at the end of the accounting period to report the revenue, expenses, and net income (loss) for that period. The income statement is sometimes called the profit and loss statement because it reports whether a business has made a profit or suffered a loss from business operations for the accounting period. The income statement has three major functions.

1. To report the sources of revenue for the accounting period
2. To report the expenses for the accounting period
3. To report the net income (or net loss) for the accounting period

The income statement for the DAVECO Corporation is presented in Figure 9-5.

You will notice that DAVECO's income statement has five major sections or lines. Let's examine each section or line.

Revenues. The revenue section reports all revenue for DAVECO Corporation for the accounting period ending June 30, 19XX. The main source of revenue is from the sale of goods and services. However, other revenue may be earned by businesses. DAVECO has earned revenue from sources other than the sale of goods and services. It has invested excess cash into various investments and saving accounts. Therefore, this revenue must be reported as other revenue. Other revenue rep-

Figure 9-5. Income Statement for the DAVECO Corporation.

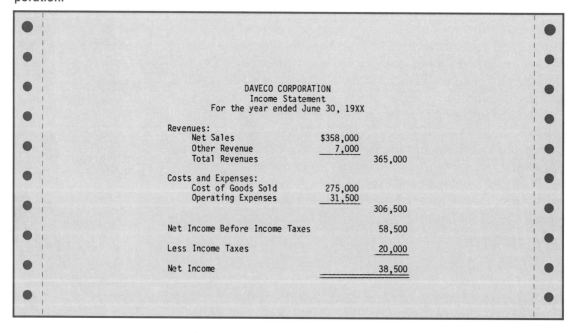

```
                    DAVECO CORPORATION
                      Income Statement
               For the year ended June 30, 19XX

        Revenues:
            Net Sales                  $358,000
            Other Revenue                 7,000
            Total Revenues                            365,000

        Costs and Expenses:
            Cost of Goods Sold          275,000
            Operating Expenses           31,500
                                                      306,500

        Net Income Before Income Taxes                 58,500

        Less Income Taxes                               20,000

        Net Income                                      38,500
```

resents revenue earned from something other than the sale of goods and services. The last line of the revenue section reports the total revenue for the accounting period.

Costs and Expenses. The costs and expenses of operating the business are reported in the next section of the income statement. In accounting, there is a difference in the terms expenses and costs. As discussed previously, expenses are assets used in the operation of the business. **Costs** are defined as amounts spent to purchase merchandise for resale. The first line of the expense section reports the cost of goods sold. This represents the total cost of all the merchandise that was sold during the accounting period. The next line reports the operating expenses for the accounting period. **Operating expenses** represent expenses incurred in the normal operation of the business. These include items such as advertising, distribution expenses, selling expenses, and salaries. The last line of this section reports the total costs and expenses for the accounting period.

Net Income Before Income Taxes. This section or line reports the net income (loss) to the DAVECO Corporation before income taxes are determined. This is computed by merely subtracting the total costs and expenses from the total revenue.

Income Taxes. This section or line reports any local, state, or federal income taxes which must be paid by the corporation. The income taxes are subtracted from the net income before income taxes to determine the actual net income or profit to the business.

▼ You are interested in purchasing a refreshment stand on a busy beach. The price the owner is asking does not seem justified based on the owner's tax record of revenues. The owner tells you confidentially that he keeps two sets of books, one for the IRS and one for himself. You are still interested in the store. What is your reaction to this finding?

Net Income. This is the "bottom line." The net income represents the profit DAVECO Corporation has made for the accounting period. The business must now decide what is to be done with the net income. DAVECO Corporation has basically three choices of how to distribute the net income.

Automating the Bottom Line

The electronic spreadsheet has become a primary tool of the accountant. The name *spreadsheet* describes a fundamental business tool for financial managers. The word has become almost a synonym for a computer software program representing the columns and rows which are laid out in a grid on a computer screen. The spreadsheet is not that new, however. For centuries business managers have used this business tool to keep track of data that could be organized in rows and columns. Using numbers and formulas, along with a pencil, eraser, adding machine, or calculator, the accountant solved financial problems. The results of the calculations were displayed on long sheets of lined paper called spreadsheets. The spreadsheet is an easy format for presenting such financial statements as the income statement and the balance sheet.

In 1979 a computer software product called VisiCalc revolutionized the manual process of creating financial reports. Now called the electronic spreadsheet, rows and columns appear on a computer screen. Each intersection between a row and a column is referred to as a cell. A movable, highlighted area (called a pointer) allows the user to move from one cell to another on the spreadsheet. Accountant's numbers and formulas are entered into cells. The most remarkable feature of the electronic spreadsheet is its ability to recalculate the formulas when new numbers are entered in the numeric cells. This makes it possible for managers to ask "what if" questions. The manager enters a new number or set of numbers, and the computer automatically displays the recalculation.

VisiCalc was discontinued in 1985, but the electronic spreadsheet appears in many more software programs on the market today. Lotus 1-2-3 is the most widely used product, but many other software companies have entered the market to provide brisk competition. Many experts believe that the electronic spreadsheet helped promote the popularity of the microcomputer for business users.

Use of the spreadsheet has caused a new set of procedures to be written for the typical financial manager. Even though the computer is a primary tool for preparing financial reports, rules for developing them are necessary. Each type of statement must be planned so that the printed copy from the computer is easy to read. Formulas must be accurate so that the calculations on the statement are accurate. The fixed and calculated numbers on the spreadsheet must be documented so that other people know what the numbers mean. In other words, a lot of work goes into the planning of financial reports on the computer. The reward for this work, however, is that the *second, third, and fourth* time the report needs to be prepared, it is easy and accurate. The power to get work done faster can help a business make great gains in productivity.

Sources: Teresa Alberte-Hallam, Stephen F. Hallam, and James Hallam, *Introduction to Microcomputer Spreadsheets*, Academic Press, 1986; "The Great Software Debate," *Computerworld*, November 2, 1987; Larry Long and Nancy Long, *Computers*, Prentice-Hall, 1986.

The first choice is to keep the net income in the business and use it to purchase new assets, purchase more merchandise, pay expenses, pay debts, or use it for any other use deemed necessary by the financial manager. The net income that is kept in the business is called **retained earnings.**

The second choice is to give the net income to the owners of the corporation. Individuals invest in businesses and expect some return on their investment. The investors, or stockholders, expect to receive some of the profit. The portion of the net income or profit given to the owners is termed dividends. In a corporation, each share of stock will receive an equal share of the net income, an equal dividend.

The third choice of the financial manager is to retain some of the net income in the DAVECO Corporation and to pay dividends to the owners with the remainder. The financial manager must determine which portion of the net income is to be retained and which portion is to be paid in dividends. This decision is based on many factors: the future plans of the business, the condition of the market, and the economic conditions of society.

The Balance Sheet

The second financial statement that we will examine is the balance sheet. The balance sheet reports the total assets, total liabilities, and the total owner's equity on a particular date. The two main purposes of the balance sheet are:

1. To show the financial condition of the business on a specific date

2. To prove the validity of the accounting equation: total assets are equal to the total liabilities plus the total owner's equity

The balance sheet for the DAVECO Corporation is shown in Figure 9-6 on page 204. Notice that the balance sheet is divided into three major sections. Let's examine each of these sections.

Assets. This section reports the value of the assets of DAVECO Corporation as of June 30, 19XX. Assets are reported on the balance sheet at their original cost. Therefore, assets are not shown at their present value or at their market value. Assets are listed on the balance sheet in the order of their liquidity. Current assets are more liquid than are plant and equipment assets; therefore, they are listed first. Cash is the first current

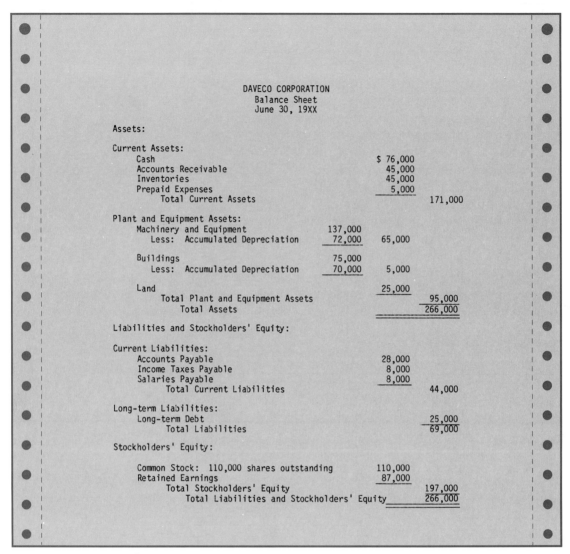

```
                    DAVECO CORPORATION
                       Balance Sheet
                       June 30, 19XX

Assets:

Current Assets:
     Cash                                      $ 76,000
     Accounts Receivable                         45,000
     Inventories                                 45,000
     Prepaid Expenses                             5,000
          Total Current Assets                              171,000

Plant and Equipment Assets:
     Machinery and Equipment          137,000
          Less:  Accumulated Depreciation   72,000    65,000

     Buildings                          75,000
          Less:  Accumulated Depreciation   70,000     5,000

     Land                               25,000
          Total Plant and Equipment Assets                 95,000
               Total Assets                               266,000

Liabilities and Stockholders' Equity:

Current Liabilities:
     Accounts Payable                            28,000
     Income Taxes Payable                         8,000
     Salaries Payable                             8,000
          Total Current Liabilities                         44,000

Long-term Liabilities:
     Long-term Debt                                         25,000
          Total Liabilities                                 69,000

Stockholders' Equity:

     Common Stock:  110,000 shares outstanding  110,000
     Retained Earnings                            87,000
          Total Stockholders' Equity                       197,000
               Total Liabilities and Stockholders' Equity  266,000
```

Figure 9-6. Balance Sheet for the DAVECO Corporation.

asset listed because it is the most liquid of all assets. Plant and equipment assets are recorded at their original value and are normally used by the business for a long period of time. Their value reported on the balance sheet may not equal the value it would cost to replace them. The amount of depreciation which has accumulated since the plant and equipment assets were purchased is also reported on the balance sheet. This is merely an estimate, but it does provide an idea of the present value of the asset. This is subtracted from the original value to provide an estimate of the asset's present value. Notice that land, as previously mentioned, does not depreciate.

Liabilities. This section reports both the current and long-term liabilities. As you can see, DAVECO owes money to creditors (accounts payable), owes salaries to employees (salaries payable), and owes income tax payments (income taxes payable) to the government. The liabilities section does not report the change in liabilities during the accounting period and does not show which specific assets were purchased on credit. It merely reports amounts owed as of June 30.

Stockholder's Equity. Since the DAVECO Corporation is organized as a corporate form of business, this section is titled stockholder's equity. As previously stated, if DAVECO were a proprietorship, this section would be termed the owner's equity section; and if it were a partnership, this section would be termed the partner's equity section. Regardless of the form of business ownership, this section reports the owner's investment in the business and any profits (losses) of the business. The owner's equity section does not show any changes in the owner's equity during the accounting period; it only reports the owner's equity as of June 30, 19XX.

Statement of Changes in Financial Position

The income statement summarizes the revenues and expenses and whether the business earned a profit or suffered a loss. The balance sheet shows the amount of owner's equity in the business. The statement of changes in financial position is the link between the income statement and the balance sheet. It shows how funds were obtained and how they were used by the business during an accounting period. Figure 9-7 shows DAVECO's statement of changes in financial position.

The statement of changes in financial position focuses on the changes in current assets and current liabilities. The difference between current assets and current liabilities is termed **working capital.** For that reason, this statement is sometimes referred to as the statement of changes in working capital.

DAVECO Corporation had a net increase in working capital during the latest accounting period. The accountant computed the sources of working capital from the income statement (revenue) and the balance sheet (new shares of stock sold and new debt). The accountant also computed the uses of working capital (dividends, building and equipment purchases) from the two statements. The final section of the statement provides

```
                        DAVECO CORPORATION
                Statement of Changes in Financial Position
                    For the year ended June 30, 19XX

Sources of Working Capital:

Revenues from operations                              $38,500
  Add:  Expenses not affecting working capital:
        Depreciation                                    7,000
Working Capital provided by operations                 45,500
From the sale of new stock                              5,000
From the sale of new long-term debt                    15,000

Total Sources of Working Capital                       65,500

Uses of Working Capital:

Purchase of machinery and equipment                    37,000
Payment of Cash Dividends                              16,500
Payments on Long-term Debt                              2,000

Total Uses of Working Capital                          55,500

Net Increase in Working Capital                        10,000

Changes in Working Capital:
  Increases (Decreases) in current assets:
    Cash                                               (6,000)
    Accounts Receivable                                10,000
    Inventories                                        10,000
    Prepaid Expenses                                    2,000
      Total Increase (Decrease) in current assets      16,000

  Increases (Decreases) in current liabilities:
    Accounts Payable                                   (3,000)
    Salaries Payable                                   (2,000)
    Income Taxes Payable                               (1,000)
      Total Increases (Decreases) in current liabilities (6,000)

Net Increase (Decrease) in Working Capital             10,000
```

Figure 9-7. Statement of Changes in Financial Position for the DAVECO Corporation. Note that numbers in parentheses—for example (6,000)—represent a loss or decrease by a given amount. Numbers not shown in parentheses represent a gain or increase by a given amount.

details on changes in current assets and current liabilities. Changes in the latest year are compared to the previous year. DAVECO had fewer changes in current liabilities, $6000, than current assets—$16,000. This meant that the assets had to be financed by some other method.

RATIO ANALYSIS

Financial statements reveal many important facts about the business. The use of ratios is a means by which the financial manager, an investor, or a creditor can more closely examine the financial condition of the business. A **ratio** is a mathematical relationship between two amounts. The ratio of 1000 employees to 100 business managers is 10 to 1 or 10 employees for every 1 manager. The relationship may also be expressed mathematically as 10:1.

Three general types of financial ratios will be discussed in this chapter: (1) liquidity ratios, (2) activity ratios, and (3) profitability ratios.

Liquidity Ratios

The cash position of the business can be measured by liquidity ratios. These ratios are used to tell the investor or financial manager the ability of the business to pay debts when they become due.

The current ratio is the ratio of current assets to current liabilities. If the current assets are greater than the current liabilities, the business is more able to pay its short-term debts. A business that is able to pay its short-term debts is said to be solvent. Likewise, a business that is unable to pay its short-term debts is said to be insolvent. The current ratio is computed by dividing current assets by current liabilities. The current ratio for DAVECO Corporation may be expressed as

$$\frac{\$171,000}{\$44,000} = 3.89$$

A general rule of thumb states that current assets should be twice the value of current liabilities. However, rules of thumb do not always apply to all industries. It is best to compare the current ratio of DAVECO with other firms in the same industry to have a more accurate picture of its solvency.

Activity Ratios

Activity ratios show how often a business is turning its assets into cash. The two assets normally examined are inventories and receivables. The inventory turnover ratio computes the number of times the inventory of a business turns over during a year. In business, inventory turnover means how quickly the inventory for sale to customers is sold. The higher the turnover, the less time merchandise sits unsold on shelves; the lower the

Information Brief
9-3

Watching for the "Trouble Spots"

"What do you mean we can't make our payroll?" the manager shouted. "Yesterday you told me that orders are up 20 percent." The embarrassed accountant could only shake his head. "And what will happen with our short-term loan at the bank—they don't take kindly to not receiving our monthly payment," the manager continued.

What happened here could have been avoided by developing a set of financial checks on potential trouble spots. These checks may include poor collection of receivables from customers, lagging performance by the sales force, or a poor delivery record by the business.

Source: Adapted from an article by Stanley R. Rich and David Gumpert, "Closely Watched Trends," *INC*, January 1987.

Start-up Statements

Income statements, balance sheets, and cash flow forecasts for a five-year period are commonly included in a business plan. The point at which the business will break even should also be included. The break-even point is determined by showing when total sales will equal total costs. Income above this point will be profit.

These statements are especially important when the new business is seeking money to start up. Reasoned assumptions about the future and how the money is to be used will most often be a key to qualifying for a loan. Further, the plan should also include projections about whether the new business will require additional funds in the future.

Source: "Your Business Plan: Put It in Writing," *Changing Times,* September 1985, p. 83.

turnover, the longer merchandise sits unsold. A high inventory ratio means the business is selling goods quickly and generating revenue. This may be a good sign; however, in some cases it could be a bad sign. If prices are too low, the business may not be maximizing its profit on merchandise sold. If the ratio is low, it may mean prices are too high, or there may be another reason that must be investigated. Regardless, the inventory turnover ratio should be compared with other businesses in the same industry. This gives an indication of how the business compares with its competitors.

This ratio is computed by dividing the net sales by the value of the average inventory for the accounting period. The average inventory is calculated by adding the beginning inventory to the ending inventory and dividing by 2. For DAVECO the inventory turnover is computed as

$$\frac{\$358,000}{(\$45,000 + \$35,000) \div 2} = 8.95$$

Profitability Ratios

Profitability ratios are used to measure the operating results of the business. In other words, they are used to determine whether a business is earning a satisfactory income. The two profitability ratios discussed here are (1) the return on sales and (2) the return on owner's equity ratio.

Return on Sales Ratio. This ratio measures the percentage of sales which is actually net income. The return on sales ratio is computed by dividing net income before taxes by the net sales. As with other ratios, this should also be compared with other businesses in the industry. The return on sales for DAVECO would be computed as

$$\frac{\$58,500}{\$358,000} = 16.3\%$$

Return on Owner's Equity Ratio. All business owners would like to maximize the return on their investment. For that reason the return on owner's equity ratio is computed by dividing the net income by the total owner's equity. The return on owner's equity for DAVECO Corporaton would be computed as

$$\frac{\$38,500}{\$197,000} = 19.5\%$$

The owners should not only compare this with others in the industry but also with other personal investments they have made.

▼ You are an accountant. The subject of accounting is being discussed at a dinner party. A friend has just made the statement that "accounting is the study of the past—not the future." How would you respond?

PREPARING A BUSINESS PLAN

Starting a new business without adequate financing is the reason many businesses fail. A detailed written business plan can enable a prospective business owner to predict cash flow and avoid mistakes. Those who have already established businesses may want to prepare a business plan to answer the questions of "Where is the business now?" and "Where is it going in the future?" These are important questions if the owner, or owners, plan to borrow additional funds or to convince additional investors to become owners. Bankers and accountants do not take individuals or businesses seriously unless they have put their plans and figures on paper. (See Information Briefs 9-4 and 9-5.)

The financial concepts discussed in this chapter may all play a vital role in the preparation of a business plan. Chapter 10 will explore where and how to get the money to begin or to expand a business.

Information Brief 9-5

Financial Aid for Female Entrepreneurs

Traditionally female entrepreneurs have had trouble obtaining funds to start up or expand businesses. Often their lack of previous business experience and of a credit history has left them at a disadvantage when seeking loans from banks. Now the National Association of Female Executives (NAFE), a New York-based group, has come along with a plan to help. In 1987 NAFE set up the first small business start-up fund "for women only."

Women looking to start new ventures must present a plan to NAFE projecting at least three years of income statements and a plan on how the funds will be used.

Source: Adapted from "Venture Capital Fund Extends Financial Backing to Entreprising Women," *Newark Star Ledger*, December 20, 1987, Business/Opinion section, p. 5.

Select Terms to Know

accounting	balance sheet	equity
assets	controller	expenses
audit	depreciation	financial accounting

income statement	managerial accounting	revenue
leverage	owner's equity	statement of changes in financial position
liabilities	ratio	treasurer
liquidity	retained earnings	working capital

Review Questions

1. List the four general responsibilities of a financial manager.

2. How does the financial manager make certain that the business is able to meet its financial obligations?

3. Describe the difference between stocks and bonds.

4. Briefly describe the relationship between the three elements of accounting.

5. What is considered the input of the accounting system? The output?

6. Briefly distinguish between managerial accounting and financial accounting.

7. What is the purpose of the income statement?

8. What is the purpose of the balance sheet?

9. What is a financial ratio? What value does ratio analysis have to financial managers and investors?

10. Why is it important for a business to develop a business plan?

Thought and Discussion Questions

1. Describe the sources and uses of working capital for an individual who opens a franchise ice cream shop. Draw a diagram which illustrates your choices.

2. Why do you think a uniform system of accounting records has been established?

3. Discuss the advantages, if any, of not distributing dividends to the owners.

4. Why must the results of financial ratios be compared to other businesses in the same industry? What cautions do you suppose should be observed in making comparisons?

5. What are some disadvantages to a business having too much cash on hand?

Projects

1. Interview a certified public accountant to find out how a person becomes a CPA.

2. NEW-WORLD Genetics Corporation is one of several firms involved in the scientific examination and testing of genetic diseases. The company has been exploring technologies that could lead to the development of new or improved products for the diagnosis and treatment of various diseases. These diseases include cystic fibrosis, sickle-cell anemia, hemophilia B, and Huntington's disease. To allow for future growth and to accommodate its expanding staff, the company recently completed a manufacturing plant for the production of clinical-grade therapeutic proteins.

a. What are some elements that the financial manager should consider when making forecasts about the company's operations?

b. What are some elements that the financial manager should consider when making forecasts about the outside environment?

3. Obtain a copy of a corporation's annual report. As financial manager, the analysis of investment opportunities rests with you. Answer the following questions about the company you have selected.

a. What are some problems and developments set forth in management's message to stockholders?

b. Compute the current ratio for the company.

c. Who was the auditor for the financial data displayed in the annual report?

4. For each of the balance sheet and income statement accounts listed below, describe how increases in these accounts could affect the business.

a. Cash
b. Inventories
c. Long-term debt
d. Cost of goods sold
e. Dividends

Case Study: The Davises Consider a Business Plan

Jane and Jack Davis own a small landscaping business which they operate out of their home in Louisville, Kentucky. The business, Blueridge Landscaping, produces less than $70,000 annually. They have four part-time employees and a 1981 Dodge pickup with 110,000 miles on it. They have a small nursery in their backyard where they grow much of their stock for the 10 to 12 customers who contract with them. When the amount of labor they put into their work is computed, they probably don't make much more than $5 per hour. Their combined wages taken out of the business were under $30,000 and were used for food, rent, and other expenses. Their owner's equity in the business is probably not much more than $15,000.

Jack has worked for other people but much prefers to be his own boss and to operate his own business with his wife. He loves his work and the schedule he feels he is allowed to keep. A short time ago he and Jane were offered an opportunity that caused them to think about business planning. A local builder asked them to consider expanding by adding a housing project to their list of customers. Land was being developed on the outskirts of the city, and the developer would be building houses in the $200,000 to $300,000 range. If the Davises decided to undertake this expansion, they would need to borrow $45,000 or so in working capital and come up with another $10,000. A contract like this should lead to others and eventually the business would take off.

Sources: Based on articles by Erik Larson, "The Best-Laid Plans," *INC*, February 1987; and James Cook, "Bring on the Wild and Crazy People," *Forbes*, April 28, 1986.

1. What should the Davises first begin considering in developing their business plan?

2. What outside environmental information should be considered?

3. What financial information should they gather in preparing this plan?

4. Would you recommend that they take advantage of the opportunity to expand? Why or why not?

CHAPTER 10

Sources of Funding

An Unusual Act of Financial Wizardry

At a bankers convention in Chicago today, John Bates, a prominent financier, recalled how the banking community was once outwitted by a brilliant business tycoon, Charles Tyson Yerkes (1837–1905). The gathering of 100 Chicago bankers seemed especially interested in the account of Yerkes' most memorable feat—an unusual act of philanthropy (gift giving).

It seems that in 1892 Yerkes was unable to finance his streetcar operations in Chicago due to a poor credit rating. Unshaken, he tried another tactic. He made an offer to William Rainey Harper, president of the University of Chicago, that was hard to turn down. He promised to give the university $1 million for an astronomical observatory. The only conditions were that the school would announce the gift immediately but wait a few months to actually receive the donation.

The announcement was made to the public. Bankers who were doubtful about his creditworthiness now concluded that a man who had a million dollars to give away must be a good credit risk. He was granted his loans, from which he gave $1 million to the university for the observatory which to this day bears his name. By this masterstroke, of course, Yerkes also secured the funds needed to finance the streetcar operations. Concluding his remarks to the convention, Bates said, "This act of derring-do payed off handsomely for the university, the city of Chicago, and, of course, for Yerkes' himself."

Businesspeople, like Yerkes, and financial managers are unavoidably concerned about ways to fund business activities. Use this chapter to learn more about sources of funding and to answer the questions in the end-of-chapter case study, "Financing the New Firm."

Source: Partly fictionalized account loosely based on Peter Baida, "Dreiser's Fabulous Tycoon." *Forbes,* October 27, 1986.

Not all businesspeople are as daring or as lucky as Charles Yerkes. Yerkes succeeded because he could tap business funds just when they were needed. Sometimes, however, funding is unavailable or business plans go astray, causing financial problems to veer out of control and eventually sink a business.

Whether business conditions are good or bad, the financial manager must help the firm meet its financial needs. Regardless of the firm's size, the financial manager has three special roles to perform:

1. Find sources to fund the company's needs, based on a working knowledge of our nation's financial system.
2. Determine the best method to finance the firm's needs.
3. Manage the firm's finances to ensure that its short- and long-term needs are met.

The profitability of the firm and its ultimate success or failure can depend heavily on how well the financial manager carries out these roles. In this chapter you will study each of these important responsibilities of financial management.

OUR FINANCIAL SYSTEM

If you were a financial manager, you would need to have a good working knowledge of our financial system. The reason is that the financial system provides businesses with potential sources of funds. The financial system also provides a means by which the funds can be transferred to businesses. Then, too, conditions within our financial system can affect the level of business activity, including the direction of spending, saving, and borrowing. Let's begin our examination of the role of the financial manager with an overview of our financial system.

The Role of Individuals, Business, and Government

A key to understanding our financial system is that individuals, businesses, and governments are both the suppliers and users of the funds within our economic system. Typically employee wages, profits from the business, and governmental tax monies are deposited in financial institutions. Once these institutions receive the funds, they must then decide what to do with them. Several choices exist. For example, after paying their own expenses, they may buy financial securities, such as stocks and bonds, on the financial markets. (Financial markets are places where funds may be exchanged or financial securities may be bought and sold.) Or these institutions can also lend excess

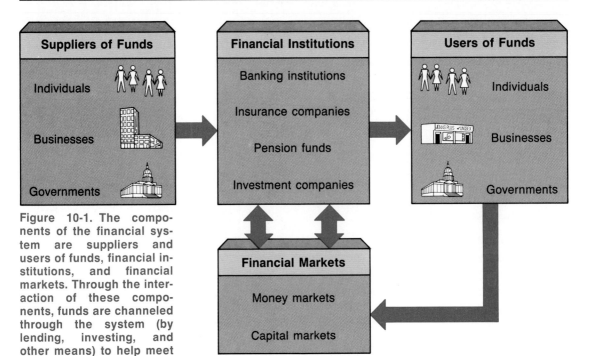

Figure 10-1. The components of the financial system are suppliers and users of funds, financial institutions, and financial markets. Through the interaction of these components, funds are channeled through the system (by lending, investing, and other means) to help meet the financing needs of individuals, businesses, and governments.

money to individuals, businesses, or governments. Look now at Figure 10-1. It shows you how our financial system is formed through the interaction of the suppliers and users of funds, financial institutions, and financial markets.

Types of Funds

Another point to remember is that within our financial system three basic types of funds are available: money, debt, and equity. As you know, the federal government issues money in the form of coin and paper currency. Money can also take the form of checks. Lenders—including individuals, businesses, and the government—are the issuers of debt. Of course, when funds are loaned to others, the lenders expect that it will be repaid with interest. Equity represents ownership in a business. Equity in a proprietorship, partnership, or a corporation can be sold in exchange for money. Today, however, equity ownership is most commonly associated with the corporate form of business. Corporations are the only ones legally authorized to issue and sell shares of stock. Such shares represent a part-ownership interest in an incorporated business.

Now, perhaps, you have a better picture of the role that suppliers and users of funds play in our financial system. But for a financial manager, would that represent sufficient "working knowledge" of our financial system? The answer is "no." If you were a financial manager, you would need to know more about the other major parts of the system.

FINANCIAL INSTITUTIONS

As illustrated in Figure 10-1, financial institutions and financial markets are the other major parts of our financial system. They provide funds to individuals, governments, and businesses. There are four key financial institutions which a business may turn to as sources of funds: banks, insurance companies, investment funds, and pension funds.

Banking Institutions

Commercial banks, savings and loan associations, and credit unions are banking institutions. Table 10-1 provides a brief description of each of these banking institutions. (Recently, too, a new type of bank has emerged, the so-called nonbank bank, or limited-service bank. See Information Brief 10-1.)

TABLE 10-1 Major Types of Banking Institutions

Commercial banks:
  Extend credit to businesses and individuals.
  Accept deposits in the form of savings and checking accounts.
  Are the primary source of capital, especially of short-term funds, for business.
  May offer a wide range of other services—insurance, credit cards, investment management, etc.

Savings and loan associations:
  Provide checking and savings accounts and loans to individuals.
  Most of their funds are invested in financing home mortgages.

Credit unions:
  Also known as mutual benefit loan companies, credit unions are cooperative lending institutions. They are operated by the members of a group—for example, the employees of a company or members of a lodge or a labor union.
  Tax-exempt status allows them to make loans on generally favorable terms.

Information Brief 10-1

"Nonbank" Banks

They look like banks. They issue savings accounts, certificates of deposit, and provide checking accounts. "Nonbank" banks may issue either savings instruments or credit instruments, but not both. That is why they are also called limited-service banks. Their services are generally offered to consumers rather than businesses.

There are fewer than 200 of these "banks." A typical nonbank "bank" is Greenwood Trust, a small commercial bank in Delaware. Greenwood was small until it was bought by Sears Roebuck, which used it to issue its Discover Credit Card. Deposits in the bank have mushroomed from $12 million to $2 billion in just a few years.

Sources: Eric Berg, "Limited Banks Giant Hurdle," *The New York Times,* July 2, 1987; Mary Rowland, "The Battle for Bigger Bucks," *Insurance Review,* July 1986.

Information Brief
10-2

Banco de Ponce

Recognizing the rapid growth of the Spanish-speaking population, banks are beginning to market to the growing Hispanic business community.

Banco de Ponce, a bank from Ponce, Puerto Rico, has launched a $600,000 advertising campaign aimed at Hispanics. The ads—in both English and Spanish—must be effective. Banco de Ponce is the leading Hispanic bank in New York. It claims that it has half of the city's Hispanic market. With a yearly growth rate of 23 percent, the bank's strategy seems to be working.

Source: Penelope Wang, "A Banco For the Big Mango," *Forbes*, May 30, 1988, pp. 260–261.

Banking institutions accept money deposits made by individuals, firms, and governments and lend this money to others. The largest of these institutions are called commercial banks. Commercial banks provide business users with about 60 percent of the money they need to borrow.

Users of savings and loan associations and credit unions are more likely to be individuals than businesses. Commercial banks, on the other hand, are often used by financial managers as the source of loans.

Insurance Companies

Insurance companies invest billions of dollars through financial markets. They can do this because they must invest the premiums from their policyholders. (A premium is a sum of money an individual or business pays to an insurance company for insurance against certain risks. You will learn more about insurance in Chapter 11.) For several reasons, which also will be discussed in Chapter 11, insurance companies invest the premiums paid to them. The heaviest investments are in corporate stock and bonds and in mortgages, a form of long-term debt on individual and business property. Insurance companies look for especially safe investments because they know that they will have to repay most of the money they invest in the form of earnings to their policyholders.

Pension Funds

Pension funds are established to provide income to retired or disabled persons. These funds are established through contributions (payments) by individuals and the organizations that employ them. The money in a pension fund must grow to meet the retirement needs of employees. Therefore, pension funds usually make investments in businesses in the form of debt or equity. Pension funds are most often managed by large commercial banks or insurance companies. The pension funds of large corporations are an especially rich source of capital. Corporate pension funds may have millions, even billions, of dollars available for investment purposes.

▼ How would you feel if you worked for a company and discovered that your company had invested all your pension funds in the stock of large corporations? Do you think this would be too risky? Why?

Investment Companies

Investment companies are corporations that accept money from individual or business savers and then use these dollars to invest in securities. The most common type of investment company is the **mutual fund.** Pooling is the key to mutual fund investing. It allows thousands of investors with varying amounts of savings to gain access to the financial markets. Different funds (over 1500) have been developed to serve the various types of investments desired by savers: short-term investments, long-term investments, debt, equity, or a mixture of these investments.

You now know that financial institutions, such as investment companies, are the second major part of our financial system. However, a study of the third and final component—financial markets—will be necessary to complete your review of our nation's financial system.

FINANCIAL MARKETS

The market for debt and equity funds is much like the markets where goods and services are bought and sold. Financial institutions and financial markets are dependent upon each other. An insurance company, for example, might have billions of dollars to invest in the debt or equity of a large corporation. The corporation's stocks and bonds could be sold directly to the insurance company. It is the more common practice, however, to use financial markets for this purpose.

There are two general types of financial markets: money markets and capital markets. Financial institutions can be found actively buying and selling funds in both types of markets.

The Money Market

The **money market** is created by the interaction between suppliers and users of short-term funds (funds needed for a year or less). The money market does not exist at a single building or in a particular trading location. Money markets exist at many locations. They serve as places where short-term debts can be traded by individuals, businesses, and the government. These markets exist because certain individuals or businesses may have excess cash and other parties, such as businesses or the government, have a short-term need to borrow these funds. The money market thus brings these suppliers of idle funds together with those users who are in temporary need of them. The suppliers loan the idle funds to a business firm or the government. The lending firm or government, in turn, agrees to repay the loan with interest.

The Capital Markets

Capital markets are created by the interaction of suppliers and users of long-term funds (those needed for more than a year). Typically, long-term funds are used by a business to develop new products, build new buildings, or replace outdated equipment. The capital market is conducted through more formally structured exchanges or markets than the money market. The stock exchange and over-the-counter markets are two important ways that long-term funds are transferred.

The Stock Exchange. A stock exchange is an organization whose members get together to provide a central trading place for selling and buying stocks and bonds. In the United States, the New York Stock Exchange (NYSE) is the largest of these exchanges. Members (most often brokerage firms) do not actually own the securities they trade—they merely provide a convenient means of matching buyers with sellers. The American Stock Exchange is another major stock exchange, but much smaller than the NYSE. Today the stocks and bonds of American companies are also widely traded on foreign stock exchanges. In fact, the Japanese stock exchange is the largest stock exchange in the world.

▼ Buying and selling securities in the financial markets has become international in recent years. More than $1 trillion of U.S. financial assets are now held by foreign investors. How do you feel about this? Do you think this is healthy for our economy?

The Over-the-Counter Market. The **over-the-counter market (OTC)** has no central trading floor. Instead, this market relies on a network of thousands of securities dealers who usually use the telephone to execute their trades. The dealers may actually buy securities, such as stocks and bonds, and hold them in their inventories for sale. (In fact, at one time dealers would actually hold the securities in their safes and trade them

Figure 10-2. Stocks and bonds are traded on capital markets such as the New York Stock Exchange, shown here.

"over the counter.") If individual sellers later want to resell the securities, the dealers will readily buy them back. This process is called making a market in the stock. The OTC market trades a high percentage of corporate bonds.

The Transfer Process

The financial system operates efficiently because it is an orderly system. Financial markets provide suppliers and users of funds with a convenient place for trading securities, such as stocks and bonds. Through this system, the financial institutions are also able to move funds back and forth smoothly and quickly. Figure 10-3 illustrates three different methods by which securities are moved from the users who create them to the suppliers of funds who invest in them. The unique part of each method is the way the funds are transferred. The suppliers and users could be either individuals, businesses, or governments. The three methods are:

1. *Direct transfer* occurs when a business sells its securities directly to the buyer. This is likely to happen in money markets between large firms.

2. *Indirect transfer* occurs when an investment bank acts as a go-between for supplier and users. **Investment banks** are in business to arrange the sale of securities from the issuing business to individual or corporate buyers (suppliers).

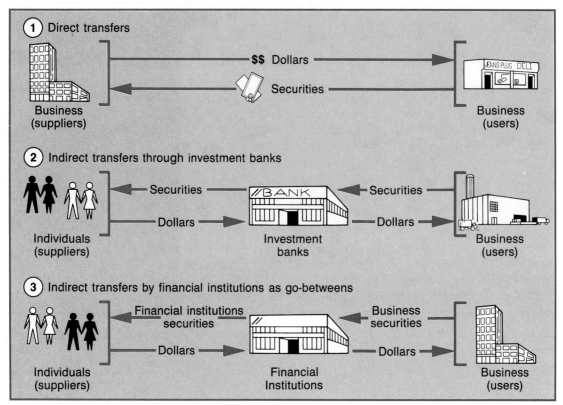

(1) Direct transfers

$$ Dollars

Securities

Business
(suppliers)

Business
(users)

(2) Indirect transfers through investment banks

Securities ← BANK ← Securities

Dollars → → Dollars

Individuals
(suppliers)

Investment
banks

Business
(users)

(3) Indirect transfers by financial institutions as go-betweens

Financial institutions
securities

Business
securities

Dollars →

→ Dollars

Individuals
(suppliers)

Financial
Institutions

Business
(users)

Figure 10-3. The three most common methods of transferring securities.

3. *Transfer by financial institutions* occurs when banks, insurance companies, pension funds, and mutual funds buy securities. These institutions often use these investments as a base for creating their own investment products, which in turn are sold to the suppliers of funds. The owner of a mutual fund share, for example, does not really own the securities the fund has bought in the money market or capital market. The owner owns a share of a product the mutual fund has created from a larger pool of securities.

THE FEDERAL RESERVE AND THE BANKING SYSTEM

Our banking system also has an effect on the financial system, especially on the cost of money borrowed from commercial banks. The **Federal Reserve System** (known as the Fed) is the central bank of the United States. As the central bank, the Fed writes the rules under which member banks must operate. It also acts as the network for processing checks throughout the banking system.

The Fed has three tools for regulating the amount of money and credit available in the economy. It controls the money reserves of financial institutions, changes the discount rate, and conducts open-market operations. These efforts to control the money supply are called **monetary policy.** The Fed's monetary policy has a direct effect on the cost of borrowing or saving money, as you will see in the discussion that follows. In a much broader sense, however, monetary policy also affects the level of business and consumer spending.

Control of Bank Reserves

The Fed requires that all member banks and financial institutions set aside a certain percentage of their deposits. This percentage, called a reserve requirement, may be increased or decreased depending on the amount by which the Fed wants to increase or decrease the money supply. For example, if a bank must increase its reserves, it will have less money to lend to business and individual customers. The effect of increasing the reserve requirement is to decrease the money supply so fewer loans will be granted for spending in the economy. This is known as "tightening" the money supply. The opposite takes place when the Fed wishes to expand the money supply. It can lower the reserve requirement and thereby make it possible for banks to lend more money to businesses and individual customers.

Changing the Discount Rate

The Fed is often called the banker's bank. If member banks need additional funds, one way they may obtain them is by borrowing from the Federal Reserve Bank in their region. The rate of interest the Fed charges its member banks is called the discount rate. Lower rates encourage more borrowing, and higher rates encourage less. The discount rate is another tool the Fed uses to regulate our nation's money supply.

When member banks make loans to their customers, they are required to charge more than the Fed's discount rate. When they loan money to business and individual customers, they put an additional percentage interest charge on top of the discount rate. The lowest resulting rate is called the **prime rate.** This rate is available to the member bank's best customers. Other customers have to pay even higher interest rates.

Financial Systems Go Electronic

Speed and accuracy are requirements for what is rapidly becoming a global financial system. Many banking customers rely on electronic fund transfers to electronically move money from one account to another without ever stepping inside a bank. Automated teller machines (ATMs) found in almost every community in the United States and other nations allow individuals to deposit and withdraw funds in a matter of seconds.

Business customers can do most of their banking via the computer. Information on checking, savings, loans, and investments is available 24 hours a day. A smart financial manager does not leave any more money in the firm's checking account than is needed to pay immediate bills. Excess money is swept out of checking and into short-term investments that earn interest for the business. The business can also use its line of credit without ever talking to anyone at the financial institution.

October 19, 1987, was a day to remember for the New York Stock Exchange and other securities markets. A record number of shares were traded as markets around the world plunged. The huge volume of trading was triggered and carried out by a sophisticated network of computers around the world.

The heavy volume of securities trading and banking transactions places even more pressure on the banking system. The Federal Reserve System's Fedwire links more than 7000 domestic banks electronically as they move Americans' money with the speed of light. The Clearing House Interbank Payments System, called CHIPS, has gone one step further. This advanced system links U.S. banks with banks around the world.

The financial network of electronic banking is rapidly becoming a reality. It will only be a matter of time before our financial system will be international in scope and electronic as a medium of exchange.

Sources: Monroe W. Karmin and Pamela Sherrid, "Risky Moments in the Money Markets," *U.S. News and World Report*, March 2, 1987; Calvin Sims, "How the Exchanges' Computers Got By," *The New York Times*, October 28, 1987; Barnaby J. Feder, "Testing the Technical Limits of Trading," *The New York Times*, January 28, 1987; Catherine L. Harris, "Information Power," *Business Week*, October 14, 1985.

Open-Market Operations

The Fed's main money decisions are made by a committee of 12 members. Each morning a Fed staff economist meets with several securities dealers to discuss what is happening in the financial markets. Information is gathered on how much demand there is for loans and the direction in which interest rates seem to be headed. This information is compared to the money supply goals set by the open-market committee. Twelve traders are directed to buy or sell a certain amount of government securities. They call about 30 securities dealers, compare their prices on government securities to get the best rates, and make billions of dollars worth of transactions each hour.

When the Fed is buying government securities, it is putting money into the economy. When the Fed is selling government securities, it is taking money out of the economy. By increasing or decreasing the supply of money available in the financial system, the Fed hopes to keep our economy sound and stable.

▼ It is said that the Fed acts as the safety net for the banking system. How do you think business would be affected if Americans felt their deposits were not safe in the banking system?

FINANCING ALTERNATIVES

Knowledge of our financial system provides a financial manager with a starting base for making financial decisions. For example, if you were a financial manager, this knowledge would be important in helping you determine where to turn for a source of funds.

As a financial manager, however, finding a source of capital would be only one of your responsibilities. You would also frequently be asked to determine the best method of financing your company's needs. Generally speaking you would have only three choices available to you: (1) internal financing, (2) debt financing, or (3) equity financing. Each method would have its advantages and disadvantages. You would have to weigh these in recommending the best method for your company.

Internal Financing

You have learned from Chapter 9 that revenue flows into a business mainly from the sale of goods and services. If a business is operated successfully, it will generate profits—capital or earnings left over after all expenses and taxes have been deducted from the firm's revenues. When these profits or earnings are kept by the firm, they are called retained earnings. If sufficient capital is retained and reinvested in the firm, it may be possible to finance business operations almost entirely from this source.

Use of retained earnings is considered a sound and conservative method of finance. There are several advantages to using it. A firm has the maximum freedom to do what it wants with its own funds. It need not worry about obligations to outside parties. This is also considered the least risky form of financing.

This method of finance, however, can only be used if the firm generates sufficient revenues and profits. Moreover this method cannot be used at all times. For example, a firm may be temporarily drained of internal funds if they are needed for some unexpected emergency. Very often, too, retained earnings are insufficient to take advantage of certain business opportunities. This seems to be especially true when firms are just starting up operations or trying to expand into new markets, improve operations, or expand facilities. Because the cost of such ventures tends to be very high, a firm will almost always rely on outside sources to finance them. This may take the form of either debt or equity financing.

Debt Financing

Debt financing occurs when a firm borrows capital to help it meet its financial needs. When the firm borrows capital, it promises to repay the borrowed funds by a certain time, usually with interest. The borrowing, for example, may take the form of a loan or the sale of bonds.

There are certain advantages to a business in using borrowed capital. Borrowing is especially helpful when financing short-term business needs. A retail store, for example, may use a short-term loan to help it purchase inventories during peak business periods. Such a loan would make it unnecessary for the firm to keep large amounts of cash on hand during such busy periods. Borrowed money also provides additional capital without requiring the owners or managers to give up ownership or control of the firm. The interest paid for the use of borrowed money is not subject to taxation. In effect, this lowers the cost of using the borrowed capital. When borrowed capital is used, the firm is also risking someone else's money, not the owner's, in activities that may earn it profits. Borrowing, then, can give a firm powerful financial leverage. Financial leverage exists when an individual or firm controls and uses another's funds to gain a business advantage or profit.

However, there is also a major drawback to debt financing. Firms that borrow must make interest payments on a regular basis, whether business is good or bad. Meeting the payments can become a major burden if there is a business slowdown and revenues are inadequate to cover the interest payments.

Equity Financing

Equity financing occurs when a corporation sells an ownership interest in the firm, usually by selling stock to shareholders. When the owners of a corporation employ equity financing, they are, in effect, allowing new owners and investors to share in the ownership, risks, and profits of the firm.

There are many advantages to equity financing. Unlike debt financing, this type of financing does not involve the payment of interest to lenders. When economic slowdowns occur, the firm will not have to worry about meeting any lending obligations. As a result, firms which rely on equity financing tend to be relatively stable and less threatened by bankruptcy in times of economic hardship. Then, too, the profits of the firm belong only to the owners of the firm. The earnings of the owners need not be diminished by loan and interest payments.

The principal disadvantage of equity financing is that it tends to dilute, or spread, the ownership and control of the corporation among many parties. Reliance on equity also means that more shares of stock will be sold. As a result there will be more claims upon the assets and profits of the firm. Although a corporation does not have to distribute profits to shareholders through dividend payments, frequent failure to do so may discourage purchase of the corporation's stock. Some investors buy stock primarily for the purpose of earning dividends.

▼ Suppose you owned 100 shares of Big Motors. The company has just earned $7 per share. The company can pay all the profit in dividends—in which case you would receive $700—or retain the earnings in the firm for further expansion. This action could make your stock worth more sometime in the future. Which would you prefer as a stockholder?

Choosing a Financing Method

It is clear then that each method of finance has its own unique benefits and drawbacks. Now, suppose you were a financial manager for a firm. How would you choose the best method of financing your company's needs? The choice would probably depend on many factors. No doubt a major consideration would be whether a particular method, or combination of methods, was likely to raise the funds required by your firm. Then, too, you would likely weigh the costs and risks associated with each method of finance. If you were like most financial managers, you would want to choose the method that involved the least cost to your firm. You would also probably opt for a method that involved the least risk to your firm's financial structure. Thus internal or equity funding, considered the least costly and safest financing method, might be your preferred choice.

How about the purpose of the funding? No doubt the purpose of the funding—for example, whether it were needed for a short- or long-term project—would also affect your decision. In fact, let's examine this a bit further. Working capital and budget management are important functions of financial management.

WORKING CAPITAL MANAGEMENT

If you were a financial manager, another of your responsibilities would be to make sure that your firm's requirements for short-term and long-term needs were funded adequately. Short-term funding refers to funding needs of a year or less. Long-term funding refers to funding needs of more than one year. More often than not, long-range financing involves funding for a period of 5, 10, or 20 years.

Short-term funds are called a firm's working capital. In accounting terminology, working capital is defined as the difference between current assets and current liabilities. However, for our purposes it's best to think of working capital as the money used to pay a firm's regular business operations. Working capital, for example, is needed to finance payrolls, inventory merchandise, raw materials, rent, utilities, and the like. In fact, funding to pay for these regular operations is so important that most companies have a separate **working capital policy.** This policy determines a target amount that the firm plans to spend on each regular business operation and how each operation will be financed. If you were a financial manager, you would help determine this policy.

Generally, short-term loans are used to provide the firm with working capital. Figure 10-4, for example, shows how one typical retail store uses working capital obtained by a short-term loan to finance its needs. It is plain to see that this particular store uses working capital to build up merchandise inventory for the busy holiday seasons. Short-term borrowing is also commonly used to take advantage of an inventory bargain or simply to cover an emergency.

Large and small business firms obtain short-term funds from three principal sources (1) short-term loans from lending institutions, usually commercial banks, (2) trade credit, and (3) commercial paper.

Short-Term Loans

Bank loans are the most common form of short-term borrowing. Loans may be either secured or unsecured. A **secured loan** pledges specific assets of the firm to the bank in case the loan is not repaid. A wide variety of assets, referred to as **collateral,** may be used to secure loans. Accounts receivable, inventory, equipment, and buildings are some examples of assets that can be pledged as collateral. In the event a loan is not repaid, the lending institution can take possession and ownership of the collateral.

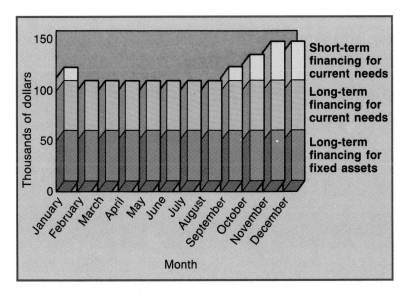

Figure 10-4. Analysis of financing needs for a typical retail store. The store builds merchandise inventories for the Christmas selling season and uses working capital in the form of short-term debt to finance this temporary need.

Information Brief
10-3

Four Keys to Credit Granting

Bankers describe a good prospect for a business loan as having the following four characteristics:

1. *Good character*. The good credit history, education, and training or experience of the firms owner(s) are considered important elements of good character.

2. *Capacity to repay*. The amount of cash flowing through the business is a key indicator that the loan can be repaid.

3. *Appropriate purpose*. The loan should be earmarked for some specific business purpose—not just for the general purpose of paying bills.

4. *Collateral*. Having the ability to provide collateral makes it easier for the bank to grant a loan—and also makes it easier for the borrower to make repayment if all else fails.

A **line of credit** is a widely used form of unsecured short-term credit. The bank earmarks a specific sum that a firm may draw on as needed over a specified period of time. For example, a commercial bank might give a firm a $25,000 line of credit to use as needed over a 12-month period. This enables a firm to plan the use of its working capital over an extended period of time.

To secure a loan, a firm must prove that it has a good credit reputation. See Information Brief 10-3, which describes some of the criteria for determining a firm's creditworthiness.

Trade Credit

Instead of borrowing from a bank, a firm may obtain credit directly from its suppliers. Credit extended by suppliers of a firm is called **trade credit.** The most common form of trade credit allows the buying firm to defer payment for 30, 60, or 90 days before payment and interest are due. Before extending trade credit to a firm, the supplier usually will check the buyer's credit reputation.

Let's look at an example of how trade credit works. A hardware store orders 100 hammers from its supplier. After checking the credit reputation of the hardware store, the supplier ships the hammers to the hardware store. A document is sent along with the hammers, stating that the hardware store has 30 days to pay the $500; thereafter interest must be paid. Notice that no money is actually exchanged between the hardware store and the supplier at this time. However, because the hardware store can use the $500 worth of hammers for 30 days without charge, it has, in reality, been given $500 worth of credit.

Commercial Paper

Big businesses have an option other than borrowing from banks and suppliers. They can borrow from each other by using commercial paper. **Commercial paper** is a company's promise to repay a stated sum of money after a specified period of time (2 to 270 days). Commercial paper is unsecured. The loan requires good faith in the strength of the business firm issuing the commercial paper. The cost of borrowing with commercial paper is usually less than the cost of a regular bank loan. For this reason this form of short-term borrowing is becoming the most popular source of short-term credit for large firms. Commercial paper may be sold directly by the lending corporation or through an investment banker.

CAPITAL BUDGETING

If you were a financial manager, the matter of long-range financing would involve you in a firm's capital budgeting decisions. **Capital budgeting** is the process of making financial decisions related to fixed assets. The budgeting part of the definition refers to the process of looking at proposed projects to decide what should be included in the firm's budget. Capital projects are long-term projects. Projects of this kind could include:

1. Maintaining and replacing equipment used to produce the company's products

2. Developing new products and entering new markets

3. Purchasing new equipment or technology to reduce the current cost of production

4. Adding new equipment or adjusting present equipment to comply with government regulations

5. Purchasing land, adding new buildings, building parking lots, and the like

If you were a financial manager, capital budgeting would require you to examine proposed projects like these very carefully. You would have to determine which project would bring the greatest return or benefit to your firm. Normally it would be impossible to fund an entire wish list of such costly projects. Therefore you would also have to decide which particular projects to fund. Most likely your decision would be based on such factors as return, risk, total cost of the project, and your firm's goals.

Your firm would probably use a combination of internal and outside funding to finance long-term projects such as these. The outside funding might take the form of long-term debt or equity financing. These methods are particularly suited to raising large sums of funds for capital projects.

Long-Term Debt Financing

Long-term debt financing is usually accomplished through the use of bonds or mortgages. Bonds are a form of long-term debt which are issued by corporations and the government. Bonds

Information Brief
10-4

Services Rate Debt

Standard & Poor's Corporation (S&P) and Moody's Investor Service, Inc., wield great power in the bond market. Nearly all corporations have one of these rating services evaluate their strength before placing bonds on the market.

S&P gives its highest rating of AAA to the companies most likely to repay the money owed to bond holders. Moody's uses a similar rating.

For corporations and governments selling bonds, the higher the rating, the more investors will be willing to pay for them. This means that it is cheaper for a well-rated company to sell bonds than it is for a low-rated company to sell risky ones.

Sources: Alexandra Peers, "Value of Bond Ratings Questioned by a Growing Number of Studies," *Wall Street Journal*, September 16, 1987, p. 33; James O'Shea, "Moody's, S&P Facing New Kid on the Block," *Chicago Tribune*, February 25, 1981; and "What Those Bond Ratings Mean," *Changing Times*, March 1980.

are certificates given by the borrower or issuer to the lender, pledging that the amount borrowed plus interest will be paid back by a certain date (the *maturity date*). The $1000 bond is quite common, but other denominations are also sold. Interest will be paid on the bond (usually twice a year) at a fixed rate.

If a bond is secured by the firm's assets it is called a **mortgage bond.** If it is unsecured, it is called a **debenture bond.** The debenture bond relies on the good credit standing of the firm issuing it.

Large corporations may sell bonds rather than equity in the form of stock because the holders become creditors, not owners, of the firm. As nonowners, the bondholders cannot participate in the operation of the firm. Almost immediately after selling bonds a firm must begin planning to repay them. Normally this means setting up a bond retirement fund, or so-called sinking fund. If you were the financial manager of the firm, you would see to it that the firm put a specific amount of money into the fund each year to retire or sink the bond by its maturity date.

Only corporations can sell bonds, however. Proprietorships and partnerships must obtain long-term debt by other means. For example, they may obtain such funds by mortgaging their real estate. Moreover, in some cases it may be impossible for smaller firms to secure long-term borrowed capital without pledging the owner's personal assets (home, for example) as collateral.

▼ How would you feel if your parents had to put up the family home or automobile as collateral to finance a business they wanted to start?

Long-Term Equity Financing

Long-term equity financing can be accomplished in a variety of ways. A proprietor may bring in a partner. A partnership may bring in additional partners. Any business also has the option of selling its assets to raise capital. To raise large sums of money, corporations may publicly sell and trade stocks on financial markets. When a corporation raises capital in this way it is said to be "going public." (See Information Brief 10-5 on page 232.)

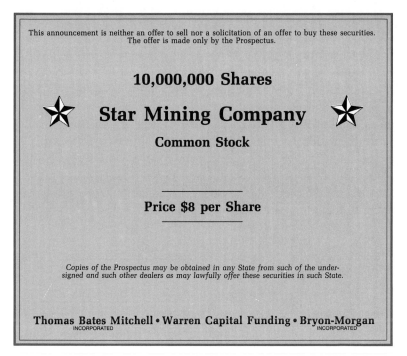

This announcement is neither an offer to sell nor a solicitation of an offer to buy these securities. The offer is made only by the Prospectus.

10,000,000 Shares

★ Star Mining Company ★

Common Stock

Price $8 per Share

Copies of the Prospectus may be obtained in any State from such of the undersigned and such other dealers as may lawfully offer these securities in such State.

Thomas Bates Mitchell • **Warren Capital Funding** • **Bryon-Morgan**
INCORPORATED   INCORPORATED

Figure 10-5. When common stock is offered for sale, the public offering may be advertised in newspapers, as it is here. The stock may be assigned a predetermined value, such as $8 per share, in which case it is called *par value stock.*

Long-term equity financing through the sale of stock is a source of funds for the corporation only. As was noted earlier, the corporation is the only form of business legally entitled to sell shares of stock.

Two types of stock are sold to investors. The first type, **preferred stock,** gives the purchaser a preferred claim on the profits and assets of the corporation. Preferred stock usually does not entitle its holders to elect the corporation's board of directors. This can be an advantage to the issuing firm because preferred stockholders, unlike holders of common stock, usually do not have a voice in controlling the business operations of a firm. The second type of stock, **common stock,** gives stockholders voting rights to elect the board of directors. Through their right to elect directors, common stockholders can indirectly influence the operations and decisions of a firm.

Preferred stockholders must be paid dividends before common stockholders. If the corporation goes out of business, the assets of the corporation would be sold. The money from the sale would be used to pay creditors first. If there were any remaining money, the preferred stockholders would be paid for their investment next. The common stockholders would be paid last.

Today many corporations raise long-term equity capital by issuing both kinds of stock. The chief advantage of long-term equity financing is that it provides an efficient means of raising large sums of capital. The firm is under no obligation to repay stockholders for their investment. In fact, the issuing firm does not even guarantee that profits will be distributed to stockholders. The board of directors can distribute such earnings in the form of dividends or it may retain them either partly or wholly in the firm. The decision as to how to distribute the earnings rests entirely with the board. However, it is common practice for the board to seek the advice of financial management when making decisions of this nature.

PUTTING IT ALL TOGETHER—THE DAVECO CORPORATION

You were introduced to the DAVECO Corp. in Chapter 9. DAVECO is a small corporation which manufactures skiing equipment. The firm is headquartered in Vermont. David O'Brien is the company president; Lisa Certo is the firm's financial manager. To gain a better understanding of the vital role of finance, let's see how Lisa puts the principles of financial management to work at DAVECO.

At the outset it must be noted that DAVECO is tied into the nation's financial system in a variety of ways. It borrows from a commercial bank when it needs short-term loans. When it sells its common stock or bonds, it does so through the OTC market.

Now take a look at Figure 10-6. This figure represents the sources of funds that DAVECO uses to finance its needs. The percentages were calculated by using Figure 9-6, DAVECO's balance sheet. Notice that trade credit is used to finance the firm's accounts payable, a short-term liability. Income taxes payable and salaries payable are also considered short-term liabilities. Long-term debt (bonds), equity (common stock), and retained earnings represent 83 percent of the funds that DAVECO uses to finance the company's long-term needs.

Closer examination of DAVECO's balance sheet (Figure 9-6) would show that DAVECO uses $171,000 out of $266,000, or slightly more than 60 percent of its capital, to fund regular business operations. Therefore efficient management of working capital is vitally important to the firm's profitability.

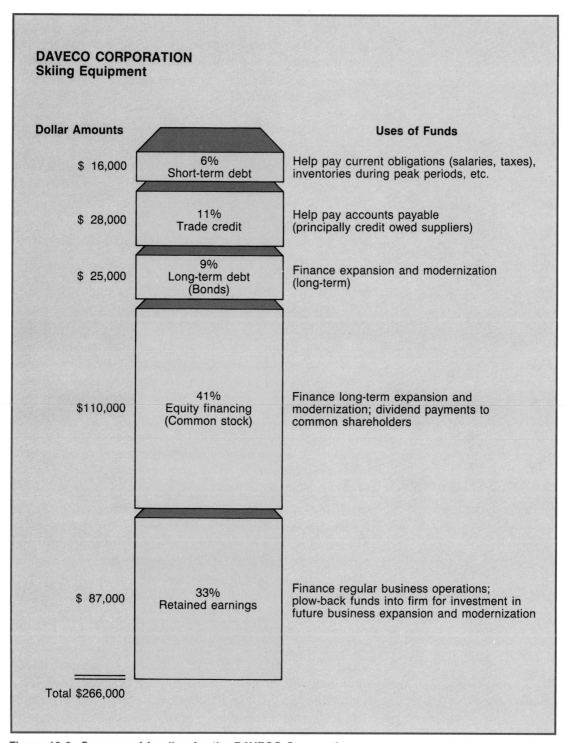

DAVECO CORPORATION
Skiing Equipment

Dollar Amounts

Uses of Funds

$ 16,000 — 6% Short-term debt — Help pay current obligations (salaries, taxes), inventories during peak periods, etc.

$ 28,000 — 11% Trade credit — Help pay accounts payable (principally credit owed suppliers)

$ 25,000 — 9% Long-term debt (Bonds) — Finance expansion and modernization (long-term)

$110,000 — 41% Equity financing (Common stock) — Finance long-term expansion and modernization; dividend payments to common shareholders

$ 87,000 — 33% Retained earnings — Finance regular business operations; plow-back funds into firm for investment in future business expansion and modernization

Total $266,000

Figure 10-6. Sources of funding for the DAVECO Corporation.

Managing DAVECO's Working Capital

Since DAVECO is a manufacturing business, Lisa is aware that the firm's working capital will be needed all during its production cycle. This cycle begins when customers place their orders for the firm's products. The production cycle unfolds in five steps.

1. DAVECO buys raw materials to use in making the ski equipment. The company uses trade credit from suppliers to buy the raw materials. The trade credit is considered a current liability on DAVECO's balance sheet and recorded in accounts payable.

2. The employees turn the raw materials into finished products. The salaries are not always fully paid when the work is completed. The company therefore has another current liability in the form of salaries payable. Revenues generated from the sale of the company's products and short-term debt are used to meet this short-term obligation.

3. The finished goods are then sold to customers who usually do not pay in cash. Most customers pay DAVECO on credit every 30, 60, or 90 days. This is considered an asset on DAVECO's balance sheet and recorded in accounts receivable.

4. Lisa makes sure that DAVECO pays its accounts payable, secured through trade credit, very promptly to take advantage of discounts offered by suppliers.

5. The accounts receivable are collected from customers in the form of cash. Frequent credit reminders are sent to customers, encouraging them to make prompt payments. In this way Lisa makes sure that sufficient revenues are generated to pay the company's other operating expenses, including salaries, rent, utilities, and the like. Short-term debt is also used to pay for these obligations.

Throughout this five-step cycle, Lisa seeks to implement the working capital policy of her firm. The goal of that policy is to ensure that the firm has a positive cash flow—that more money is coming into the firm than leaving it. DAVECO uses the excess cash generated in this way together with some short-term borrowing to finance its inventory needs, especially during peak business periods. It is clear that Lisa manages the firm's working capital effectively to meet the company's short-term needs.

Capital Budgeting at DAVECO

Lisa is also involved in capital budgeting decisions for DAVECO. The firm has adopted a five-year plan for modernizing its equipment and expanding its facilities. Internal financing, in the form of retained earnings, the sale of stock, and long-term debt (bonds), will be used to finance these long-term projects.

Lisa is conservative in her approach to finance. She believes that overreliance on long-term debt will saddle the firm with burdensome interest payments for years into the future. Repayment of the loan with interest could become a problem if there is a slowdown in business. An inability to repay the debt might result in the bankruptcy of the firm. Therefore, she is determined to use only a modest amount of debt, through the sale of bonds, to finance the firm's long-term projects. The firm's current level of long-term debt is just 9 percent for this reason. Clearly, increasing amounts of long-term debt will be needed to finance the projects in DAVECO's capital budget. Lisa has put a ceiling of 25 percent as the portion of long-term debt that can be used to fund the company's long-term needs.

The firm also has plans to "go public" with a new offering of common stock to be sold on the OTC market. Lisa has studied conditions on the stock markets, and she believes that many thousands of dollars in equity capital can be raised in this way. Investors are attracted to DAVECO's common stock. The company has paid dividends for five straight years, a sign of its financial health and good standing in its industry. That is one reason why DAVECO has been able to finance 41 percent of its long-term needs by equity financing. (See Figure 10-6.)

Internal financing will also be used to fund the company's long-term projects. Thanks largely to Lisa's sound financial management, DAVECO for many years has been able to retain about 33 percent of its profits even after paying out dividends. As a result, the company has built up a cash reserve large enough to help it fund many of its short- and long-term needs from retained earnings.

DAVECO, then, projects an image of a well-run and a well-financed company. However, this is more than an image. It is a reality. The firm has a positive cash flow. It is profitable. DAVECO's financial statements indicate that it is a strong company. DAVECO and its managers have a motto, "Pride in Performance." Thanks to Lisa Certo, DAVECO can take pride in its favorable performance, based largely on the application of sound financial principles and practices.

Select Terms to Know

capital budgeting	investment banks	pension funds
capital market	investment companies	over-the-counter market
collateral	line of credit	preferred stock
commercial paper	monetary policy	prime rate
common stock	money market	secured loan
debenture bonds	mortgage bonds	trade credit
Federal Reserve System	mutual fund	working capital policy

Review Questions

1. What is the main purpose of banking institutions within our financial system?

2. Name the three ways the Fed controls the money supply.

3. List and briefly describe each of the three general financing alternatives available to a business firm.

4. How does an investment bank differ in purpose from a commercial bank?

5. How does trade credit differ from a short-term loan?

6. What is the difference between an unsecured loan and a secured loan?

7. How is a line of credit used by a business firm?

8. What is the main difference between the financing methods used in working capital policy and capital budgeting?

9. What is the difference between a mortgage bond and a debenture bond?

10. What is the main purpose of long-term equity financing? What effect does it have on the business firm?

Thought and Discussion Questions

1. Why does a corporation hire an investment bank to place its securities into the marketplace instead of doing this on its own?

2. Of the three methods of money control, which do you suppose is most effectively used by the Fed? What are the drawbacks in using the other two?

3. Do you think that the interest rates for short-term borrowing should be higher than that for

long-term borrowing? Why or why not?

4. What factors about a corporation would cause it to sell mortgage bonds or debenture bonds? What factors would be considered in determining the interest rate of bonds?

5. What capital budgeting decisions would have to be made in changing the name of a corporation?

Projects

1. Corporations often advertise the fact that they are attempting to sell debt and equity securities. Page through the *Wall Street Journal*

and other business publications and record the following:

a. The names of companies who are selling

short- and long-term debt. Be sure to name some of the investment banks listed in the advertisements.

   b. Where would you purchase these securities?

   c. What are the conditions of the bond sales (interest rate, maturity date, face value, and so forth).

   d. Find and report on an article which describes the sale of debt or equity financing.

2. Interview financial managers or accountants of several business firms in your community to investigate the use of trade credit.

   a. Does the firm extend or receive trade credit or both?

   b. How do firms encourage buyers to speed up their payments rather than let them have the whole 30-, 60- or 90-day period to pay?

   c. Are there any other forms of trade credit used by the firm?

3. The Nebraska Corn Company lists its sources of funds as short-term borrowing ($50,000), common stock ($10,000,000), retained earnings ($400,000), long-term borrowing ($50,000), and trade credit ($100,000). Prepare a chart that illustrates these uses of funds. The chart numbers should be expressed as numbers and percentages. Use Figure 10-6 as a guide.

4. Use newspapers, periodicals, and discussions with investors to prepare a list of products sold by financial institutions. Include one or two products each for commercial banks, nonbank banks, insurance companies, pension funds, and investment companies. Provide a brief description of each product, advantages of the product as an investment, and fees or costs in purchasing the product.

Case Study: *Financing the New Firm*

Most people would find the formula for a large loan acceptance used by Mr. Yerkes difficult to pull off today. Many people find themselves new to the business community and local lenders. The Chen brothers were no exception. Jim Chen, an accountant, prepared the start-up requirements for their new 2000-square-foot clothing store to be opened in a surburb of a large eastern city. The budget is shown below.

Answer the following questions based upon your opinion and the chapter content:

1. What is the main source of financing for this new firm?

2. Which of the start-up costs would most likely be funded with short-term debt? By long-term debt?

3. The figures listed in the budget are maximums. How could the brothers cut some of the start-up costs?

4. Where would the Chens be most likely to look for financing to start their business?

Advertising	$3,000
Deposits on rental property, telephone, utilities and insurance	4,000
Inventory	60,000
Office supplies	500
Professional services (lawyer, etc.)	3,000
Working capital	115,000
Furniture and equipment	12,000
Improvements to the leased property	130,000
Total	$327,500

CHAPTER 11

Risk and Insurance

"Swinging" into a Liability Suit

It was a pleasant summer afternoon in 1972. Children were busily playing in the backyard of the house owned by Morris and Rosalyn Friedman in Staten Island, New York. Nine-year-old Sylvia Ashwal was one of the visitors to the yard that day. She was riding on a swing that was being pushed by two other visitors, Deborah and Lisa Rosenberg. The swing Sylvia was riding on was purchased from Sears Roe-buck and manufactured by the Turco Manufacturing Co. of Illinois.

When Sylvia somehow broke her leg, Rosalyn Friedman rushed her to the hospital where she was promptly treated. The Friedmans thought the episode was over and would be forgotten. But three years later they were surprised to be in the middle of a huge lawsuit that involved Sears Roebuck, Turco Manufacturing, and neighborhood children Deborah and Lisa Rosenberg.

Learn what happened when the lawsuit went to trial and how risk and insurance fit into this story when you read the end-of-chapter case study, "Playmates or Plaintiffs?" Study this chapter to learn more about how risk and insurance impact business and to help you answer the questions in the end-of-chapter case study.

Business firms face the constant threat of accidental loss. If a firm is unprepared, losses can cost millions of dollars and could even force the business to close. The following incidents, all reported in different states within a recent one-week period, demonstrate the exposure of businesses to potential losses:

- In Indiana, a machine operator was hurt while operating equipment at work. When he sued, the court decided that the manufacturer of the equipment was responsible. The manufacturer, in turn, sued the worker's employer for failure to operate the equipment properly.

- In Vermont, a bus company suspended its formerly profitable bus charter service to hilltop ski resorts. The bus company feared lawsuits resulting from crashes on icy hilltop roads.

- In California, a creative and energetic business partner died, leaving a large void in the management of the business. The business had to call a halt to its plans for expansion.

- In Utah, more than 10 inches of rain fell in 24 hours and flooded a hardware store. The store's entire inventory was destroyed.

From these examples, it's easy to see that business losses can come in many destructive forms. Without some means of protecting itself against such losses, a business would be in a very unsafe position.

In this chapter we will identify some of the major risks and hazards that businesses face. We will also look at several ways to handle these risks, including insurance. You will learn about the major types of insurance available to businesses today.

THE NATURE OF RISK

All of us are faced with risks every day of our lives. If we drive a car, we face the risk of getting in an accident. If we go to a movie rather than study for our math test, we face the risk of failing that test. Or if we simply do anything that we are not supposed to do, we face the risk of being caught.

What Is Risk?

From the examples presented above and from your own experience, you might define risk as the chance of something bad happening. In terms in which insurance companies use it, **risk** is the chance of a loss. The important part of this definition is the word *chance*. When there is risk, there is uncertainty. A loss may occur or it may not. Without the uncertainty, there is no risk. If a delivery truck is totally destroyed in an accident, the risk is turned into reality. If a factory is heated by oil, there is no risk of business interruption through a coal strike because the element of uncertainty would not exist.

Even though you may be uncertain about the possible outcomes of a business situation, you probably have an idea of the different things that could happen. Let's look at a very simple example. Say that you own a department store in the middle of a busy downtown shopping area. During each of the past few years, several of your store windows have been accidentally broken. One time you had trouble with the heating system at the store and had to close for a day. Both a broken window and a bad furnace caused your business to suffer losses.

Loss is the accidental decrease or total disappearance of value. When the window is shattered, it is worth nothing and must be replaced. When the furnace breaks down, it is worthless until it works again. And the furnace causes additional loss because you have to shut the doors to the store if it breaks down during the winter months.

Some losses such as broken windows, a building that has burned down, or an automobile that has been smashed are easy to see. Other losses are more difficult to see. A person may be unable to continue working as a carpenter, for example, because of a back injury. Or a child who has been injured in an accident within a retail store may need professional counseling to overcome the fear of entering a store again.

Clearly, then, there is a relationship between risk and uncertainty of loss. Typically, a business like the department store described above is not concerned about all risks that might result in loss. Usually, a business seeks to protect itself against the most common risks. Let's examine these common risks a bit further.

What Are Common Business Risks?

The most common business risks are personal risks, property risks, and liability risks. **Personal risks** involve the uncertainty of loss due to premature death and physical disability of key people. Death or disability of a company's owner or key employees may leave a serious void in that area of the company. Many firms rely on the unique and specialized talents of individuals such as designers, tailors, and artists. These companies have a high degree of risk in this area.

Property risks involve the direct or indirect loss of property. Property includes such things as a building, land, equipment, and company-owned vehicles. A direct loss may result from the physical damage, destruction, or theft of property. A hailstorm destroying a farmer's crop or a boiler explosion that destroys a company's building are both examples of direct losses. Indirect loss may also result from direct loss of property. For example, if a valuable road working machine is stolen, there is a direct loss because the company no longer has the machine. There is also an indirect loss if the company loses the road building contract because it doesn't have the equipment to finish the job. The salary of the operator may also have to be paid even though the machine is gone.

Liability risks involve financial losses that a firm might suffer if it is held responsible for property damages or injuries suffered by others. In recent years, liability risk has become a growing source of concern to businesses. Juries have awarded huge sums of money to parties suing firms for property damage or personal injury. As a result, the cost of insuring against this risk has risen to unacceptable heights for some firms.

▼ How would you feel if a court has ordered your firm to pay $1 million to an individual who was injured using your company's product? The individual used the product in a manner other than how it was intended to be used. Nevertheless, the court ruled that your company was liable because it did not print a warning notice that the product should not be used in ways other than those for which it was intended.

What Are Methods of Handling Risk?

Once you have identified the potential risks that your business faces, what should you do about them? Most of this chapter is devoted to insurance, which will be explained in detail in a few pages. Your first answer to the question of what to do about risk might be "buy insurance." That's one possible solution but

Figure 11-1. Businesses face many risks. For example, oil spills create a liability risk for shippers because they can be sued for physical and other damages they cause. They may be held responsible for the costs of any required environmental cleanup.

not the only one. What you really need to do is "manage" the risk. **Risk management** is the process of using available sources to minimize the risks faced by a company.

There are four ways that a company can handle risk: avoid it, reduce it, assume it, or transfer it.

Avoiding Risk. When you avoid risk, you eliminate the possibility that it will occur. If you are afraid that the windows of your store will break, you can have them all removed and replaced by solid walls. If you are afraid that one of your employees might be killed in a plane crash, you could tell all your employees that they are not allowed to travel by plane. Although avoiding risk is one possible way to manage risk, it is usually not very practical.

Reducing Risk. Another possible way to manage risk is to reduce it. If you are afraid that the store window might be shattered, you might invest in a special type of glass that is more difficult to break. If you are afraid that the furnace might break down, you can have it serviced regularly and replace the old or worn-out parts. If you are afraid that machinery may be stolen, you can keep it in a closely guarded area. Risk reduction is often a very practical way to manage risk. Some companies install burglar alarms to reduce the risk of break-ins. Others install sprinkler systems to reduce the risk of damage in case there is a fire.

Assuming Risk. You might decide to manage risks by paying for losses directly from company funds. If you set aside a sufficient sum of money every month, for example, you might be able to handle the cost of breakage to the $2000 plate glass window in the front of your store. When you assume the risk yourself, you are actually using **self-insurance.**

For some companies, self-insurance is a practical option, but for others it is too risky. A small company, for example, would probably find it impossible to set aside enough money to cover the huge lawsuit that might be filed by one of its customers or to replace a building destroyed by fire. For this reason, the company may decide to assume some of the risk by setting up a fund of $100,000, for example. It would then buy insurance to pay for the cost of defending itself in lawsuits or a fire where losses might be over $100,000.

Assuming risk is considered a sound way of managing risk when it is planned for in advance. If a firm does not develop a plan to assume certain risks, it is unlikely to set aside the funds needed to pay for possible losses. When this happens, the company can be exposed to very large potential losses.

▼ How would you feel if you had $50,000 set aside as a form of self-insurance but were sued for $150,000 by a customer who was injured in your store?

Transferring Risk. The most popular form of risk management is transferring the risk. When a company buys insurance, it transfers the risk of loss to the insurance firm, which pays for certain types of losses.

To get a better idea of the way that insurance works, let's look again at our department store example. Say that you and 19 other store owners in your area were all concerned about having to pay $2000 to replace broken store windows. You could all set up a special "broken window fund" and each of you could contribute $100 to the fund. The fund wouldn't protect you from having your windows broken, but it would protect you from having to pay the full $2000 to have them replaced if they were broken. You are sharing the risk with the other store owners who contribute to the fund. If your windows are broken, the fund will pay you the $2000 to have them replaced, even though you have only paid $100 into the fund.

What happens if two or three stores have their windows broken at the same time? Then the broken window fund wouldn't work as well. But insurance companies share the risk among many thousands of businesses.

You will be better equipped to understand a discussion of insurance, if you understand some basic terms. Those terms are defined in Table 11-1 on page 244.

RISK MANAGEMENT AND INSURANCE

Today there is a widely held view that every business should be engaged in risk management to some degree. Generally speaking, the more a business is exposed to financial loss due to risk, the more it needs to be concerned about risk management. With that in mind, let's look a bit more closely at the goal of risk management. Then we will discuss insurance, the major tool of risk management.

TABLE 11-1 Definitions of Some Basic Insurance Terms

Term	Definition
Insurance	A system for protecting against losses by sharing the risk. Those that seek protection pay regularly into a fund that is used to pay for losses they suffer.
Premium	A regular payment made by an insured business to the insurance company.
Insurer	The company that sells the insurance.
Insured	The person or organization covered by insurance.
Policy	Legal contract to provide insurance.
Deductible	The amount that the insured agrees to pay per accident toward the total amount of the loss.
Damages	The amount a court awards the person who brings suit (the plaintiff) in a successful lawsuit.

The Goal of Risk Management

Management of risk involves a specific goal. This goal is to maintain enough cash flow for the firm to operate following a loss. A substantial loss may result in the interruption of business activity. Many companies have a risk manager who specializes in the following activities:

1. *Studying the risks associated with doing business and identifying the specific areas where the firm is exposed to risk.* This requires knowledge of the firm's equipment, operations, income, products, employees, customers, and industry. Fraud, physical damage to assets, product liability, potential lawsuits, death of owner or employees, and management of employee benefit plans are all areas to be investigated by the risk manager for potential risk.

2. *Selecting the best means of protection against the risks faced by the firm.* After identifying the exposure to risk by the firm, the firm's management must determine the level of protection it desires.

3. *Implementing and evaluating the form of protection.* Many risk managers undertake a yearly risk management review. They do so because the nature of business constantly

changes and new risks may emerge. The costs of insurance and employee benefits need to be reviewed periodically too. Based on such reviews, some firms may find that it is less costly to set aside money to cover losses rather than to pay insurance premiums.

Insurance Protection

Insurance is best used where the risk of loss is low but the cost of a loss would be catastrophic. Insurance companies are in business to assume risk. There are certain conditions, however, that must be present for insurance companies to survive. The most important of these conditions is the principle of insurable risk. The principle of insurable risk states that the risk of loss cannot be covered unless there is the possibility of an economic loss. An insurable risk is distinguished from other types of risk by one major quality or characteristic.

The risk must be "pure" and not "speculative." A *pure risk* is one that can result in loss but cannot result in gain for the business. The risk of fire is a pure risk. If your business burns, it will probably cost you a great deal of money to repair it. If it does not burn, you won't necessarily profit from the fact that a fire did not occur. A *speculative risk* is one that offers both the chance of loss and the chance of profit. If you are in the candy making business and decide to introduce a new type of candy bar, there is a risk. You have to invest money in such things as the ingredients, wrapper design, advertising, and marketing. Your new candy bar may be a success or it may be a failure. If it is a failure, you lose money. But if it is a success, you make a profit. Because there is a chance that you can make a profit, the risk is not insurable.

There is another condition of insurance to consider. It is too expensive to purchase insurance for very small losses. The paperwork necessary to file for or repay this type of loss would be too costly. Therefore, most insurance policies are sold with a **deductible clause** in which the policyholder pays part of the loss and the insurance company will pay any amount over that amount. Automobile and certain other kinds of property insurance policies usually include deductible clauses.

▼ How would you feel if you just purchased a new car and your insurance agent suggested a policy with a deductible of $2,000—that is, you pay for the first $2,000 of damage to the car?

Information Brief 11-1

The New Role of the Risk Manager

The risk manager is beginning to assume a high degree of visibility in business. When Gina Pauli first began her job as risk manager at DataPhase Corporation, she was expected to protect the firm from catastrophic loss. Now, however, risk management involves more than using insurance to protect a firm. It means managing risks which at one time were unforeseen or considered unimportant.

Pollution, which is not insurable; political risk, which may not be insurable; and liability, which may be too costly to insure, all pose new problems for the business firm. Employee benefits and pension fund management are also part of Gina's duties.

Source: Derived from Mary Rowland, "The Changing Role of the Risk Manager," *Insurance Review*, January 1987, pp. 26 and 28.

Using Cellular to Sell Insurance

Working longer hours and still going home early! Seems like a contradiction doesn't it? Insurance agents are finding that they can do both with the help of cellular mobile telephones.

Before the cellular phone, insurance agents had a difficult decision to make. The more days they can spend getting out and visiting clients, the more sales they can make. But three or four days each week should be spent making telephone calls to prospective clients and setting up appointments. And when the telephone was connected by a long cord to the wall of an office or a house, agents had to make most of their calls from there.

The cellular phone has solved the problem. This phone can be used just about anywhere. Now insurance agents can set up appointments from wherever they are on the road. If they are away from the car, they can use their briefcase phones. Agents with cellular phones can make important calls while driving, sitting in traffic, or waiting for meetings with clients. They can confirm appointments on the way to them and change appointments as necessary.

Cellular phones send messages via radio waves. They go from the agent's car or portable phone to "cell" stations that are placed at convenient locations throughout the calling area. A central switching station automatically connects the radio waves to the regular public phone network. It also switches the signal from one receiving tower to the next one as the car travels along the road.

With the help of cellular phones, insurance agents can receive calls from clients while they are driving. In the past, they received messages when they called in from pay phones and generally returned the calls later.

Agents can also receive quick answers to questions by using their cellular phones. The agent who had just visited a client can call the office and get answers to technical questions. Then, he or she can call the client back in a matter of minutes. If a specific price quote is needed, the information can be gathered quickly—often quicker than other agents who have to drive back to the office. Time, in this case, leads to greater sales volume.

What technology is expected next? The *(Continued)*

Japanese are now selling facsimile machines that can transmit documents from a car phone to a destination over the cellular phone network. We can soon look for ultralight portable cellular phones that are no larger than a wallet. All these advances will help insurance agents to better serve clients as they use their "offices on the go."

Sources: Adapted from Ellen Ryan, "Take Your Office on the Road," *Insurance Review*, January/February 1985; Berton G. Latamore, "Cellular Systems Ease Mobile Phone Woes," *High Technology*, July 1986; Gary W. Ozanich, "Trafficking in Cellular Radio Technology," *Computerworld*, no date available; and John Keller et al., "Hello Anywhere," *Business Week*, September 21, 1987, pp. 84–92.

TYPES OF INSURANCE PROVIDERS

You may think only of private insurance companies when you think of insurance. But insurance is provided by both private companies and government agencies. In fact, the government is the largest single provider of insurance in the United States.

Government Insurance

The main types of government insurance are social security, workers' compensation, and unemployment compensation.

Social Security. Social security is designed to provide Americans with some economic insurance against loss of income from retirement, disability, illness, and the death of a wage earner. The funds for social security come from a payroll tax shared equally by employees and employers. Social security taxes withheld from a worker's wages are identified as **FICA** (Federal Insurance Contributions Act) taxes. Deductions are deposited in social security trust funds.

Workers' Compensation. **Workers' compensation** is insurance which compensates employees who are injured on the job regardless of fault. This form of insurance is considered public insurance because it is required by law. The actual insurance is purchased from private firms. Medical expenses and a portion of lost income are paid while the worker is out of work due to the injury. If an employee is killed from a work-related accident, the survivors receive workers' compensation payments. Business firms pay the premiums for workers' compensation insurance. The original intent of workers' compensation laws was to provide a predetermined schedule of payments for workers while they were injured or disabled. In turn, the employee gave up the right to sue the employer.

Information Brief 11-2

The Crisis in Workers' Comp

Is workers' compensation (workers' comp) growing beyond its original design? Some employers think so.

In its early years workers' comp was seen as an effective solution to on-the-job injuries. Now, however, some employers think they are the injured ones. Why? Costs for this type of insurance have risen steeply as the definition of injury has been broadened to include such things as mental and emotional stress to injured workers and occupational diseases.

This has led to a crisis in workers' comp. Some businesses will not locate in states where workers' comp benefits have been expanded. The high cost or difficulty in obtaining the insurance is the prime reason.

Sources: Resa W. King, "The Worsening Ills of Workers' Comp," *Business Week*, October 12, 1987, p. 46; Carey W. English, "Cutting Costs, Abuses in Disability Insurance," *U.S. News and World Report*, May 28, 1984; Mary Rowland, "Workers' Comp Under Stress," *Insurance Review*, December 1986.

Unemployment Insurance. Unemployment compensation programs provide weekly income benefits to unemployed workers. Each state has its own program which is financed by employers. Unemployed workers are usually compensated up to two-thirds of their regular income. Business firms can reduce their unemployment compensation premiums by providing a stable work force. They must also cooperate to prevent payment of unjustified claims.

Private Insurance Companies

Private insurance companies are organized either as stock companies or as mutual companies. A **stock company** is a corporation which is owned by its stockholders and operated to make a profit. A **mutual company** is a corporation which is owned by its policyholders, not by stockholders. The policyholders are paid dividends or given reductions in premiums if excess money is available. Both types of companies sell various types of insurance. They are involved mainly in the business insurance programs described in the next section.

BUSINESS INSURANCE

Business insurance protects against losses in four major risk areas: loss of property, liability losses, loss of earning power, and loss due to dishonesty or nonperformance.

Loss of Property

There are many forms of insurance available to protect against property losses. The two most common are fire and marine insurance.

Property (or fire) insurance policies cover loss or destruction of buildings, fixtures, machinery, equipment, or other property resulting from fire. These policies may be extended to cover losses resulting from hazards associated with fire, such as wind, water, smoke damage, and explosion. Special terms may even be added to fire insurance policies to protect business property against other kinds of disasters, such as lightning, earthquakes, and hailstorms.

Fire Insurance. Each policy describes the perils covered, property covered, types of losses covered, person or persons named in the policy, location of property, the time the insurance begins, and hazards not covered by the policy.

Fire insurance policies also cover **consequential losses** which are those resulting from but not directly caused by the fire. A fire which destroys a refrigeration unit in a restaurant is covered by fire insurance. If food is spoiled due to the fire damages to the refrigerator, the restaurant has suffered a consequential loss.

Most fire insurance policies are sold with a coinsurance clause. **Coinsurance** means that the insured must maintain a certain amount of insurance based on the value of the building. This amount is expressed as a percentage of value. For example, a retail store is valued at $100,000. The firm is insured by a policy that contains a coinsurance clause of 80 percent. If the owner buys $80,000 of property insurance on the store, any loss of up to $80,000 will be covered in full by the insurance company. However, if the store purchases less than the required $80,000 coinsurance amount, the insurance company will pay only a specified portion or percentage of any fire loss. The owner of the store would bear the burden of paying for the remainder of the loss as a coinsurer.

To illustrate how coinsurance works, let's use the example of the retail store again. Suppose the store purchased only $40,000 of fire insurance and not the required $80,000 amount. In that case the insurance company would pay the store for only one-half of any fire loss because $40,000 is one-half (50 percent) of the required $80,000 coinsurance amount. The remainder of any loss would be the responsibility of the store owner as a coinsurer. Suppose, then, that a fire causes a $40,000 loss to the store. How much of this loss would the insurance company actually cover? The answer is $20,000, or just 50 percent of the loss and no more. The store owner would be responsible for the remaining $20,000 portion of the loss as a coinsurer.

▼ The premiums on your fire (property) insurance policy have been steadily increasing for the past five years, but you have never experienced a major loss. One of the managers has suggested that you drop your insurance coverage and that you self-insure against property loss. Would you go this route, taking the risk of not knowing how much it may cost you in claims, or would you stick with the insurance policy that will cover all your losses, regardless of how large they might be?

Marine Insurance. **Marine insurance** covers perils to goods being transported by water or land. Risks in shipping goods exist on all waterways as well as by ground transportation. The two branches of marine insurance are ocean and inland.

Ocean marine insurance covers vessels and the cargo they carry. The coverage includes time when they are at sea, on lakes, and in inland waterways.

Inland marine insurance is somewhat of a contradiction in terms. It really has nothing to do with insuring ships or their cargoes. Instead, it provides financial protection for anything you can ship. This includes contractor's equipment, jewelry, and cargo carried by truck or railroad.

Liability

A second major risk area that is covered by private insurance companies is liability. Liability risk arises from tort law. (See Chapter 7 for an explanation of tort law.) Liability insurance and workers' compensation normally fall into this category. While property insurance repays business owners for direct or indirect losses to property, liability insurance protects them from claims made against their companies by others. General liability insurance covers losses resulting from (1) conditions of the business property, (2) business operations, (3) products liability, and (4) completed operations. Let's look more closely at these areas.

Liability for Business Premises. The first two risks involve the business premises itself. Businesses are expected to maintain their property so that customers will not be hurt. A faulty elevator, a loose tile on the floor or ceiling, or an unmarked glass door all represent hazards for which the business could be sued if injury to customers result.

A firm may also be held liable for injuries resulting from the actions of its employees. For example, suppose an employee is repairing a light fixture in a store and drops it on a customer. The store can be held liable for injuries to the customer resulting from such employee actions.

Liability for Goods and Services. Product liability involves products after they have left the firm. A retail, manufacturing, or wholesale business may be liable for injury or damages from defective products. The defect may result from improper testing or design. The liability may even result from failure of the business to foresee possible abuse or even misuse of the product.

Liability may also apply to completed operations. Typically such liability arises from work completed by professionals in the plumbing, electrical, or repair businesses. For example, suppose a hot water heater explodes after it has been installed in your store by a plumber. If the installation was faulty, the plumber can be held liable for any damage to your store or injury to persons resulting from the explosion.

Another important type of liability insurance protects professionals such as doctors, lawyers, and architects from losses. **Malpractice insurance** covers losses due to damages or injuries caused by the insured while performing professional services for clients.

Liability Insurance Costs. Liability insurance has become a center of controversy in recent years. Huge settlements in lawsuits have increased the cost of premiums and decreased the availability of certain types of insurance. The most affected areas are insurance for product liability, workers' compensation, and malpractice. Figure 11-2 shows how members of the Small Business Service Bureau are coping with the high costs of liability insurance. The organization has 35,000 members who are firms with less than $3 million in annual sales.

Figure 11-2. This survey shows what some small businesses are doing in response to soaring rates for liability insurance. (Source: Small Business Service Bureau.)

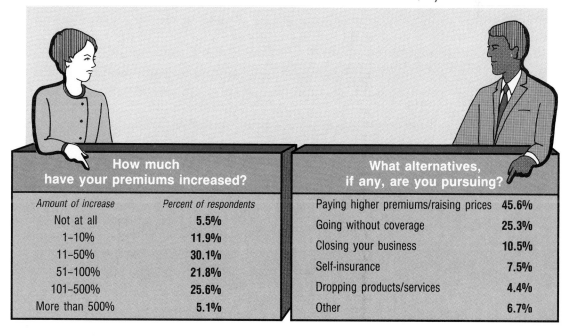

How much have your premiums increased?		What alternatives, if any, are you pursuing?	
Amount of increase	*Percent of respondents*		
Not at all	5.5%	Paying higher premiums/raising prices	45.6%
1–10%	11.9%	Going without coverage	25.3%
11–50%	30.1%	Closing your business	10.5%
51–100%	21.8%	Self-insurance	7.5%
101–500%	25.6%	Dropping products/services	4.4%
More than 500%	5.1%	Other	6.7%

The cost crunch has caused some firms to adopt nontraditional methods to insure against liability losses. One nontraditional method even has members of industrial groups or associations forming their own insurance companies. The companies are run for the benefit of the policyholders—all members of a specific industry group. Still another nontraditional method involves individual firms using large deductibles. They thereby make themselves coinsurers for any liability losses.

Loss of Earning Power

Another major risk area that can be protected by insurance is loss of earning power. Life insurance, annuities, and retirement plans are part of the employee benefit package offered by many firms. Benefits provide money, when needed, to employees and management. These forms of insurance along with health insurance make up the typical employee benefit package. Together they represent almost 40 percent of all payroll costs to employers.

Life Insurance. **Life insurance** pays a set amount to survivors in the event of death. In a business firm it is used in two ways. First, it is offered to employees as a fringe benefit. Secondly, the firm becomes the policyholder for life insurance on its key employees. The firm has an insurable interest in the lives of top managers or owners whose financial interest or expertise are key to the firm's continued operation.

Health Insurance. Employers paid over $90 billion to health insurance benefit plans in one recent year. Business firms are under heavy pressure from high costs to provide new and less expensive types of health benefits. The health care industry has also undergone changes that have introduced more competition based upon cost. Among the more rapidly growing trends are:

1. *The use of preferred-provider organizations* in which firms buy care at a discount if they use physicians and hospitals listed by the insurer. Employees may be nonparticipating members, but they typically have to pay twice as much to use the same physicians and hospitals.
2. *Health-maintenance organizations (HMOs)* are clinic-type operations which require employees to pick and use doctors

and hospitals from a prescribed list. HMOs may be available for dental insurance, too.

3. *Set-asides of cash funds for employee health care needs.* After the employee pays a deductible, all additional costs are drawn from the health care fund. If money remains at the end of the year, the excess funds are paid to the employee or put into a retirement plan.

Many firms are attempting to reduce health care loss by starting wellness programs, including tests for high blood pressure, in-house gyms, nutrition clinics, and health counseling. Antismoking programs have also been introduced to lower health costs and to increase employee productivity.

Annuities and Retirement Plans. An **annuity** is investment income that is payable to a person at regular intervals over a period of time. Annuities are often used as part of employee retirement plans. Through these plans persons pay into the annuity while they are employed. Then annuity payments are made to them when they retire. For example, a person may receive $300 per month for a number of years. Insurance companies sometimes manage annuity and retirement plans for client firms. The insurance company must invest annuity and retirement funds wisely. Funds earned from such investments must allow the insurance company to meet the retirement needs of the client firm's employees and at the same time earn a profit for the insurance company itself.

Loss Due to Nonperformance or Dishonesty

Dishonest people both inside and outside the company can also be serious risks to a business. Bonding and crime insurance can protect against losses caused by such risks.

Bonding. A **bond** is a legal agreement where a party agrees to reimburse another party for losses resulting from an individual's failure to fulfill an obligation. Bonds provide guarantees against loss through incapacity or dishonesty of individuals who are entrusted with money, property, or some major responsibility and who violate their trust. Surety and fidelity bonds are most commonly used by business firms.

A **surety bond** is typically used to insure that someone fulfills an obligation. These bonds are issued by surety companies. The company agrees to make good any default on the part of the person for whom the bond was issued. For example, a building contractor may commit to constructing a building meeting certain specifications. A surety bond may be issued to guarantee that the contractor fulfills his or her part of the contract. If the building does not meet the required specifications, the individual with whom the contractor entered the agreement may receive payment from the surety bond.

The second type of bond, a **fidelity bond,** is similar in nature to a surety bond, but is used to protect a company from dishonest employees. Should a company experience a loss due to an employee's dishonesty (for example, if an employee embezzled money from the company), the company could recover the loss from the fidelity bond. Fidelity bonds may be issued to cover a single employee or a whole group of employees within a business firm.

Crime Insurance. Finally, the area of **crime insurance** is primarily concerned with losses experienced due to robbery, burglary, or theft. Burglary is defined as the unlawful taking of property when the business is closed. A burglary also includes the forced entry into the business. Robbery takes place when the robber takes property by force or by threat of violence. Theft is a very broad term that describes taking of property that is not classified as either burglary or robbery. A swindle that results in lost property is an example of theft.

A business can purchase a variety of insurance products to protect itself against criminal losses. The insurance coverage can be narrow or broad in scope. An example of narrow coverage is insurance against property loss from the break-in of a safe. Broad coverage would allow a business to protect itself against most forms of crime.

The types of insurance described in this chapter are only representative of the total insurance offering. Many other risks may be measured and insured. Lack of risk management can only hurt a firm—there is no chance to reduce or avoid losses resulting from risks that can hamper or destroy a business.

Select Terms to Know

annuity	damages	insured
bond	deductible	insurer
coinsurance	fidelity bonds	liability risks
consequential losses	insurance	life insurance

loss
malpractice insurance
marine insurance
mutual company
personal risks

policy
premium
principle of insurable risk
property risks
risk

risk management
self-insurance
stock company
surety bond
workers' compensation

Review Questions

1. What is risk?

2. Classify and briefly discuss the three kinds of business risks.

3. What are the four methods of handling risk?

4. Briefly describe the elements of an insurable risk.

5. Describe the main difference between a stock insurance company and a mutual insurance company.

6. How are consequential losses tied to direct losses?

7. What is coinsurance?

8. What risk is insured under marine insurance?

9. Cite one example of when a business firm can be held liable for (*a*) the conditions of the firm's premises and (*b*) goods or services it provides. Give one example of liability that may be imposed on a business firm or individual for malpractice.

10. What are the two major forms of bonding?

Thought and Discussion Questions

1. Some argue that insurance and gambling are the same. Why are such arguments incorrect?

2. Do you agree with the idea that insurance actually reduces competition because it reduces the risk of business losses? Explain your answer.

3. Describe some ways that individuals can avoid, reduce, assume, and transfer risk.

4. How can a mutual insurance company be a corporation when it has no stockholders?

5. If workers' compensation insurance premiums are based on job injuries, what is the effect on business, workers, and society if the definition includes emotional and mental stress?

Projects

1. Assume that a group of homeowners agree that if any owner's home is damaged by fire, the other owners will cover the losses. From data gathered by the group, there would probably be 100 fires each year with an average cost of $20,000 (homes are rarely completely destroyed). There are 10,000 homeowners in this pool, and each home has a value of $80,000.

a. What is the total amount of estimated losses each year?

b. To compute the pool of funds needed, how much would it cost each homeowner to cover the anticipated losses?

c. What are the shortcomings of such a plan?

d. What other categories would an insurance company need to add to the estimated dollar figure to arrive at a premium?

2. Visit several local business firms to find out how they manage risk. Prepare a list of questions in advance, which may include:

   a. What types of risk management tools are used for various kinds of perils?
   b. In what ways is insurance used to manage risk—types of insurance, deductibles, and so forth?
   c. Is the firm covered by workers' compensation insurance? What are some of the state regulations regarding the collection of this type of insurance?
   d. What is the employer contribution toward unemployment insurance?

3. Obtain a property insurance policy and make a list of the direct and consequential losses which are covered.

4. The Dataflow Company has a building valued at $500,000. Their insurance company asks that they maintain a coinsurance percentage of 80 percent. Dataflow has not checked its coverage in several years and thinks that its building is worth $300,000. If they sustain a fire loss of $50,000, how much would they collect? If Dataflow wanted to purchase coverage at 100 percent of the value, the premium increase between the 80 percent and full coverage would be quite small. Why?

5. Sally Dennis, the new risk manager for the Tower Bottling Company, has decided to evaluate the present risk handling techniques of the firm. She has been told that there has been some employee dissatisfaction with the current plan. During the past year, the firm has seen a larger-than-normal turnover. The chief financial officer has also made the statement that the business assumes too much risk for a firm of its size. Management is willing to make some changes—even spend more money to improve employee morale. Sally surveyed the company's risk management plans, and her findings are presented

TABLE 11-2 Tower Bottling Company: Risk Management Survey

Type of Risk	Method of Handling Risk
Fire damages	100 percent coverage on buildings, but only direct losses are covered.
Product damages during transportation	Ocean marine insurance.
Worker injuries on the job	Workers' compensation insurance; the firm does only what is required by law, no more.
Legal liability	Covers accidents on the premises up to $1 million in combined claims per year.
Death of workers or key personnel	Life insurance is provided as a fringe benefit to employees.
Retirement of employees	Pays into social security fund.
Illness of employees	Offers choice of regular health insurance plan or HMO to its employees.

in Table 11-2. Analyze the risks and risk handling techniques and make recommendations for each risk regarding:

   a. Alternate methods of handling the risk

   b. Suggestions for saving money consistent with the goal of protecting cash flow

   c. Changes in the current plan that would improve employee morale

Case Study: Playmates or Plaintiffs

In the chapter opening, you learned about 9-year-old Sylvia Ashwal's broken leg. Morris and Rosalyn Friedman were shocked when they were named in a lawsuit three years after the accident. But they weren't the only ones sued. Sears Roebuck, which sold them the swing, Turco Manufacturing Company, which made the swing, and the little Rosenberg girls who pushed the swing were also sued.

Why did the Ashwals file suit? Sylvia's fractured leg had stopped growing. She walked with a limp, couldn't sit or stand for very long, and had continuous back pain. The family even resorted to an operation on Sylvia's good leg but couldn't correct the problem.

Sylvia's lawyer contended that the swing was so poorly designed that Sylvia's leg could easily be caught between the seat and the platform below. But both Sears Roebuck and Turco Manufacturing said that the accident was really Sylvia's fault. She should have been sitting on the swing and she was standing. The Rosenberg children who were pushing the swing said they didn't cause the accident. They just pushed the swing.

The final outcome of the trial was a $2.5 million verdict awarded to Sylvia. Most of it was to cover her medical care. And who paid for the suit? Not the Friedmans or the Rosenbergs. They were cleared! Turco was told to pay 80 percent of the amount and Sears was told to pay the remaining 20 percent.

Although both companies believed that they were not to blame, they chose to settle the matter for a lesser amount ($1.35 million) rather than take the matter through the appeal process.

Source: Adapted from "From Playmate to Plaintiff," *U. S. News and World Report,* January 27, 1986, p. 37.

1. Why do you think that the jury decided that Sears and Turco Manufacturing should have been held liable for Sylvia's injuries?

2. Do you feel that they should be held liable and asked to pay?

3. What parts of a liability insurance policy would probably have covered this lawsuit?

4. If you were Sylvia Ashwal's parents, would you have sued? If so, whom would you have sued?

5. Do you think Sears or Turco should have appealed the verdict and gone back to trial?

Analyzing a Corporation's Annual Report

Public corporations issue quarterly or annual reports to their shareholders. The annual report is a comprehensive report that contains valuable financial information. Much of this data is found on the balance sheet, income statement, and the statement of changes in financial information, which generally appear in the annual report. (See Chapter 9 for an explanation of these financial statements.) In addition to these statements, the annual report usually includes a section titled "Notes to the Financial Statements." This section provides useful information about how and why the firm is handling financial and risk management the way it is.

So you can understand their usefulness to shareholders and others, let's take a look at the notes found in the annual report of one typical but imaginary corporation, the WEBCO Corporation. As you read on, notice how often the terms and concepts that you studied in Unit 4 appear in the notes.

FINANCIAL CONDITION OF THE WEBCO CORPORATION

Our corporation required cash before financing activities of $70 million compared to $10 million last year. The cash use this year was primarily due to continued implementation of our manufacturing restructuring program begun last year. The program was designed to streamline our design, purchasing, manufacturing, and distribution networks so that they operate at substantially higher efficiency levels.

WORKING CAPITAL AT WEBCO

Another reason for increased cash use was our greater working capital needs. The higher accounts receivable level this year was primarily the result of increased sales in the fourth quarter as compared to last year. The increase in our inventories was less than that of the past two years. Our corporation maintains a bank line of credit of $3 million. The unused portion at the end of the year was $500,000. Periodic borrowing under the line of credit is at the bank's prime rate. Borrowing institutions may also be used to support the issuance of commercial paper in the United States and European markets through dealers at the best market rates.

The current assets–to–current liabilities ratio was 1.6 for the year ended compared to 1.4 last year. The change was primarily the result of high accounts receivable levels.

CAPITAL BUDGETING AT WEBCO

Of the $67 million charged against restructuring reserves, $50 million related to spending for the manufacturing restructuring program, with the remainder relating to the acquisition of the Arch Corporation. Improved earnings and reduced dividends partially offset the effects of these increased cash requirements.

Cash requirements this year were financed primarily by the issuance of long-term debt. This year and last our corporation reduced certain higher-cost, long-term debt with the proceeds from sales of equity and through borrowing. This borrowing included the issuance of $90 million of 10-year debenture bonds. Our corporation's debt to total capital was 40 percent at the end of the year compared to 38 percent last year. Our corporation has one class of common stock with 60 million shares outstanding. Our corporation also has 7 million shares of preferred stock available, but no attempt has been made to raise capital by this method.

RISK MANAGEMENT AT WEBCO

Our corporation and its subsidiaries (smaller companies that are part of a larger company) have pension plans covering substantially all their employees. As of the latest valuation, the market value of the assets exceeded the values of guaranteed benefits. In addition to pension benefits, our corporation provides postretirement health care and medical benefits to employees.

DISCUSSION QUESTIONS

It is easy to see that financial notes cover a great variety of financial activity for the year. Read the case again and answer the following:

1. Make a list of terms in the case which were introduced in Unit 4.

2. Would you describe the WEBCO Corp. as a growing business? Explain your answer, citing evidence in the case to support your viewpoint.

3. How is WEBCO financed?

4. What are some of the risk management costs of WEBCO?

american dairy association®
Milk – "The South" :30

MUSIC: UNDER

SING: M-M-M-M-MILK!

MUSIC: FIDDLE SOLO

SFX: COW BELLS

SING: C'MON EVERYBODY...

DO THAT KICK...

HEALTH KICK, MILK'S THAT KICK.

MUSIC: FIDDLE SOLO
SING: WE'RE ALL ON A HEALTH KICK SO COME ON Y'ALL.

MILK'S VITAMINS AND CALCIUM ARE PART OF IT ALL!

SFX: CANNONS

SING: MILK!

WAY DOWN SOUTH TODAY THERE'S JUST ONE THING TO SAY...

AMERICA'S FAVORITE...

HEALTH KICK...

MILK!

U N I T   5

Marketing Management

Marketing personnel are charged with the mission of promoting products and services so as to let customers find out what is available and how to get what they want. Marketing personnel include managers, entrepreneurs, and employees involved in marketing, selling, and distributing products and services. Marketing personnel, especially marketing managers, are usually able to communicate well, both in written and spoken form. An ability to work well with people, information, and technology is also a vital key for success in marketing.

Marketing functions include: advertising (via print, television and the like), promotion, packaging, pricing, market research, selling, and distributing goods and services. The overall objective of Unit 5 is to help you understand these various marketing functions.

UNIT OBJECTIVES

1. Identify the components of the marketing manager's job.
2. Explain the elements of marketing, including the marketing mix.
3. Understand the uses and applications of market research.
4. Describe how pricing and packaging decisions affect the marketing of goods and services.
5. Understand the role of advertising, promotion, personal selling, and distribution in the process of marketing.

The Elements of Marketing and Marketing Research

Software Firm Targets a Market with Built-in Sales Leads

The Gale Research Co. counts over 19,000 associations in the United States. Computer marketers often target promotion of their computer products and services to members of these groups.

Sometimes a "pot of gold" can be earned by those who market to such associations. The Menlo Corporation, a software firm, learned this the hard way, however.

Menlo markets a software program called Pro-Search PC. This software makes it easy for customers to tap into Dialog Information Services, an electronic library of hundreds of journals and research reports. (In fact, as of 1988, Dialog was the world's largest electronic information service. With over 91,000 subscribers in 86 countries, it collects information from more than 320 databases worldwide.) At first Menlo tried to market Pro-Search to many different types of customers. But after burning through $4 million of its $4.5 million in start-up funds (with minimum sales), the firm realized that only librarians were actually buying the software. Then, Menlo did something smart. It began to market its software package to library associations, which usually have many hundreds, even thousands, of members. It would even tailor its marketing campaigns to appeal to such associations.

Study this chapter to learn more about how firms like Menlo apply the elements of marketing and marketing research to business. Also, use the contents to help you answer the questions in the chapter case study, "Tapping a Ready-Made Market."

People engaged in the marketing function are concerned with providing goods and services that consumers need and want. If this concern is not the central focus, then marketers and their firms cannot get customers to buy. In meeting this goal, a marketing manager and his or her staff gather and study data that will help them answer these questions:

- Can our products and services be improved or expanded to reach more people?

- Is there a less costly or better way to market this service or that product?

- Can product and service problems be solved?

- Can the problems in our selling program be solved?

- Can shopping be made more convenient to our customers?

In this chapter you will learn how marketing managers try to answer these and other similar questions.

COMPONENTS OF THE MARKETING MANAGER'S JOB

All managers work through people to get things done, which calls for supervising subordinates. In the marketing department these subordinates constitute the marketing manager's staff. Marketing managers, like managers in other departments, also do planning, organizing, directing, and controlling.

Planning. All managers plan how they and their subordinates are going to reach individual objectives, which is one of their major tasks. An example of a marketing goal is to sell 10,000 products in one month. Marketing managers have a responsibility for achieving goals like this.

For ease of understanding, let us compare the tasks of a marketing manager (such as planning) to those carried out by the chairperson of a student organization when managing a fund-raising activity.

Suppose, as a money-making venture, your student organization decided to sell homemade candy door-to-door. Clearing $3000 profit is the goal. Plans are made for achieving objectives such as buying ingredients, pricing, packaging, and assigning tasks. A committee chairperson (manager) is appointed. This chairperson, together with committee members (subordinates), plan the separate tasks needed to achieve each objective.

Organizing. Managers start putting their plan into action by organizing people, resources, time, and the details of each task. They identify and list needed resources, like materials, machines, records, and people. Resources help people carry out each task. Then a time frame is determined—when tasks are scheduled to start and finish. Likewise, marketing managers organize resources and activities.

For the student fund-raising project, the chair assigns committee members to tasks. Members get needed resources—the candy ingredients and packages and a calculator and typewriter for the people assigned to keep the records and type reports. Other people organize transportation and establish each sales territory. If all goes well by the end of the organization stage, everything is ready to go. Cooks and salespeople are trained. Car drivers know which sales routes to follow. Record-keeping people have set up various accounts. And the advertising people are ready to start the advertising program.

Directing. Managers direct those under them in starting, pursuing, and completing the tasks assigned during the organization stage. Each set of tasks comes under one of the objectives established during the planning step. Managers lead, motivate, and supervise the progress of the plan toward reaching the ultimate goal. The plan is put into action. Similarly, marketing managers direct and activate plans.

The student project chairperson works with subcommittee chairs, who in turn supervise their committee members. Additional resources are obtained, if needed, and progress along the time line is checked to see that everything is on schedule.

The advertising people have made and gotten permission to place posters and have written advertising copy. Fliers are distributed, and announcements are broadcast over the radio. The candy is made and packaged. Salespeople are out selling. Record keepers are keeping track of expenses and revenues and tallying the results against the remaining inventory. Cooks are making more candy to keep up with the demand for products from the salespeople.

Controlling. Managers monitor and evaluate progress. They control costs and evaluate both processes and people. They identify errors and problems and supervise those who work for them in correcting mistakes or solving problems. Marketing managers do this too.

Suppose that, when the student salespeople get out in their territories, they find that another organization has just passed through the neighborhood selling the same type of candy. The potential customers are not buying. Here is a problem! Because this market may be saturated (oversold), the chairperson should look for new markets—new customers and sales territories. (Actually, it would have been better, during the planning and organizing steps, if they had studied the competition and the sales potential of each territory.) See Table 12-1, which depicts how the student organization met its goal.

TABLE 12-1 Student Organization Fund-Raising Planning Chart
Goal: Clear $3000 in net profits from selling homemade candy door-to-door

Function	Objectives	Time	Resources	Assignments
		Week 1		
Planning	Choose ingredients		Parents' menu(s)	Joan and Bob
	Price (to cover expenses, clear profit, etc.)		Going store prices	Paul and Nan
	Choose packages		Check stores	Karl and George
	Check territories		Members' neighborhoods	Sue and Lucy
	Plan advertising		See media people	Chang and Kim
	Design record system		Accounting teacher	Chair
	Get approval		Advisor	Chair
		Week 2		
Organizing	Buy ingredients		Stores; treasury	Joan and Bob
	Set price		Advisor approval	Chair and staff
	Buy packages		Stores; treasury	Karl and George
	Write advertising copy	Week 3	Marketing teacher	Chang and Kim
	Get calculator, typewriter; supplies		School, homes	Paul and Nan
	Line up cars		Homes; members	Pat and Lou
	Train cooks		Home economics teacher	Joan, Bob, Pat
	Train salespeople		Marketing teacher	Kim, Karl, Nan, Chang, Sue, Lucy
	Periodic check of all *organizing* activities	Week 4	Advisor	Chair
		Week 5		
Directing	Place posters		Store windows	Advertising staff
	News releases		Newspapers	Advertising staff
	Radio spots		Radio	Advertising staff
	Cook candy		Chair, advisor	Cooking staff
	Package candy		Chair, advisor	Cooking staff
	Sell candy		Chair, advisor	Sales staff

TABLE 12-1 Student Organization Fund-Raising Planning Chart (continued)

Function	Objectives	Time	Resources	Assignments
	Drive cars		Chair, advisor	Transportation staff
	Keep records		Chair, advisor	Records staff
	Periodic check of all *directing* activities		Advisor	Chair
		Week 6		
Controlling	Check *everything* above		Advisor	Chair
	Check sales staff		Advisor	Chair
	Check records staff		Advisor	Chair
	Verify progress		Advisor	Chair
	Identify problems		Advisor	Chair
	Propose solutions		Brainstorm, check competition	Chair and all members
	Implement Changes		Advisor	Chair, members

Experience and the results of studying the market help managers foresee problems and plan how to effectively overcome them. Once any program is in operation, it's harder to correct errors, including those of misjudgment. Nevertheless, effective managers also *un*plan, as well as plan. Unplanning implies flexibility. As problems emerge, the manager adjusts by making new decisions to solve the emerging problems in order to control the plan toward reaching the established goal.

Knowledge and Skills Needed by the Marketing Manager

The marketing manager draws heavily on knowledge and skills obtained from the academic fields of communications, mathematics, psychology, and sociology. The marketing manager should have the ability to:

- Communicate well and use math correctly.
- Work well and effectively with people.
- Promote products and services.
- Take calculated risks based on sound research data.

According to one national marketing consultant, the most important of these abilities is communication. For example, marketing managers cannot promote their goods and services if messages sent out over TV, radio, and other media are garbled through the use of improper words.

MARKETING ELEMENTS

The marketing elements of product, price, promotion, and place cannot be separated in the decision making process. Therefore, when taken together, these elements are called the **marketing mix.**

Product. Product planning focuses on finding out, mainly through marketing research, which goods and services consumers need and want. The products are then selected and designed, or the services chosen, that will meet these needs and wants.

Price. Setting prices accurately is critical in the marketing mix. If prices are too high, customers won't buy. But if prices are too low, the firm cannot pay all its expenses, and therefore the possibility of making a profit is decreased.

▼ How would you feel if you'd spent a year inventing a new and better device for washing cars, but your car washing service didn't make a profit because you set your price too low to cover expenses?

Promotion. The promotion element in the marketing mix addresses advertising, promotion, and personal selling.

Advertising uses the media, such as radio, television, and magazine and newspaper ads. The logo (symbol) a company uses on its business papers, products, and advertisements promotes the business to its customers. Distributing posters and fliers are other means of promoting a product or service. Billboards, located on highways that approach a town where businesses are located, help promote businesses since they let people know what a firm has to offer. Even the sign a firm uses can be a tool for promotion.

Direct-sales promotion includes but is not limited to:

- Designing displays inside a store and in store windows
- Giving away free samples
- Providing discount coupons
- Offering discount sales

Information Brief 12-1

Keys to Marketing Success

A person with a good idea has to communicate it to others in order to turn dreams into reality. A marketing consultant has these tips for new owners:

1. Prepare an in-depth plan with facts about advertising, market potential, and future growth.

2. Then be able to sell (communicate) the plan to bankers and investors.

3. Look to successful competitors for ideas on how they market their products and services.

4. Find out from consumers what they like.

5. By researching the market, find out about consumer groups and then target them by customizing your marketing campaigns to appeal to their wants and needs.

Sources: "Marketing Consultant Says the Key to Success Is 'Work,'" *Laramie Boomerang,* May 6, 1987, p. 10; and seminar presented by the University of Wyoming Cooperative Extension Service, May 5, 1987.

Figure 12-1. The logo or symbol that a firm uses on its business products or in its advertisements helps promote the company's identity and its products and services to customers. Here NYNEX, a telephone and information services company, uses its "let the fingers do the walking" logo to help promote its yellow pages directory.

Your opportunity to reach the rapidly growing New Jersey Hispanic market

NYNEX
Yellow Pages

- Using games, contests, and sweepstakes

Personal selling takes place when:

- Salesclerks deal directly with customers inside the store.
- A door-to-door sales representative contacts customers at their homes.
- A company's sales representative calls on business customers in their offices. (See Chapter 14 for more about personal selling.)

Place. The place element has to do with getting the right goods and services in the right place for the right customers so that they can buy. Place and distribution are closely related. Marketers decide where to store goods and whether their products will be sold directly, indirectly, or at one versus several locations.

For a mail-order business, the place includes in which parts of the country or world the product will be marketed. Owners of local businesses also try to choose the best location in order to attract customers and strategically place their products.

▼ How would you feel about opening a fast-food service in the garage of a house located 15 miles away from any town? How many customers could you reasonably expect to get?

PRODUCT TYPES

New products and services emerge and old ones wane because of fads and fashions and the needs and whims of consumers.

All products and services, therefore, have a life cycle. All goods and services are produced and sold to either the consumer market or the industrial market.

Consumer Goods

Consumer goods are bought by individuals and families to satisfy their needs and wants. Hundreds of thousands of goods and services are manufactured and distributed by firms which go into business to try to meet consumers' needs. Consumer products are divided into three types, based on the buying habits of individual and family customers: convenience, shopping, and speciality goods.

Convenience or Impulse Goods. Typifying the category of **convenience goods** are low unit price, frequency of purchase, low selling effort, habit buying, and availability in numerous stores. Consumers tend to be familiar with these items and will accept substitutes (for example, a variety of brands) rather than going to another store. Examples are nonprescription drugs, snacks, and household staples like milk.

Shopping Goods. **Shopping goods** typically have a high unit price, are purchased infrequently, and require an intensive selling effort. Sale of shopping goods is usually limited to only certain kinds of establishments. Usually consumers spend a lot of time in comparing prices, features, and quality before purchasing these type of products. Vehicles, furniture, appliances, and higher-priced apparel are examples of shopping goods.

Speciality Goods. Typifying the category of **speciality goods** are high unit price, infrequency of purchase and a more intensive selling effort. Few if any substitutes are considered and sold via brand name. Examples are jewelry, perfume, stereo sound equipment, photographic and computer equipment, and sports equipment.

Industrial Products

Industrial products are used to produce other goods or services. Or they are used in the general operations of an organization. Supplies that are used up, like paper and typewriter ribbons, come under the category of general-operations' products. Industrial products are classified as either raw materials or component parts.

Raw materials are unprocessed natural resources, such as the products extracted from within or off of the land by mining, farming, ranching, fishing, and timbering operations. Oil, tin, wood, wheat, and beef are examples of raw materials.

Component parts are made from raw materials and go into other products. For example, electronic parts are used to make video games, computers, appliances, and automobiles.

THE LIFE CYCLE OF A PRODUCT

Companies continually develop new products or change or discontinue old ones. Thus all products have a life cycle from birth to death. Manufacturers decide when to produce new products, when to pull mature products, or when to stop spending money to promote them. New products are introduced in hopes of replacing or outshining the less-profitable older products or to fulfill new consumer needs and wants.

The **life cycle of a product** includes the phases of introduction, growth, maturity, and decline. The Boston Consulting Group, a marketing consulting firm, has nicknamed products in each of the life cycle phases. The nicknames are "stars," "cash cows," "problem children," and "dogs."

The Introduction Phase

It takes money to conduct research, gear up the plant with new equipment and processes, produce a new product, and promote it. These new products (stars) are supported by their companies in order to build a profitable market position and thereby reap future revenues. Thus, during the introduction phase, a new product or service might produce a loss rather than a profit. Indeed, most newly introduced products or services are expected to generate losses at first.

The Growth Phase

A product is successful when it produces a constant demand for it from consumers. Nicknamed a cash cow, the product enters a period of growth. Sales and revenues increase, and the profit picture looks good. By now, however, competitors enter the market with their own versions of the product or service.

The Mature Phase

Product maturity occurs when sales growth reaches a plateau. Market demand becomes satisfied. Profits start to dwindle as the results of the competition are felt. Products that are in this phase are nicknamed problem children. At this point, the manufacturer might decide to stop supporting problem children or new strategies are introduced to change problem children into stars or cash cows.

The Declining Phase

Because of intense competition, sales and profits fall rapidly during this phase. Products in the declining phase are nicknamed dogs.

The first Apple computer is an example of a product that passed through all four phases. Steve Jobs and Steve Wozniak got A. C. Markkula to invest $250,000 of his own money in the new venture. Several million dollars of additional investment money were needed to manufacture and introduce the first Apple. This desktop computer moved rapidly through the cycles of introduction (star), growth (cash cow), and maturity (problem child). It reached the declining phase (dog) when International Business Machines (IBM) and other computer competitors entered the market with desktop computers. Later, Apple would replace its first computer with new "stars," such as the MacIntosh Computer.

MEETING CUSTOMER NEEDS WITH GOODS AND SERVICES

It's difficult, and often impossible, to sell products and services to people if they cannot afford to buy them. The ability to buy, having purchasing power, is the factor that puts people in the consumer market. Potential customers usually get their purchasing power from the income they receive.

From a job that pays you wages, you get the money to pay for basic necessities. Whatever is left, after making these payments and purchases, is yours to spend any way you like. This amount is called **discretionary income** because you spend it at your own discretion, or based on personal decisions.

People buy goods and services to satisfy certain needs and wants, categorized as physical, social, and psychological.

Physical Needs

Physical needs are needs related to one's body, security, safety, and mobility or movement. The basic or physical need level is represented by basic needs for food, shelter, clothing, and, in today's mobile world, transportation. Goods in this category include groceries, housing, and clothing.

Also in this category are needs for security and safety. Thus consumers need insurance (for example, life, medical, auto, theft, fire); security devices for their homes, cars, and businesses; fire and police protection; schools and churches; hospitals and dental clinics, and the like.

Social Needs

Social needs have to do with our need for affiliation with others and our need to be loved, accepted, or recognized by others. People need to have friends and do things together. They need to love and be loved. The deep need for a sense of belonging is paramount at this need level. The desire to look physically attractive is one outgrowth of the social need.

Among other reasons, people try to be attractive and personable so that they can attract someone of the opposite sex in order to develop relationships that can lead to courtship, marriage, and the raising of a family. Thus beauty aids and attractive clothing may help one fulfill this social need.

Psychological Needs

Once the satisfaction of physical and social needs are pretty well ensured, people are more likely to demonstrate needs at the psychological level. Included in this category are the **psychological needs** for self-esteem, approval, and prestige. One way of developing positive self-esteem comes through getting approval. Children first seek approval from parents and then from teachers. As we grow older, we want approval from bosses and other authority figures.

To ensure that people think well of us, as consumers, we often try to show, through our purchases and activities, that we have achieved something in life. These achievements usually center around one's occupational, educational, and income level. Psychological motivations are often reflected in our need or desire to gain respect, prestige, and status.

Consumer Motivations

One way people express human needs is through buying products and services. Three motives help determine what and where customers buy. These can be described as rational motives, emotional motives, and patronage motives.

A *rational motive* causes consumers to think logically. A comparison of prices with quality and durability is made before buying. Often marketers try to provide sound, rational reasons for buying a product or service in order to appeal to rational consumers.

Even before deciding to spend money on something, though, rational consumers carefully calculate the returns in relation to needs and wants. For example, rational consumers make sure they have sound savings and investment plans before they go very far beyond satisfying their basic and social needs. Thus banks, brokerages, real estate agencies, accountants, and investment planners provide services in response to this need.

An *emotional motive* for making consumer purchases is based on feelings, attitudes, values, and habits. Some psychologists claim that these motives are housed in the subconscious mind. They mostly come from family and peers in the early stages of childhood and adolescence. Consumers in this type of mood often buy on impulse, because an advertisement or TV commercial makes the product or service sound irresistible. See Information Brief 12-3, for example, which tells how the "Snuggle" bear appeals to consumers' emotional motives.

A *patronage motive* is born out of loyalty—to a person, place, brand-name product, or company. When a favorite lawyer, hairdresser, mechanic, or doctor leaves one establishment and moves to another, many of their clients follow. Even convenience becomes secondary, because often these loyal clients have to travel across town to the new location.

Loyalty to place can also be a primary consideration. Some consumers are motivated to shop in a favorite shopping mall.

Many consumers want certain brands and will accept no others, even if the prices of their favorite brands are higher or the quality is lower. The trade name of products is closely allied with the company name. Thus companies spend part of their advertising funds to promote the reputation of their company as well as their products and services.

The war between Pepsico and Coca-Cola is an example of the patronage motive. Some people swear by Pepsi, while

Information Brief 12-3

Rational and Emotional Symbolism in Advertising

Lever Brothers built a $300 million fabric softener brand using a teddy bear named "Snuggle." Turning to a psychology consultant, Lever marketers had learned that their teddy bear acts as a bridge between the consumer's rational and emotional sides.

Social scientists help marketers communicate specific messages to consumers through advertising symbols. One psychologist, who is a consultant to marketers, says that as a symbol of tamed aggression, the teddy bear is a good image for a fabric softener that takes the rough texture out of clothing.

Source: Ronald Alsop, "Agencies Scrutinize Their Ads for Psychological Symbolism," *The Wall Street Journal*, June 11, 1987, p. 27.

others claim that Coke is better. Yet even Coke fans were ready to desert the company when the familiar formula (recipe) was changed. Responding to consumers' protests, the Coca-Cola Company again provided its tried and true recipe but renamed it Coca-Cola Classic (turning a problem child into a star).

Effective marketing people use all available resources to help them to identify what consumers want and need. Besides understanding these general needs and motivations, as discussed above, successful marketers can also identify the needs that typify their target market population. This information, and much more, usually comes from market research.

THE USEFULNESS OF MARKET RESEARCH

Market research is the systematic study that has as its goal the identifying and characterizing of markets and the forecasting of future market trends. Through market research, marketers gather data to produce useful information about markets and the marketing process.

Market research is not a perfect science. Marketers study people and their constantly changing likes and dislikes. These personal preferences can be affected by literally hundreds of influences, many of which cannot be determined specifically. Some marketing experts say: "Market research tries to find out how things are, not how you think they are or would like them to be. It tries to find out what people want to buy, not just what you want to sell them."

A market study focuses and organizes market information. It ensures that data are timely. It helps reduce business risks and the potential of failure by providing the information needed to make better decisions and establish plans for action.

Types of Research

Market studies can be categorized as either primary or secondary research. The primary method is when marketing people collect their own data. The secondary method focuses on printed information. With both methods, these data are analyzed, interpreted, and applied in the specific company regarding specific products and services.

Primary research involves collecting data directly by conducting interviews, making surveys, and observing people, communities, and the competition. Primary market researchers use city, county, and state maps and census reports. They gather data from chambers of commerce, utility companies, and railroads. They regularly call, write to, and poll businesses in various industries to get reports on sales, profits, problems, and potential solutions. Mailing out questionnaires to consumers and interpreting the responses is another means of collecting data.

The Nielson Company, for instance, surveys TV viewing habits and publishes the ratings. Companies and advertising agencies use this information to decide where to place their TV commercials. Market researchers ask consumers to react to commercials. Based on their responses, many ads are modified before they are aired. Consumers also taste-test food products before they are put on the market.

By standing on street corners or in shopping malls, clipboard in hand, market researchers count pedestrian and vehicle traffic and stop shoppers and survey their opinions on various matters. Pedestrian traffic tells how many people walk by a given store or through a shopping mall. The vehicle traffic count tells the number of vehicles passing by a business or business area. The pedestrians and drivers are all potential customers. These and other methods of primary research give marketers information about the consumer groups.

Figure 12-2. Marketers conduct market research at shopping malls and other places to help determine consumer wants, needs, and preferences. They also gather valuable data about consumers' reactions to existing products and services.

High-Tech Marketing Revolutionizes the Supermarket Industry

Not all supermarkets use computer-linked cash registers and optical character readers, but those that do are discovering that customers are fascinated by high-tech marketing. The optical character reader (OCR) uses a laser beam. Cashiers pass products over the beam in a certain way. The OCR must be able to "read" the computer code, which is placed on products in a series of bars.

Voice-activated systems provide a voice that speaks the product and price, so both the cashier and customer can hear the message. Some stores, however, have omitted the voice because marketing surveys have shown that some customers find this extra marketing service to be a nuisance. They'd rather talk to the cashier or to fellow shoppers and not be interrupted by the artificially created voice.

With a computer-linked cash register, the sale of each product is automatically subtracted from the store's inventory. Products and prices are also recorded automatically and tallied. Thus at the end of every day, week, month, or quarterly period, the sales manager can see which products (at which prices) are moving the fastest. Marketers can then make decisions about pricing and relocating products on the store's shelves.

Armed with this information, marketers can also make timely decisions about how to market and advertise the store's products effectively. Customers benefit, too. Using the information gathered, marketers can advertise the products customers are most likely to need and place them in the most convenient store locations. That can save customers precious time.

But this is not the only way that high-tech equipment helps. More-advanced optical scanners exist that not only track which items sell best in each store but also calculate precise profit margins on each product. By monitoring the pace of sales, such scanners identify peak buying periods, which helps marketers determine when to bring in more workers. And other innovations in OCR technology

(continued)

Technology Feature *(continued)*

provide for the direct linkup of stores and warehouses. Such linkups allow for speedier, more automatic, and more systemized reordering of goods.

Indeed, technology has become the unseen hand that has brought big changes to an industry where companies are grateful for a profit margin of merely 1 percent. The supermarket's typical 1 percent profit margin is less than a tenth of what most businesses consider attractive. Thus we can see that the optical scanning equipment that makes today's checkout counters work is revolutionizing inventory, merchandising, advertising, and business and labor practices in the vitally important supermarket industry.

Sources: Andrea Gabor, "The New Supermarket Sweepstakes," *U.S. News and World Report*, August 11, 1986, pp. 38–39; and interviews and observations conducted at Safeway in Laramie, Wyoming, and at Alco in Witchita, Kansas, January and February 1988.

Watching people in stores, as consumers react to displays, special sales, games, and free samples, is another way of conducting primary research. One retailer passed out unshelled peanuts at the door and told customers to drop the shells anywhere. At the end of the day, he simply followed the path of the densest shells to know what displays had attracted most of the consumers' attention.

Secondary research involves data that already have been organized and published. These reports come from professional market researchers who conduct primary research regarding trade, business, economic, financial, and demographic news.

Webster defines **demographics** as "the statistical science dealing with distribution, density, and vital statistics of populations." These data describe the trade market area and the people living and shopping in various areas. Pertinent data cover the number of people in different age groups, their occupational and educational and income levels, the types of dwellings they live in, and whether they own or rent.

Marketers read trade publications and get data from the marketing departments of universities and professional market research firms. These firms and organizations conduct primary research.

▼ How would you feel if, after taste-testing a new candy bar and finding it tasted awful, the food company introduced it anyhow?

Marketing Research Applications

Gathering market research data is pointless unless the data is translated into relevant and timely information. By using more market research in the beginning, Menlo Corp. marketers might have helped their company avoid "burning through $4 million of its $4.5 million in start-up funds" (see the article that opened this chapter).

By following the peanut shell path, as described earlier, the retailer learned which store displays were most appealing to customers. This enabled the retailer to duplicate the successful methods in displaying other products.

Thus, when interpreted and applied properly, marketing research can be an important ingredient in the marketing success of an enterprise. When misinterpreted or misapplied, however, marketing research can be costly, wasteful, and yield unpleasant consequences.

Select Terms to Know

component parts
convenience goods
demographics
discretionary income
industrial products
life cycle of a product

market research
marketing mix
patronage motive
physical needs
primary research
psychological needs

raw materials
secondary research
shopping goods
social needs
specialty goods

Review Questions

1.   Tell how the marketing manager uses the steps of planning, organizing, directing, and controlling. Use the example of the student organization and make comparisons with a business.

2.   What knowledge and skills does the marketing manager need? Why is using correct and effective communication important?

3.   Describe the marketing elements. How, as a marketing mix, do they relate to each other?

4.   Describe and give examples of consumer products and industrial products.

5.   Describe the four phases of a product's life cycle. How can each of the nicknames used for

these phases help you to remember them?

6.   How are the following terms defined and what do they mean to marketers—purchasing power and discretionary income?

7.   Give examples of products and services that consumers are likely to buy to meet their needs and wants at these levels: physical, social, and psychological (prestige, status, or self-esteem).

8.   What is the difference between primary and secondary research? Give examples of actions that marketers are likely to take by applying each of these research methods of gathering and studying data.

Thought and Discussion Questions

1. Discuss the marketer's interest in and involvement with each of the four marketing elements.

2. Which of the four marketing elements do you consider to be the most important? Explain your answer.

3. In your opinion, how would the marketing of consumer products differ from the marketing of industrial products? Who are the typical target customers of each of these types of products?

4. In your opinion, why is it important to understand people through identifying different human needs? What impact does this understanding have on the people who are marketing goods and services?

5. Consider three products that you have purchased recently. Which consumer motivation (rational, emotional, or patronage) do you think had the greatest affect on your purchasing decision for each product? Explain your answer.

6. Why is it important to conduct market research? In your opinion, what is the significance of collecting data and then storing (filing), processing, analyzing, interpreting, and applying all this information to the marketing of goods and services?

Projects

1. Identify products in your home and school that represent the phases of a product's life cycle: introduction (stars), growth (cash cows), maturity (problem children), and decline (dogs).

A Rubic's Cube, for instance, can now be called a dog. A new blouse or shirt style that's just come into fashion this season is a star. Explain why you have identified each item according to its life cycle phase (and nickname).

2. Watch and analyze television commercials. Have paper and pencil at hand, ready to record and classify data from the selected commercials. Use the following guidelines:

a. At the top of three sheets of paper, write one human need category: physical, social, and psychological.

b. Select commercials that appeal to each human need.

c. Record the names of each company and the products and services being marketed in each TV commercial. Record these data on your separate sheets of paper, opposite each itemized commercial.

d. Compare your primary research findings. Report the findings to your class.

3. Locate several magazine ads. (Use old magazines from home or the classroom or photocopy ads from magazines in the library.) Select ads that demonstrate appeals to consumers' motivational buying habits, namely: (*a*) rational, (*b*) emotional, and (*c*) patronage.

(Note that the copy—written matter—might provide facts and figures as an appeal to consumers' rational side. The pictures, however, might have been selected to appeal to consumers' emotional side, as well as to the three categories of human needs. Ads that promote a company's reputation are designed to appeal to consumers' patronage motive.)

4. Find articles that report market research. The articles can address trends in business, economics, finance, and demographics that affect marketers in specific trades (industries). Report on and discuss the impact of marketing research on marketers and entrepreneurs.

Case Study: Tapping a Ready-Made Market

The Menlo Corporation (described in the chapter-opening article) uses a direct-mail campaign to sign up library associations to help promote and sell the firm's Pro-Search software. Menlo treats the library associations just like retail dealers, giving the associations a 30 to 40 percent discount on each software program. The associations can then resell the software to their members for a profit. If a library association is unable to handle invoicing and inventory, Menlo makes arrangements for these tasks. However, if that occurs, Menlo treats the association like a sales agent. In other words, it pays the association a 20 percent commission on sales.

Sources: Russell Sabin, "Marketing by Association," *Venture*, November 1984, pp. 131–133; and "The Media Business: Knight-Ridder to Acquire Dialog," *The New York Times*, July 12, 1988, p. D24.

Review the chapter-opening article together with the facts presented in the case above. Be ready to answer the questions and carry out the assignments below.

1. Why were library associations a natural and ready-made market for Menlo's Pro-Search software? Why would marketing through such associations give Menlo "built-in sales leads?"

2. Imagine you are the writer of direct-mail ads for Menlo Corp. How might you take advantage of the linkage between Menlo's Pro-Search software and Dialog Information Services in your direct-mail campaigns to library associations?

3. Assume you are placed in charge of Menlo's plan to market its software program to a professional association of librarians. (a) Tell how you would persuade officers of this association to purchase your product. (*Hint:* As part of your plan, you should help the association officers appreciate and understand the value of your firm's discount policies and the benefit of reselling the software to association members.) (b) To make your plan more appealing to the association and its members, outline some specific ways that nonprofit libraries might use the Pro-Search software as part of their fund-raising activities. Note that nonprofit libraries almost always need to raise money to cover their operating expenses. (*Hint:* Review the fund-raising activities of the student organization described in this chapter and Table 12-1 for activities of a similar nature that might apply to fund-raising projects for nonprofit libraries.)

CHAPTER 13

Packaging and Pricing Decisions

The Packaging and Pricing Knockoff War

While Avon Products markets its Giorgio perfume at $135 an ounce, Parfums de Coeur Ltd. lets consumers smell like Giorgio for $7.50 an ounce. The original designers claim that knockoff artists are getting a free ride from the millions of dollars spent by the originals to advertise their brands. (A "knockoff" here refers to a copy of an original product that is offered at a lower price than the original to make it more attractive to targeted consum-

ers. Sometimes the knockoff comes in packaging that closely resembles that of the original, too.)

The Stamford, Connecticut, company that sells Primo, the Giorgio imitation, is the leading maker of designer-brand fragrance knockoffs. Primo is sold in drugstores and discount outlets. "We're like guerrilla warriors fighting the U.S. Army. Every time they come at us, we just change the packaging," says the marketer of an imita-

tion fragrance whose company was involved in a legal war with Calvin Klein, another famous designer-brand firm.

Study this chapter to learn more about the impact that pricing and packaging have on the marketing of products and services. Use the contents to help you answer the questions in the end-of-chapter case study, "The Knockoff Wars Leave a Bitter Scent."

During the product development stage, there are numerous decisions to make and lots of opportunity for creativity. Two major decision areas address packaging and pricing. Marketers participate in deciding what a product's package will look like and how it will be priced. The marketing staff is involved because people in this department conduct marketing research and also work directly with consumers. They usually are in a good position to know what factors appeal to customers and therefore what is likely to sell.

Unlike products, services do not come in physical containers or packages. Nevertheless, marketers advertise and promote services, too. Marketers are also concerned with pricing services and with developing a positive perception and image for the services their firms offer for sale.

In this chapter you will study some of the factors that guide marketers in pricing and packaging goods and services.

PACKAGING DECISIONS

Packaging involves the design and production of the physical container that holds a product. Major matters addressed in making packaging decisions are: (1) the desired product perception and image, (2) cost, and (3) quality.

Desired Product Perception and Image

To gain consumer acceptance and thus sell products, the package has to be appealing. But looks are not the only criterion that gets customers to buy one product over another. Consumers don't usually accept a product unless they have a positive perception or image of it. Packaging decisions focus on appearance and familiarity, protection and safety, labeling, customer use, and distributor and retailer use.

Appearance and Familiarity. Suppose the consumer wants to try a new fragrance but has little perception about which one among several is preferable. The package's appearance draws attention to the product. The color, shape, and attractiveness all catch the consumer's eye. To make their product competitive with many other brands, marketers try to apply creativity to the development of an appealing package.

Once consumers decide they like a product, they have to be able to find it again. If familiar with the packaging, they can locate it on the retailer's shelves among dozens of other brands.

Protection and Safety. Packages are designed to protect the contents. Bottles are designed so that they won't break or spill. Liquids cannot be allowed to evaporate. Soft contents are protected by the packaging's configuration so that they won't get crushed. Packages have a long route to travel. They move from the point of manufacture and packaging through storage, transportation, display, and into the consumers' hands. Thus one of the marketer's goals is to create a sturdy package.

Safety is another protection goal of packaging. Food, drugs, cleaning products, and cosmetics are all vulnerable because they can easily be misused. If not used correctly, their contents can cause sickness, even death. So packages are designed to protect children from getting into them and to avoid accidental spills. The health and safety of people is usually a major concern of manufacturers and marketers. Pharmaceutical firms, for example, try to package drugs in tamper-proof containers that children cannot open.

▼ How would you feel if a child got into a package you helped create—especially if the product were dangerous and the child was badly injured? Do you think enough is being done today to package products safely? Why do you feel as you do?

Labeling. **Labeling** is that part of a product which carries verbal or other information about the product or the seller of an item. Consumers need labeling for several reasons. Any product that's potentially dangerous is carefully labeled so that people won't misuse it. A product that's designed to be rubbed on the body could be very harmful if taken internally. Therefore, the language used in labeling products has to be correct and clear. Consumers need to be able to understand what they find printed on product labels.

Legal requirements cover the labeling of food and drug products and of cleaning and industrial products that affect health and safety. The disclosure requirements mandated by state, local, and/or federal agencies direct manufacturers to label products to protect users.

The label advertises the product. The company's familiar **logo** (symbol) and the brand name of the product appear on the package. Consumers locate familiar products by the brand and logo labeling as well as by their color, shape, and appearance. New products consumers have seen advertised in the media can be located by their labels.

Labels also give information and directions. This information tells consumers how much of a product to use for given circumstances and how to use it. For example, food products may include the ingredients and nutritional values on their labels.

Labels explain the potential benefits and important characteristics of a product. Thus consumers get news about the

Information Brief
13-1

The Quest for Quality

Companies are developing computer systems that are "smart" enough to analyze the quality of a product and its packaging while it still exists on a computer screen.

Quality experts say that no more than 20 percent of quality defects can be traced to the production line. The other 80 percent is locked in during the design phase. The core of the quality revolution can be captured in a phrase: customer satisfaction. Whether buying automobiles or life insurance, stereos or hamburgers, millions of shoppers won't plunk down their money until they check a product's reputation for quality by reading magazines such as *Consumer Reports* published by the Consumers Union.

Sources: Otis Port, "The Push for Quality"; and Mimi Bluestone, "When *Consumer Reports* Talks, Buyers Listen—And So Do Companies," *U.S. News and World Report,* June 8, 1987, pp. 130–135.

product. However, from a marketer's viewpoint, the label also serves to promote the product in comparison with the competitions' products.

Customer Use. The package has to be easy for the consumer to use. First, a package needs to be opened to get to the contents. Pasteboard and plastic containers and plastic and cellophane wrappings are used to protect fragile contents or bottles and other types of inside containers. Consumers need to get through all these outside packages and wrappings before they can get to the actual product contents. Soap, cereal, and frozen food packages, for instance, have to be opened before their contents can be used.

Consumers are often in a hurry. They don't want to have to read a lot of instructions or try first one kitchen utensil and then another to get to the product. Getting into products includes finding and uncovering spouts, locating rip-off strips, pulling strings, and punching holes. All these things are a nuisance unless they are convenient to find and easy to use. Consumers might not purchase the same products again, simply because they get irritated and frustrated trying to get the package open to use them. Thus, ease of use is an important factor in designing a package.

Distributor and Retailer Use. Distributors and retailers also want packages that are convenient and easy to use. Transporters and warehouse people dislike handling products that will accidentally spill, evaporate, or make messes. Retailers want attractive, easily manageable products that will display well and stack easily.

Many factors affect the consumer's perception of a product. But while marketers and manufacturers are dealing with these concerns, they also have to ensure that the cost of packaging is not excessive.

Cost

Production costs need to be covered in the price. If the retail price is too high, consumers won't buy products. Packaging is included in the costs of production. Controlling costs is a constant marketing challenge. It is this challenge that directs marketers to search for less expensive and more efficient ways to package products and services.

Suppose that after designing a product to meet all the packaging factors, the cost is too high. If you were the marketing manager, which packaging factors would you attempt to cut back on—appearance, safety, labeling, or convenience? Maybe a two-color package for a toy would be almost as attractive as one with three colors. But the instructions about how to assemble the parts of a toy could not be omitted. Nor, legally, could the protective seal and danger label be eliminated from a potentially poisonous cleaning product.

Quality

Quality begins with product design and continues with production and packaging. Each product has numerous competitors, including many from abroad. To meet consumer needs and beat the competition, maintaining quality is critical. (See Information Brief 13-1.)

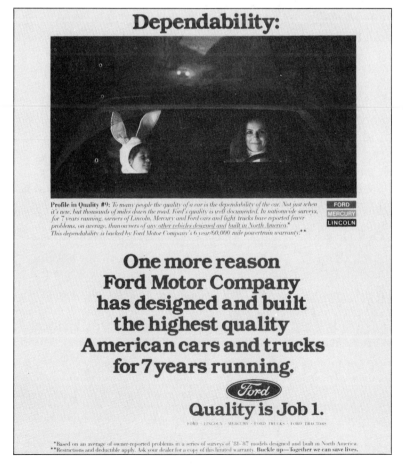

Figure 13-1. Businesses in the United States are increasingly emphasizing the importance of quality in the packaging and design of their products, as shown by this advertisement for Ford automobiles and trucks.

Marketers Design Products and Packages With Computer Graphics

What kind of sweater designs will appeal to consumers and beat the competition? What colors and shapes are appealing on the fabrics of furniture? How must a bottle or package look to promote its contents when placed on a shelf beside its rivals?

To help marketers design more eye-catching products and packaging, an image-design computer system can simulate what a shopper should see when strolling through a supermarket. Steve Jobs, founder of Apple Computer, helped develop the Pixar, a powerful image-design computer.

The Pixar, and similar computer systems, are changing the way marketers work, especially the way they design products and packages. Marketers used to design products and packages with paper and pencil.

Now marketers create images 100 times faster than they could with the old paper-and-pencil method. Pixar, a large version of the personal computer, is a super workstation that lets marketing designers create a three-dimensional model on the screen. Marketers can change a design into a hundred different shapes, in dozens of color combinations.

Designers at Levi Strauss use the computer systems to try out the look of different fabric textures and patterns on three-dimensional images of jeans designs. All this is done before the jeans are even sewn. Aerospace and automobile companies use the system to simulate the look and design of automobile and airline interiors. These 3D systems are revolutionizing and improving the design of countless other products as well.

Sources: Katharine M. Hafner, "Computer Graphics Are Animating Another Market," *Business Week*, March 16, 1987, pp. 88–92; and Phillip Elmer-Dewitt and Charles Pelton, "Computers," *Time*, September 1, 1986.

Many trade-offs are made in designing and producing a product's package. And all these decisions impact on the prices that manufacturers and retailers establish in order to realize a profit.

PRICING CONSIDERATIONS

Price is an important factor in the consumer's decision to buy. Consumers are bombarded right and left by news about prices. They see prices displayed in stores and newspapers and hear about prices from radio and TV commercials. They compare prices through direct contact with products and services and by discussing prices with friends.

The Meaning of Price

Price is the amount of money—or value of a transaction—for which something is bought, sold, or offered for sale. Price is the value placed on any product or service. If you and a neighbor agree to exchange services, such as lawn mowing for garage cleaning, you've just made a **nonmonetary exchange.** The value of the exchange is based on the time and energy each task takes. These tasks need to be somewhat equal, or one of you will feel shortchanged and not agree to the exchange.

Price serves as a communication vehicle, a measure of value, and a competitive strategy. All businesses, whether they offer products or services, face pricing decisions.

Price Affects Exchange

Lacking enough money to buy everything one wants is a problem many people face, consumer and business customer alike. Before deciding to exchange money for goods or services, many consumers shop around. They seldom pay high prices for shoddy merchandise or services. Consumers look for the best combination of price and quality before buying.

Price as a Communication Vehicle

The price communicates a message to consumers. This message may say that the product or service is of high or of low quality. Price helps the marketer create an image of his or her company. A very high price may create an image of prestige and exclusiveness. A very low price may suggest a bargain basement image.

Price as a Measure of Value

Two similar products or services that range widely in price can give consumers the impression that the higher-priced item is worth more, even if it isn't. From an analysis of contents and making comparisons, for example, market research found that Ponds face cream is even better than some of the more expensive brands. When the comparison study was conducted, Ponds was priced at less than half the prestigious brands.

The prices of services may also vary a great deal. The more valuable the service, the higher the price. For example, discount stockbrokers charge lower prices for their services, but they merely enter orders for the buying and selling of shares of stock. Investors who want financial advice, as well as the buying-and-selling service, are willing to pay more. They are more likely to use full-service stockbrokers.

Thus experienced consumers expect to pay for value. Suppose a lawyer charges only $6 an hour for legal services compared to other lawyers who charge from $50 to $300 an hour. Potential clients would probably decide that the low-priced lawyer has no experience, has a shifty reputation, or has a record of losing every case. Thus, we see that price is often a key indicator of the value of a product or service to the customer.

▼ How would you feel if a young person with no baby-sitting experience advertised his or her service at the same price per hour as you charge? Suppose you'd been baby-sitting in your neighborhood for the past three years. You're very experienced and have established a fine reputation for your service. Considering the difference in value, would you expect this inexperienced person to charge as much as you?

Pricing as a Competitive Strategy

No industry is immune to the competition's prices. Even where value and high quality are desirable, some consumers desert a favorite brand or company to purchase a lower-priced version of the same product or service. Besides, consumers know that not everything needs to be bought in the more expensive versions. Many consumers have little money to spend on extras. So there's a ready-made and very large market for low-priced goods and services.

Figure 13-2. Evidence of price competition is seen almost everywhere today. To attract customers, some businesses deep discount their goods and services. Their advertisements often play up the idea that their prices cannot be beaten by the competition.

PRICING POLICIES

Price is one element in the marketing mix. Many pricing methods are complex because of how the four marketing elements in the marketing mix impact on one another.

Policies used to establish the product's price include follow-the-leader pricing, penetration pricing, cost-oriented pricing, demand-oriented pricing, and break-even point. Both product and service marketers are involved with setting pricing policies.

Follow-the-Leader Pricing

Follow-the-leader pricing means that businesses follow an industry or market leader in establishing prices for goods and services. This is one of the most popular methods, because it focuses on the competition and strives to stay in line. Industries where there is concentration of players is where price leadership predominates. Examples include the steel, lumber, automobile, and computer industries.

Desktop computer companies that competed with IBM's personal computer (PC) tried to stay in line pricewise. In offering similar benefits and quality, they priced their computers just a little bit less than the PC to make their versions attractive to consumers. Yet they followed IBM as the leader.

Penetration Pricing

When new products are introduced to the market, the goal is to penetrate that market. Thus, with **penetration pricing,** the price is set as low as possible while still covering the costs of manufacturing and promotion. This is an ideal method when market penetration is good and the sales volume is high. Low prices help to discourage competitors from entering the market with their own versions of the product or service.

Cost-Oriented Pricing

With **cost-oriented pricing,** an arbitrary amount is added to the cost of producing the product or service. The cost per unit is calculated. This procedure means collecting all the cost data regarding purchasing (of raw materials or component parts), manufacturing, packaging and promotion, plus determining the operating expenses. **Operating expenses** include rent or mortgage payments, utilities, wages, advertising, insurance, and supplies. Then the number of units is divided into the total cost, producing a cost-per-unit figure. The math formula looks like this:

$$\frac{\text{Operating expenses}}{\text{Number of units}} = \text{Unit cost}$$

See Figure 13-3 to learn how widgets were priced. The total cost of producing each widget is $62.25. To arrive at this individual cost figure, suppose that 100,000 widgets are produced, with direct and indirect costs totaling $6,225,000. The math

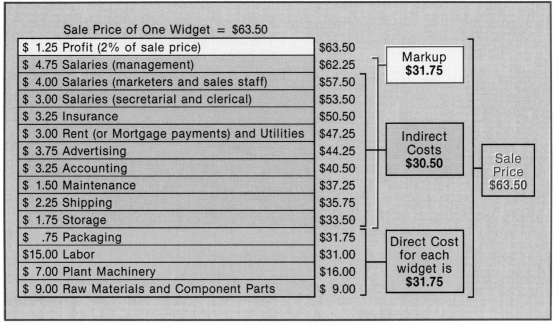

Figure 13-3. What is markup? Here is a visual example to illustrate what markup is and how it is computed. Widget, Inc. produces widgets. The markup on each widget is $31.75. *Markup* is the difference between direct costs and sales price. Markup must cover all indirect costs in addition to profit. Note that the profit on each widget is only $1.25 out of a markup of $31.75. This $1.25 profit, per unit, is roughly 2 percent of the sales price.

formula is therefore $6,225,000 ÷ 100,000, for a unit cost of $62.25 per widget.

Markup is the amount needed to cover indirect costs, plus profit, after all direct costs are covered. **Direct costs** refer to the production of a product, including raw materials, plant machinery, wages for the manufacturing workers, and packaging. The markup also covers the indirect costs of doing business. **Indirect costs** include storing, shipping, advertising, maintenance, accounting, rent or mortgage payments, utilities, and insurance. The wages and salaries paid to the sales force, the clerical personnel, and management are included.

Demand-Oriented Pricing

Demand-oriented pricing tries to identify what prices customers are willing to pay. The prestige factor is part of demand-oriented pricing.

"Whatever the traffic will bear" is a phrase that implies the use of demand-oriented pricing. This means that marketers try to determine the price level beyond which customers will refuse to buy. Besides some other method, both manufacturers and retailers are likely to consider demand-oriented pricing.

A Boston service station sold its gasoline for 12 cents more per gallon than most other stations in the city, including those within a half-dozen blocks. Asked why they bought their gas there, the reasons customers gave ranged from "I don't know, I've always come here" to "The gas must be better if it costs more."

In fact, some consumers are dazzled by those companies that offer their goods and services at the higher prices into believing that the product is superior. This impression is reinforced regularly by advertising campaigns. Some products, however, are actually considered to be superior in certain respects, such as the Lincoln Continental, Mercedes Benz, and BMW automobiles.

Retail Pricing

Retailers usually follow the pricing policies recommended by manufacturer and franchise marketers. For example, at shopping malls a single chocolate chip cookie sells for 55 cents in Casper, Wyoming, for 65 cents in Kansas City, Missouri, and for 85 cents in Washington, D.C. Each of these chocolate chip cookie shops represents either a franchise or one among a chain of shops, with the producer providing the pricing. Obviously these retail outlets do not compete with one another. But if all three shops were located within 10 miles of each other, some chocolate chip cookie buffs might willingly drive across town to buy the higher-priced cookie. Of course, one reason the 85-cent cookie is priced higher is that it's fatter and has more chips, so each unit costs more to produce.

Retail marketers can be guided by industry standards and by carefully studying the results of marketing research. The U.S. Small Business Administration (SBA) is one agency that provides many types of guidelines, including those related to pricing.

Wholesaler and Shipping Policies

Factors that contribute to pricing in the wholesale trade and shipping industries include the costs of storage facilities, operating transportation systems, time, government regulations, and promotion. Distribution marketers in these industries promote their companies' services. Transportation includes trucks, trains, planes, and ships.

TABLE 13-1 Factors Retailers Consider in Setting Prices

1. Is the price very important to consumers in the target market?

2. Are prices based on estimates of the number of units that consumers will demand at various price levels?

3. Has a price range for the product or service been established by the manufacturer or by industry standards?

4. What price strategies are compatible with the store's total retailing mix (merchandise, location, promotion, and services)?

5. Does the retailer have final pricing authority? Or must the retailer assign prices according to a franchisor's or manufacturer's recommendations?

6. What prices are direct competitors charging?

7. Does the retailer regularly review competitors' ads to check on their prices?

8. Should competitors' temporary price reductions ever be matched?

9. Has a profit objective been established for the first few months of the store's operation and of the new-product introduction period?

10. Has the retailer estimated sales, operating expenses, and reductions, on an annual or per-season (for seasonal firms) basis?

11. Given estimated sales, expenses, and reductions, has the retailer calculated the markup into the pricing strategies?

12. Would it be appropriate to have different initial markup figures for various lines of merchandise of services?

13. Are additional markups called for because wholesale prices have increased or because an item's low price causes consumers to question its quality?

14. Will the retailer consider the cost of merchandise before setting markdown prices?

15. Has the retailer established procedures for recording the dollar amounts, percentages, and probable causes of markdowns?

16. If the state(s) in which the retail outlet operates has an unfair-sales-practices act that requires minimum markups on certain merchandise, will the retailer's prices comply?

17. Are economic conditions in the trading area abnormal?

18. Does the retailer display and promote prices in a way compatible with consumerism (e.g., providing straightforward price information)?

Source: Adapted from Bruce J. Walker, "A Pricing Checklist for Small Retailers," *Management Aids,* no. 4.013. U.S. Small Business Administration, U.S. Government Printing Office.

Transportation is used to get goods from one place to another, and numerous competing carriers. Many of the same policies used in manufacturing apply to how wholesale trade and transportation firms establish prices. Direct costs include facility storage and handling, vehicles and fuel, and wages of warehouse workers and transportation drivers. The markup covers indirect costs and profit.

Wholesale marketers promote their services with values like these: speed, on-time deliveries, care of products in storage and transit, and price. Shippers have to meet government regulations regarding such things as load weights, speed limits, and certification and licenses.

Pricing for Services

Service firms sell services (naturally) plus expertise and time. The length of time involved in preparing for a career contributes to the price of services in the professional fields. The clients who purchase the services of professionals are usually willing to pay for considerable expertise.

Pricing That Includes Expertise. Expertise is a combination of formal education and in-depth experience covering a wide range of knowledge and background within a given field. A lawyer with no trial experience, for instance, would likely charge lower rates until he or she had gained that experience.

Pricing That Includes Time. Time is used in establishing service prices. Doctors, repair operators, and hotels all establish prices on the basis of time. So do dentists, consultants, accountants, lawyers, mechanics, beauty operators, and the like. In hotels and motels, guests are told that if they don't check out by a preestablished time, they will be charged an additional night's rate. These guests are using the establishment's services—taking up space, or using a room—for a longer amount of time.

Pricing for Repair Services. The cost of providing repair and related services has three parts: (1) materials cost, (2) direct labor cost, and (3) operating expenses. Materials cost cover parts and supplies used to provide the service, plus their shipping and storage. Direct labor cost covers the wages paid to the workers providing the service. Operating expenses are the indirect costs of the service, whether for materials, labor, or other items. (Refer again to Figure 13-3.) The profit margin is also included.

Table 13-2 shows how profit can be applied independently to all three costs—materials, labor, and operating expenses. See how the final price was determined. Assigned are a 10 percent profit from material, a 30 percent profit from direct labor, and a 30 percent profit on operating expenses.

TABLE 13-2 Building a Profit Percentage Into Repair-Related Service Pricing

Cost Factor	Cost	Percent	Price	Profit
Materials cost	$20	10	$22	$2
Direct labor cost	10	30	13	3
Operating expenses	10	30	13	3
Totals	$40		$48	$8

Break-Even Point

The **break-even point** identifies the quantity of a good or service that must be sold at a given price so the producer gets enough revenue to cover all the costs of production. Let's use the operation of a motel belonging to the Gehrings to illustrate how break-even analysis is applied to a service business.

When the Gehring family bought an old run-down motel in west Texas, family members knew that to survive they would have to reduce their break-even point to a bare minimum. First, they had to take in enough income to meet their monthly mortgage and utility payments. Repairing the dilapidated facility, using their own labor, was another high priority. Meanwhile, they were promoting the business as "under new management." This priority addressed rebuilding the goodwill the former owners had lost for the business. By doing all the work themselves, the Gehrings were able to lower the break-even point to an average nightly rental of four rooms.

Although the motel had 40 rooms, the previous owners were seldom renting any rooms at all. That was because the facility had been allowed to deteriorate, the owners' reputation for service was very poor, and they had made no effort to market their services. Even the big neon motel sign was broken.

The four-room rental average brought in just enough income for the new owners to meet their monthly mortgage payments and to pay the high cost of utilities. Especially important was keeping on the big neon sign in order to attract and pull in guests. Any money earned over the income from these four rooms was used for capital investment. The Gehrings tackled the motel's exterior first. Projecting a good image was essential to draw in trade from the street to rent their rooms. Except for buying groceries (the family lived in the motel's apartment), the Gehrings spent every cent of what they took in from room rentals on the motel. They upgraded furniture and carpeting, asphalted the driveways, and repaired the swimming pool and restaurant.

To keep operating expenses down, Mr. and Mrs. Gehring and their two teenage children did their own laundry, room cleaning, and grounds work. They simultaneously operated the motel and cafe single-handed. They also reasoned that any income was better than none, so they sometimes negotiated on the price per room. That is, instead of always sticking to an established price, they were willing to negotiate, to haggle. Lots of times the Gehrings dropped the established room-rental price to whatever price their transient guests were willing to pay. This practice also served to undercut the competition.

Soon the motel was averaging more nightly room rentals. By then the Gehring family business's break-even point had risen. From the income derived from renting five rooms nightly (on average), the Gehrings could hire one part-time employee. With a six-room average, they hired two workers, and so on. They soon needed to rent 10, 15, 20 rooms per night to pay for the additional direct and indirect costs of doing business.

Sometimes the break-even point for a good or service can be lowered, but only when owners and employees are committed to cutting costs, boosting sales revenue, and promoting their goods and services. In many businesses, however, reducing the break-even point is far more difficult than it was for the Gehrings. The direct costs may be so high or be such a high percentage of the total costs that it's not possible to reduce the break-even point.

Marketers Get and Give Information

The ability to promote and price goods and services to cover costs and operating expenses and still make a profit is based on getting sound information. However, marketers also give information. Through various means, marketers inform customers about how their companies' goods and services will meet human needs and wants.

Customers get this information in many ways. They are attracted to a wide range of packages and prices. By meeting consumer needs, companies can stay in business, sell beyond the break-even point, pay all costs and expenses, and still make a profit.

Select Terms to Know

break-even point
cost-oriented pricing
demand-oriented pricing
direct costs

follow-the-leader pricing
indirect costs
inventory
labeling

logo
markup
operating expenses
penetration pricing

Review Questions

1. Name the packaging issues related to gaining desired product perceptions, and give examples of each.

2. How can marketers use packaging to protect consumers?

3. What does price mean?

4. How does price serve as a communication vehicle? As a measure of value? As a competitive strategy? Give examples.

5. How does price affect exchange?

6. Describe the cost-oriented pricing method. Give examples.

7. How is the demand-pricing method used? For example, what impact do the concepts of "what the traffic will bear" and prestige have on consumers and thus on pricing policies?

8. Relate the pricing-policy decisions that affect manufacturing to those of wholesale-trade, shipping, retail, and service firms.

9. Explain why expertise is a factor in setting prices for services.

10. Explain how time is used in setting prices for services.

Thought and Discussion Questions

1. Express your opinion about the impact packaging can make in creating familiarity of a product among self-service shoppers. Discuss the importance of communications in designing a product's label.

2. Discuss how marketers can balance the need to keep packaging costs under control with meeting the criteria of getting the desired product perceptions from quality packaging.

3. Refer to Figure 13-3. Interpret the data in this illustration, and discuss how these terms apply: markup, direct costs, indirect costs, and profit.

4. Of what significance is the break-even point on profit? Discuss how small-firm owners and their employees, including members of family-owned businesses, can help to lower the break-even point.

Projects

1. Locate and study products found in your home and in stores. Record and compare data about the packaging of competitive products. At the completion of this activity, express your opinion regarding which product is packaged the best and be ready to tell why.

In relation to the product(s) selected, use the following criteria in judging and reporting how marketing decisions might have been made. Notice the effect of these possible factors in gaining positive customer perceptions of each product:

a.   Appearance: color, shape, and attractiveness of design
b.   Protection and safety
c.   Labeling: warnings, instructions, company logo and product brand name
d.   Ease or difficulty of customer use

2.   Collect data from watching and analyzing TV commercials and from magazine advertisements. (Or refer to the data collected in Chapter 12, projects 2 and 3.) Note and record data about packaging in response to the same criteria listed in project 1 above, and be ready to report your findings to the class.

3.   Locate price data for two comparative products. Use actual products, and commercials and ads from TV, magazines, and newspapers. Upon completing the activity, express your opinion about each product, and which is better, on the bases of collecting and recording the following comparative data:

a.   The measures of value the prices communicate
b.   The competitive strategies that might be in effect
c.   Examples of follow-the-leader pricing

d.   Examples of penetration pricing (new products)

4.   You are the marketing manager of a toy and game manufacturer. Your task is to use the cost-oriented pricing method to establish a price for a new game called "Planet Wars." From the data given below, construct a chart like the one in Figure 13-3. Use these steps:

a.   Show what items are covered under direct cost, indirect cost, markup, and profit.
b.   To get the figures at the side, add each new figure to the one below.
c.   Set the price and calculate the profit (aim for a 4 to 12 percent profit).

Financial data per unit:

Raw materials, $3.00
Plant equipment, $1.50
Labor, $5.50
Packaging, $0.40
Storage, $0.35
Shipping, $0.42
Maintenance, $0.21
Accounting, $1.77
Advertising, $0.83
Utilities, $0.44
Insurance, $0.31
Salaries (clerical), $1.13
Salaries (sales), $1.88
Salaries (management), $1.97

Case Study: The Knockoff Wars Leave a Bitter Scent

Parfums de Coeur declares on its packaging, "If you like Giorgio (or Opium or Dior's Poison), you'll love Primo (or Ninja or Turmoil)." Most imitators put disclaimers on their product packages. These state that the copycat fragrances are not actually the same as the original designer-brand products. However, the original designers say that such disclaimers may not be read by consumers. Such disclaimers may be printed in type too small to be read or even noticed by consumers. Moreover, the designer-brand makers argue that disclaimers are intended more to

help copycat makers avoid legal problems than to provide consumers with needed information.

Scents can't be patented. But Calvin Klein Cosmetics keeps trying to protect its image and products. The company has sued five imitators. Calvin Klein's lawyer claims that the appearance of the designer's trademark in bold letters on a knockoff's packaging confuses consumers. "It is a threat to the goodwill of the brand."

Calvin Klein Cosmetics—whose imitators of Obsession (for men) produced Confess and Enamoured—charged that the copycats misused

Klein's trademark. The courts, however, have not shown much sympathy for such arguments.

The knockoff marketers claim, in rebuttal, that they are targeting a different market from the original designers. According to a spokesperson for F. W. Woolworth Co., who sell fragrances for both men and women: "The average working person who can't afford Obsession or Giorgio is the one buying our quality alternatives."

Even the designer-brand marketers concede that knockoffs aren't stealing customers. Rather, the imitations appear to be getting consumers from the moderately priced lines, like Revlon and Coty.

Mark A. Laracy, one-time president of Parfums de Coeur, is credited with creating the copycat business. He helped launch Yves Saint Laurent's Opium in 1978. Parfums de Coeur spent $5 million for advertising in one year. Next there were copycats imitating copycats. In one year alone 41 such companies introduced new imitation products. Many of these companies, though, were poorly financed, had limited distribution, or produced cheap-smelling imitations. The bet-ter knockoffs soon began to knock off much of their competition.

Source: Amy Dunkin, " 'Obsession' by Any Other Name Sells Sweetly," *Business Week*, June 1, 1987, p. 97.

Who do you support in the knockoff war? Adopt the viewpoint of either the original higher-priced design fragrances or the low-cost copy-cats. Then defend your position with supporting arguments on the following matters:

1. Is the packaging and pricing of the copycat brands proper and fair?

2. Are the target markets for the copycats and designer fragrances the same or different?

3. Which side has the most defensible legal position? Which side is most likely to win in court? Why?

4. Are the legal implications good or bad for other types of companies and products? (For example, consider the legal implications for IBM's personal computers (PCs) and IBM copy-cats or clones, so-called PC-compatibles.)

CHAPTER 14

Advertising and Sales Promotion

Shopping by TV

With telephone and credit card at hand, today's shoppers don't even have to leave their homes. Several TV shopping channels bring the products to viewers. The typical TV sales pitch includes product and label displays, explanation of the product's use and price, and why a particular product is better than a competing product.

Shopping by TV can result in big price discounts, sometimes on brand name products. Often the price is lower than what one might pay for the same product at a neighborhood store, even at a discount store. Why are the price discounts possible? Because advertising and promoting goods and services in this way eliminates or sharply reduces the need for store and display space, thereby reducing a company's operating expenses. This permits the TV shopping service to pass on some of the resulting cost savings to customers in the form of lower prices.

How do TV viewers order products and services? Customarily, a toll-free 800 phone number is displayed on the TV screen. If the viewer wants to order a product, he or she simply phones that number, reports his or her name and address, credit card number and its expiration date, and places an order for the item by product name and stock number. Typically, the product is then sent to the customer at his or her address within a specified period of time.

Study this chapter to learn how businesses, such as TV shopping channels, promote, advertise, and sell goods and services. And use the contents to help you answer the questions in the end-of-chapter case study, "Using TV and Computers to Tune In Shoppers."

When you see commercials on television or ads in magazines and newspapers, do you sometimes wish you could buy the products or services advertised? If so, you're not unusual. Through advertising, we find out about new items offered for sale. Through advertising, we get news about where to go or how to buy the goods and services we already need or want. So that's what marketers do. They give us commercial news.

The next time you watch TV, notice how announcers lead into a commercial break. They don't say, "Here are some commercials." Instead, they often say, "Stay tuned for these messages." TV commercials are one of many ways marketers promote goods, services, and ideas.

Promotion means to communicate news about products and services and also to further advance their popularity—through advertising and publicizing. In this chapter we'll address promotion, competition, meeting the needs and wants of customers, and sales techniques.

MARKETERS PROMOTE GOODS AND SERVICES

Promotion, as one element in the marketing mix, includes advertising, publicizing, and budgeting. From Chapter 9, you know that a budget is a plan or a forecast, usually containing financial data. Thus marketing managers predict what they need to spend on promotional activities, and then they plan their activities to fit the planned expenditures.

Advertising

Advertising is marketing's most visible form of communication. The American Marketing Association (AMA) defines **advertising** as "any paid form of nonpersonal presentation and promotion of ideas, goods, or services by an identified sponsor." Nonprofit and public organizations, individuals, and businesses all use advertising to communicate messages about their services, ideas, and products.

Marketers, including entrepreneurs, get involved with various aspects of advertising, which include the following tasks:

- Selecting which products or services to advertise
- Selecting the media
- Sketching the ad with artwork, graphics, copy, or computer
- Writing the copy by hand, typewriter, or computer
- Creating a TV or radio commercial
- Writing a direct-mail letter
- Establishing and staying within the advertising budget
- Coordinating advertising with other promotional activities

- Working with people from within and outside the firm (e.g., media people) and following ads through to publication or broadcast

Promotion

The **promotional submix** is a component of the promotion mix that relies on advertising, personal selling, packaging, and sales promotion to transmit messages to the public. These messages can promote ideas as well as goods and services.

Promoting Ideas. Government agencies, endowed charities and research foundations, educational institutions, and political candidates all have ideas to promote. For example, government promotes the ideas of buying savings bonds and of joining the armed forces.

Cancer research institutions tell people to stop smoking and to avoid taking drugs. Educational groups promote staying in school to get knowledge and skills for life and work. Political candidates promote their platform to get votes and thus get elected. Companies also use slogans to promote ideas. See Figure 14-1.

▼ How would you feel if you were running for president of the student organization and your opponents (competitors for the office) show up with professionally printed posters? If you could not afford posters like theirs, how might you try to promote your candidacy and ideas?

Promoting Goodwill. Business marketers promote goodwill for their companies. **Goodwill** is the value of a business's reputation, other then tangible assets. Few things are more important to a firm than its reputation. A positive reputation comes not only from offering quality goods and services at affordable prices but also from the benefits a company provides to society. Examples of these benefits include environmental and energy conservation, pollution control, and contributions to charitable groups. By gaining goodwill, a company can motivate customers to patronize the firm.

The Identifying Sponsor Companies wouldn't be willing to pay for advertising if the sponsoring company's name was not promoted.

Figure 14-1. Some familiar logos and slogans used by companies in an effort to communicate a positive message about their respective businesses, create a favorable image of its products or services, and build brand name recognition.

Sponsors are identified by their logotypes. A **logotype** (**logo** is the short version) is a distinctive design that depicts a firm's name, a brand name, or a trademark. The logo is reproduced on all print advertisements, including packaging and labels, stationery, envelopes, and other business papers that go outside the firm.

▼ How would you feel if, during your campaign for student organization president (described previously), you enlisted your friends to prepare your campaign posters but they forgot to include your slogan or name on them?

A **trademark** is a registered name, symbol, or design. The U.S. government registers such names and brand marks to protect their sponsors. Although states have different requirements, a trademark registration usually lasts for 20 years with an option to renew.

Radio stations are required to announce a firm's name or the brand name. Television has more flexibility than either print or radio media because it's both an audio and a visual medium. Repetition, the soul of memorizing and remembering, is used everywhere in advertising. Also, in recognition of both the hearing- and the visually impaired among the TV audience, advertising sponsors use both print and audio.

Sweepstake and Mail-Order Promotions. Sweepstakes and contests have grown in popularity. People subscribe to magazines and order jewelry, perfume, and so on as a result of mail-order promotions. Some of the revenue obtained by getting orders in this way goes to pay for the cost of the prizes. Some of the revenue goes to defray the costs of advertising.

Telemarketing. **Telemarketers** sell goods and services over the telephone. This job emerged during the service and information eras (see Chapter 2). Telemarketers use information and technology in selling and taking orders.

Perhaps you've answered the telephone at home only to find that the caller's purpose was to sell you magazines or to get your family to contribute to a charity. These telemarketers sometimes work on **commission**, getting a percentage of the income earned from each sale. They sometimes work out of their homes. Other telemarketers have full-time jobs working in their companies' offices. These telemarketers use a computer to retrieve customer accounts (from computer storage) and to enter new accounts from first-time buyers. Telemarketers take orders when callers are ready to buy. (See the case at the end of the chapter.) So telemarketers use these skills: polite and

Figure 14-2. Some businesses depend heavily on telemarketing to sell their goods and services. Timely and effective use of information technologies (the telephone, computer, etc.) are the keys to running a successful telemarketing operation.

articulate telephone manners, quick and accurate computer techniques, and effective selling strategies. They should also be effective with human relations, since sometimes callers are irate customers who complain about problems.

Wholesalers' Promotions. Manufacturers sell to wholesalers and retailers by phone and also in person. Sales representatives (reps) travel in the field to call on business customers in stores, plants, and offices.

Wholesalers and shippers advertise in trade journals and by word of mouth. They promote the idea that their services are faster, better, and more courteous than those of the competition. Both reputation and services are addressed in their promotional activities.

Cooperative Promotion. Manufacturers, wholesalers, and franchisers often provide promotional ideas and help to the retail outlets that sell their goods or services. This practice is known as **cooperative promotion.** Many preprinted signs and ads, as well as promotional ideas, come to retailers from these three sources. The next time you're in a grocery store or a McDonald's, look around at the signs that promote goods and services with special displays, games, and contests.

For example, retail firms use direct-sales promotion when they display products attractively inside the store and in store windows. Many ideas for displays come from producers, if not from the retail headquarters. Consumers get free samples, which are made available by someone representing the identifying sponsor of a particular brand of product. Retailers advertise games and contests, which also are often designed by marketers who represent the chain or franchise sponsor.

Retailers print discount and special-sale coupons in local newspapers. But national marketers take responsibility for printing coupons in magazines, distributing them through direct-mail advertising, and describing national contests on network, independent, and cable television stations.

Unusual and Special-Service Promotions. To attract and keep customers, marketers use many promotional strategies. Among these are special and unusual promotions (see Information Brief 14-1). Extra or special services, provided free or at a nominal charge, include:

• Accepting credit cards and offering credit

Information Brief 14-1

Unusual Places and Ways to Advertise

Besides along highways, billboards also appear on the roads themselves. New York's Prestige Panels hauls standard-sized billboards on trucks. A fee of $4500 for a 50-hour week gets Prestige Panels to roll its trucks nonstop through neighborhoods anywhere in the country. For example, New York rock station WNEW-FM sent these trucks to such teenage hot spots as the beaches of Long Island and the New Jersey shore to advertise for the station.

Phonograph albums and compact discs are other unusual places to advertise. There usually are 30-second spaces between each song—a spot to stick in an ad. Why do marketers advertise this way? Said one group's marketer: "We're here to make money. That's the bottom line."

Source: Julia Reed, "Ads Where You Least Expect Them," *U.S. News and World Report*, March 9, 1987, p. 46.

- Allowing exchanges and refunds on returned merchandise
- Gift wrapping
- Free deliveries
- Advice about how to access, use, install, or repair data banks, computers, software, appliances, etc.

Publicity

Publicity involves getting favorable news printed or broadcast at no cost to the advertising firm. **Public relations (PR)** is a business activity designed to get public understanding and acceptance of a firm's goods, services, ideas, and contributions to society. PR people try to get **publicity** (nonpaid space) accepted for publication or broadcast.

PR people write **news releases** (news articles). News releases are submitted to newspapers and magazines to be printed or to radio and television to be broadcast as news or public-service announcements.

PR people deal with the media, consumer groups, stockholders, government, suppliers, dealers, employees, and especially the community at large. Examples of business-related publicity and news include:

- Company announcements dealing with new products and services
- A drop or rise in revenues and profits that affect the company's investors, its employees, or possibly the price of goods and services that therefore affect consumers
- Mergers and acquisitions that affect the company's investors, employees, and possibly the community where the firm is located
- Contributions and services provided as a public service

The Advertising Budget

Advertising costs money. In the **advertising budget,** the following items represent expenditures:

- Space in magazines, newspapers, yellow pages, catalogs, and on billboards or advertising vehicles
- Time on radio and television
- Printing and postage for direct mail, catalogs, and brochures
- Salaries of people involved with advertising

Factors to be budgeted appear under the broad categories of media, promotions, and expenses. Representative costs by category include:

Media: newspapers, magazines, radio, television, direct mail. Included are the related production costs and ad-agency and media billings. (See Information Brief 14-2.)

Promotions: exhibits, displays, contests, games, sweepstakes.

Operating expenses: salaries and wages, supplies, printing, postage, utilities, telecommunications, travel, entertainment, insurance, subscriptions, dues, etc.

IDENTIFYING AND ADDRESSING THE MARKET

Marketers identify the target market in as much detail as possible. Then they zero in on specifically identified groups with the type of advertising that's most likely to appeal to people in these groups. In accomplishing these objectives, marketers deal with market segmentation, market share, and the selection of media, methods, and timing.

Market Segmentation

If your company markets disposable diapers, the target group would be parents of infants. Demographic data describing one town or neighborhood would be insufficient for a national marketing campaign like that used by disposable-diaper manufacturers. Local data is needed by local merchants. A collection of such data from many locations is used by mass marketers.

The process of dividing the total market into smaller parts is called **market segmentation.** Marketers are interested in finding customers with similar characteristics. Each identified segment is made up of people who are similar to one another in behavior, life-style, hobbies, and values. For example, marketers of diapers concentrate on families with babies. These specific types of families constitute the market segment for diapers.

Market groups may be segmented by age, geographical location, sex, education, occupation, ethnic background, income level, and other characteristics. (Take the photo opening Unit 5. It is an example of an advertisement directed at a market group segmented by geographical location, those who live in the South.)

The best segment would produce positive answers to all four of the following questions:

Information Brief 14-2

Hotshot Ad Agency Wins Some, Loses Some

The Miami-based Beber Silverstein & Partners Advertising, Inc., spared no expense to produce a 60-second TV spot for one client. But all that creativity never made it to the TV viewers' screen. The advertiser had to cut back on the ad budget. Beber Silverstein got only a small sum of money from the client up front—not enough to cover the costs of making the TV commercial.

When the duo made the cover of *Advertising Age,* Beber Silverstein was Florida's biggest ad agency and one of the nation's largest female-owned agencies. Silverstein says that in business, you have to be a risk taker. "But risks don't always pay off—sometimes you lose."

Source: Pete Engardio, "Did Success Spoil Beber Silverstein?" *Business Week,* June 1, 1987, p. 98.

Information Brief
14-3

Huge Hispanic Market Segment Attracts Advertisers

The Hispanic population is growing at four times the national rate. Despite this, Spanish-speaking Americans have long been overlooked by American businesses. Today there are signs that this is changing.

In 1987, U.S. companies were expected to spend $450 million on Spanish-language advertising. They knew the Hispanic market represented 18 million consumers. It had a purchasing power of $120 billion.

Companies such as Procter & Gamble, McDonald's, and Kraft have been increasing their Hispanic-advertising budgets. They are turning to agencies specializing in Spanish language advertising.

Source: Pete Engardio, "Fast Times on Avenida Madison," *Business Week,* June 6, 1988, pp. 62–67, and Scott Brown, "Madison Avenue's Big Latin Beat," *Time,* July 20, 1987, p. 57.

- Is the segment measurable? Populations within groups can be counted and their needs and wants surveyed.
- Is it large enough? The market segment has sufficient buying customers. (See Information Brief 14-3.)
- Is it reachable? Advertising and promotional activities can be placed so that customers can learn about the products and services available and can also get to the selling places or order from home.
- Is it responsive? Customers must be interested, willing, and able to make sufficient purchases to enable the offering company to make a profit.

Market Share

The **market share** is that part of the market which buys a firm's products. Market share is often expressed as a percentage of the market. Using a local example, suppose that a community has a population of 100,000. Market research data suggests that it takes a certain number of people to support various types of businesses. Although only 1200 people are needed to keep a gas station in business, at least 25,000 people are needed to support a gift shop.

Four gift shops could probably survive in a city of 100,000 people. Provided that all were similar in size and in quality of products and services and situated in good locations, these gift shops could reasonably expect to divide the market share somewhat equally. Earnings data collected in the community reveals that annual revenues for these shops totals $500,000. Each gift shop, in sharing the market, sells about $125,000 worth of goods each year, representing a 25 percent market share.

Suppose however that a fifth shop opens and enters the competition. Assuming that location, products, and services are equal and that advertising and promotional activities draw enough trade, one can assume that each store's market share will change. The same number of people live and shop in the community. Just because there's another gift shop does not mean that more people will buy more gifts. Thus each of the five stores now sell only $100,000 worth of merchandise per year, and their market share has dropped from 25 to 20 percent.

▼ How would you feel if you owned one of the existing gift shops and the fifth shop, a new store, opened across the street from yours?

SOLE MATES.

Bare your sole in one of four fabulous colors. Introducing White 'n Brights." The good-time white hi-tops with splashes of turquoise, rose, yellow or midnight blue. Go ahead, knock their socks off.

Reebok

Because life is not a spectator sport.®

Figure 14-3. An example of advertising targeted to a specific market segment— the nation's teenage popu- lation—a very powerful consumer group which spends billions of dollars each year.

The Nielsen company rates TV shows in terms of the numbers in the viewing audiences. Collectively, these data tell which of the networks are rated highest—has the highest market share. Advertisers are interested in these data, because they make choices about where their advertising dollars will do the most good. For example, toys are advertised during children's shows.

Selecting the Right Time to Advertise

Timing has several implications. It can refer to the time place- ment of TV and radio spots within a day's or week's program- ming. Time can refer to seasonal promotions. For example, a florist chain will try to place its advertisements in time to precede holidays, such as Easter and Mother's Day. Stores pro- mote seasonal items well in advance of their actual purchase and use dates, including Christmas merchandise, lawn and gar- den products, and fashions for the upcoming season.

Timing can also be critical in the introduction of new prod- ucts to the national and international markets. Suppose Com-

Source: Alvin P. Sanoff with Cynthia Kyle, "Zapping the TV Networks," *U.S. News and World Report*, June 1, 1987, pp. 56–57.

Information Brief 14-4

TV People Meters and Viewer Clout

Determining market share is a big headache to TV networks. But the results of market research, from so called people meters, give viewers more clout. The people-meter device electronically records TV viewers' choices.

Advertising rates are based on the size and composition of TV audiences. If the networks fail to lure enough viewers of a particular age group, sex, and income level, they generally must give advertisers free spots to make good. When that happens, it takes a big bite out of network profits. It's a frantic time to be in the television business for the networks and the independents, but also for advertisers. Viewers are fickle, because they have so many options vying for their restless viewing habits—cable, VCRs, and the like.

puter Co. A is determined to introduce its desktop computer to the market in time for students to find out about it and buy it before heading for college. But because of packaging and promotion problems, Company A's computer is not available until October. Meanwhile, Computer Co. B, with a product that's similar in usage and price, introduces its computer in June. Which computer are college students most likely to buy, if they want to purchase everything they need before the fall semester starts? Marketers are always alert to the competition, especially when two or more producers are designing and producing a similar new item. The first to get to market—global or national—invariably has the advantage.

Selecting the Media

Advertisers use the media of television, direct mail, newspapers, radio, magazines, trade publications, outdoor space, fliers, and so on. The more people a medium reaches, the higher the cost of ad fees charged to advertisers. Thus magazines and newspapers with a high circulation (number of readers) charge advertisers more than those with lower readership. And TV shows with a high viewing audience charge higher rates to air commercials than those with lower viewing numbers.

Television and Radio. National advertisers who can afford it often prefer prime-time TV slots. Advertisers select their ad spots based on the identification of market segments and the products offered.

▼ How would you feel about decisions to advertise soap during a football game? Or denture cleaner during a teen show? Or a stockbroker's services during a show for young children?

National and global commercials appear on network and broad-range distribution channels. But local advertisers use the local media. Local advertisers include car and appliance dealers, local businesses, consumers, public services, and the like.

Newspapers, Magazines, and Other Print Media. About 30 percent of money spent on advertising goes to local newspapers. Here's where many local merchants, service firms, organizations, agencies, and individuals place much of their print promotions.

But you wouldn't choose a single local newspaper in which to advertise your company's disposable diapers. Not if marketing efforts are supposed to reach the national, even global, young-family market segment. *Parents Magazine* might be a good place to advertise disposable diapers.

Other print media include the yellow pages of telephone directories, as well as direct-mail and outdoor advertisements. (See Information Brief 14-5.)

Direct Mail. Known as "junk mail" to some consumers, many companies and organizations rely heavily on direct-mail advertising. Sweepstakes, games and contests, and coupons are distributed through the mails, in addition to straight copy and graphic ads that provide no gimmicks, just information. Non-profit organizations and associations use direct-mail promotions to recruit and retain members and solicit contributions.

Every possible method is used to get consumers to, first, open their mail; second, read it; and, third, respond—the quicker the better.

Outdoor Media. Outdoor advertising includes signs, billboards, printed balloons, and the like. Some signs stand up high and flash in colored neon. Other signs are small and nondescript. Billboards decorate roadsides, and airplanes and balloons trail banners across the sky.

SALES TECHNIQUES

Meeting the customer's needs and providing courteous, considerate service are the first two premises of personal selling around which other strategies are developed.

The Customer Is "Always Right"

Customers might not always be right, but "the customer is always the customer." This means treating them with respect and courtesy. Customers are more likely to return when their needs and wants are satisfied by courteous, sensitive, empathetic, and patient salespeople.

Courtesy. Courtesy is a constant. When wares or services are advertised, the effect is that of inviting anybody and everybody in to browse, question, compare, and shop. Some customers know what they're searching for—whether through a store,

Information Brief 14-5

Yellow Page Advertising— Confusing, but Necessary

A typical quarter-page ad in one yellow page directory costs $4956 a year. "One book used to be all there was; now nobody knows where to look," says a Los Angeles taxicab marketer.

Many marketers wonder which directories they should use for advertising. NYNEX has a Spanish yellow pages, a directory aimed at the college student market, and another targeted to marine businesses and boat owners.

An east coast employment agency spends $120,000 a year to get their ads in four yellow page directories and is confused about which ad brings the best results. But even at steep rates, businesses find advertising in the yellow pages a necessary expense.

Source: Manuel Schiffres with Lisa J. Moore and Esther Pessin, "Mining for Gold in Yellow Pages," *U.S. News and World Report,* October 13, 1986, p. 53.

a catalog, or a computer data bank. They still appreciate advice and guidance. Some customers need to know how to order. Others want to know about price and quality. Still others want time alone to examine products, to make comparisons, and to arrive at their own decisions without interference. The successful salesperson is alert, knowledgeable, and pleasant.

Sensitivity. **Sensitivity** can be defined as an awareness of the needs and emotions of others. Salespeople often walk a narrow line between absolute truth and sensitivity. The salesclerk might want to make a sale and also to please a customer. But what if an obese man tries to stuff himself into a suit that's too small and then asks the clerk how he looks? The response can be sensitive and tactful, while avoiding the complete truth. For example, the smart clerk avoids saying "You look dreadful in that thing. You need a suit at least three sizes bigger!"

Without being unduly humble, subservient, or apologetic, the wise salesclerk puts the customer's needs first. Notice the differences between sensitive and insensitive responses, as they appear in Table 14-1.

Empathy and Patience. Empathy means putting oneself in the customer's shoes. It's not hard to think of all sorts of

TABLE 14-1 A Comparison of Sensitive Versus Insensitive Responses in Sales Situations

Situation	Sensitive Response	Insensitive Response
The customer complains about a product	"Perhaps this particular item is faulty; would you like to exchange it?"	"It's not my fault! Don't blame me."
The customer misunderstands the sales representative	"Perhaps I didn't make myself clear."	"You didn't listen to me!"
The customer mumbles and cannot be understood	"I didn't understand; would you repeat that please?"	"Speak up! You're talking too quietly."
The customer complains that she was taken out of turn; another customer arriving afterward was served first	"I might have taken you out of order; step right this way, please."	"I'm only human. Why didn't you speak up?"

examples of poor and inefficient service, impatient and insensitive salespeople. Treating customers the way you'd like to be treated is the best clue to positive sales techniques that can win friends and sell goods and services.

Being patient in the face of rude and irate customers is more difficult. But putting oneself in their shoes helps. A hard day of facing problems, of traffic and lines, of heat and hunger can make any customer touchy and ill-mannered. They need patience more than ever.

Making the Sale

Selling large-item industrial and consumer goods requires some special sales techniques. Yet getting a business customer to buy a $2 million item is sometimes no more difficult than persuading a consumer to buy a year's membership in a health spa. The idea is to stimulate action. Until the customer signs on the dotted line, the sales objective has not been met. Successful personal-contact sellers use the following seven-step plan:

- Meet the customer
- Talk the customer's language, and listen
- Establish credibility by demonstrating knowledge of the company and its goods and services
- Get the customer to perceive a need or want
- Handle objections by proposing solutions
- Close the sale
- Provide follow-up services to customers

Meet the Customer. Successful salespeople are courteous, respectful, and businesslike, while still being friendly. They wear appropriate clothing and do not overuse gestures and mannerisms. They compliment the customer with sincerity, saying something nice about the office decor or home (for house-to-house selling), or the courtesy of receiving personnel.

Personal-contact salespeople make customers feel comfortable and at ease. Through informal conversation, they find out something about their customers. For example, a real estate agent wants to learn something about the client's life-style. Showing $200,000 houses to people whose financial picture permits a less-than-$75,000 purchase is insulting. It shows a lack of consideration for the client.

Talk the Customer's Language, and Listen. People in the same industry use **jargon**—abbreviations and terms used in any given industry or field. People who have similar work backgrounds can share problems and interests. For example, a former teacher who sells textbooks to teachers can understand a teacher's problems and sympathize, and sometimes even offer solutions. Thus the textbook salesperson establishes rapport by talking the teacher's language.

Good salespeople are good listeners. They listen to the spoken word and also interpret nuances, gestures, and facial expressions. They are ready and able to respond to the customer's needs, wants, or doubts. They let customers ask questions.

Establish Credibility. Knowledgeable sales reps keep abreast of innovations in their own companies and also from the competition. They subscribe to trade literature, attend seminars and trade conventions, and maintain active membership in appropriate business and professional associations. They know how their products operate and the various uses that can be made of them. They describe, illustrate and demonstrate products efficiently. They can explain the benefits of company services.

Get the Customer to Perceive a Need. Based on human needs, as discussed in Chapter 12, effective salespeople know that people seldom buy either a product or a service for its own sake. They buy to meet other needs. Thus effective salespeople describe the benefits their goods and services can provide. Benefits address such things as:

- Saving money, time, and effort
- Contributions to health, safety, physical attractiveness, leisure-time activities, self-esteem, prestige
- Learning tools that develop life-coping and work-enhancing skills and knowledge

Handle Objections by Proposing Solutions. Because of budgetary limits and other problems, customers might raise objections to buying the product or service. Objections usually refer to cost and quality, or they make comparisons with competitors' products and services.

At this point, provided the salesperson has gotten the customer to perceive a need, the customer could be eager and willing to buy. But the customer might not have final authority to make a buying decision. For example, a purchasing agent could be required to check first with a manager, or a married person could be in the habit of discussing purchases with a spouse. The sales rep helps the customer hurdle the last obstacles by being frank but supportive when objections are raised.

Admitting to problems, the sales rep uses "Yes . . . but" phrases:

"Yes, our product costs more (than brand X), but it's likely to last three times longer." (This solution addresses durability and quality.)

"Yes, our product is new, but already there's a long list of satisfied customers." (This solution addresses the needs for prestige and reassurance.)

Close the Sale. The experienced salesperson knows when the customer is ready to buy and does not oversell or delay the final decision. Urging the customer along, the sales rep provides positive options. The following questions, for example, are good.

"Do you need one or two items (or dozens of units) right now?"

"Would you prefer to pay cash or use our easy-payment plan?"

Questions about delivery, installation, use, and service will usually already have been covered. The wise salesperson tucks the sales contract away and departs quickly but politely. For door-to-door sales, however, consumers have three days (72 hours) to change their minds. This is the law, because consumers sometimes get overenthusiastic and sign a sales contract to buy something they neither want nor can afford.

Provide Follow-Up Services to Customers. Follow-up services include helping customers solve problems and getting their questions answered. In the computer industry, this follow-up service is essential. Many enthusiastic customers, inexperienced in the ways that computers work or how to get the most out of their software, get easily frustrated. Follow-up services also include checking with a former customer to see how he or she likes the product and whether other new and related products and services might meet additional needs.

Information Brief 14-6

Tips for Personable Follow-Up

Out in Los Angeles, Dave Smith, sales manager of the largest real estate sales force in the United States, uses these customer follow-up tips:

When Dave leaves his office every day, he takes along a stack of blank 3 × 5 cards and a stubby pencil. He drives by houses he's already sold and notes (on a card) a new tree or shrub. When he sees a former client walking down the street—one who just got out of the hospital—he notes that data too. Because of these personable follow-up techniques, Dave's former clients send many other real estate clients to him.

Laptops Help Sales Reps

Today it is not uncommon to see sales reps equipped with laptop computers like that shown in the photo above. These portable computers are changing the way reps do their work. Sometimes businesses create whole systems or networks of these computers. The Dendrite system is an example.

The Dendrite system, a computer network, was developed in Australia by a United Kingdom international pharmaceutical giant. A Somerset County, New Jersey, firm that uses the system explains the origins of the system's name. A dendrite is the treelike set of connections that carries impulses from the body to a nerve cell. And that's what the computerized technology does for the pharmaceutical firm—it connects each sales rep to the home office, and vice versa.

How do the reps use the system? Pharmaceutical sales reps need to save time out in the field, especially when they call on doctors whose time is also valuable. These sales reps hope that doctors will prescribe their pharmaceutical companies' drugs over those of the competition when they write prescriptions for patients. Merck Pharmaceutical has 1500 sales representatives in the field, and Parke-Davis has another 1000. Time is money, especially when it's estimated that sales calls cost about $120 each to make.

At one time, all pharmaceutical sales reps had to keep records by hand. And that was time-consuming, too. This recordkeeping (obtaining and keeping or processing of information) covers names, addresses, doctor specialties, hospital affiliations, former contacts, future appointments, number and type of free samples, and much more. Now the Dendride system helps the reps record and track this information automatically.

Pharmaceutical firms aren't the only ones that use portable, or laptop, computers. Salespeople who are out in the field representing all sorts of companies use the laptops to conduct business in a time-saving and cost-effective way while on the road.

Sources: John T. Harding, "Dendrite Promotes Computers as Selling Tool for Drug Industry," *Newark Star Ledger*, October 4, 1987.

Dissatisfied customers can cause a business to lose goodwill in a hurry. A satisfied customer returns again and again. Satisfied customers also provide valuable (and free!) word-of-mouth advertising. For an example, see Information Brief 14-6 on page 315 to learn how one enterprising real estate Sales Manager benefits from good follow-up with his customers.

The Excitement of Selling

Whether selling over a counter or in the offices and homes of customers, many salespeople are successful because they're good at their trade. These salespeople say their field is both exciting and fun. There's the technical aspect of knowing all about the company and its products, services, and ideas. Then there's the people side. Successsful salespeople are masters at using psychology and human relations in meeting the needs and wants of customers.

Select Terms to Know

advertising	logotype (logo)	public relations (PR)
advertising budget	market segmentation	publicity
commission (sales)	market share	sensitivity
cooperative promotion	news release	telemarketer
goodwill	promotion	trademark
jargon	promotional submix	

Review Questions

1. Describe the purpose of advertising, and give examples.

2. Explain the marketer's typical advertising tasks. Give examples.

3. Give some examples of promotional activities, including those used by individuals as well as by public and other nonprofit organizations.

4. Give examples of publicity and public relations activities.

5. Why is it important for marketers to stick to their budgets?

6. What is market segmentation, and how is it used? Give examples.

7. What is market share? Give examples.

8. Describe how the media are used in advertising. Why is timing important? Give examples of both media use and timing.

9. Explain and give examples of the seven-step plan in personal-contact selling. Why do consumers who buy at home get 72 hours to make a decision?

Thought and Discussion Questions

1. Discuss the similarities and differences between and among advertising, promotional activities, and publicity.

2. What methods do advertising sponsors use to get identified? If you were designing an ad, how would you identify your company?

3. Assume you are in charge of advertising at a local grocery store, which is one store among a chain of retail outlets. Discuss how you would cooperate with headquarters' marketers on a cooperative promotion campaign.

4. Discuss how you would train a telemarketing clerk to handle telephone customers, meet customers' needs, and make sales. Review the opening news item, the description of the telemarketer's function, and the section on sales techniques. (See also the case discussion.)

Projects

1. In a city with a population of 1 million people, there are 14 information processing service firms. Their target market includes 6 percent of the total population. Yours will be the fifteenth firm. Current total annual revenues amount to $1,225,000. Assume that once your firm is operating at full capacity, you will obtain an equal market share, or 1/15th of total revenues. Use these steps to determine your firm's market share.

a. What dollar amount of the market share do the existing firms now hold, assuming that each shares equally, or 1/14th each of the market?

b. How much will each firm's share be once your firm is operating at full capacity?

2. Collect examples of direct-mail advertising. Report your findings to the class. Observe and record the methods advertisers use to get reader consumers to:

a. Open the mail.
b. Read the mail.
c. Want the product or service.
d. Respond quickly and positively to the offer.

3. Get your notes from analyzing TV commercials (activities in Chapters 12 and 13), or select new TV commercials to study. Choose a product or service that interests you and that's familiar to you. Analyze the commercials and do the following:

a. Organize your notes according to these categories: target market, method, timing of each commercial.
b. Record ideas, while observing commercials, about how you would redesign the commercial.
Report your findings to the class.

4. Listen to advertisements aired on a local radio station. Write a script for a 30-second spot that promotes one of the following options:

a. Recruiting students into a student association
b. The purposes of getting an education—the benefits of staying in school compared with the disadvantages of dropping out
c. Developing a healthy body—avoiding the misuse of drugs and alcohol

Case Study: Using TV and Computers to Tune In Shoppers

The practice of shopping by TV, telephone, and credit card has grown in popularity. Points in the sales pitch typically refer to time and limited supply. Viewers are usually urged to act now "while the supply lasts" or "during the limited time that this price applies." The promise of quick delivery is also often used in the selling pitch.

TV shopper services like catalog and door-to-door selling give consumers a chance to return products for refunds or credit. This practice is used to assure consumers that if they don't like a product after seeing it, they won't be stuck with having to pay for it.

Comp-U-Card provides another kind of home shopping service. Comp-U-Card's customers use computers. The customers pay $39 a year for access to its database, which lists a quarter-million items and hundreds of brands. The bulk of Comp-U-Card's revenues come from membership fees and also from commissions. Comp-U-Card itself handles no goods.

Members call the 800 number and order from the telemarketer (telephone sales-order clerk). A computer combs a list containing the latest bids from 500 independent distributors, wholesalers, and retailers. Then it reveals the best deal. Comp-U-Card then places the order to the low bidder. Consumers get up to 50 percent discounts.

Yet by targeting only consumers who had computers at home, their market was limited. Revenues from membership fees were slow coming in. The company was about to fold. A name change to CitiShoppers and a link to banks, however, gave the computer shopping firm access to mailing lists containing more than 2.7 million Visa and Master Card holders. This helped restore the computer shopping service to relative health.

Sources: CVN, Home Shoppers' Channel; and Russell Mitchell, "How Comp-U-Card Hooks Shoppers," *Business Week*, May 18, 1987, pp. 73–74.

---

1. If you owned or managed a TV shopping service, what type of salespeople would you hire to present products and services to the TV viewing audience? What qualifications would you look for in interviewing and hiring these TV salespeople?

2. What tasks and procedures would you use to ensure that orders from TV shoppers were processed quickly and accurately?

3. Now assume you were a Comp-U-Card marketer. Why do you think a name change to CitiShoppers might help your firm obtain increased business? How would getting access to a mailing list of 2.7 million Visa and Master Card credit card holders help your company?

4. In order of frequency, what media would you recommend that your newly named firm, CitiShoppers, use to promote its computer shopping service? Explain your answer.

CHAPTER 15

Channels of Distribution

Thomas's Distribution Promises

"Thomas's Promises" is a familiar slogan to English muffin lovers throughout the country. But back in 1987 some distributors who delivered Thomas's English Muffins to stores in Florida and North Carolina complained that the S. B. Thomas Company had broken some of its promises to them as regards the firm's use of channels of distribution. The distributors started grumbling shortly after the owners of Thomas acquired another baking company. Thomas and the newly acquired company were then merged (joined together) into one baking operation. As a result, the merged company wound up with duplicate channels of distribution in the same territories in Florida and North Carolina.

Study this chapter to find out more about the importance of channels of distribution to businesses such as S. B. Thomas. And use the contents to help you answer the questions to the end-of-chapter case study, "The Questionable Distribution Promises."

How many different products can you find in one supermarket or department store? Hundreds? Thousands? Millions? One of the factors that attracts us to this type of store is its selection of products. Did you ever stop to think where all those products are produced? In just one aisle of the supermarket you might find cookies from New York, potato chips from Illinois, pretzels from Pennsylvania, raisins from California, nuts from Georgia, and items from 30 or 40 other states and countries.

How did the products get to the shelves of the supermarket or department store? It would be almost impossible for the store manager or owner to contact all the producers whose products are sold there, buy the products, make arrangements to have them shipped, and handle the paperwork involved with paying for them.

Now let's look at the situation from the producer's viewpoint. Imagine how difficult it would be for the Wrigley Company in Chicago to sell directly to the millions of supermarkets, convenience stores, variety stores, theaters, restaurants, and vending machine companies that sell Doublemint chewing gum. Just naming all the locations where Doublemint is sold would take weeks or months. Instead of selling directly to each location, producers use the services of channels of distribution.

What are channels of distribution? In a sense they are the paths, or routes, used by businesses to move products and services to customers. In this chapter you will look at different types of channels and learn how they are used in carrying out the distribution function of marketing. The central goal of that function is most vital: to get goods and services to customers *at the right place at the right time*.

WHAT ARE CHANNELS OF DISTRIBUTION?

Almost everything that you buy when you go shopping has passed through a well-organized system that moved it from the producer, or manufacturer, to the location where you can buy it. This system is made up of wholesalers, agents, and retailers who specialize in getting products (and some services) from the producer to consumers like you who want to buy them. These businesses use the services of truckers, railroads, airlines, cargo ship lines, and pipeline owners to move products quickly and efficiently. The system that producers use to get their products to the consumers who want them is referred to as the **channels of distribution.** These channels may differ from producer to producer, depending on the products that they are marketing. A shoelace manufacturer, for example, will probably use a different channel of distribution than a sports car manufacturer.

Channels of distribution typically have several different types of members, each of whom serve a unique role in the distribution system. Members include producers, intermediaries, and consumers. Each of these will be discussed in detail in the next section.

▼ How would you feel if there were no channels of distribution to get the products you want to the stores where you want to buy them? Could you manage if you were able to buy only those products that are manufactured in your neighborhood? Would you be willing to contact the manufacturers of shirts, jeans, cassette tapes, and magazines in order to buy them if you couldn't get them in local stores?

PRODUCERS

Producers, or manufacturers, are firms that create products and services which are distributed through the marketing channels. Many manufacturing firms produce only a limited number of related products. The Wrigley Company in Chicago produces fewer than 10 brands of chewing gum; James Industries in Hollidayburg, Pennsylvania, produces Slinky Toys and several other types of toy sets; and Bumble Bee Seafoods in San Francisco produces fewer than 10 brands of canned and frozen fish products. You can buy Wrigley's Spearmint gum, Slinky Toys, and Bumble Bee tuna in locations throughout the United States as well as in other countries thanks to intermediaries.

INTERMEDIARIES

Intermediaries, also called middlemen, are companies or people that help to move products and services from producers to consumers. In the process of doing this, they perform some important services for the producer, for other intermediaries, and for the consumer. We will examine these services after we look at three important types of intermediaries: wholesalers, retailers, and agents. Wholesalers and retailers actually purchase products from the producer or from other intermediaries and sell them again. Agents help buyers and sellers to get together without actually purchasing the products themselves.

Wholesalers

Wholesalers are intermediaries who sell products to companies or individuals who are not consumers or industrial consumers. Instead, these companies or individuals resell them directly to the final consumers or process them further and then resell them. Wholesalers are sometimes referred to as **distributors.**

A wholesaler, for example, might gather merchandise such as gum, soft drinks, stationery, health and beauty aids, and tobacco from a variety of producers. The company would then offer a selection of the products that it had gathered to several hundred retail stores. Another wholesaler might buy a variety of small industrial parts or plumbing and electrical supplies from many different producers. The wholesaler would then sell the parts or supplies to industries for use in manufacturing products that will later be sold to industrial customers. In the next section of the chapter, we will look at the various services that the wholesaler performs for the retailer.

Retailers

Retailers are intermediaries who sell products to the ultimate consumer. Today's retail stores include a mix of department stores, mass merchandiser department stores, supermarkets, specialty stores, and convenience stores among others.

The traditional **department store** offers a wide assortment of merchandise including home furnishings, appliances, apparel, and housewares in price ranges that appeal to the general public. This merchandise comes to the store through wholesalers who gather it from a wide variety of different producers. For some large stores, the wholesaler that services the stores is a company-owned intermediary.

Mass merchandiser department stores are willing to price merchandise lower than the traditional department store but sell at higher volume levels. The supermarket was the earliest form of mass merchandiser. The typical supermarket makes approximately 1 cent on each dollar of sales in order to sell its products in large volumes. This is one-tenth of what most businesses consider attractive. Today many other forms of mass merchandisers include superdrug stores such as Osco, discounters such as Kmart and Target, and catalog showroom retailers such as Service Merchandise.

In contrast to the mass merchandiser, the **specialty store** is usually small and offers specific goods and services to select end-users. The specialty store offers fewer types of merchandise items but specializes in those items that will appeal to certain groups of people who might not be satisfied with the products offered by the department store. A small specialty clothing store, for example, might offer 25 varieties of the most popular type of jeans in all the latest colors and a wide selection of sweatshirts and sweaters but no other merchandise. To assemble this merchandise assortment, the owner-manager may have to work with several different wholesalers, each of whom deals with jeans and tops along with other items of merchandise.

Information Brief 15-1

Exporting Channels

Business owners are beginning to realize that exporting their goods and services outside the United States offers many advantages. More than 95 percent of the world's population lies outside our country, a rich prize for the aggressive businessperson.

Exporting is no longer the sole province of the large business firm. Small and medium-sized firms are finding encouraging acceptance for their goods and services. These businesses are finding that their foreign channels of distribution may need to be quite different from those at home.

Exporting can be profitable, but is also hard work. Local customs, tax structures, legal restrictions, transportation systems, and business practices are all hurdles which must be overcome to secure a marketing channel.

Sources: Christopher Knowlton, "The New Export Entrepreneurs," *Fortune,* June 6, 1988; "The Long Arm of Small Business," *Business Week,* February 29, 1988.

Convenience stores may be open 24 hours a day and usually offer bread, milk, coffee, and other staple items of merchandise at high prices. The attraction of most convenience stores is that the customer can get in, buy, and get back out of the store in a hurry. These stores are beginning to offer a broader selection of merchandise and services such as video tape rentals and meals that customers can heat in the store's microwave oven.

Convenience stores and most other retail members of the channels of distribution use the services of wholesalers to gather products for their customers.

▼ How would you feel if you had to do all your shopping between the hours of 9 a.m. and 6 p.m.? Would you be able to manage without the convenience of supermarkets and convenience stores that often stay open 24 hours a day?

Agents and Brokers

Agents and brokers are intermediaries who do not buy and take possession of the products that they help to distribute. Instead, they bring buyers and sellers together and help to arrange for the sale. **Agents** are salespeople who represent a number of different companies that produce similar, but non-competing, products. Agents are particularly helpful to producers in sales areas where there are not enough clients to justify the use of a full-time sales representative. A textile company, for example, might have a sales staff of five full-time representatives who serve the five largest territories. Their clients include clothing manufacturers and fabric stores. The company might also use several agents to sell to the same type of clients in areas where there is no need for a full-time sales representative. Because these agents represent the textile company, they do not need to buy the fabric. They simply arrange the sales and ask the manufacturer to ship the fabric. As an additional service to their clients, these agents may also represent other companies that manufacture patterns, sewing needles, thread, bobbins, and other related products.

Brokers are agents who specialize in the food area. They usually represent several noncompeting food producers within a specific geographic location. Their clients include supermarket buyers, managers of independent food stores, and institutions that have food service programs.

CONSUMERS

The final member of the channel of distribution is the consumer. The **consumer** actually uses, or consumes, the products and services made by producers and distributed by intermediaries. There are two basic types of consumers, those who buy consumer goods and those who buy industrial goods.

Consumer goods are products and services that are used by the ultimate consumer. Consumer products include toothpaste, food, television sets, VCRs, cars, records, and lamps. Consumer services include car repair, dry cleaning, entertainment activities such as bowling, insurance, telephone systems, private education such as piano lessons, and personal business services such as legal or financial counseling.

Industrial goods are products and services that are used to run a business or organization or to produce other products and services. Industrial products include farm products such as wheat or corn that are made into food; zippers and fabric that are made into clothing; and equipment such as tools, forklift trucks, and cash registers. Industrial services include insurance, accounting, building maintenance, display services, transportation, and computer services.

WHY DO PRODUCERS USE THE SERVICES OF INTERMEDIARIES?

The first member of the channel of distribution is the producer of either goods or services. By using the services of intermediaries rather than selling directly to consumers, producers can make larger sales with fewer transactions. They also gather more information about consumers from the intermediaries than they would be able to gather themselves. Still another benefit of using intermediaries is the ability to keep a smaller number of products on hand.

Larger Sales With Fewer Transactions

By relying on intermediaries, companies such as James Industries are able to sell their Slinky Toys in large quantities with relatively few sales transactions. They might deal with 200 wholesalers instead of 10,000 retailers or 3 million consumers each year.

Figure 15-1 shows the number of transactions that four producers would make if they each sold one product to four

Figure 15-1. This diagram shows that producers can make a larger quantity of sales to consumers, efficiently and with fewer sales transactions, by using the services of intermediaries.

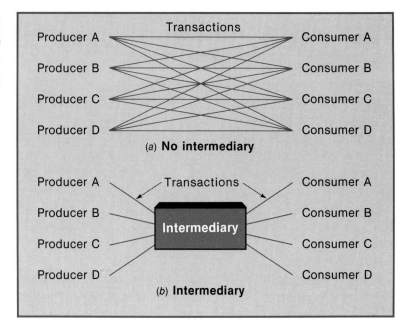

different consumers without the services of a marketing intermediary. The figure also shows the number of transactions that the same four producers would make if they used the services of one marketing intermediary who, in turn, moves the products to each of the four consumers.

More Information About Consumers

Producers also benefit from the fact that intermediaries are closer to the consumers. Because they talk with consumers on a daily basis, wholesalers and retailers have a better understanding of the needs and wants of the market. When intermediaries communicate these needs and wants back to the producers, all channel members, as well as the ultimate consumers, benefit. Producers are able to tailor their production of products to the wants and needs of consumers. As a result, they make a higher profit and are better able to produce the amounts of their products that consumers will buy. This means that they will be able to save money by keeping a smaller inventory.

Intermediaries are able to buy products that move quickly off their shelves and into the consumers' hands. This increases their level of profit. And the consumers benefit because they are able to buy products that more closely meet their needs and wants.

WHAT SERVICES DO INTERMEDIARIES PERFORM?

If you were to visit the warehouse and offices of a busy wholesaler, what would you see? Just what services do the intermediaries perform? Intermediaries perform various activities including buying and selling, financing and risk bearing, bulk breaking, and transporting and storing goods.

Buying and Selling

Wholesalers make direct contact with the producers of goods and services. Because they specialize in buying goods in large quantities from a variety of different suppliers, they are more likely to have current information about the best suppliers. This information may not be available to retailers or to individual consumers.

Retailers, who are also intermediaries, specialize in selling directly to consumers. They offer services such as alterations, gift wrapping, store credit, and personal sales attention that wholesalers and producers are not able to offer.

Financing and Risk Bearing

Some intermediaries offer their customers attractive credit policies. Manufacturers could not possibly offer credit to all the retailers that sell their products. To offer credit to several hundred thousand retail stores would be a paperwork nightmare and would be much too risky financially.

Most intermediaries are prepared to assume risk when they buy the products that they sell. If they select products wisely, they are confident that their product assortments will sell. If they do not sell, it is the intermediaries who lose money because a product spoils, goes out of style, or becomes obsolete. The producer assumes no risk after the intermediary has purchased the products.

Bulk Breaking

Bulk breaking consists of breaking down large quantities of goods purchased from producers into smaller quantities. Wholesalers purchase products by the carload or truckload at reduced freight rates. Then they divide up the total shipment into smaller quantities that can be used by the retailer.

One wholesaler may buy gardening gloves, fertilizer, seeds, and bedding plants from producers and divide them into quantities that are suitable for small retailers. Retailers, then, can contact one wholesaler for all five items rather than five different producers. And the small retailer doesn't have to buy a carload of gardening gloves to get three dozen pairs to sell during the gardening season.

▼ How would you feel if you had to buy the products you need in large quantities directly from the manufacturer? Instead of buying one loaf of bread, you would have to buy a dozen. And instead of buying one Hershey bar, you would have to buy a case of 36. What would be the advantages and disadvantages of buying in this manner?

Transporting and Storing Goods

Both wholesalers and retailers may provide delivery services for their customers. Because wholesalers store products and have them ready to deliver when they are needed, retailers can keep a smaller inventory. With a simple phone call or computerized order, the retailer can get products quickly and efficiently, often within a day. Retailers also store products and deliver them, such as a new refrigerator.

WHAT ARE THE CHANNELS OF DISTRIBUTION FOR CONSUMER PRODUCTS?

How do the channel members work together to get products and services from the producer to the consumer? Because services cannot be stored and shipped in the same way that products can, they will be discussed in a separate section.

There are four different channels that a product can follow as it travels from the producer to consumer. The simplest is from the producer directly to the consumer, and the most complex is from the producer, to an agent, to a retailer, and to the consumer. All four channels for consumer products are described below and shown in Figure 15-2.

Producer to Consumer

Sales directly from producers to consumers often take the form of mail-order or catalog selling. Billions of catalogs are mailed to households each year. It is possible to buy everything from

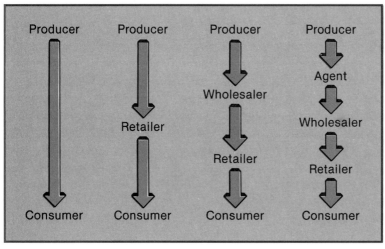

Figure 15-2. Four different marketing channels of distribution for consumer products.

an African safari to robots that flip tennis balls at the player without a partner. Direct mail particularly appeals to customers who put a premium on time.

Sales directly from producer to consumer may also take the form of door-to-door sales or sales to a small group in a "party" setting. (See Information Brief 15-3 on page 330.) Avon, Tupperware, Mary Kay Cosmetics, and Amway are but a few of the producers who market directly to consumers in this manner.

Producer to Retailer to Consumer

Some producers choose to sell directly to retailers. This is a particularly attractive alternative for producers when they can sell goods that are expensive or in large-enough quantities to make the effort worthwhile. Automobile manufacturers, for example, often sell their cars directly to retail car dealers. When a producer selects only one dealer in a geographic area, it is a strategy called **exclusive distribution.** Furniture and clothing may also be channeled from producer to retailer to consumer through an exclusive distribution arrangement.

A channel arrangement that is similar to the producer-retailer-consumer route is the use of manufacturer's outlet stores. **Manufacturers' outlets** are retail stores owned and operated by producers and manufacturers. Although these outlets are technically a way of channeling products from the producer directly to the consumer, they do make use of retail stores.

Information Brief
15-3

Fuller Changes Channels

The Fuller Brush Company, which is over 80 years old, has made its reputation through the years by selling its brushes and home cleansers directly to consumers door-to-door. But times have changed even for this highly respected old company.

In more recent times Fuller has used direct-mail catalogs to help distribute its products. And you now can add another twist to the story of Fuller's marketing channels. The company that once shunned retail stores, now wants to modernize its distribution channels even more. How? It will begin opening retail stores to help market its famous product line!

Sources; Adapted from "Fuller Brush to Open 2 Stores," *Chicago Tribune,* July 26, 1987 (Reprint from the Dallas Morning News); and Sara Rimer, "Barred Door: Fuller Brush Is a Passkey," *New York Times,* August 1, 1987.

The 1.3-million-square-foot Potomac Mills Mall in Dale City, Virginia, is currently the world's largest off-price shopping center. **Off-price** stores provide fewer services than conventional stores but also have better prices. Potomac Mills features 180 factory-direct, discount, and off-price stores. Since opening in September 1985, it has attracted 12 million visitors. More than 500 other such malls are currently in operation across the United States.

Even manufacturers of better clothing are opening their own stores. Recently Polo/Ralph Lauren, Inc., opened their own 20,000-square-foot retail emporium in New York City. The store is owned directly by Mr. Lauren and his company.

▼ How would you feel if you owned a retail store in New York City and sold Polo/Ralph Lauren products in your store? Would you consider the new Polo/Ralph Lauren emporium to be in competition with your store?

Producer to Wholesaler to Retailer to Consumer

The producer-wholesaler-retailer-consumer channel of distribution is a common one for consumer products. As an intermediary, the wholesaler buys products from the producer. The wholesaler then performs many of the services described earlier in this chapter, such as breaking bulk packages and making assortments that are convenient for retail use, transporting and storing, and taking the responsibility for risk. The wholesaler then sells the products to the retailer, who is also an intermediary.

Producer to Agent to Wholesaler to Retailer to Consumer

For some specialized products such as textiles, grocery products, furniture, and electrical goods, the channel of distribution also involves an agent or broker. This channel member arranges for the sale between producers and the wholesaler. An agent or broker will handle a variety of related items. In some cases, the agent or broker will bypass the wholesaler and sell directly to the retailer.

WHAT ARE THE CHANNELS OF DISTRIBUTION FOR INDUSTRIAL PRODUCTS?

The channels of distribution for industrial products are similar to those for consumer products. Figure 15-3 shows the industrial channels that are most frequently used.

Producer to Industrial User

The most frequent industrial channel is from the producer directly to the industrial user. This is because many industrial products such as complex machinery and construction equipment require the personal attention of the manufacturer to tailor the product to the user's needs.

Producer to Industrial Distributor to Industrial User

Industrial distributors are comparable to wholesalers. This channel is helpful for industrial products such as cleaning supplies or office supplies. By contacting one distributor, the industrial user can buy a selection of supplies from a wide variety of producers.

Producer to Agent to Industrial Distributor to Industrial User

Still another industrial channel involves the services of an agent who arranges for the sale of products. The industrial distributor

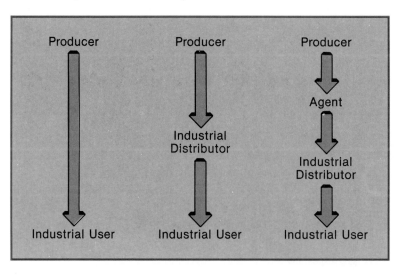

Figure 15-3. The marketing channels of distribution used most frequently for industrial products.

then stores them until the consumer needs them and provides quick delivery service on command.

WHAT ARE THE CHANNELS OF DISTRIBUTION FOR SERVICES?

The channels of distribution for services are unique because services cannot be stored in a warehouse and repackaged to suit the needs of the consumer or industrial user. The channels of distribution for services, shown in Figure 15-4, are described below.

Producer to Consumer (or Industrial User)

The most frequently used channel of distribution for services is direct distribution from the producer to the consumer or industrial user. For consumer services such as car repair, piano lessons, and legal or professional counseling, this direct contact between the producer of the service and the consumer is essential. Similarly, for industrial services such as accounting, building maintenance, and display services, there has to be direct contact.

▼ You arrange to take private piano lessons from a teacher that you respect and like. When you go to her home for your first lesson, you find a note on the door that directs you to a large, impersonal piano studio in another neighborhood. The note indicates that she has decided to buy the services of a larger producer of piano lessons instead of teaching piano herself. How would you feel?

Figure 15-4. Channels of distribution for services.

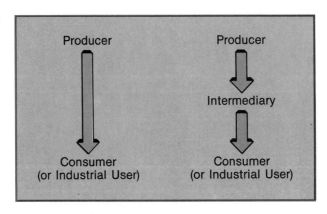

Compact Disks Alter a Distribution Channel

The NYNEX corporation has made a name for itself selling telephone information to both business consumers and ultimate consumers. The company has traditionally sold printed directories to businesses for use in verifying names, addresses, and phone numbers of consumers. This is particularly important when the customers are applying for credit. Unfortunately, printed directories can become outdated almost the moment they are published.

Now the company is offering business consumers its white page telephone directory on a compact disk with related software. The system will allow companies to retrieve information from personal computers. This way businesses will always have up-to-the-minute information about their potential credit customers as well as other consumers and companies with whom they do business.

The product is based on a compact disk read-only-memory technology. The disk is placed in a drive that is connected to a personal computer. The drives resemble compact disk audio players. They use tiny lasers to read data that is held in microscopic pits inside a spinning plastic disk. The disk can hold the equivalent of 200,000 single-spaced typed pages.

With the software program, users can call up names, phone numbers, and addresses with the touch of a few buttons. Customers receive a new disk each month containing updated information.

To receive up-to-date information from NYNEX when the printed directories were outdated, business customers had to contact information operators for each name and number. This meant that they might have many contacts with the supplier of the information service in a single day. Now, with the new system that NYNEX is offering, they are able to alter the channel of distribution to the business customer. Once the system is set up, they will no longer have to go to the producer each time they need updated information.

NYNEX is optimistic about the demand for this new service because people and companies are constantly changing locations. Companies need a quick, accurate way of updating names, addresses, and phone numbers and this service should help them do this.

Source: Adapted from "NYNEX Corp. to Sell Phone Directories on Compact Disks," *The Wall Street Journal,* November 16, 1987, p. 41.

Figure 15-5. Computerized warehouses, such as the one shown here, allow for quick and efficient tracking of inventory.

Producer to Intermediary to Consumer (or Industrial User)

Sometimes, the producers of consumer services use intermediaries in the channel of distribution. For example, a small dry cleaner may collect clothing from the consumer and send it to a large plant to be processed. Another may send shirts to a separate plant that specializes in washing, starching, and pressing them. In these cases, the dry cleaners are intermediaries who act as retailers.

Another intermediary who is used in the sale of services is the agent or broker. When securities, travel arrangements, entertainment, and housing rentals are sold, an agent often works between the producer and the consumer or industrial user.

PHYSICAL DISTRIBUTION OF GOODS

Finally, an important aspect of the channels of distribution is the storing and moving of the products that are sold.

Storing and Handling Merchandise Efficiently

Products that are held in inventory must be stored in efficient, well-managed warehouses. Companies that need storage facilities may use either their own private warehouses or public warehouses (warehouses operated by other companies for profit).

Computerized systems that are appearing in greater numbers every year help warehouse managers keep track of goods on hand quickly and efficiently.

Selecting the Best Modes of Transportation

A wide range of possible modes of transportation is available for the shipment of goods. These modes include trucks, railroad, water (primarily cargo ships), airlines, and pipelines. Figure 15-6 shows the advantages and disadvantages of each of these modes of transportation.

MODE OF TRANSPORTATION	ADVANTAGES	DISADVANTAGES
Railroad	Low cost shipment of heavy goods over long distances. Reliable schedules. Little damage to goods.	Access to terminals sometimes difficult. No service in many small towns. Less suitable for small shipments and short distances.
Motor trucks	Provide door-to-door delivery. Can ship to and from nearly any point. Frequent service. Little damage to goods.	Less suitable for shipping very large quantities and for some bulky or large goods. More affected by weather than railroads.
Water transportation	Low cost. Can handle very large quantities.	Slow speed. Infrequent service. Not available in many places. Damaged goods more likely.
Airlines	High speed. Frequent service. Little damage to goods.	High cost. Access to terminals sometimes difficult. Not available in many small towns. Schedules affected by weather.
Pipeline	Low cost. Continual delivery. Not affected by weather.	Only suitable for liquids or gases. Slow delivery.

Figure 15-6. The advantages and disadvantages of different modes of transportation. (Source: Lester R. Bittel, *Business in Action,* Third Edition, McGraw-Hill Inc., © 1988, p. 182)

Select Terms to Know

agents	consumer goods	intermediaries	retailers
brokers	convenience stores	manufacturers' outlets	specialty store
bulk breaking	department store	mass merchandiser	wholesalers
channels of distribution	exclusive distribution	off-price stores	
consumer	industrial goods	producers	

Review Questions

1. What are the three different types of members in the typical channel of distribution?

2. What are three different types of intermediaries? Explain the differences among them.

3. How do the four different types of retailers discussed in this chapter differ from each other?

4. Explain why producers often use intermediaries instead of selling directly to customers.

5. What are four services performed by intermediaries?

6. Briefly describe one of the channels used to distribute consumer goods.

7. Briefly describe one of the channels used to distribute industrial goods.

8. Briefly describe one of the channels used to distribute services.

Thought and Discussion Questions

1. If you were a producer of school notebooks and filler paper, what channels of distribution might you use to get your products to the consumer? Who is the consumer for your products, and where will this person likely buy them?

2. If you were a producer of fabric, could your product be considered both a consumer product and an industrial product? Explain your answer. How would the channels of distribution differ for your fabric in each instance?

3. If you were a producer of expensive watches, what type of marketing channel would you use? Describe the channel and what each channel member does to help distribute your watches.

4. Assume that you work in a busy wholesale warehouse which handles candy, gum, soft drinks, and stationery supplies for independent supermarkets and convenience stores. One of your friends has asked you what a wholesaler does. Explain the services performed by the wholesaler, using your own words and examples from this type of business.

5. Give two examples of products that would best be distributed under each of the consumer distribution channels explained in the chapter.

Projects

1. Excell Inc. is a distributor of electric motors, fans, air compressors, paint spraying equipment, lighting fixtures, and 12,000 other products. Their customers are mainly contractors and other small businesses.

While Excell has several branches in larger cities, they found that their customers valued a convenient location over lower prices. The branches serve walk-in business, the bulk of their sales.

Excell wishes to analyze its marketing channels to increase its exposure to its customers.

a. Where does Excell fit into the marketing channel of a paint sprayer manufacturer?

b. How would you describe Excell: producer, wholesaler, agent, or retailer? Why?

c. What channels should Excell explore to increase its sales?

2. In 1986, two firms, Harris and 3M, formed a joint venture to manufacture and market copiers and facsimile equipment. Both products are rather technical and sold in small numbers to end-users.

a. What are the advantages of direct sales to end-users? What personnel would be necessary to sell in this manner?

b. Would it be possible to sell the equipment indirectly as well? Who would handle the equipment and what would the channel participant be called?

c. Why would the marketing channel for such equipment probably be limited in levels of participants?

3. The Safe-Line security system hit the market with considerable fanfare. The producer advertised heavily in the media, and its sales force was active in the field. The owners of the firm decided that they would sell their product through dealers in every major U.S. city. They also sold the system directly to business firms and by mail order in specially prepared catalogs. The system was also distributed by industrial distributors who were outside the company's regular sales force.

a. Outline the advantages and disadvantages of the marketing system used by Safe-Line.

b. What is your opinion of the marketing system? Explain your answer.

Case Study: The Questionable Distribution Promises

In 1987, distributors who delivered Thomas's English Muffins to stores in Florida and North Carolina felt that the slogan "Thomas's Promises" no longer was an accurate slogan when it came to the company's dealings with them. That year Thomas's parent company, food industry giant CPC International, had acquired another specialty baker, Arnold Foods Co., in a merger. In the process of merging the two baking operations, the company discovered that the distributors for Arnold's and the distributors for Thomas's covered the same basic territories. Because they felt this was inefficient, the company decided to eliminate from its distribution network all but one of the 25 independent wholesaling companies that distributed their products in these states.

Many of these distributors protested loudly. The reason for this protest was that they had formed their distribution businesses solely to distribute Thomas's English Muffins. This company decision would wipe out their businesses.

A few of these distributors had even uprooted their families and moved to Florida from other states four years previously at the urging and encouragement of the company.

Source: Adapted from "The Merger of Two Bakers Teaches Distributors a Costly Lesson," *The Wall Street Journal*, September 14, 1987, p. 27.

1. Do you feel that the S. B. Thomas Company was justified in deciding not to allow the Arnold distributors and the Thomas distributors to continue working in duplicate territories? Explain your answer.

2. If you were one of the distributors who was being eliminated, how would you feel? Why?

3. If you owned S. B. Thomas, would you have made a different decision than the one that had been made? What decision? Why?

Marketing in Your Community: An Exploration Exercise

This is an opportunity for you to learn more about marketing as it is being used by businesses or nonprofit organizations in your community and to investigate possible career areas in which skills in marketing may be beneficial. This project calls for you to visit a business or organization and conduct a semistructured interview with the person responsible for marketing in that organization.

CHOOSE AN ORGANIZATION TO INTERVIEW

With the help of your business teacher or a counselor at your school or college, select a profit-oriented business or a nonprofit organization in your city or community that will cooperate with you in your search for further information on how marketing is being used today. It is suggested that you and your classmates identify several different types of businesses and nonprofit organizations from which you would like information. Such a list should include production, distribution, service, and people-oriented businesses as well as nonprofit organizations such as the Red Cross, the Rescue Squad, and the local United Fund.

Divide these among your classmates for the purposes of this project. This will ensure that information about marketing and marketing careers is obtained from a variety of organizations in your community.

DEVELOP INTERVIEW QUESTIONS

Develop a list of questions about marketing that could be answered appropriately by a person on the marketing or marketing management staff in that business or association.

In developing your questions, remember that this project has two major objectives: (1) to determine how marketing is being used by businesses or nonprofit organizations in your community and (2) to investigate possible career areas in which skills in marketing may be beneficial. For example, suppose you decided to find out more about marketing in a financial institution, let us say a credit union. The following are a few questions that might appropriately be asked of someone responsible for marketing the services of a credit union.

1. How does your firm decide which services should be offered to your members?

2. Does the credit union do any type of marketing research, such as conducting surveys or interviewing possible customers, to determine which services to offer?

3. How are prices for the various services determined?

4. How is the credit union promoted? How do you decide when and where to advertise? Do you make personal selling presentations to individuals or groups? Are there other promotional techniques?

5. How important are people skills in your organization?

6. What types of entry-level jobs as well as advancement opportunities are available in your firm for someone who has studied marketing?

As another example, the following questions might be asked of someone responsible for marketing the continuing education program for a community college.

1. How does this school decide which courses should be offered?

2. How does the college decide where and when to offer courses?

3. How are the course fees determined?

4. How are courses promoted? How do you decide when and where to advertise? How do you go about obtaining publicity for the college's courses and programs?

5. Can you think of other ways in which marketing is used by this community college?

6. What career opportunities are available in education for people with backgrounds in marketing?

ARRANGE FOR THE INTERVIEW

It is suggested that you phone the firm or nonprofit organization and make appropriate arrangements for your visit. Your teacher or counselor may be able to suggest a name or office for you to phone. Be sure to explain the purposes of the visit. You also may wish to provide the person whom you will be interviewing with a few sample questions ahead of time.

FOLLOW-UP

After the interview, be sure to write a thank-you note to the person(s) you interviewed. Then, as directed by your teacher, organize your notes from the interview in preparation for a class discussion or prepare a written report.

Source: Lynch, Ross, and Wray, *Casebook for Introduction to Marketing,* prepared by Robert J. Welsh, McGraw-Hill Book Company, 1984, pp. 19–20.

UNIT 6

Human Resources and Operations Management

You will now learn about two more functional areas of business, human resources and operations. Human resources—people—are considered the most valuable resource of any organization. Therefore, it is crucial to manage them effectively. Organizations would not need to worry about the other functional areas if there were no goods or services to be produced. The activities related to the production of goods and services are commonly referred to as the operations function and the management of these activities as operations management. This unit will help you to become more familiar with the management of the human resources and operations areas of an organization.

UNIT OBJECTIVES

1. Describe the process involved in forecasting human resources needs, and in recruiting, hiring, training, and developing employees.
2. Discuss why human resource and other managers need to be familiar with human behavior and leadership traits and styles.
3. Identify practical suggestions for helping managers motivate people and help employees get along with their managers.
4. Describe how the collective bargaining process works and identify the tactics and settlement procedures used by unions and management during disputes.
5. Discuss operations activities and operations management techniques.

CHAPTER 16

Employment of Human Resources

Cutthroat Competition for Craftspersons

Tom Kelly was sure that his staffing problems were over when he heard that 97 craftspersons were being laid off at a neighboring Groton, Connecticut, plant. As human resources manager of Electric Boat in Groton, Kelly had always had more applicants than he needed for jobs. Just by opening the front door of the huge shipbuilding company he could get thousands of applicants who were eager to be hired. Kelly was confident as he planned to select the best 30 workers from those who had been laid off.

But when Kelly started arranging to interview the laid-off workers, he had a surprise in store. He found himself in cutthroat competition with 50 other companies who were also looking for craftspersons. Instead of expanding his staff by 30 workers, he was lucky to get two.

Learn more about the problems experienced by human resources managers in selecting a work force when you read the end-of-chapter case study, "The Wanted Workers." Study this chapter to learn more about the vital role played by human resources managers in business and to help you answer the questions in the end-of-chapter case study.

Tom Kelly and other human resources managers like him play an important role in businesses of all sizes. **Human resources** are the people who work for an organization. The **human resources manager** is a special type of manager who is responsible for hiring the people to work for an organization and for keeping a well-trained and happy staff of workers on the job. This person may also be called the personnel administrator or the personnel director.

In this chapter you will learn about the human resources manager's responsibilities for employing the company's staff. These responsibilities include planning and estimating employment needs and managing the actual employment process. In addition, the human resources manager may have other duties such as training and developing workers, appraising personnel work performance, and coordinating job changes.

THE IMPORTANCE OF HUMAN RESOURCES MANAGEMENT

Until this present century, most companies paid little attention to human resources (or personnel) management. Workers were often selected randomly, without much thought. To enforce work standards, employers tended to discipline workers in a harsh manner. Workers who questioned ways of doing things were considered uncooperative and were fired. If you didn't have a job, you and your family would have to live in poverty. There- fore, the last thing workers wanted to do was lose their jobs.

Businesses today recognize the importance of a dedicated work force and pay more attention to hiring and training work- ers. A recent survey by *INC.* magazine showed that the real secret of successful firms is their motivated and enthusiastic employees. The magazine surveyed the 500 fastest-growing small and midsized private companies in the United States. These successful companies pay their employees somewhat less than larger companies. However, they make up for this lack of pay by providing jobs that offer challenges and a sense of accomplishment. The satisfied employees in these companies know that their employers value ideas and hard work, produc- tion of quality products and services, and that the firms treat employees with respect. Evidence shows that employee moti- vation is a major force behind the extraordinary growth of these companies, rather than just the result of it.[1]

Human resources managers work in a staff, or advisory, ca- pacity as they assist the other managers in the company. Al- though all company managers are responsible for managing people, human resources managers are experts in hiring, train- ing, motivating, and counseling employees.

▼ Would you rather work for a rude, demanding employer who would pay you $250 per week or a kind, thoughtful em- ployer who would pay you $175 per week? Why do you feel as you do?

[1] Information from Curtis Hartman and Steven Pearlstein, "The Joy of Work- ing," *INC.*, November 1987, pp. 61–70.

WORK FORCE PLANNING

Fortunately, not all human resources managers have the type of difficulty Tom Kelly (who was described in the chapter introduction) did in scrambling to get the few qualified employees who were available.

The human resources manager is responsible for planning the size and nature of the company's work force. This planning includes studying the qualifications and skills the company requires of its employees. It also includes knowing how many people are actually needed. This information becomes the basis for the manager to use in hiring, training, and developing the company's human resources.

In planning and hiring employees, managers must be aware of the numerous laws and federal executive orders that protect employees against discrimination. The Equal Employment Opportunity Commission (EEOC) administers most of the federal laws that prevent employers from failing to hire or promote because of sex, age, race, religious beliefs, or other similar reasons. These regulations usually apply to companies that have 16 or more employees, to public institutions such as local governments, to labor unions, and to organizations that have federal grants or contracts or operate across state lines. Some of these organizations may be required to have **affirmative action plans** that spell out positive steps to increase the hiring and promotion of minorities and other groups, such as females. (See Figure 16-1.)

▼ Do you think human resources managers should be able to hire anyone they want, or do you think they should be required to hire females and minorities in certain special situations? What are some of the special situations? Why do you feel as you do?

Estimating Qualities Needed in Employees

Almost every job in a company requires a different type of person. Each job usually requires a worker with a unique combination of physical, mental, creative, social, and personal knowledge and skills. To decide just what qualities are needed in an employee, the manager should carefully analyze each of the jobs that must be done.

The systematic study of the characteristics and activities required by each specific job is called **job analysis.** The job

Figure 16-1. Under federal law, managers in some organizations must implement affirmative action plans. These plans are intended to increase the hiring and promotion of minorities and women in industries once considered white- or male-dominated.

analysis is usually done by a specialist who carefully observes the job as it is being performed, interviews the person doing the job, and talks with the supervisor of that position. The purpose of job analysis is to find out exactly what a person in a given job does and what qualifications are needed.

The human resources manager then summarizes the information in a job description. A **job description** is a written listing of the activities and responsibilities of the job as well as the skills and characteristics the worker should have to do it. The job description is often expanded into a **job specification,** which is a written listing of measurable information such as the years of schooling, length and type of experience, and essential physical abilities necessary for the job. The job specificaton is used in the actual hiring process because it clearly describes the type of employee who is most likely to be suitable for a given job. Table 16-1 shows a combined job description and job specification for a shipping clerk. Notice the detailed breakdown of duties performed. The job supervisor and human resources manager often work together to determine the percentage of working time that is devoted to each duty.

TABLE 16-1 Sample Job Description/Job Specification

Position: Shipping Clerk
Department: Shipping and Receiving
Location: "C" Building Warehouse

Job Summary
Under general supervision of warehouse manager, processes shipments to customers in accordance with shipment authorization forms forwarded by the sales department. Together with other clerks and packers, removes goods from shelves by hand or by powered equipment and packs them in containers for shipment by truck, rail, air, or parcel post. Prepares and processes appropriate paperwork and maintains related files.

Education
High school graduate.

Experience
None required.

Duties Performed
1. The following represent 70 percent of working time:
   a. Removing stock from shelves and racks and packs into proper shipping containers.
   b. Weighing and labeling cartons for shipment by carrier designated on the shipping order.
   c. Assisting in loading carriers.
2. The following represent 15 percent of the working time:
   a. Preparing and/or processing authorization forms including packing lists, shipping orders, and bills of lading.
   b. Maintaining shipment records by tally sheets or data entry.
   c. Doing miscellaneous typing of forms and labels.
   d. Maintaining appropriate files.
3. The following represent the balance of working time:
   a. Driving company truck to post office or for an occasional local delivery.
   b. Assisting in taking inventory.
   c. Acting as checker for other shipping or receiving clerks.
   d. Keeping workplace clean and orderly.

Supervision Received
Except for general instructions and special problems, works mostly on his or her own.

Relationships
Works in close contact with packers, material handlers, and other clerks. Has contact with truck drivers when loading. Has occasional contact with order department personnel.

Equipment
Operates mechanized stockpicker, powered conveyor belts, carton sealing machinery, data entry (computer) and/or typewriter.

Working Conditions
Clean, well-lit, and heated. Requires normal standing, walking, climbing, and lifting. Subject to drafts when shipping doors are open.

Estimating the Size of the Work Force

Estimating the number of people needed for the company's staff is a difficult task. In developing an estimate, managers must first look at how many goods or services the company plans to produce. In a company that has been in operation for some time, it is possible to estimate fairly accurately how much each employee can produce in a certain amount of time. If managers know how much the company will produce and how much each employee can produce, they can figure out how many employees are needed to meet production goals.

Unfortunately, estimating the size of the work force is seldom as easy as the process described above. A number of complications come into play. Employees may be ill or absent from time to time. Some may quit and need to be replaced. The number of workers who leave and must be replaced is referred to as *employee turnover.* Others may be promoted, be dismissed, retire, or die.

Changes in equipment or products that are produced sometimes call for a change in the number of employees needed. As new equipment is purchased, there may be a need for fewer employees of one kind but more of another, for example. Sudden changes in economic conditions may also affect the work force needs of a company, positively or negatively.

One recent study indicates that 40 percent of America's largest corporations have either too many or too few employees. (See Information Brief 16-1.)

MANAGING THE EMPLOYMENT PROCESS

After careful work force planning, the company is ready to manage the actual employment process. Managers need systematic procedures for recruiting, hiring, and orienting new employees.

Recruiting

A manager looking for candidates to fill job openings will probably look first at current employees. By promoting someone from within to fill a vacancy, the company gains some important advantages. Present employees will already be familiar with company operations and will usually need less orientation and training. Also, supervisors will be familiar with employees' work habits, interests, and abilities.

Information Brief 16-1

Corporations Can Learn From Goldilocks

Goldilocks spent her time looking for a chair that was just the right size, and corporations spend their time looking for a staff that is just the right size. Four out of every ten companies have either too few or too many employees.

According to some experts, one way to figure out whether a staff is too large or too small is to watch what happens at quitting time. If workers all stay late and act frazzled or distracted, the firm may have too few of them.

On the other hand, if a firm's whole staff is out the door at the stroke of 5:00 p.m. or they can't describe what they do all day, the firm may have too many workers.

Source: Adapted from "Companies Can Learn a Thing or Two From the Three Bears," *Working Woman,* September 1987, p. 20.

Company morale is also improved by promoting from within. Workers see that it is possible to progress in their work and may remain more loyal to the company. Moving a current employee into an open position also saves the time and expense of recruiting from outside the company.

If it's not possible to find a current employee who is really suitable for an open position, the company will have to look outside the organization.

Human resources managers are familiar with organizations and other sources of qualified employees in their areas. Some of the most frequently used are listed below:

Private or state employment agencies

Colleges, universities, vocational schools, and trade schools

Advertisements in newspapers or in trade and professional publications

Labor unions

Friends of present managers and employees

Unsolicited applications from interested candidates

Selection

Selection is the process of picking one candidate who seems to best match the job specification and is the most likely person to succeed in the job. It is probably the most important task of the human resources manager.

In many companies, the human resources manager screens applicants who come into the company looking for employment and sends them to the department where they seem best-suited for work. Then, the manager in that department makes the final employment selection. In smaller firms, there may not be a human resources manager or specific departments. In these firms the owner may have many roles. Owners are often the human resources manager, department manager, and supervisor at one and the same time.

No matter how large or small, a thorough selection procedure typically includes a résumé, application, interviews, and investigation. In some larger firms, applicants may also take tests related to job activities and be required to pass a physical examination before beginning work.

Résumé and Applications. The résumé is a written summary of education and experience prepared by the job applicant. It is a valuable tool for helping to select the best candidates for jobs. Résumés are discussed in Chapter 20.

The application for employment is a preprinted form which is completed by all persons interested in working for an organization. Although not all organizations ask for exactly the same information, there are some things they all want to know. Therefore, the application for employment usually asks candidates for personal information such as name, address, phone number, and so on. Candidates are also asked to describe their job interests, education and training, work history, and other experience that may relate to the job. And, finally, they will probably be asked to give the names, addresses, and phone numbers for some business or educational and personal references. By reviewing applications, managers can usually eliminate applicants who are clearly unsuited for a job opening. Often the human resources manager reviews the applications first, selects the most promising applications, and then sends those on to the department manager or supervisor.

Employment Tests. Testing is the process of asking applicants to demonstrate their ability to perform in a joblike situation. For example, an applicant for a secretarial job might type a sample letter or an auto mechanic might repair a carburetor. Some companies may also use personality, motivation, or intelligence tests in the selection of salespeople and managers. A complaint sometimes heard about these tests is that they generally reflect the values and interests of white, middle-class Americans. As a result, some believe that such tests may unfairly penalize minorities who may not necessarily share the same cultural background as middle-class whites. For this reason, there has been active pressure from some sources, such as the Equal Employment Opportunity Commission (EEOC), to limit or stop the use of tests unless an organization can clearly show that they are a necessary and vital part of the selection process.

▼ Do you feel organizations should be able to require people to take a personality or intelligence test as part of the job application process? Why do you feel as you do?

Interviews. The interview is a face-to-face meeting between the applicant for a job and someone from the organization. It is probably the most important part of the employment process. Careful interviewers can learn important information about a

Information Brief 16-2

To Lie or Not to Lie

Business is growing by leaps and bounds for professional résumé checkers. In the early 1970s credential checking was considered "not nice." Now it is considered bad business *not* to check credentials.

A company can be sued for "negligent hiring" if one of its employees injures someone and the employer should have known that the employee had a history of this type of behavior.

Recently 100 résumés that were all submitted to the same company were checked. A surprising number of untruthful statements were found. There were 41 wrong employment dates, 26 wrong dates of educational study, 13 errors reporting the size of previous salary, and 7 incorrect grade-point averages. In total, there were 129 major errors on 68 résumés.

Source: Adapted from "A Tissue of Lies," *Fortune*, November 9, 1987.

candidate's attitudes, experience, interests, and desire to succeed.

Careful interviewing is a technique that can be learned. Human resources managers sometimes run special sessions to train the other managers in the company in interviewing techniques. If you are an interviewer or if you are being interviewed, you should be aware of questions you should *not* ask or be asked in an interview. There should be no question in an interview about:

Race	Child care problems
Age	Housing
National origin	Health status
Religion	Arrest records
Marital status	Type of discharge from the military
Dependents	

See the Technology in an Information Economy feature for a description of a new type of interviewing system that can save time and money for both the employer and those applying for jobs.

Investigations. Most companies carry out at least a brief investigation of the information given by the applicant. The investigator may contact past employers, former teachers, or other people who know the candidate. One goal of the investigation is to check the accuracy of the information that is given on the application and in the résumé. An investigation can uncover facts that might point to future problems with the applicant, such as a poor attendance record or dishonesty. See Information Brief 16-2 for a description of the growing need for professional credential-checking companies.

Physical Examinations. Many companies require a physical examination before hiring. The major reason for this exam is to eliminate candidates who may be physically incapacitated in the future because of an existing health problem. However, it may also be required where heavy physical labor is part of the job. Organizations need to carefully determine the physical needs of each job. Many firms today have found that persons with physical handicaps or impairments perform all the duties of many jobs very well. In fact, some companies have policies

Job Interviews on Video

A hidden camera captures every move as employment candidates answer a series of interview questions. Are you watching the taping of an episode of Candid Camera? No, it's a new and exciting way of interviewing job candidates.

Corporate Interviewing Network Inc. (CIN) has developed a system of interviewing that saves both the company and the candidate a great deal of time and money. When a company has narrowed its candidates down to about four people who are being considered for a managerial job, the usual procedure is to fly the candidates to corporate headquarters for an interview. Unfortunately, it is not always possible to get all the decision makers who do the hiring together for the interview, so a second trip may be necessary for the top candidates. And some of the best candidates may have been screened out in the process of identifying four people because it is not economical to bring in more than four.

As an alternative, the company can now narrow its list of candidates down to 12 possible people. Instead of flying them to headquarters, the company turns the list over to CIN together with the name and address of each candidate. CIN invites those people to one of its 24 franchised nationwide locations where they are interviewed with questions written by the company. Each candidate is asked the same questions in the same order.

This process enables the company to "see" more candidates and compare them fairly. The best candidates are then invited to headquarters.

When they use the services of CIN, employers can watch the job interviews whenever and wherever they want. It can be done at their convenience. If they need to, they can rerun a tape as many times as they want.

Creative human resources managers can use the services of a company like CIN to save themselves time. Instead of spending undue time screening people, they can concentrate on recruiting candidates.

Source: Adapted from Paul B. Brown, "Every Picture Tells a Story," *INC.*, August 1987, pp. 18–21.

---

of affirmative action that encourage hiring physically impaired employees. (See Figure 16-2 on page 352.)

Salary Decision

Each time a new employee is hired, the company must decide how much it will cost to have that person working. It costs organizations more than the salary or wages regularly paid to the employee. For example, companies usually pay for life and health insurance, vacations, and such. These and any other

Figure 16-2. Many firms today have policies that encourage the hiring of physically impaired employees.

benefits employees receive are referred to as compensation.
Compensation includes everything of monetary value that
employees receive for their work. In addition to the benefits
already listed, some companies make regular contributions toward a **pension,** which is a fund that provides for retirement
income for an employee. Others might offer profit sharing,
Under **profit sharing,** employees receive a share of the company's profits even if they are not shareholders or owners.

Most companies offer some type of benefits to all their full-
time employees, but rates of pay differ from employee to employee. Regular pay to employees takes a number of different
forms including salaries, wages, piece rates, bonuses, and commissions. **Salaries** are a set amount of money paid to employees at regular intervals no matter how many hours they work.
Salaried employees are usually paid every week, every other
week, or once a month. Their pay is not based directly on the
number of hours worked or on the amount produced. Management and professional employees are usually paid salaries.

Wages are an amount of money paid to workers based on
the number of hours worked during a period of time. The
period of work is often referred to as a pay period and is
usually one or two weeks. The wage per hour that an employee

earns is multiplied by the number of hours that employee worked during the pay period. Production workers and laborers are usually paid wages.

Piece rates are a way of paying workers based on the number of units that they produce. Piece rates are common in certain skilled and semiskilled manufacturing jobs, such as garment making.

Bonuses are often paid in addition to regular wage or salary as a way to compensate for outstanding performance or unusually high production. These extra payments are usually thought of as incentives for better performance.

Commissions are amounts of money paid to certain kinds of workers to reward them for desired performance. Salespeople often receive commissions based directly on the volume of business that they have done.

Large companies often assign a level to each job title or job specification. Then they decide on a range of salaries or wages that are acceptable to each level. Let's say that the job of secretary is in level 6 and will earn between $18,000 and $24,000. The exact salary offered will depend on the experience each person has had and the skills that the person brings to the company.

Orientation

After an employee is selected and an agreement on the compensation package has been reached, it is time to introduce that person to the company. The process of helping the new employee learn about and adjust to the company is referred to as **orientation.** This process usually includes the bookkeeping chores of putting the new employee on the payroll. It also includes instructing the employee about the work to be done, the people to work with, and company policies and rules. Time taken to explain a worker's responsibilities and rights at this stage will usually avoid serious management problems later.

During orientation sessions, enough time needs to be spent to make sure that the new employees understand the business. Everyone involved must be ready and willing to answer questions and tell employees where they can get the answers to questions as they may arise. The orientation discussions should be in a language the new employee will understand. A nontechnical presentation with written materials to enforce what has been said is usually the best type of orientation.

▼ It's been said that orientation to a new job is something like orientation to a new high school. Do you think this is true? Why or why not?

TRAINING AND DEVELOPMENT

A well-trained employee will be a valuable asset to a company for many years. For this reason, it is sound business practice to have a planned training program for new employees rather than just letting them "sink or swim" on the job.

Many companies have formal programs to teach new employees specific job skills and to retrain present workers to use new technology. Companies may also have special programs to develop better managers.

Employee Training

Companies may use a number of different approaches to teach specific job skills such as those used by operations workers. One popular type of training is the vestibule method. The **vestibule method of training** sets up a simulation of the work environment and allows trainees to perform actual job activities in a classroom. To train a computer operator, for example, an actual console and equipment would be used. The trainee would receive simulated jobs to process and would be taught to use the equipment in the proper way. This method is useful when employees must be taught specific skills such as piloting a plane or computer operation.

Another common type of training is on-the-job training (OJT). With **on-the-job training,** new employees are placed right into the job situation and learn what is expected of them by working closely with skilled employees. There are two major disadvantages of on-the-job training. The trainee may not have an opportunity to receive enough actual training before being assigned to a regular work assignment. In some operations areas, this possible lack of training could even be hazardous to a new employee who has not learned all the safety precautions. The other disadvantage is that on-the-job training may cause disruption of the normal work routines while experienced employees are showing the new employee what to do and how to do it.

Another form of training which combines on-the-job training with classroom work is the apprenticeship program. With **ap-**

Figure 16-3. The vestibule method is used to train production and other kinds of workers in a simulated environment. Here pilots are trained at the controls of a simulated airplane.

prenticeship training new employees work as an assistant to a skilled worker for a specified length of time and complete supplementary classes related to the job. The length of time often ranges from two to six years. The classes teach additional aspects of the job that cannot be learned as well through actual work experiences. Electricians and plumbers are commonly trained through this type of training.

Supervisor and Management Training

An increasing number of companies have formal training and development programs for their supervisors and managers. These programs, commonly referred to as management-development programs, use a variety of techniques. One is formal classroom training. This training may be given by the company, by colleges or universities, or by special consultants that specialize in management training. These courses usually aim at teaching specific information and management techniques.

One particularly valuable training method is role-playing, which requires trainees to act out various management roles in a training situation. Role-playing helps manager trainees develop a greater ability to deal with people. When they receive feedback on how they handle specific situations, they are able

Information Brief 16-3

Help! You've Promoted the Wrong Person

You certainly thought that your hardworking and dedicated employee was ready for a promotion. But now you know that your talented rising star just isn't ready for the responsibilities of this new position.

You can't ignore the situation because it affects the performance of your entire department. Instead, you should talk candidly with the employee. He or she may already sense that the promotion isn't working out and be willing to step back down to his or her former job.

But if the employee is unwilling, don't force the issue. Instead, plan to train the employee so that he or she can handle the promotion. You might use special classes or seminars. Or other staff members might help.

Source: Adapted from Henry C. Rogers, *The One-Hat Solution*, St. Martin's Press, copyright © 1986, as reported in "You Promoted a Weak Person? Here's How to Set Things Right", *Working Woman*, August 1987.

to adjust their techniques for handling employees while working with people in a safe training atmosphere.

Coaching in actual work situations is still the most common management-development technique. Managers with more experience and responsibility usually make a conscious effort to advise, guide, and train younger managers.

Many companies give managers special assignments that will broaden their experience and skill. One common practice is **job rotation,** in which manager trainees are placed in a number of different jobs in different parts of the company, one after another. This type of training can widen the manager's experience and give him or her a broad perspective on company operations. At the same time, it is a good way to teach many management skills.

No matter which techniques are used, the goals of development programs are usually the same. They attempt to give managers the insight and maturity they need to deal with many different people in many different situations.

▼ Do you think a supervisor or manager should have worked in one or more of the jobs which are included in the unit or department before becoming the boss? Why do you feel this way?

Performance Appraisals

An important responsibility of both managers and supervisors is judging the quality of the work people in their unit do. By checking and evaluating the work of these people on a regular basis, they can maintain general productivity at as high a level as possible. These activities are referred to as **performance appraisals,** which are carefully planned and conducted evaluations of employee performance based on measurable behavior rather than on opinion. They stress measurement of the results of an employee's work. In doing this, they strongly emphasize the objectives of the department or company and the extent to which each worker participates in reaching those objectives. Most managers, at least in theory, now try to avoid the type of evaluation that is largely based on personal opinion. Performance appraisals are used in decisions about salary increases, training, promotions, assignment changes, and dismissals.

HANDLING JOB CHANGES

The work force of a company seldom remains stable or unchanged from year to year. Changes normally result from transfers and promotions and from employees leaving the company for a variety of reasons. Human resources and other managers must set up procedures for making these type of decisions and for administering the changes which they bring about.

Transfers

A transfer is a move of an employee from one job to another at the same level within an organization. When employees transfer, they work for approximately the same salary and have the same amount of responsibility or authority. When a company is involved in job rotation, transfers can be a common occurrence. They also result from the changing needs of the company. There may be a need for more people to work in one department and fewer in another, for example. As a result of transfers, companies are often able to take better advantage of the abilities and interests of employees as they move to different jobs.

Promotions

A change by an employee to a job at a higher level within an organization is a **promotion.** The employee who is promoted is given more responsibility and authority. In addition, this person usually receives more pay. Many companies tie promotions closely with the employee appraisal system. As a regular part of the appraisal, each employee is evaluated in terms of suitability for promotion. Another typical reason for promotion is **seniority,** or length of service an employee has with an organization. An employee who has more seniority in addition to a favorable performance appraisal will probably be the best candidate for promotion.

Separations

A separation occurs when a worker leaves the company. **Layoffs** are temporary separations of employees from an organization. Layoffs occur when a certain number of employees are told not to come to work. This happens because the company has declining demand for its products or services and must reduce production. When sales increase, workers who have

Information Brief 16-4

The "No Layoff" Pledge

The New United Motors Manufacturing Inc. has made an unusual pledge to its employees. Even though sales of the Chevy Nova are slipping, the company has promised no layoffs unless it is forced to do so by severe economic conditions. And even then, the company will take extreme actions such as cutting management salaries before it will lay off workers.

The company, which is actually a joint venture between Toyota and General Motors, is known as Nummi. It scheduled three "nonproduction workdays" just before the usual Christmas break. On those days, workers who showed up were asked to perform construction work and were given further training instead of being sent to the employment lines.

Source: Adapted from Jacob M. Schlesinger "Nummi Keeps Promise of No Layoffs by Setting 'Nonproduction Workdays'", *The Wall Street Journal*, October 29, 1987, p. 36.

been laid off are usually given the first chance to come back to take their former jobs.

Terminations are permanent separations of employees from an organization. Some workers may also decide to leave their jobs because they are able to get higher salaries, faster advancement, or greater benefits at other companies. Other workers may have lost interest in their present jobs or may have decided to change careers altogether. When the employee makes the decision to leave, the termination is considered "voluntary." Each year thousands of workers resign and leave their jobs voluntarily for many different reasons.

"Involuntary" terminations, commonly referred to as "firings," have various causes also. Workers may have to be permanently let go if part of a business fails or if new procedures or products eliminate certain jobs. Poor attendance, dishonesty, or poor work performance may cause workers to be fired. Well-managed companies usually have a procedure for warning employees that performance is poor and giving them the opportunity to improve. If no improvement results, they are usually fired after a certain amount of time.

Like most people, human resources managers do not enjoy unpleasant situations. Therefore, they do not enjoy making decisions related to layoffs and terminations. In the next chapter you will read more about human resources management and some of the things organizations are doing to help workers enjoy their jobs more.

Select Terms to Know

affirmative action plans	job rotation	profit sharing
apprenticeship training	job specification	promotion
compensation	layoffs	salaries
human resources	on-the-job training (OJT)	seniority
human resources manager	orientation	termination
job analysis	pension	vestibule method of training
job description	performance appraisals	wages

Review Questions

1. Even though some companies pay less than others, their employees are more satisfied. How do businesses that pay less make their employees feel more satisfied?

2. What are some of the human resources manager's responsibilities in an organization?

3. What is the difference between job analysis and job description?

4. What are some ways to tell if your staff is too small? Too large?

5. If you were responsible for recruiting candidates to apply for a job opening at your company, where are some places you would look?

6. The process of picking a candidate for a job opening is called selection. The selection process includes a series of different activities. What are those activities?

7. What is a résumé? Why is it a good idea for everyone who is looking for a job to prepare a résumé?

8. What are some topics that interviewers cannot legally ask job candidates about?

9. What are some things other than pay that are part of an employee's compensation?

10. How are wages and salaries different?

Thought and Discussion Questions

1. Companies often test their candidates for employment by having them demonstrate their ability to perform in a joblike situation. A salesperson, for example, might have to do some simple business math problems or a secretary might have to type a letter. Some people might feel that these tests are unfair because some people are uncomfortable in a testing situation and are unable to do their best work. If you were an employer, what would your opinion on the fairness of these tests be? If you were a candidate for employment, what would your opinion on the fairness of these tests be?

2. One candidate for employment said, "I hate to talk with the personnel people in the companies where I'm applying for work. They usually don't know anything about the jobs I'm applying for, and they ask dumb questons." What is your opinion of this statement? Why do personnel (or human resources) managers screen candidates before they are interviewed by the managers in the departments where they hope to be working?

3. Information Brief 16-2 describes the growing need for professional credential-checking companies. Why do you think that candidates for employment falsify their credentials? Why do companies spend extra time and money to check credentials?

4. When you answered review question 8 above, you listed questions that an interviewer should avoid asking in an interview. Why should these questions be avoided?

5. Information Brief 16-3 describes what to do when you have promoted a weak person. What are some suggestions for setting things right? Which of these suggestons do you feel is the most promising course of action? Why?

Projects

1. The sample job description/job specification shown in Table 16-1 is for a shipping clerk in the shipping and receiving department. Look carefully at that description/specification. Then assume that you are the human resources manager for a company that produces office supplies. Where would you look to recruit candidates for the job described? What are two questions you might ask a candidate for this position? What employment test could you give?

2. Firing an employee is never a pleasant task for a manager. Assume that you are the human resources manager in a small company. One of your employees, Janet Randall, has a very poor attendance record and has been transfered from job to job in an effort to find one for which she is suited. In each position, she exhibits poor work performance and is frequently absent. Today is the first day that Janet is back on the job after an absence of three days for "health reasons." You have decided to have a conference with her to warn her that she must improve her performance or you will have to fire her. You intend to follow up your conference with a written notification that will be filed in her permanent file. What will you say to Janet during your conversation? Write the exact words you will use.

3. You are in the process of hiring a secretary for the busy office at your company. Brenda Wells is under consideration for the position together with two other candidates. Brenda scored better than the other two candidates on her employment test, interviewed well, seemed very interested in the position, and had a pleasant, professional appearance. But when you investigate Brenda's résumé and application, you learn that she falsified two of her previous job references. At one company she was let go because of cutbacks in staff, but she indicated that she left to return to school full-time. At another company she worked as a file clerk, but she indicated that she was the personal secretary to the vice president. Would you hire Brenda despite her falsified records? Why or why not?

Case Study: The Wanted Workers

Tom Kelly's staffing problems at Electric Boat company in Groton, Connecticut (which were described in the chapter opener), certainly came as a surprise. Kelly, and other human resources managers like him, have been used to being able to find as many workers as they want to fill their employment needs. But some situations have changed dramatically. For example, Kelly and other managers are learning that there is a growing shortage of skilled craftspersons from which to attract qualified and willing employees.

Some labor economists feel that we are facing a serious situation. Within 10 years we may not have anyone who knows how to build an airplane engine or cut precision metal parts. This labor shortage could eventually lead to an economy with modern factories that don't work.

The problem is due, in part, to the fact that apprenticeship programs have steadily decreased in recent years. In addition, young people are shunning jobs in factories, even in cities that are traditionally made up primarily of blue-collar workers. Many younger workers feel that factory jobs are dirty and boring. But, at the same time, these young workers are not able to pass the reading and math tests that are necessary for entrance into apprentice programs. In past years, academic skills were not considered of primary importance for apprenticeship positions. But manufacturing has become increasingly sophisticated. Workers have to run computer equipment that is numerically controlled and requires an understanding of math. You used to be able to get a job if you knew someone in the company. Now you have to know algebra.

Although many companies are resisting the temptation to raise wages to attract workers, some find that this is a possible solution to their problems. One lumber company in Suffield, Connecticut, has extended its average workweek from 40 to 55 hours and increased its begining pay from $6 an hour to a scale ranging from $7 to $9, depending on the position. The company is even considering paying new recruits $1500 bonuses in three installments during their first year on the job.

Other companies have begun advertising outside their traditional recruiting areas. Tom Kelly at Electric Boat had always recruited from the Connecticut and Rhode Island area. Now he is advertising jobs in newspapers as far away as

Sturgeon Bay, Wisconsin, and western Pennsylvania. Other companies make even more dramatic efforts to solve their labor problems—they move their factories to where the workers are. One publishing company from northern New Jersey, for example, relocated its plant to Allentown, Pennsylvania, where there was a recent plant closing. This guaranteed them an ample supply of pressworkers.

Source: Adapted from Constance Mitchell, "A Growing Shortage of Skilled Craftsmen Troubles Some Firms," *The Wall Street Journal*, September 14, 1987, p. 1.

1. Summarize in your own words the problems facing human resources managers as they attempt to hire skilled craftspersons.

2. What are some of the reasons for this shortage of craftspersons?

3. How have some companies tried to solve the problems created by a shortage of workers?

4. If you were a human resources manager for a company that needed skilled craftspersons, how would you attract these workers?

CHAPTER 17

Management of Human Resources

Game Play to Combat Employee Stress

The group watched their leader with undivided attention. "Put one hand on top of your head," the leader instructed, "with your fingers toward your face. Now take your two middle fingers and hook them into your nostrils and pull them up. Now stick out your tongue. Congratulations! You've just made a bat face."

Is this a kindergarten class, or maybe a children's recreation group? Not by a long shot! It is a group of adult employees who are making bat faces as part of a stress management workshop in Seattle.

Employee stress has been referred to as the "disease of our era." Today stress management could be referred to as the "boom industry of the century." Learn more about this new business and the unusual methods that are used by human resources managers to combat stress and increase employee productivity when you read the end-of-chapter case study, "Curious Cures for Corporate Stress."

Study this chapter to learn more about how human resources managers try to create conditions conducive to work and to help you answer the questions in the end-of-chapter case study.

In chapter 16 you learned about the employment of human resources. But planning staff needs, hiring employees, and training are just a few of the responsibilities of human resources management. It is also the responsibility of the human resources manager to make sure that the people within the organization work well together and remain happy. This may sound like a simple task, but remember the human resources manager works in a staff, or advisory, position. He or she has no direct authority over the employees in other departments of the company. However, human resources managers have the opportunity to work with employees at all levels in formal training situations, workshops, conferences, and daily contact. As they help all employees work well together, they help the entire organization to be more productive.

In this chapter you will learn about the different levels of employees within each company and the responsibilities of the human resources and other managers toward workers.

WHO ARE THE EMPLOYEES WITHIN A COMPANY?

We can divide the employees of most companies into four basic groups: managers, professionals, salespeople, and hourly workers. Although these categories may not fit every company, they are appropriate for most.

Managers

Managers include all people who have other employees reporting to them. As discussed in Chapter 8, there are top-level, middle-level, and first-line managers in most organizations. All of them have the responsibility for motivating their employees to be productive and for keeping them happy. Many middle managers are caught between their own demanding superiors and a staff of not-too-enthusiastic subordinates. The human resources manager can help the management staff learn how to communicate better, manage more effectively, and establish more realistic goals. He or she may also be able to help other managers overcome the problems of stress that are closely associated with many management positions.

Professionals

Professionals include such people as computer programmers, lawyers, accountants, and marketing specialists. Often these people are also in a staff, or advisory, position. They need help in learning how to communicate their ideas to the rest of the company because they usually do not have authority over the people who ask for their help. Many of these professionals are very dedicated to their companies and want to see that their ideas are accepted and put into practice. As a result, they, too, may need help overcoming stress.

Salespeople

Salespeople include the outside sales force of a large company who travel the country representing the company's products as well as the people who may work in sales positions where customers come into a store or showroom to buy. The salespeople of a company are often quite satisfied with their jobs, dedicated to their companies, and strong promoters of their products. Salespeople are a critical link between the customer and the rest of the company. The human resources manager can help salespeople to communicate more effectively. Effective communications by the salespeople can bring customers the products they want, keep managers alter to trends in the marketplace, and benefit the company as a whole.

Hourly Workers

Hourly workers include office workers, factory workers, and all other employees who are paid on the basis of the number of hours they work. Many of the hourly workers in companies are there because they like the hours and the location of the job. These workers often experience many of the disadvantages of a company and few of the advantages. Human resources managers can help these workers learn how to communicate with their managers. In a later section of this chapter, you will learn how labor unions can affect the communications between hourly workers, a firm's management, and the rest of the company.

WHAT ARE THE CURRENT ATTITUDES THAT AFFECT EMPLOYEES?

The expectations and goals of American workers have changed a great deal over the years. Required education together with a changing attitude about which students should receive higher education have helped to create a highly trained work force in the United States. Today's workers can handle technical jobs and expect greater rewards. Many of them are looking for advancement and an opportunity to express their own ideas.

Business managers are also changing their values. Many of them feel a sense of social responsibility and concern for the welfare of their employees and people outside the organization. (See Chapter 7.) This has helped to make positive human relations a desirable goal rather than just a tool for increasing the productivity of the company workers.

▼ How would you feel if you had some good ideas that could make work easier and faster to do but nobody listened to them?

THE STUDY OF HUMAN BEHAVIOR

To help them understand human behavior, human resources managers often look to the studies of well-known psychologists. These studies give them general guidelines on how to motivate individual employees, understand group dynamics, boost morale, and manage more effectively.

Meeting the Needs of Individual Workers

Psychologist Abraham Maslow studied the needs of human beings. He discovered that people have five different levels of needs. These needs are shown in Figure 17-1. Maslow believed that the needs on the lowest level must be satisfied before those on the next higher level are addressed. Similarly, the needs on the second level must be satisfied before the needs on the third level are addressed, and so on.

On the lowest (or first) level are very basic needs such as food, clothing, and shelter. The need to be safe from physical danger and the need to be emotionally secure are on the second level. The third level includes the need to be accepted

Figure 17-1. Maslow's hierarchy of needs.

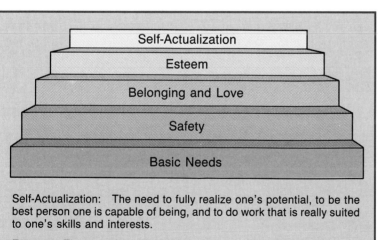

Self-Actualization

Esteem

Belonging and Love

Safety

Basic Needs

Self-Actualization: The need to fully realize one's potential, to be the best person one is capable of being, and to do work that is really suited to one's skills and interests.

Esteem: The need for self-respect and for the esteem and respect of others and the desire for recognition as a skilled and useful human being.

Belonging and Love: The need to be truly accepted by one's peers, the desire to be liked and loved, and the desire to give love and affection to others.

Safety: The need to be safe from physical danger and to be assured of emotional security.

Physiological Needs: The need for satisfying bodily functions, such as needs for food and drink, shelter, warmth, and rest.

by your peers and the desire to be liked and loved. The next level up includes the need to respect yourself and the need to be respected by other people. On the highest level is the need to be the best person that you possibly can and to realize your potential.

Human resources managers can use Maslow's theories to help them learn how to motivate employees. A person who is not earning enough to afford adequate housing probably will not be motivated by the opportunity to be recognized by his or her peers until the housing problem has been solved. And someone whose basic needs for food, clothing, housing, and safety have already been met and who is well-liked by his or her peers can best be motivated in another way. This person may respond better to public recognition than to a pay raise that is presented to him or her privately.

▼ If you were selected as your department's outstanding employee, would you rather be given a $300 increase in pay for the year or an award and public recognition at a big dinner in your community? Why do you feel as you do?

Understanding Group Dynamics

The studies of other psychologists have helped human resources managers understand the ways that people react to and influence other people. This is particularly important because employees generally work in a group setting, not just individ-

Figure 17-2. According to Maslow, some people respond very favorably to praise and public recognition. Human resources managers sometimes use both to help motivate employees. Here an employee is honored for outstanding work performance by managers and peers, a form of public recognition that can boost morale and motivate employees.

ually. All the interactions among the members of a group are called **group dynamics.**

Groups are made up of individuals who interact with each other. When an individual is a member of a group, his or her behavior will be partially influenced by the group. The amount of influence a group has on a person's individual behavior depends on:

- How close-knit the group is
- How forceful the group members' individual personalities are
- How different the group's goals, motivations, and behaviors are from those of the individual members

Some people are more likely to be strongly influenced by groups because their needs for love, esteem, and acceptance are strong. They are often willing to give up the satisfaction of other desires to gain acceptance by members of the group.

It is important for managers to understand group dynamics because they can take some practical steps to make the group work better. A manager can almost always get better cooperation from a group if he or she:

- Helps establish clear goals
- Treats group members fairly and consistently
- Encourages communication (See Information Brief 17-1.)
- Does not treat individuals so poorly that they seek all their rewards solely from the group rather than from both their work and the people they work with.

Boosting Morale

Human resources managers are also concerned with morale of an organization's employees. **Morale** is defined as the level of satisfaction with and enthusiasm for an activity. In organizations, managers are concerned with both individual and group morale. It is hard to evaluate morale because it is largely emotional. Workers with high morale will usually be cooperative and committed to their work and to mutual goals. Usually they are loyal to the organization, confident, and self-motivated also. Low morale will cause a change in these behaviors sooner or later.

Some studies have shown that low morale is not always related to low wages or salaries. Instead it is related to problems with the work activity itself. Generally speaking, workers do not like positions in which they lack responsibility, must do exactly the same tasks over and over, and have no opportunity to use their initiative to decide how to do the job better. Workers also do not like positions in which they cannot work up to what they feel is their ability. In other words, most workers like to be challenged in their jobs.

▼ Assume you were trained to run a sophisticated computer and enjoyed working on one but were working as a file clerk with no chance of advancement to computer operator, even though you were getting paid as much as a computer operator. Would you stay at your file clerk job or seek another job? Why?

Managing More Effectively

Psychologist Douglas McGregor studied management styles. He found that the way managers try to motivate people is partially determined by their attitudes toward people. He identified two common attitudes as Theory X and Theory Y. Theory X managers believe that most people dislike work and have to be pushed into doing it. They also believe that people really prefer to be directed by others and would like to avoid responsibility whenever possible. On the other hand, Theory Y managers believe that mental and physical work is as natural as play or rest. They think that employees who commit themselves to goals satisfy their need for self-respect and personal fulfillment. They believe employees readily accept responsibility for this type of work. They also believe that these employees discipline themselves as they work to achieve these goals.

As you might expect, Theory X and Theory Y managers use entirely different methods to motivate employees. Theory X managers are more likely to stress job security, salary or wage increases, and employee benefits. If these methods don't work, they will rely on strict discipline, threats of job loss, and other punishments. By contrast, Theory Y managers usually try to create work conditions that will bring more fulfillment to workers. They are often more democratic and encourage workers to participate in planning and management.

Another psychologist, Rensis Likert, studied the positive effects of letting employees participate in the management process. He found that when employees have an opportunity to participate by sharing their ideas with management, there is greater group loyalty and more cooperation. He also found that employees who share their ideas with management produce more and do better work than employees who don't have this opportunity.

Human resources managers can gain valuable background in management theory with the help of studies such as the ones mentioned above. With this background, they can help other managers and all the employees of an organization work together more effectively.

LEADERSHIP TRAITS AND STYLES

To work effectively with managers, professionals, salespeople, and hourly workers, human resources managers have to be effective leaders. Therefore, they should understand the personal traits of leaders so that they can work on developing these traits in themselves and others. They should also be able to evaluate situations and select a style of leadership that is appropriate for the circumstances. Possessing these abilities will enable human resources managers to help other managers in the company work more effectively with the rest of the staff.

Personal Traits of Leaders

To be an effective leader, a manager must use complex intellectual and social skills to deal with different kinds of people in a wide variety of situations. An effective manager must be able to adapt his or her style and approach to many different situations.

A leader and successful manager should have human relations skills, emotional and social maturity, intelligence, and self-motivation.

Human relations refer to how able and willing a person is to be sensitive to the needs and feelings of others and genuinely respect these feelings. These skills are essential if you hope to deal effectively with other people. Leaders know how to discover others' needs and feelings by communicating effectively and encouraging them to communicate.

Leaders must have emotional and social maturity. They must accept their own feelings and control their own behavior. Even when they are angry, they must be reasonable. And they shouldn't be the kind of people who are easily defeated by frustration and stress. Leaders should be able to work with people who are unlike themselves and even with people who are disagreeable.

▼ Do you think you could work for a manager with a very "short fuse" who would yell at you in front of other staff members when you made a mistake? Why do you feel as you do?

Good leaders must be intelligent to be able to analyze complex situations and discover relationships, causes, effects, and solutions. In some cases this analysis and an appropriate response must be made very quickly. Other situations involve long-range planning and more time to study or analyze a problem or opportunity before a decision needs to be made.

Finally, good leaders need self-motivation. Anyone who is in a leadership position will face stress and anxiety. Politicians, high-ranking military officers, presidents of organizations, and other leaders are all under lots of pressure. Moreover, the rewards for being a leader are often intangible or hidden. The rewards may not come often or in a way a leader would prefer them. To function well as a leader, a manager must have a strong inner determination to succeed.

Situations and Leadership Style

A good leader must be very flexible and willing to change. Leaders must be able to change their leadership behavior to suit different situations. Despite what certain theories say about one management style being more effective than others, this is simply not true for all situations.

Those who study management styles describe them as ranging from autocratic to participative. **Autocratic managers** make decisions by themselves and then tell others what to do. Employees are required to obey. If they do, they will be rewarded, usually with money. **Participative managers** invite others to take part in making decisions so that they work together in deciding what to do. They encourage initiative and self-direction in their employees. Participative managers try to provide their employees with positive motivators. For example, these might include a chance to work on a new machine, to be a leader of a small group working on a project, or to attend a workshop or training program for a day.

In practice, however, good managers are neither autocratic nor participative all the time. Rather, they are flexible enough to shift from autocratic to participative and back as specific situations require. In extreme situations (either very favorable or very unfavorable), an autocratic type of management usually is more effective because rapid decisions must be made. But in most situations, a participative style is probably more effective. It is in these situations where long-term relationships between managers and employees are developed. These situations also allow managers and employees to work together and to determine how jobs may be changed to help the employees and the organizations as a whole.

▼ Do you think you would be more like an autocratic or a participative manager? Why do you feel as you do?

MAKING JOB CHANGES TO HELP EMPLOYEES

Despite management efforts, many jobs remain boring and uninspiring. A human resources manager may be the first person to know that an employee is unhappy in his or her position. The simplest solution to the low morale that may result from a job someone considers boring may be to make changes in the job itself.

Human resources managers often have an opportunity to encourage company managers to redesign jobs to make them more satisfying and challenging. These jobs can continue to require certain basic activities but be changed in some way to make them more satisfying to the employees. Job enlargement and job enrichment are two popular ways of doing this.

Job Enlargement

One way to make a job more interesting is to have an employee do more and some different things. Increasing the number and kinds of activities performed by one employee in a job is called **job enlargement.** This can give employees more personal responsibility, more opportunity for achievement and recognition, and more of a feeling of making a real contribution. At one IBM plant, for instance, managers redesigned jobs so that machine operators now do their own setup work and actually deliver the goods they have finished to the next workstation. And some machinist jobs were even enlarged to include sharpening tools and doing certain machine maintenance.

Job Enrichment

Job enrichment is another technique for making a job more interesting. **Job enrichment** is making a job more satisfying

Information Brief 17-2

The Wilderness Lab—A Communications Tool

Can a trip into the wilderness increase business communications? Supporters of the "wilderness lab" say that it is an excellent way to develop executive ability and team spirit.

In the wilderness lab, members of a team boost each other over a 13-foot wall, cross an imaginary alligator-ridden swamp, or fall backward into the arms of teammates from a 5-foot perch. Each wilderness activity is related in some way to the activities one might encounter in a business setting.

Participants identify the "dragons" that must be overcome both in the wilderness and in the work world. They learn to choose appropriate goals, ask for help, and offer help to others. They also learn to assess, and if needed, change their goals as they work on accomplishing them.

Source: Adapted from Janet W. Long, "The Wilderness Lab Comes of Age," *Training and Development Journal,* March 1987.

by allowing the employee to be more involved in deciding what activities to do and how to do them. Knowing how an individual job contributes to the entire production process is important. Allowing workers to choose how to do the job or encouraging them to make improvements in how it should be done also humanizes work.

Texas Instruments, for example, trains employees how to do work more simply and then encourages them to make changes to improve their own jobs. Managers there also meet regularly with employees to ask directly for their help in solving department and company problems. General Motors' Rochester Products Division uses hourly workers to train other hourly workers and includes the training assignment as a recognized part of the job. This is another example of job enrichment. When a firm acknowledges that a worker has the ability to train someone else, it is providing a form of praise.

STRENGTHENING COMMUNICATION

One of the most threatening positions human beings can face in ordinary life is to be shut off from information that affects them. Employees at all levels in the company—managers, professionals, salespeople, and hourly workers—must have information in order to carry out their activities. They obtain much of this information from the other people in the organization.

Human resources managers can help people at all levels to become better communicators. By encouraging open communications and providing an opportunity for employees to discuss their ideas, make suggestions, bring up problems, and search for solutions, the human resources manager can help to develop a stronger organization overall.

HELPING MANAGERS MOTIVATE PEOPLE

The job of a human resources manager is a complex one. We have already discussed the fact that human resources managers may identify factors that affect employees, study human behavior, study leadership traits and styles, suggest job changes that can help to motivate employees, and work on strengthening communication. Although human resources managers deal with workers at all levels, they are often in the position of advising managers on the ways in which they can improve their management skills. The following practical suggestions for main-

Satellite-Delivered Learning

A valuable corporate training and communications tool is orbiting over your head right now. With a satellite receiving dish, any company can instantly begin taking advantage of some unique training opportunities and can increase its capacity for internal communications. Satellite-delivered learning is also referred to as business television.

With satellite facilities, departments within the same company that are geographically scattered can participate in the same training program at the exact same time. This means that small staffs in remote locations can receive training that they might otherwise not receive. Travel time and money can be greatly reduced because employees can stay at their own work locations for the training. Neither the employees nor the trainer has to travel.

All this is made possible by two differ-

ent kinds of satellites. One is called a C-band satellite, and the other a Q-band. C-band is similar to AM radio, while Q-band is similar to the special radio bands used by police departments. Each of the two satellite bands uses a different frequency. These satellites, which are located about 22,300 miles above the earth, receive and retransmit programs that are made by third-party sources (such as professional training companies) or a corporation's own television studio.

Using satellite dishes, companies can receive a wide variety of general-interest programs. These include management, sales and marketing, effective communication, and computer literacy programs.

Other programs delivered by satellite are very specific. The National Technological University in Fort Collins, Colorado, sends engineering courses for graduate students to participating companies around the country. Satellite students take the course right along with those students who are actually in the classroom.

Some companies, however, are having a difficult time deciding on the most effective way to use satellite-delivered learning. Some companies select programs that address training needs they are unable to fulfill. Others select programs to enhance their own planned classroom instruction. Still others produce their own half-hour programs that can be watched by their employees before work or during lunch.

Source: Adapted from Gail C. Arnall, "Satellite-Delivered Learning," *Training and Development Journal*, June 1987, pp. 90–94.

Information Brief 17-3

Big Ears Bring Ideas

You can take advantage of the acute hearing of your employees together with human nature as a management tool. Let's say your company has a new group of trainees. You might let them overhear as you tell another manager outside the training classroom, "I'm really impressed with this group of trainees. They're very careful about details and have a great attitude when it comes to learning. I'll bet some of them go a long way in this company." You could have told the class the same thing, but they may not have believed you. If someone tells you in private that they admire you, it's nice, but you may question their motives. If they tell you in front of someone else, or you hear them tell someone else within your earshot without their realizing it, it's really believable.

Source: Adapted from Kenneth Schatz and Linda Schatz, "How to Get Big Results From Little Actions," *Working Woman,* February 1988, p. 27.

taining a motivated and happy staff are adapted from those developed by Thomas L. Quick of Resource Strategies Institute.[1]

1. *Make sure that all employees know what they are expected to do.* Although this may sound like simple common sense, it is surprising how many times this step is forgotten. Management consultants are often called to correct problems of low productivity, poor work performance, and employee resistance. When they investigate, they find that employees think they are doing just what management wants them to. Somehow management never sat down with the employees and explained just what they were to do and how they were to do it.

2. *Make the work valuable to the employees.* Give the staff work that promotes self-esteem and a feeling of achievement. Professional pride is a strong motivating factor. Be sure that employees know that a job well done is appreciated. Come right out and say things such as "Thanks for the great job." When possible, reward good work with money or special benefits, although this type of reward is not essential.

3. *Make sure the work is "do-able" and that the employee understands how to do it.* Most people want to do a good job. Often people who don't do what is expected of them either don't know what is expected of them or are afraid that they can't do what the manager wants. A good manager describes the work that is to be done in detail and asks the employee to discuss the assignment.

4. *As they work, tell employees how they are doing.* This calls for both positive and negative feedback. Employees will be more responsive if managers praise them for doing a good job as well as correcting them for problems.

5. *When employees have done what you want, give them a reward.* Be both prompt and consistent with rewards. It can be in the form of simple, oral praise, but it should be genuine. For example, tell an employee something like, "Thanks for the great job on that report. I really appreciate your thorough research and well-thought-out presentation."

[1] "How To Motivate People," *Working Woman,* September 1987, p. 15.

▼ Suppose you did a job just as you thought your manager wanted you to, but then you found out that she was really unhappy with your work. Assume the job was already over half-completed when you were told this. Who would you blame for this situation? Why?

HELPING EMPLOYEES GET ALONG WITH THEIR MANAGERS

Human resources managers are also in the position of helping hourly workers learn how to get along better with their supervisors or managers. The following suggestions were adapted from those developed by communications expert Don Bagin[1] of Glassboro State College in New Jersey:

1. If you're upset with the boss, it's OK to let him or her know it, but do it constructively. Keep in mind that your boss may not even know that there is a problem, so keep your cool. Explain the problem and suggest a solution.

2. Be observant and select the best time for your discussion with the boss. It is not a good idea to bring up a problem with the boss if he or she is tired or angry. Also avoid times when the boss is rushed, preoccupied with other matters, or right after the boss has made a mistake.

3. Don't "beat around the bush" by beginning with a long speech about how great the boss is. He or she will see through your strategy and may be offended. Instead, get right to the point and discuss the work habits that are bothering you.

4. Resist the temptation to bad-mouth the boss with your co-workers. Instead, go right to the person with whom you have a problem and work on straightening it out.

▼ If one of your friends is upset with you, would you like it better if that person told you what was wrong or would you rather hear about it from someone else before talking to your friend? Why?

[1] "Workers Needn't Suffer if the Boss Is a Boob," *Supervision: The Magazine of Industrial Relations and Operating Management,* December 1987, p. 13.

THE EFFECT OF LABOR UNIONS ON MANAGEMENT

In many businesses, the hourly workers are represented by organized labor. The main goal of the organized labor movement in the United States has been to get fairer wages, better hours and working conditions, more job security, and protection from discrimination for its members. Because they often must work with unions and union members, human resources managers should be familiar with unions and the collective bargaining process.

Types of Unions

Labor unions may be organized according to the skills performed by members (such as carpenters) or by the industries in which members work (such as automobile manufacturing).

Unions may be local, national, independent, or affiliated with the AFL-CIO (American Federation of Labor–Congress of Industrial Organization). About three-quarters of the unions in the country are members of the AFL-CIO.

How Union Representation Works

When the workers in a company are represented by a union, leaders of the union and management of the company use collective bargaining to reach agreement on a labor contract. **Collective bargaining** is a process by which decisions about wages, hours of work, and working conditions are made for a group of employees through negotiations between union representatives and management. It is called "collective" because union negotiators represent all the workers who are members of a certain group. The issues negotiated revolve around rights and responsibilties of the workers the union represents and the managers, who are not in the union group.

A human resources manager's responsibilities for participating in union negotiations will depend on the company involved. Sometimes there is direct involvement as part of the management negotiation team. In other cases, there may only be indirect involvement.

The first bargaining issue must always be the recognition of a union as an agent of the workers in a company or industry. Management, in general, doesn't encourage the organization of workers. Some of the initial goals sought by unions are the right to represent workers, the right to collect dues, and the right to exchange information about union activities.

Figure 17-3. Shown here is a collective bargaining session between representatives of union and management. Collective bargaining can help the parties reach agreement on a labor contract or on other matters of mutual concern.

Once recognition is achieved, negotiations are usually aimed at four basic issues: wages and wage policies, hours of work, working conditions, and job security. When union representatives and management have agreed on each issue, they prepare a labor contract. A **labor contract** is a written agreement specifying the rights and responsibilities of workers and management related to employment conditions for a period of time. It is usually in force for a period of one, two, or three years. At the end of this period it may be renewed or renegotiated. Although it is given little if any attention by others, both unions and management consider the procedure for settling disagreements related to the contract as being one of the most important parts of a labor contract.

Labor Disputes and Their Settlement

Serious disagreements, or disputes, sometimes occur between labor and management. Although they occur and are handled very quietly during the life of a contract, disputes about the contract often attract attention from the news media and the public when the contracts are being negotiated. Both unions and managers use a variety of tactics and strategies for furthering their own cause when a new contract is being negotiated.

Union Tactics. The methods most often used by unions to achieve their goals are strikes, picketing, and lobbying. The strike is the strongest action union members can take. A **strike** occurs when all workers in the union group refuse to work. The goal of a strike action is to force management to give in to union demands. If there is no production, the company will lose money and its profits will be decreased. **Picketing** is the practice of advertising a union's complaints against management by displaying signs near the entrances to a company's facilities. Picketing usually accompanies a strike. When picketing occurs, the union hopes that other union members and other people in general will "honor" the picket line. This means that they hope no one will enter the facilities of the company to do business there.

Still another technique used by unions is lobbying. **Lobbying** is any effort by a group to influence legislators and government administrators to pass laws and interpret them to the advantage of that group.

Unions are not alone in conducting lobbying. Business groups such as the U.S. Chamber of Commerce and the National Association of Manufacturers are among the most powerful lobbying groups in our country.

▼ If you were a member of a union, would you be willing to go on strike and to picket in front of the company headquarters? Why or why not?

Management Tactics. The chief methods management uses to combat union demands and to strengthen its position are lockouts, strikebreaking, injunctions, industry associations, and lobbying. A **lockout** occurs when management refuses to allow workers into a plant to work. The lockout is to management what a strike is to a labor union. In other words, it is management's strongest tactic. Although lockouts have grown less common as a management tactic in recent years, when they are used they can force economic hardship on workers by cutting their wages.

Strikebreaking is the practice of hiring replacement workers to do the jobs of the striking union workers. Since strikebreaking is designed to have the exact opposite effect of the strike and picketing, there may be trouble when the two are used together. Replacement workers and regular workers who cross the picket lines are called scabs by strikers. (See Information Brief 17-4.) Strikers may resist the efforts of scabs to undermine the effectiveness of a strike. At times this can lead to stormy confrontations between strikers and scab workers.

Court injunctions are court orders that forbid workers to strike while negotiations on a new contract continue. To get an injunction, management must be able to convince a judge that the strike will be harmful to many people other than the workers and owners involved. Sometimes it is possible to obtain injunctions against strikes in industries critical to the national defense or welfare.

Industry associations may help strengthen management's position during labor disputes. These large and powerful groups provide bargaining information, make appeals to public opinion, and generally help the management of the company as it works to offset the demands of the union.

▼ How would you feel if you had a critical production schedule and your workers went on strike? Would you try to hire replacement workers to continue production while the union workers were on strike? Why or why not?

Settling Disputes. When labor and management just can't reach an agreement there are two basic procedures available to help bring about settlements: mediation and arbitration.

When a neutral third party attempts to work out the settlement of a dispute by getting union and management representatives together to discuss the issues to be resolved, the process is called **mediation.** The third party clarifies issues, brings in new information, and generally influences the negotiators to compromise. However, either of the two sides can decide to stop meeting at any time. Moreover, they do not have to accept any of the mediator's suggestions or recommendations.

Another more formal and more powerful method of settling labor-management disputes is called arbitration. **Arbitration** occurs when union and management agree on a neutral third party who will hear both sides of the dispute and make a decision on how to settle which must be accepted by both sides. Arbitrators may attempt to achieve a voluntary settlement first. However, arbitrators usually are not selected or become involved until the situation calls for someone to make a final decision in the labor dispute.

Human Resources Management and the Union

In a unionized company, management usually cannot ignore the framework of union rules and regulations. However, skillful human resources managers can help management operate suc-

---

Information Brief 17-4

Football Players Find They're Replaceable

When the National Football League (NFL) went on strike in the fall of 1987, team owners quickly filled their rosters with nearly 1600 eager substitutes (scabs). After two weekends of "scab ball," the players surprised everyone by turning the walkout into a walk-in.

To the players' surprise, their decision to scrap the strike and return to work came too late. The owners decided to let some replacement players continue with the games scheduled for the following Sunday and get paid for them.

NFL strikers were surprised to learn that many of their fans backed both management and the substitute players. One fan's sign at Mile High Stadium in Denver read, "Our Scabs Can Beat Your Scabs."

Source: Adapted from Michael Satchell with Sharon F. Golden, "The Strikers Strike Out," *U.S. News and World Report*, October 26, 1987, pp. 41–42.

cessfully within the framework. They can also help managers understand the rules and regulations and, where possible, how to use them to advantage. For example, at times the rules and regulations can help management in establishing work contracts and in handling some major day-to-day work problems.

Select Terms to Know

arbitration	job enrichment	participative manager
autocratic manager	labor contract	picketing
collective bargaining	lobbying	strike
court injunctions	lockout	strikebreaking
group dynamics	mediation	
job enlargement	morale	

Review Questions

1. How is the relationship between the human resources manager and the employees in other departments of a company described?

2. What are the four basic groups of employees in each company? Describe each group and the ways that human resources managers can help them.

3. What are some of the factors that affect the performance of employees? How have the changing values of business managers affected their goals?

4. Why do human resources and other managers study human behavior?

5. What are psychologist Abraham Maslow's five different levels of needs? Briefly describe each of them.

6. What factors determine how much influence a group has on a person's behavior?

7. Why is it hard to evaluate morale? How does morale show itself on the job?

8. Describe in your own words the attitudes of managers that Douglas McGregor calls Theory X and Theory Y managers.

9. What is the difference between job enrichment and job enlargement? Which one of these two techniques can relieve low morale?

10. What are the main goals of the organized labor movement in the United States?

Thought and Discussion Questions

1. Some managers feel that human resources managers are unnecessary. What do you think? Do they serve a valuable role in most companies or are they really duplicating (and sometimes complicating) the efforts of the other managers in the company?

2. The chapter indicates that managers should be flexible enough to shift from autocratic to participative and back as specific situations require. What does this mean? Do you agree with this statement? Give an example of a situation that you feel calls for an autocratic management style and one that calls for a participative management style.

3. What would you do if you were told that you absolutely had to complete an assignment in a week when you were sure (from past experience) that the assignment would take at least three weeks to complete?

4. Communication is considered an important ingredient for success in any business. Who

should be communicating, and why is communication so important?

5. When employees have done what they are expected to do, they should receive a reward. As an employee, would you rather have (*a*) a bonus but no words of encouragement or thanks from your manager or (*b*) sincere appreciation and encouragement from your manager but no bonus? Explain your answer.

Projects

1. The chapter describes the five levels of needs that were identified by Abraham Maslow. Apply these levels of needs to your own life by drawing a figure similar to the one in Figure 17-1. Write in examples of your own needs at each of the five levels. Explain how a knowledge of Maslow's levels of needs can help you as you deal with other people.

2. You are a human resources manager in a small manufacturing company. One of the factory supervisors has come to you with some problems. His staff has been producing less than the expected output, and their work performance has been lower than usual. He feels that they are resistant to his suggestions when he

tries to get them back on track. What will you tell this manager to help him regain a motivated and happy staff of workers?

3. You are the human resources manager in the large production plant of a toy manufacturing company. One of the office employees, Susanne Blackstone, has come to you for some guidance in dealing with her supervisor. "I just can't seem to talk to my boss," Suzanne explains. "Sometimes she gives me assignments that don't make any sense and expects me to do them right away. Then she disappears. What can I do? Maybe I should transfer to another department." What suggestions do you have for this employee?

Case Study: Curious Cures for Corporate Stress

Stress management has become such a serious problem in today's business world that hundreds of companies are now providing stress management programs. Many of these programs include such unusual activities as juggling and humor workshops (where participants make bat faces, as described in the chapter opening).

At Corning Glass, Citibank, and at least 30 other firms, employees juggle tennis balls and scarves as a way of relieving stress. Juggling helps you laugh at yourself, and when you laugh, you are better able to deal with stress. Other companies take a more conservative approach.

They give employees workbooks to be used with a videotape, with step-by-step instructions for combating stress.

Stress is a costly problem. Employee tension and burnout have increased sharply in recent years. Studies estimate that the cost of stress, including factors like absenteeism and rising stress-related compensation claims, now average about $150 billion a year.

With billions of dollars at stake, companies are rushing to develop cost-effective programs to reduce stress. AT&T includes stress reduction as a part of a larger "wellness" program. The

Long Island Lighting Company spends $200,000 a year for a biofeedback consultant.

Critics of the trend toward stress management say that there is no proof that it works. Although many employees say that they have been helped by programs such as these, few companies can prove that stress management is really paying off. Dr. Paul J. Rosch, president of the American Stress Institute, says that "Companies are throwing away millions of dollars on programs that don't work." Yet many companies cite figures showing both improved productivity and reduced absenteeism as a result of stress management.

Medical experts indicate that companies can design good stress management programs if they follow some basic guidelines. First, they should do a stress audit to determine the sources of tension in their businesses. Then they should give employees a wide choice of programs to use in combating stress. Then, they should do a follow-up evaluation to determine how effective the stress management program has been.

Source: Adapted from Penelope Wang, Karen Springen, Tom Schmitz, and Mary Bruno, "A Cure for Stress?" and "Tension? Lock Your Boss in a Mason Jar," *Newsweek,* October 12, 1987, pp. 64–65.

---

1.   Why are companies concerned with stress management? Why is stress considered a costly problem?

2.   What are some of the objections voiced by critics of stress management programs?

3.   What guidelines do medical experts offer for the development of effective stress management programs?

4.   Have you ever been in a stressful situation in school or on a job? Do you feel that a program that provides humor and helps you relax might have been helpful to you?

CHAPTER 18

Production and Operations Management

Soft Automation Has Hard Consequences

Automated factories are not new. Robots and machines have long been used to do a repetitive task on an assembly line. This was referred to as hard automation. The machines did the kind of work that would bore a person. Hard automation was viewed as a step forward for human dignity. The thinking went: "People should not have to do the repetitive, boring tasks. They should be involved in the tasks that change, have variety, and call for judgment."

Now there is soft automation. And workers are becoming concerned.

With soft automation, machines and robots are able to handle a much wider variety of tasks. Companies that produce goods are using soft automation because it increases productivity, often decreases costs, and usually increases product quality. However, it also can eliminate jobs—many of them.

Learn more about production issues such as productivity, costs, and quality in this chapter. Then use the chapter contents to help you answer the questions in the end-of-chapter case study, "Machines or People?"

In previous chapters, you read about financial management, marketing management, and human resources management. While you were reading, it may have occurred to you that very little was said about managing the actual production of a good or a service. What kinds of things are involved in managing the production of goods such as steel, cars, and bridges or paper, magazines, and houses? Are there different things involved in producing services such as medical care, airline transportation, and income tax preparation? And does producing government services such as national defense, social security, and highways provide yet another set of challenges?

This chapter on production and operations management is the last of the chapters dealing with the functions of management in business. The first section of the chapter will help you become familiar with what is meant by production and operations. Then you will learn about designing an operations system. After a comparison of the operations systems for manufacturing and service businesses, you will learn about controlling and maintaining effective operations. Finally, you will read about some trends and questions related to production operations management.

PRODUCTION AND OPERATIONS

In most cases manufacturing a good or product is a more complicated process than the person who purchases it realizes. Think about one of the canned or packaged food items your family had for a meal recently. A check of the label would probably indicate that the manufacturer had to bring several different ingredients together to create the item you consumed. Each of those ingredients, plus the can or package, had to be produced by the manufacturer or purchased from another company. However they were obtained, they had to be brought to the place they were to be used and stored until they were needed. Then they had to be combined or changed in some way and put into a can, box, plastic or other container by people using various types of machinery or equipment. Finally, the can or package was probably packed with several others, sent to a wholesale warehouse, and distributed to the local retailer where your family picked it up.

Some basic production operation activities were identified in the above example. The term **production** refers to any business process used to produce a physical good. Generally, production activities are considered to be those processes that change the physical form of materials. Operations, on the other hand, is commonly used as a more general term which includes production. The term **operations** refers to any business process used to produce either a physical good or a service. Because production is a type of operations, many people use the term production operations as a way of distinguishing those operations that produce a physical good from those operations that produce a service, which are referred to as operations.

Whether producing a good or a service, producers must obtain the natural, human, and capital resources needed to accomplish a task. Then they must design a system in which these factors of production are combined and processed to produce the desired good or service. Once the production system is designed and begins to operate, it must be continually reviewed and evaluated to determine if it is operating effectively.

As is true for the financial, marketing, and human resources activities of a firm, the operations activities must be managed. Someone must be responsible for planning, organizing, directing, and controlling the operations activities—managing the operations. For our purposes, **operations management** refers to managing the process of obtaining and transforming resources to add value to them before they are output as goods or services. From your study of the economic environment of business, you already know about resources, goods, and services. Now you will learn about designing an operations system.

▼ How many services do you use on a regular basis? Do you think that the average American family's use of services has increased or decreased over the last 50 years? Why do you think it has increased or decreased?

DESIGNING AN OPERATIONS SYSTEM

Before goods or services are available for purchase by consumers in the market, someone must produce them. To do this, someone must design an operations system. An **operations system** identifies the facilities, processing, and people needed—and the relationships that must exist between them—to produce the desired goods or services.

The major components of an operations system are facilities, processing, and people. Operations managers must make decisions related to each of these components and to the relationships between them. The components must support one another to achieve the planned objective of the system. Of course, the planned objective of an operations system is to produce a good or provide a service.

Facilities

Operations facilities consist of such things as land, buildings, machinery, equipment, and trucks. Two big decisions related

**Figure 18-1. Three compo-
nents of an operations system.**

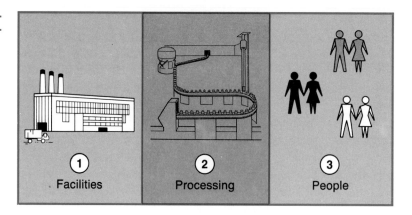

①	②	③
Facilities	Processing	People

to facilities are location and layout. This is true for systems that produce goods or services, or a combination of the two.

A great deal of analysis and planning goes into deciding where to locate a manufacturing plant, stationery store, gasoline station, or bank. Many factors affect location. Some of the factors are what is being produced, the type of raw materials needed, the availability of labor, the local cost of energy, and the closeness to consumers. If it is not possible to be near the raw materials or consumers, the availability and cost of using various types of transportation are important.

Once a location is selected, managers need to plan the physical layout of the facilities. This includes deciding what type of building to construct, if a new building is involved, or what changes are needed to an existing one. Then the location of equipment, machines, and furniture in the facility must be planned. The operations system designers must decide how and where to store raw materials and finished goods. Finally, they have to decide where and how people will work. Layout decisions affect how efficiently raw materials are handled, equipment is used, and people work.

The layout of the facilities is dependent on the type of processing that the business uses. For example, a manufacturing business using an assembly line will require a completely different type of layout than an advertising agency. The processing component of an operations system is the factor that most affects the layout of operations facilities.

Processing

The processing component of an operations system consists of all the activities involved in transforming or combining resources to create the final goods or services. The processing activities actually transform raw materials into goods or services in some way so that value is added. There are many types of processing which add value. One of the tasks of operations managers is to decide how best to use factory resources for processing. (See Information Brief 18-1.)

Almost everyone is familiar with the assembly process used to produce goods such as cars, TVs, washing machines, and personal computers. Although the exact process is less familiar, most of us realize there are chemical processes involved in producing food, beverage, and health products. The processing activities for delivering various services are much more difficult to identify and describe.

People

As was stated in Chapter 8 and again in the previous two chapters, human resources are considered the most valuable asset of any organization. People are also the most important component of an operations system. Even in systems where most of the processing is done by machines, people are needed to operate, monitor, and generally keep the machines functioning properly. No matter how automated a system becomes, people are responsible for programming the computers: starting and stopping them and repairing them. Because people are involved, operations managers are concerned with such human resources management activities as job design and labor standards.

Job design is planning the content and methods of work in a job. Job design involves identifying what task or tasks are to be done, how to do them, and, if appropriate, when and where to do them. Over the years there have been two approaches to job design. In one, the objective approach, jobs are designed on the basis of the most efficient performance of the tasks involved in the job. Getting the job done in the best way is the focus of this approach. In the other, the behavioral approach to job design, the focus is on the individual doing the job. Here training and motivating workers to do the job most efficiently are the most important activities. Those favoring this approach are concerned with how satisfied workers are with their jobs.

Sometimes job design identifies how things are to be done. In other cases, workers decide how best to do the job based on their knowledge and experience. Operations managers

Information Brief 18-1

Playing on the Job

The factory manager and several engineers were huddled around a computer screen. They were watching little symbols thread their way through a series of mazes. Were they playing a video game on company time?

They were playing a game of sorts. It was actually a "simulation." The screen displayed an image of their factory floor. It very accurately showed all the machines, tools, robots, and vehicles used for handling raw materials.

The computer program simulates the process of manufacturing a product. The goal of the simulation is to determine how best to use the factory resources to produce the best quality product at the lowest cost.

Source: "This Video 'Game' Is Saving Manufacturers Millions," *Business Week*, August 17, 1987, p. 82.

Information Brief 18-2

Teaching Machines to Work With People

Nobody can work as fast as a machine. That's why General Motors carried out an experiment at its plants that assemble the Baretta and Corsica models. GM tried to teach machines to work at a human rate.

Information about the plant's nearly 700 robots, automatic guided vehicles, automated welders, and modular paint sprayers was fed into a data base. The computerized system was then able to track each car as it was being assembled. The system automatically brought parts to workers when they were ready to assemble them.

The experiment has produced one very interesting result. When the machines were slowed down to work at a human pace, the workers achieved great productivity gains.

Source: "How to Teach Machines to Work With People," General Motors advertisement, *Time*, May 4, 1987.

study how work is being done and determine the best methods for getting the most production of quality goods or services at the lowest cost. (See Information Brief 8-2.)

▼ If you were given the task of designing jobs, which approach would you use? Which do you think is better, and why do you feel that way?

Computers and Robots

As you saw in the beginning of this chapter, in recent years many businesses have started to use computers and robots in their processing activities. Computer-aided design (CAD) and computer-aided manufacturing (CAM) play an important role in the processing activities of many of today's businesses.

Figure 18-2 shows how robots are being used in U.S. industry. Robots can do physical work. The simplest robots can do manual manipulations or complete a fixed sequence of activities. More intelligent robots have microprocessors that can store, manipulate, and react to information about materials, times, locations, and various activities. As you read, the smartest robots can pick up and assemble or sort and inspect a wide variety of materials. Some can even recognize voice commands and respond to questions by using a speech synthesizer. Many people

Figure 18-2. How U.S. industry is using robots. (Source: Dataquest, Inc., 1986.)

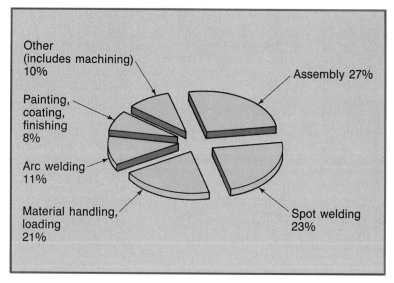

Other (includes machining) 10%

Painting, coating, finishing 8%

Arc welding 11%

Material handling, loading 21%

Assembly 27%

Spot welding 23%

Figure 18-3. As shown here, robots are being used to weld the chassis of cars at a highly automated automobile factory.

feel that it is a benefit to have robots do boring, repetitive manual work or some of the hazardous jobs which used to be done by humans. However, there are also concerns that the increased use of robots will put people out of work and increase the level of unemployment.

Not every type of operations system uses robots. In fact, many service businesses may have little need of sophisticated computers and robots. It all depends on the type of operations system used by the business. You'll be reading more about the two basic types of operations systems in the next section.

▼ What are some other good and bad things you can think of related to the increased use of robots? Do you think organizations should continue to increase their use of robots? Explain your answers.

COMPARING OPERATIONS SYSTEMS

Many different types of operations systems are used to produce the millions of different goods and services available in our society. All organizations that manufacture goods or provide services are similar because their operations systems include facilities, processes, and people. However, there are also some distinct differences between operations systems for manufacturing companies and for service companies. (See Table 18-1.)

TABLE 18-1 Differences Between Operations Systems	
Manufacturing Systems	**Service Systems**
Produce goods	Provide services
Tangible (physical) product	Less tangible product
Often standardized	Often customized
Quality depends on materials	Quality depends on people
Product, in itself, has value	Service has value only if used.

Source: Adapted from Joseph G. Monk, *Operations Management: Theory and Problems,* McGraw-Hill, 1987, p. 161.

Manufacturing Systems

Manufacturing systems are arrangements of facilities, processing systems, and people designed to produce physical goods. Many people think manufacturing involves a large factory, a long assembly line, and lots of people doing boring work on a single product as it moves past them. There are, of course, many manufacturing systems that do resemble this perception. However, manufacturing systems may also be designed for producing a single large product. They may produce a bridge, a paper mill, or a supercomputer, for example.

The buildings, machinery, and other capital resources are very important in most manufacturing systems. They determine the capacity and fixed costs of a system. **Capacity** refers to the maximum amount of goods a system can produce during a specified time period (perhaps an hour or a day). **Fixed costs** are costs which do not vary regardless of the operations' activities or the level of output. The costs of buildings and most machines are examples of fixed costs. The other costs in the system are referred to as being variable. **Variable costs** are costs which change depending on the operations' activities or the level of output. Raw materials and labor costs are the most important variable costs in a manufacturing system.

Manufacturing systems are usually organized and operated in a way that makes it fairly easy to measure and determine values. It is relatively easy to determine the costs of the inputs (natural resources, capital resources, human labor) and the value of the outputs (the finished goods). The difference between these two is considered to be the *value added* during the production process.

The output of a manufacturing system, the physical goods, can also be stored. These systems store the value they add when they put finished goods in inventory.

Service Systems

Service systems are arrangements of facilities, equipment, and people designed to provide services to consumers. Hospitals, law firms, airlines, and banks are examples of businesses which provide services to their customers rather than products. In addition, almost all local, state, and federal government agencies and offices provide services rather than goods.

Most people never really think about all the factors involved in providing services. This is especially true for government services such as national defense, the weather bureau, and education. These services are not bought directly, and there are no physical goods to hold or see. It is easy to forget that there are buildings, equipment, and people involved in providing them just as there are in producing goods. In many ways the operations system of a service organization is similar to that of a manufacturing firm, but there are some distinct differences.

When consuming a service such as hairstyling, the consumer must come to where the service is offered. To add or withdraw money from a savings account, people must go to the bank or to an automatic teller machine. Services are often produced and consumed with the consumer present, and the consumer is usually actively involved in the activities. Because of this, the people who actually provide the service, the human resources, are much more important than the materials and capital resources involved in the process. The skill and reputation of the nurse, dentist, stockbroker, auto mechanic, cook, or maid are much more important to the consumer than the type of office or equipment involved.

Services usually cannot be produced and stored up to be shipped or sold later. Most services cannot be produced until the consumer wants them. Therefore, there are not warehouses of stored-up services, waiting to be distributed to consumers. This makes it difficult to accurately match capacity to demand for a service. How do operations managers at hospitals, restaurants, or funeral homes determine what capacity they will need to best serve their consumers? Similarly, it is difficult to accurately determine and control the costs of providing services. The largest share of the costs is for labor. But it is not possible to know exactly how much time a nurse or psychiatrist will

Using Technology in a Service Industry

The airline industry overall has grown very rapidly in recent years. A decrease in government regulation, an increase in demand for air travel, and several mergers have all contributed to the growth. However, airlines have also done an outstanding job of using technology to improve passenger reservations and scheduling of flights. Since both of these directly affect customers, many analysts believe the increasing use of technology in these areas may be the key factor in the rapid growth of passengers, passenger miles, and revenues.

Today's airline reservations systems are excellent illustrations of how technology can be used to improve a service. Using a terminal at their desk, airline or travel agents are able to retrieve any information they need about the flights of an airline. The information is then displayed on their screen in seconds. The agent can tell a customer what flights are scheduled between two cities, when they leave and return, whether there are seats available, and the cost. If a reservation is desired, the passenger can select and be assigned a seat on a specific flight. The agent can then direct the automated system to print the ticket and boarding pass that will be needed to board the plane when it leaves.

In addition to using technology to make the reservations process so convenient for passengers, airlines have also used it to make their operations more efficient. By using computer systems, they have been able to maintain accurate and timely records of the number of passengers on various flights. This information is used to determine when a flight should be permanently canceled because it is not profitable. The amount of passenger revenue must cover the fixed costs of the flight and provide for some profit. They have also used computer systems to plan the arrival and departing time of flights so that they allow passengers to make the connections they need. This is especially important at the "hubs" of the various airlines, where there are many arrivals and departures by the same airline each day.

Passengers using commercial airlines today enjoy the benefits of convenient reservations and efficient scheduling of flights. These benefits have come about primarily because of the increasing use of technology in the airline industry.

Source: "A Special Report: Technology in the Workplace," *The Wall Street Journal,* June 12, 1987, pp. 5D, 56D.

need to spend with a patient. Because it is hard to estimate what the largest share of the costs will be, it is hard to predict the operations costs for providing services.

▼ Would you prefer to be a worker on an assembly line or someone who had direct contact with customers in providing them with a service? Why?

PRODUCTION AND INVENTORY CONTROL

Once an operations system has been designed and begins to function, those managing the system must take steps to control it. Formal controls are used in an operations system for the same reason they are used in any business. As you learned in Chapter 8, the control function involves checking to see how well a business is doing in relation to a plan and making changes if things get too far out of line. Production and inventory management are the two important aspects of an operations system. In very large organizations, each of these aspects may involve very specialized control techniques. In smaller organizations, one person may be responsible for all the control activities in an operations system.

Forecasting

One of the most effective ways to control production costs is to know what amount of goods or services to produce. A business would like to produce the exact quantity of goods or services consumers will buy at a price which provides a reasonable profit. In our economy, people can choose from among several different producers of the same good or service. This makes it impossible for a business to know the exact quantity of a good or service that will be demanded.

Because of this uncertainty, producers must estimate how much of a good or service will be demanded. They call the estimates demand forecasts. A **demand forecast** is a prediction of the future demand for a good or service based on the likelihood of certain events occurring.

Business forecasters use many methods to predict demand. Some simply look at what has happened in the past and assume demand will be the same as last month or last year. Others try to find out as much as they can about things which will affect demand in the future. They gather information from inside as well as outside the organization. Then they predict what will happen to demand based on what they think will happen to the things affecting it. For example, if they believe that consumers' income is likely to go up, they may predict demand is likely to increase.

However they are done, demand forecasts provide the basic information for deciding what and how much to produce.

Master Scheduling

The information from the demand forecasts is used to put together a rough production plan. From this rough plan, an important control tool called the master schedule can then be developed. The **master schedule** identifies the specific goods or services and the exact quantity of each to be produced or provided in a given period of time. For example, the rough production plan may indicate that 9000 refrigerators should be produced in the next week. The master schedule would show exactly how many of each model, color, and size are to be produced. The amount of each specific good or service to be produced is based on the quantity consumers have already ordered and on the demand forecasts.

The master schedule becomes the guide for all operations activities. Therefore, it is an important control device. The quantities of each good or service to be produced determine how many and what type of human, capital, or natural resources are needed. The business must then decide whether there are enough, too many, or too few of certain resources available.

The development and use of a master schedule is dependent upon the availability of accurate and timely information. Information is needed about the quantities of a good or service already ordered, demand forecasts and their basis, the organization's existing resources, and its current levels of output. Because master schedule activities are based on information, the computer has been widely used as an aid in this area for many years.

Inventory Management

Operations management also involves making decisions about inventory. In this case, **inventory** means the amount of raw materials, supplies, and partially completed goods used in production and the finished goods which are produced. There are two different types of inventory to manage: production (or manufacturing) inventory and finished goods inventory. Since neither of these is usually an important part of service operations, the inventory primarily relates to producers of goods.

Raw materials, supplies, and partially completed goods are all needed for production activities. Producers need to have a certain amount of these available to use at all times. The amount needed at various times is determined by how much is needed to produce the goods indicated in the master schedule.

A business must make some basic decisions about its manufacturing inventory. It must decide what amount of different types of raw materials and supplies to order and who to order them from. It must decide when to have them delivered and what amount to keep on hand in a storage area. And, it must decide what amount of partially finished goods and finished goods to keep in inventory. If the appropriate amount of raw materials and partially finished goods is not in inventory when needed, production will stop. If production stops, a business will not have a supply of finished goods to sell and the business will begin losing money. Most businesses try to avoid stopping production at all costs.

One way to avoid inventory shortages would be to keep large quantities in inventory at all times. However, having too many materials and partially finished goods in inventory can be as unwise as having too few. A business must pay to store the items, and no value is added to a product while it is in inventory. Further, the amount spent to buy or produce a product is not recovered until it is sold. The amount spent for raw materials and partially completed goods is said to be "tied up in inventory" until the finished goods are sold. Using computerized systems, many U.S. firms now use the Japanese just-in-time (JIT) inventory approach. As its name suggests, with a JIT inventory approach suppliers are required to deliver inventory items very close to when they are needed. This decreases the need for storage space and the amount tied up in inventory.

Firms want to produce the right amount of finished goods. Producing too few means the loss of sales income which could have been earned. Producing too many means additional inventory costs. Finished goods sitting in inventory do not generate income. The goal of the operations system is to produce goods which will be sold, not stored in inventory. Both shortages and surpluses of inventory items are undesirable because they decrease earnings. Figure 18-4 shows the processes involved in inventory management.

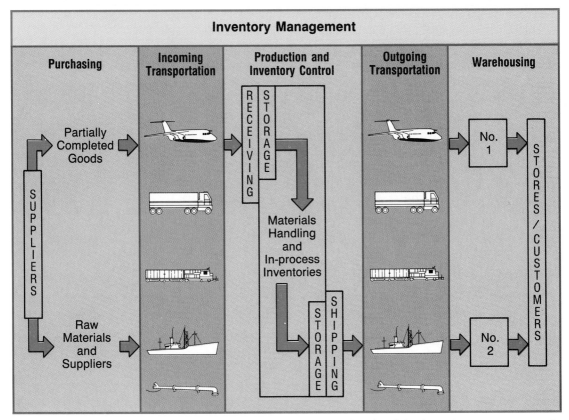

Figure 18-4. The processes involved in inventory management, from purchasing to production/inventory control to transporting inventory to warehouses for distribution to stores and customers.

Material and Capacity Requirements Planning

There are two closely related production and inventory control techniques which tie together the master schedule and inventory information. They are referred to as material requirements planning and capacity requirements planning.

Material requirements planning uses information from the master schedule and the inventory system to produce the material requirements plan. The **material requirements plan (MRP)** identifies what, how much, and when materials are needed to produce the finished goods indicated in a master schedule. It identifies the quantities of all the raw materials and partially finished goods needed to produce the finished goods shown in the master schedule. It then matches the materials needed against what is already in inventory or on order and calculates what is needed. The MRP also specifies exactly when the materials are needed to produce the finished goods by the dates given in the master schedule.

A master schedule indicates how many and what kind of finished goods are to be produced in a given period of time. The MRP identifies what and when materials are needed to produce those finished goods. Note that neither of these looks specifically at whether enough equipment and people are available to produce the desired amount of finished goods. These are capacity concerns, and a formal plan similar to the MRP is developed to address them. A **capacity requirements plan (CRP)** identifies what amount and type of equipment and personnel are needed to produce the finished goods indicated in a master schedule. A firm's production capacity is the maximum quantity it can produce during a specified period of time. Production capacity is determined by the amount and type of equipment and people available.

The MRP and CRP are planning and control tools that together identify what specific materials and capacity are needed and when they are needed. If either the MRP or CRP indicates there will be a problem in achieving the production goals, a manager must take corrective action. The production goals in the master schedule may need to be changed. Maybe different or additional sources of raw materials need to be found. Perhaps the business needs to purchase more equipment, hire more people, or have some of the current workers put in overtime.

▼ Do you feel it would be easier to control the operations of a company that was just starting up or of a company that had been in existence for a while? For which would it be easier to develop a demand forecast? A master schedule?

MAINTAINING EFFECTIVE OPERATIONS

Careful design of an operations system and wise use of production and inventory control techniques help an organization produce goods and services efficiently and effectively. However, they do not guarantee that the operations of an organization will produce high-quality goods and services at low costs. This goal requires focusing attention on the operations activities themselves. Quality control, maintenance, and cost control are three major areas of concern in the operations activities.

Quality Control

Unless you are different from other consumers, you are interested in getting the best good or service you can for the money you spend. You don't want to buy cassette tapes or compact disks that sound bad after playing them three times. Nor do you or your family want to take a car to a service center for repair and have the same problem come up again in two weeks. Since consumers want to get the best quality they can for their money, producers strive to produce the best-quality goods and services possible.

Consumers think of quality in many different ways. One person may think a pair of shoes or a movie is great, while another thinks they aren't. However, producers generally think of quality in the same way. They consider it to be a measure of how closely a good or service meets specified standards. Standards for size, shape, and other physical attributes are established for goods. Standards are also developed for speed, reliability, durability, and other measures of performance. All these are standards related to material characteristics which are present in the physical good. They can be stated in numeric terms and can be measured in some way.

Services are consumed as they are produced, and there are fewer physical aspects involved in their use. Therefore, it is more difficult to establish standards for services. This is especially true for services intended to make one "feel good," such as medical services, or to increase one's intellectual ability, such as education. Because quality standards are so important, however, producers of services have also developed and used them. Standards could involve when and how long it takes to provide a service to a consumer. Or they could measure the skill with which the person providing the service performs. As you can see, it is difficult to clearly define and state the more subjective standards related to providing a service.

Setting standards is the first step taken to control the quality of the goods and services being produced. The second step is to determine whether the finished goods and services meet the specified standards. There are two major approaches to doing this. One approach involves taking samples of finished goods and comparing them to the standards. The other approach is to take samples at various times during the processing or transformation activities. Taking samples and making inspections increase the cost of operations.

However, there are also costs involved when an organization produces goods and services of poor quality. These costs might be in the form of having to repair or replace defective goods or being sued for damages caused by an unsatisfactory service. Moreover, if consumers feel a good or service is of poor quality, they will not buy it. So producers must weigh the costs of quality control against the costs of producing poor-quality goods and services. A certain amount must be spent on quality control to consistently produce high-quality goods and services.

Maintenance

Once an operations system is producing quality goods and services, it must be kept running smoothly. This is referred to as maintaining the system, and the activities involved are called maintenance. More specifically, **maintenance** is any type of activity designed to keep an organization's resources in working condition or to put them back in such condition. This includes things done to prevent a breakdown, **preventive maintenance,** as well as those done to get something back in operating condition, **breakdown maintenance.**

Preventive maintenance consists of inspection and service activities designed to detect potential problems and correct them before they cause a breakdown. Breakdown maintenance, on the other hand, includes activities necessary to repair a resource which has broken down. Taking a car to a dealer or service center for an oil change and checkup after each 5000 miles of driving is preventive maintenance. Having to call someone to come to work on the car or to tow it in for service because it has stopped running is breakdown maintenance.

Like other operations decisions, those related to maintenance are difficult to make. There are human resource and monetary costs involved in preventive maintenance. However, the costs associated with breakdown maintenance may be even greater. Having to stop operations because of an emergency breakdown can be very costly for a business. Therefore, decisions must be made about how much preventive maintenance is needed to prevent breakdowns. Managers have to make tough decisions such as when to replace old resources with new ones. Machines and equipment need to be replaced before they break down, but producers want to use them as long as they can. A manager must also decide who will do the maintenance as well as when and exactly how to do it.

Information Brief 18-4

Saving Through Cost Control

Three years ago Lichty Mfg., a small equipment manufacturer, was told by its parent company that it had to improve its operations. After some study, they decided to discard their manual production control system and develop a computer-based system to gain better control of their costs.

First, the material requirements and inventory records were computerized. Then the labor cost information was automatically interfaced to the job costing system. Finally order entry and invoicing was incorporated. Now all managers can get accurate cost information quickly.

The new operations control system took about two years to develop and implement. Was it worth it? Says Rick Lichty, the firm's president, "the system saved us over $152,000 in the first year of operation."

Sources: P&IM Review, 1986 Reference Guide, p. 88; and Joseph G. Monk, *Operations Management: Theory and Problems*, McGraw-Hill, 1987, p. 256.

Cost Control

As you have seen, all operations decisions are affected by costs. Costs are important whether a business is producing goods or services. They are also a concern for government and nonprofit groups. Managers in government or nonprofit organizations try to keep cost below budget levels. Those in profit-oriented organizations must keep costs below income or the business will lose money.

Organizations are concerned about the cost of materials, labor, equipment, and facilties. The amount of material and labor used in production is usually easy to identify and varies with the quantity of goods produced. These are variable costs. Costs for equipment, a building, or supplies are not as easily identified with producing goods. An organization has these costs no matter how many goods and services it produces. These fixed costs are often referred to as **overhead.** Managers who have analyzed production costs have discovered that the costs for labor and materials are more than for equipment and facilities. In fact, it has been estimated that they are as much as two to three times as high.

Managers in charge of cost control work with two different types of cost information: budgets and cost standards. A **cost budget** shows the estimated costs of materials, labor, and overhead to produce a certain amount of goods or services in a given period of time. Budgets are usually used when services are provided. Your school district, for example, prepares a budget for educating all the students in your area each year. **Cost standards** specify the cost of the materials, labor, and overhead used to produce one unit of a good or service under normal conditions. For example, to produce a television set may require $33 of materials, $22 of labor, and $11 of overhead. To control operations costs, managers need accurate information on how much is spent on materials, labor, and overhead. Then they compare the actual expenditures with the amounts shown in budgets or cost standards. If the costs are too high, the manager must find out why they are high and decide on what measures to take to bring the costs back in line with the budget.

▼ How important do you think quality control should be to a company? If a company is to cut back on costs, do you think cutting back on quality control is a good idea? Why or why not?

SOCIAL ISSUES IN OPERATIONS MANAGEMENT

There are some major social issues related to the way operations activities are changing in our country. First, there is concern about the long-run effects of robots and other automated equipment replacing people in the workplace. How will those who are replaced earn income? Second, there is concern about the long-term psychological effects of dealing with machines rather than other people. Will workers lose the ability to work with other workers? How will the day-to-day dealing with machines affect workers' social and family lives? Third, there is a concern that the increasing use of computers centralizes the control of too many important areas of our society in the hands of a few technical people. Should we move more slowly toward automating parts of operations systems? Will those programming the machines gain too much power? These are only a few of the issues we are going to have to address in the future.

▼ How do you feel about these concerns? What are some other concerns related to the increasing use of automation in operations?

Select Terms to Know

breakdown maintenance	fixed costs	operations systems
capacity	inventory	overhead
capacity requirements plan (CRP)	master schedule	preventive mainte-
cost budget	material requirements plan (MRP)	nance
cost standards	operations	production
demand forecast	operations management	variable costs

Review Questions

1. How are production and operations related as these two terms are commonly used today?

2. What is the most important component of an operations system, and why is it the most important one?

3. What are the two basic approaches to job design, and how do they differ?

4. What types of things are robots being used for in operations systems?

5. List three things that are likely to differ in the operations activities of a manufacturing firm and an organization providing services.

6. What are some things business forecasters do to make their predictions of demand for goods or services more accurate?

7. Why do organizations try to keep inventory levels as close as possible to the amount of materials and finished goods needed?

8. Why are the MRP and CRP considered to be "control" tools in an operations system?

9. How do producers define quality? Give an example of a good or service, and describe some production quality standards that the producer might be using.

10. What is the difference between a cost budget and a cost standard?

Thought and Discussion Questions

1. Some people say that the purpose of operations systems is to take certain inputs and add value to them before they become outputs. What do you think it means to add value to something? Choose a good or a service as an example, identify the inputs, and explain how value is added before the inputs become an output.

2. What factors do you think were involved in deciding where to locate your school? List as many as you can, and indicate why you think each affected the location.

3. Who do you think should decide how work is done in a job, a manager or the one doing the work? Why do you feel as you do?

4. How do you think the manager of a restaurant decides how many waiters and waitresses to schedule for the times food is served? What factors are considered? When do you think the most are needed? When are the fewest needed? Why?

5. What are some advantages and disadvantages of having preventive maintenance on typewriters, microcomputers, and other office equipment done by those who use them? By a technician specially trained to do it? Which approach do you think is better? Why?

Projects

1. Select a service that you purchased recently and think about how it was provided to you. Write a brief report in which you identify and describe as completely as possible:

  a. The service
  b. The location and layout of the facilities involved
  c. Any equipment or machines which were used
  d. The person or persons who actually provided the service
  e. The type of social interaction which was involved
  f. How you felt about the level of quality

2. Talk with the owner of a small business in your community and ask why she or he decided to start the business at its present location. Write a brief report summarizing your talk and your general feelings about the location which includes:

  a. The name and address of the business and the name of the person you talked with
  b. As many reasons as possible for choosing the present location
  c. An explanation of why each reason was a factor
  d. Which of the reasons was the most important factor and why
  e. How you feel about the location of the business
  f. Why you feel as you do about the location

3. Visit a small business in your community and study the layout of the facility. Draw a rough sketch of the layout showing the different areas of the facility and where equipment, machines, inventory, and other things are located. Discuss the layout with the owner to find out why he or she has arranged things as they are. Write a brief report in which you:

a. Identify the name and address of the business and the name of the person you visited with.

b. Briefly describe the layout of the facility (include the sketch you made).

c. Summarize your discussion with the owner about why the facility is laid out as it is.

d. Indicate how you feel about the layout.

e. Describe why you feel as you do about the layout.

Case Study: Machines or People?

After reading this chapter you can begin to see why soft automation is attractive to manufacturers. Soft automation uses a totally new type of machine (often controlled by a microprocessor) that can do an incredible variety of tasks. Tools that were once controlled by human operators are now controlled by microprocessors. Machines now perform applications that were originally performed by human workers.

Robot arms load and unload machine tools and pallets in addition to assembling products. Robot arms also perform such specialized functions as drilling, grinding, polishing, welding, and painting.

Automatic storage and retrieval systems (ASRS) are used to store incoming materials, parts, or products and to remove the items for processing. ASRS use computer controls and automatic devices rather than a human and a forklift to manage the movement of items.

The need for people is also reduced by automatically guided vehicles (AGVs). These are computer-controlled carts that are used to transfer tools, fixtures, parts, and material in the factory.

Soft automation means that a company requires less workers. In fact, many of the cost advantages of soft automation are a direct result of decreased costs for human resources.

Soft automation allows factories to run shift after shift with fewer breaks and vacations and less time off for illness. The equipment's accuracy and consistency leads to increased product quality. Costs are reduced because there is less waste, and the amount paid for employee benefits, recruiting costs, and training costs is decreased.

U.S. industry needs to increase its ability to compete with other countries where labor is cheaper. It needs to increase its productivity. There is a nationwide move to increase the quality of products. And, companies always need to keep costs down. But the United States also has a real problem with unemployment.

Operations managers must face some very difficult questions. Should they increase their use of soft automation to increase their companies' competitiveness? Or, should they be concerned about their workers—even if it means the company suffers? This could very well be one of the most important questions facing American business today.

Source: Mark Bronakowski, "The Automated Factory," *Technical Education News,* Winter 1988, pp. 25–27.

1. How important do you think the following issues are for operations managers: keeping costs down, increasing productivity, and improving quality?

2. If you were faced with the decision whether to use automated processes or to provide for full employment, what would you do?

Managing the Techies

If you have seen the movie *Cool Hand Luke*, you may remember the line. After beating his defiant prisoner nearly senseless, the warden dryly explains, "What we have here is a failure to communicate."

All too often, that seems to sum up relations today between many technical staffs and their corporate managers. The technical staff consists of people who are closely related to the computer hardware and software in an organization. These are the hardcore people in the data processing area—programmers, engineers, technicians, operators. Since they are most directly concerned with the technical activities related to keeping the hardware and software operating, they may be called "techies."

The techies and the more generally oriented managers are both trying to achieve the same organization objectives, supposedly. However, members of the two groups seem quite different in personality and often come from very different education and training programs. Generally, they seem to approach tasks in different ways.

In addition, each group seems to use a language with a vocabulary or jargon the other group doesn't recognize or understand. Sometimes misunderstanding has led to arguments between the programmers in technical support and the managers in operations. In severe cases, some companies have failed because of the lack of communication between groups. Brilliant technical ideas were never accepted by managers who did not understand them, thought they were too costly to use, or could not see how they would improve a firm's operations.

So whose responsibility is it to bridge the apparent gap between the two groups? Both general managers and the technical leaders, say the experts. They offer the following tips on how to close the gap:

1. *Expand the circle.* Technology seems to breed mistrust. Yet technical managers must be included in the inner circle of managers who make the important decisions. "It's not a question of how you prevent technical people from impacting on business but how to make sure you get technical input into business decisions," says Gerald P. Dinneen, corporate vice president of science and technology at Honeywell Inc.

2. *Show them the big picture.* Engineers are not usually taught to think in what managers refer to as "strategic" terms. "They're very project-oriented. They don't deal with other people and concerns and issues until they get to the top spot," says Bruce L. Miller, head of information services at Aon Corp., a Chicago insurer.

3. *Stick to the road.* The best operations managers don't try to grab the steering wheel away from technical managers. They don't change signals, and they don't try to rush projects. When working with technical people, "You have to set a goal and let them work at it," says Lawrence W. Shearon, vice president of corporate technology at Medtronic Inc., a health care devices concern.

4. *Say that again?* Technical and nontechnical people often speak different dialects. "It's vital that technical people clearly explain what they're trying to do in terms of

the business," says Honeywell's Mr. Dinneen. He adds that many managers are technical dummies and suggests that "they learn something about calculus and physics."

5. *Let techies manage techies.* Putting a nontechnical manager in charge of a laboratory or techies in any other situation is risky. "The person without a technical background can be eaten alive," says a vice president of technology. Experts especially advise against starting MBAs (people with master of business administration degrees) on the technical side.

Managers in an organization need to think of the data processing department and its technical staff as an asset which they can use to help them do their jobs. Aon's Mr. Miller thinks too many managers treat data processing like a pizza parlor. In his words, "Instead of saying, 'Send me a pepperoni,' managers should ask, 'What are today's specials?'"

Managers and the technical staff need to make an extra effort to establish good lines of communication. Unless they are able to communicate with one another easily, it will be difficult for managers to take advantage of the expertise the data processing department and staff can provide. Similarly, a lack of communication prevents the technical staff from understanding the organization well enough to make the best contribution it can. The techies and managers must work together if the organization is to get the most benefits from their efforts and achieve its overall objectives.

Source: Adapted from Richard Gibson, Managing the Techies—Closing the Lab Coat–Pinstripe Gap, in "Technology in the Workplace," a special report, *The Wall Street Journal,* June 12, 1987, pp. 23D, 26D.

1. What are some reasons why techies and managers have difficulty communicating?

2. Whose responsibility is it to improve communications between members of the techie and manager groups?

3. Do you agree with the statement that "engineers are not taught to think in what managers refer to as 'strategic' terms"? Why or why not?

4. Why do you think Mr. Dinneen suggests that managers should "learn something about calculus and physics"?

5. Why do you think the experts say putting a nontechnical person in charge of a group of techies is "risky"?

Working in an Information Economy

People join together to form organizations which develop goals that can only be achieved by working together. Information is the lifeblood of the organization. Information as knowledge can only be applied to organizational goals when it is communicated in a timely, accurate, and understandable fashion. Therefore, organizations depend upon efficient systems to gather, communicate, and protect the information needed to meet their goals. Chapter 19 discusses the elements and uses of information systems.

In the 1990s most U.S. workers will spend a good portion of their work day interacting with a computer or other information technologies. Preparing for one's work and career requires an individual goal-oriented system. Chapter 20 outlines a strategy for career preparation, and jobsearch in our information economy.

UNIT OBJECTIVES

1. Explain the purpose of an information system and how it is used in a business organization.
2. Identify the elements of a computerized information system.
3. Discuss career opportunities in our information economy.
4. Learn how to use the self-assessment process as it applies to career paths and goals.
5. Describe the job search process and outline techniques for finding a job.

CHAPTER 19

Computerized Information Systems for Business

Computers Keep Patients Healthy

The computer can be used to record, store, and analyze just about any kind of data generated by an organization. The City Central Clinic is convinced that this is true. They feel their new computer system can provide an almost limitless variety of service to the clinic.

Using a computer system, the clinic maintains records of its 100 staff members and 3000 outpatients who make 55,000 visits per year, yet the administration of the clinic is convinced that they have barely touched the many uses for the computer in their organization.

In this chapter you will learn how computers help businesses like City Cen- tral Clinic manage huge amounts of information.

Study this chapter to learn more about the use of computerized information systems in business and to help you answer the questions in the end- of-chapter case study, "Computer Systems in the Medical Profession—Is It Healthy?"

You walk to your desk past rows of desks which all have computer terminals or personal computers (PCs) on them. John and Kathy are already working away at their terminals updating the latest repair schedules and getting ready to transmit the information via computer to the repair shop this morning. You sit at your desk and type in your log-on identification code to access the computer system in order to read the daily company newsletter. After noting the current stock prices, you check your electronic mailbox to see if anyone has responded to the requests you transmitted yesterday. You decide to send a few reminders via the electronic mail system to coworkers in Swit- zerland and Holland who are late in sending product infor- mation that you requested a few days ago. After that's done, you settle down to work on the monthly forecasts using the data you loaded into your PC yesterday.

A computer on every desk? Electronic mailboxes? A company newsletter on a computer system? Sound like years in the future? It's actually the way things are done in many companies today. Computers have revolutionized the way we do our jobs and have provided us with the capability to do a vast array of tasks electronically.

Completing tasks, either with or without electronic equipment, does not happen by accident. Managers or specialists hired by managers must carefully study the process of work to find ways to be more productive. Information must also be organized in a manner which will promote sound decision making. The study of systems has gained in importance as business seeks to improve its productivity in the face of world competition.

In this chapter you will study what an information system is. You will also learn about the function of the information systems manager. And you will learn how information systems help business to carry out many practical and vital tasks, including decision making.

WHAT IS A SYSTEM?

A rather broad definition of a **system** is that it represents a group of elements or parts that work together for a common purpose. People working together within a particular department, an assembly line, or the procedure for producing weekly paychecks are all examples of systems.

Definition of an Information System

An **information system** is composed of a group of elements that work together to produce information. In an information system, the elements are data (facts). Information is useful knowledge that is communicated accurately and understandably when it is needed. It is made up of data. In fact, at times data and information can be identical. Information tells us something that we did not previously know. Data that have been processed in some way (added together, averaged, or summarized in a report) convey information.

Let's use an example to clarify this seemingly confusing concept. Consider the situation where a manager knew that last week's sales were $6000. This $6000 represents a fact, one piece of data. Alone, it doesn't really tell the manager anything except how much was sold last week. If the manager was concerned

Information Brief 19-1

Information Systems— An Old Idea

Many of us make the mistake of thinking there were no information systems before computers, or that in order for a company to have an information system, it must first have a computer. Both viewpoints are wrong.

The main idea of an information system is to organize information in a manner which will make it useful for any number of purposes. While the computer makes this organization a whole lot easier, there are many examples where a manual method can be just as effective. For example, accounting systems in some firms (especially smaller ones) are not computerized today. Yet these manual accounting systems may still provide necessary, timely, and effective information.

Information Overload

As information processing continues to grow and the technology that makes a lot of it possible (namely, computers) becomes more sophisticated, the processing of data has almost gotten out of hand. We are almost to the point where the information generated by the information system is as useless as the data from which it was derived!

The problem is information overload. The problem occurs when too much irrelevant information is generated for the problem at hand. When this happens, the relevant information gets lost in the shuffle, and we're almost no better off than we were before we processed the data.

about next week's sales or next year's sales, this piece of data doesn't really provide any information. If the manager collected data on weekly sales for the last year, added them together, and averaged them, the result is information. Why? Because it now provides the manager with something that has more meaning than the separate data did.

The ultimate function of an information system is the transformation of data into knowledge. Knowledge can be retained for use in future decision making.

Recently, however, information overload has made it difficult for information systems to transform data into usable information because of the overwhelming amount of irrelevant data that computers can generate. The responsibility of the information systems manager is to strike a balance between the quantity of data that is processed and the quality of the information produced.

▼ How do you feel about information overload? Have you ever experienced it yourself? How did you react to it?

Managing the Information System

By now you are probably beginning to appreciate the complex job of managing information systems. Figure 19-1 illustrates how a large firm might organize its information management process. A manager at the vice presidential level is assigned to the management information systems (MIS) department, which usually has responsibilities for consulting, projects, long-range planning, operating the firm's information center, and providing technical services support. Employees of the MIS department consult with information users throughout the company to solve problems and develop new systems projects, help top management plan for the firm's information needs, and provide assistance to the firm in matters concerning technology.

The **information center** also provides valuable technical training, assistance in purchasing computers and other technological equipment, and systems help for users. The information center is located within the MIS department where computers and software are available for all employees in the firm. The information center concept has spread rapidly with the introduction of microcomputers. It has gained wide acceptance as more employees have become knowledgeable

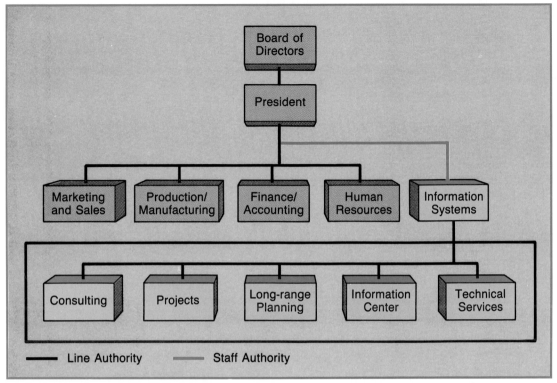

Figure 19-1. Information Systems Department within the organization of a large firm.

about microcomputers and have learned to use them to handle their information needs and solve technical problems.

Figure 19-2 shows the relationship between the MIS department and other functional areas in the organization. The information systems department may be placed on an equal footing with the other functional areas—marketing, production, finance, and human resources. (See Figure 19-2*a* on page 412.)

Firms can also organize information management in other ways. The MIS function may also be handled within one or more functional departments. (See Figure 19-2*b*.) Under this arrangement, a group of information experts would be housed within each department to fulfill many of the same functions as a specialized information systems department. This is particularly common where the microcomputer is the dominant information processor.

However, the most common practice is to organize information management as a staff or service department within a firm. (See Figure 19-2*c*.) Under this arrangement, the infor-

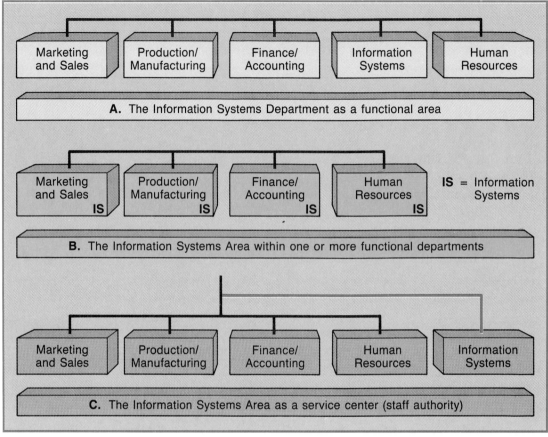

Figure 19-2. Location of Information Systems Department within various business organization structures.

mation systems department provides service and advice to all the other functional departments of the business. It also advises personnel at all levels of the firm, including top management, about information management.

The Information Manager's Functions

As you learned in Chapter 8, management functions can typically be classified into four categories: planning, organizing, directing, and controlling. These same functions exist in information systems management but in a special way.

Planning. In Chapter 8 you learned that of all the management functions, planning was the most important. In the case of information systems management, this is also true. However, planning in the area of information systems is made more difficult due to the constant interaction with so many departments in the organization. Planning what the information systems department will be doing in the next 5 to 10 years is often very dependent on what the other departments will be doing.

Why do the other departments have such a great effect on information systems management? It all boils down to two things: time and money. Depending on what the various departments' information systems requirements are, the information systems manager must be sure there is enough time to develop the system they desire, and enough money to pay for it. This may not seem like such a new concept, but information systems development is often backlogged from three to five years.

It might be hard to believe that it would take so many years before a desired information system is put in operation, but due to the complexity of the task, it is usually the case. Along with developing the new information systems, the information systems manager is responsible for keeping the old ones running, as well as planning for their eventual replacement as the technology of the old equipment becomes out of date.

Money, too, complicates the planning task, primarily due to the large costs of equipment to support information processing. The initial cost of many computer systems can run into millions of dollars, and that is strictly the cost of the physical equipment. Add to that the cost of personnel to design the system, write the programs, and run it.

So the planning function of the information systems manager involves developing realistic goals and objectives considering the long time horizon that must be considered and the high costs associated with information processing.

Organizing. After hearing some of the things that make planning difficult for the information systems manager, it will come as no surprise that organizing is also made more difficult by some of the same factors.

The information systems manager needs to organize the company's information resources in a manner in which the maximum benefit to the firm is realized. This is no easy task considering the limited nature of information resources and the very many requests from departments for new systems.

Directing. The directing task of the information systems manager primarily involves coordinating the development and maintenance of the information system. Quite often, a good deal of the leading and directing is left to project teams.

A **project team** is simply a group of information systems personnel that is temporarily assigned to work together on the development of an information system. Each team has a leader, and it is that leader's responsibility to make sure the system development stays on schedule and that the members of the team perform their duties. This arrangement frees the information systems manager from being heavily involved in the somewhat routine tasks of developing the actual system and allows the manager to spend time planning and coordinating the various teams.

Controlling. The final broad category of management tasks is controlling. Some of the aspects of controlling as it relates to information systems management have already been mentioned. The project team allows much of the controlling task to be moved to the level of the team leader. The information systems manager, however, still may set standards of performance for various tasks within the department. It is not uncommon for standards or goals to be set in terms of the number of lines of a computer program that should be written each day. Overall, the length of time it takes to develop a new system is also monitored and more or less subjectively evaluated in terms of the amount of resources it took to complete it.

In addition to monitoring the performance of personnel involved with systems development, the information systems manager also maintains close contact with the departments and individuals using the systems to ensure their expectations are met. Table 19-1 shows the range of information systems projects which would involve systems managers and their project teams. In small organizations this responsibility may fall to the owner or manager. The systems would appear smaller, but the challenge may be even greater if the owner-manager is not technology-oriented.

ELEMENTS OF A MODERN INFORMATION SYSTEM

In the previous section we spent a good deal of time discussing what an information system is and describing the tasks associated with managing the system. In this section we will describe the physical components of an information system, including people, software, hardware, and communication systems.

TABLE 19-1 Major Systems by Functional Area	
Name of Functional Area	**Type of Major System**
Marketing/sales	Product planning and development Pricing strategy Promotion (advertising) system Channels and distribution system
Production/manufacturing	Engineering design system Inventory and purchasing system Quality control Production cost system Employee scheduling system
Finance/accounting	Forecasting system Funds management Financial control system (audit) External relations (stockholders, government, etc.) Payroll System
Human resources	Recruiting and hiring system Promotion system Employee benefits

People

Whenever we hear someone talking about information systems or computer systems, typically the last thing we think about is people. We naturally associate information systems with computers and the various physical components that make up an information system.

The problem with this attitude is that without people, we wouldn't have an information system. Behind the scenes there are many people keeping the current systems running, developing new systems, and planning for the purchase of new equipment. On the other side, we have those people using the systems—the **end-users.** Without their need for the information systems, what use would the systems have?

Information Brief
19-3

The Systems Analyst

The systems analyst determines what the end-user ultimately wants to accomplish in an information system.

The analyst responds to a request from a department or end-user. A preliminary visit is necessary to get a grasp on the problem to be studied. Once the problem has been determined, a preliminary investigation is conducted which includes gathering the facts and eventually estimating the possible cost of change.

If the go-ahead is given, the new system is designed and programmed to the user's specifications. The new system is tested and implemented. In the months and years to come, the new system must be maintained and adjusted when the need occurs.

Analysts must be able to listen to others carefully and communicate with them clearly to get the best results.

Source: John Kador, "Up Close and Personal", *Information Center*, October 1987.

Some people believe that computers have caused a drastic reduction in the number of jobs available. In reality, computers have created more jobs. What has changed as a result of computers and the development of information systems is a demand for different types of people with different skills. The computer is more likely to displace people than to replace them.

The end-user is the person using the information system. There are increasing numbers of end-users who are developing their own systems (typically by using personal computers.)

The majority of end-users still depend on someone else to write the programs that handle their information processing needs. While the end-users may not be involved with the actual writing of computer programs, they play an important role in the systems development process by explaining to information systems personnel what they would like the system to do.

Software

One of the most often used and misunderstood terms related to information systems is software. Some people think it refers to programs you buy that are prewritten, while others believe it refers to programs that you write yourself. **Software** includes computer programs and the procedures and manuals which assist people in working with computer systems.

You probably already know that a **computer program** is a set of instructions for the computer to file. These instructions range from telling the computer to add two numbers together to telling the computer to print something out on a printer. Typically the instructions follow a standard format which is often referred to as a programming language. BASIC, COBOL, FORTRAN, and PASCAL are examples of programming languages. Each of these languages has rules and procedures for its use, much like English and other languages.

Computer programs can be further broken down into application programs and utility programs. **Application software** are programs written for a particular situation. Examples include a program to handle accounts receivables or a program to handle names and addresses on a mailing list. The primary characteristic is that this program has a specific function and is often written for a particular end-user.

Systems software refers to programs which run the computer itself. For example, when the computer is turned on, it's the systems software which gets the computer ready to process data.

Software also refers to rules, procedures, and documentation. Rules refer to the written and unwritten guidelines of the information system. For example, one rule might be that no one without a valid password can access the payroll system. An example of a procedure would be that in order for passwords to be issued to employees, they must submit an approval form signed by the payroll manager. As you can see, neither the rule nor the procedure is actually a computer program. Rather they provide useful guidelines and controls for the proper use of a particular system.

Documentation may be a little harder to understand. **Documentation** can be defined as any material (diagram, words, etc.) that (1) explains to the end-users how to use a system, (2) explains to the systems operators how to operate the system, and (3) explains to the programmers how to modify or change the system.

Another form of documentation is the user's manual which accompanies each software application. The manual could be a step-by-step set of instructions for making the system operate. It would explain in more detail what the different functions of the system are and how the user can make them work. Just as you would look at the owner's manual of a car to find out how different features work, you would use the manual to see how the different parts of the system operate.

Hardware

You may already have an idea of what is meant by hardware. **Hardware** simply refers to all the physical equipment used in an information system. The common mistake people make is in thinking that hardware only refers to the actual computer where the processing occurs. But it includes everything that is part of the computer system including printers, monitors (screens), and storage devices.

The heart of the computer system and probably the single most important part of the hardware is the **central processing unit (CPU).** The CPU is where the actual instructions contained in the computer program are interpreted and executed. Without the CPU there would be no computer.

The CPU controls and/or manages all the hardware that is part of the system. This includes input-output devices and storage devices. Figure 19-3 illustrates the parts of a hardware system.

Input-Output (I/O) Devices. **Input-output (I/O) de-vices** are units where data can be input to the CPU, and where data and/or information can be output from the CPU. The most common form of an input device is a terminal which has a keyboard and a monitor that displays what is keyed.

The terminal is also used for output from the CPU, but equally common is a printer. The obvious difference between the terminal and the printer used as output devices is that with a printer we receive a printed copy of the CPU output. The terminal only maintains the information as long as it's on the screen.

Storage Devices. Storage devices can also serve as I/O devices. As the name implies, a storage device stores data. These data can be sent to the CPU, and similarly the CPU can send data to the storage device. A storage device provides us with a permanent, reusable copy of the data as opposed to the temporary nature of both printed and displayed output. Output may be stored on various types of computer disks and tapes. The major choice in storage depends upon the speed needed in retrieving data and the security needed to protect the data.

Communications Systems

A CPU and I/O device or a secondary storage system is of little use alone. A microcomputer on one desk in an office may not be of much use either. A large firm with many branches would be helpless if their computer systems only functioned in the central office. The process that transmits and receives data from one device in an information system to another is called **data communication.** This process also makes it possible for data to be transmitted from one physical location to another. The use of special wiring, telephones, and satellites are tools in the communication process.

USE OF INFORMATION SYSTEMS IN BUSINESS

Business information systems are used by all levels of management within an organization. Table 19-1 looked at major systems by functional areas. In this section we will be looking at information systems at the different levels of management within the organization: first-line or supervisory management, middle management, and top-level or executive management.

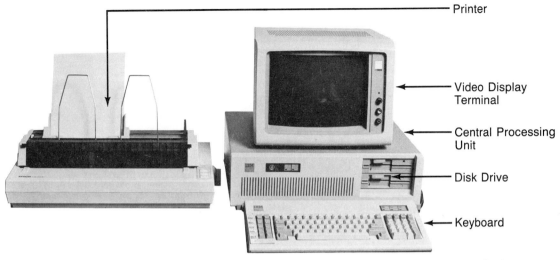

Printer

Video Display Terminal

Central Processing Unit

Disk Drive

Keyboard

Figure 19-3. Components of a typical microcomputer hardware system.

First-Line Management

Probably the most well-developed business information systems exist in this area. The systems used in this category are primarily focused on handling the day-to-day operations of the firms. Often, it is in this area that the value of using a computer is first realized because the computer provides a means for handling an enormous amount of data collection, analysis, and storage.

One of the first departments to successfully use information systems was accounting. Initially, computers were believed to have been designed to handle "number crunching" functions, and accounting was the natural place to look for an application. In addition, the standard procedures utilized in accounting were more easily translated into an information system because computers work best with set rules.

Another supervisory-level area that has used computers is inventory management. Again, we have a situation where a large quantity of data needs to be handled, in this case, inventory information. We also have a standard procedure to follow with handling the information. If the amount of inventory we have on hand drops below a certain point, we need to reorder it. If we could maintain the record of inventory on a computer, then we could leave it up to the computer to tell us when we need to order more.

In general, a first-line manager's use of information systems tends to focus on the processing of large quantities of data in

Information Brief 19-4

More Than Just "Number Crunchers"

Computerized information systems are often viewed as high-powered machines that crank out endless computations and generate pages of reports. While the majority of information systems functions revolve around the processing of data, there are many new components and features emerging in this area that are revolutionizing the workplace.

Voice messaging/voice recognition is but one exciting area that ultimately will allow direct communication with the computer simply by speaking to it. Through synthesizing the human voice, we will be able to work with computers as easily as talking with our coworkers.

a somewhat standardized fashion. The information systems provide managers and workers at this level a means to evaluate the company's performance. The use of the computer has greatly reduced the quantity of clerical people necessary to maintain manual records. The computer has, however, increased the need for people experienced in the use of computers or the aptitude for working with them.

▼ How would you feel if the retail store at which you work as an inventory clerk made the decision to automate the inventory function? You have been assured that you will still have a job, but you will need to be retrained on the computer when the system is implemented.

Middle Management

It may be apparent that if we processed the data at this level in the same way we did at the supervisory level, we would experience the problem of information overload described in Information Brief 19-1. Unfortunately, as more and more aspects of the company become part of the information system, the natural tendency is to produce more reports showing every conceivable summary of the data. This, however, does not serve the goals of middle management or the need to implement the goals at the lower level.

Many experts believe that middle management is best served by reducing the quantity of data in favor of improving its relevance. They argue that when this occurs, an organization tends to move successfully toward the truly professional use of information systems.

An important thing to recognize is that at this level, the information generated at the first-line manager's level becomes the data at the middle-manager level. In other words, the information generated for the first-line manager needs to be processed again in order for it to have value and relevance to the middle manager.

Some of the applications of information systems that have been developed for middle management include inventory forecasting systems, budgeting systems, and cost accounting systems. These systems represent the processing of first-line management information by yet another system.

Some examples might help to clarify this point. At the supervisory level we discussed the use of information systems to

Expert Systems for Complex Problems

Traditional software programs are designed to solve well-defined problems. End-users utilize application programs as tools to solve the problems of storage and analysis of data. This information is then reported in meaningful form inside and outside the organization. Supervisors and middle managers have found existing software the most applicable to their problems. The high-level executives are next in line for some much needed help.

Expert systems are computer programs that use human traits to solve problems. Expert systems represent one branch of the technology called artificial intelligence. Other branches include natural interfaces (brain waves) between computers and users and voice recognition systems (computers responding to human voices). Expert systems have progressed more rapidly than other branches. These programs enable computers to perform tasks that require reasoning skills to solve problems. The development of expert systems will help managers access more information quickly and easily to make business decisions.

Just what is an expert system? It is a computer program that pools the knowledge of an expert or group of experts on a certain subject. This so-called knowledge is stored so that the computer program can manipulate it to formulate answers to questions asked by end-users. For example, a farmer would have to go through a certain decision process in de-

ciding when to plant a field. The farmer would have to consider the weather conditions, time of year, condition of the soil, and other factors. The expert system helps with the decision making process by implementing its rules. The rules might be IF the temperature is greater than 75 degrees, THEN plant seeds; IF it is later than April 30, THEN plant seeds; and so on. The program is a series of IF-THEN statements based on expert information stored in the program.

What does it take to develop an expert system? The most important ingredient is a problem that human experts have mastered. The problem should be small enough to be well-defined with many possible solutions but big enough to interest management. Secondly, the firm would buy a software program called an **expert system shell** that stores knowledge. The most important step then is to find a cooperative human "expert" who is willing to share knowledge and expertise. Finally an engineer must design the system so that it can easily respond to questions asked by end-users who want to use the finished product to make decisions.

Sources: Sharong Efroymson and David B. Phillips, "How Would You Like a Crash Course in the Most Economical Application of Artifical Intelligence Research?" *Information Center*, March 1987; Harvey P. Newquist III, "Expert Systems: The Promise of a Smart Machine," *Computerworld*, January 13, 1986; Andrew Kupfer, "Now, Live Experts On a Floppy Disk," *Fortune*, October 12, 1987; Rick Minicucci, "Artifical Intelligence: Fact vs. Fantasy," *Today's Office*, September 1986.

Information Brief 19-5

Are You Being Watched?

Computers are often praised for improving productivity. Productivity is not always easy to measure, especially in an office setting. Lately, however, new methods have been devised to measure the amount of work employees do during the workday.

New systems have also been devised that can monitor the amount of time employees spend on certain tasks. This includes employees who are measured for each keystroke they make in an office setting, the amount of time they spend in customer service calls, or the time spent on the telephone for nonbusiness purposes.

Some think this is needed to increase worker and managerial productivity. Others view this as spying, and an invasion of privacy. What do you think?

Sources: Beth Brophy, "New Technology, High Anxiety," *U.S. News and World Report,* September 19, 1986; and "Study Says Computers Are Watching 7 Million U.S. Workers", *The New York Times,* September 28, 1987.

manage inventory, more specifically to handle the tasks of reordering when stock is low. At the middle-manager level, we could use the information maintained by the inventory system of how much stock was being used to forecast what we thought the usage would be for the next month or next year. Similarly, in the accounting system, we could again use these data in preparing our budgets, using the records of previous activity as a predictor of what might happen in the future.

Top-Level Management

By now you may have guessed that at the top-management level of information systems use, we will be processing information from first-line and middle-management levels. Typically, top-level management is involved with the most abstract level of strategic planning and therefore would want data that provides the broadest possible picture of the organization and its operations.

It is highly unlikely that top-level managers are interested in daily inventory usage or even the tracking of routine accounting activity. More typically, they are interested in information that provides a comprehensive summary picture of the organization. For example, top-level management might use the information generated at lower levels in an attempt to predict what future financial outlays might be required given the present rate of business activity. Or top-level managers might base their plans for future company expansion on sales-related data which have been processed into meaningful projections of company growth 5 or 10 years into the future.

In essence, top-level managers try to use data to make long-range projections. They do so because it is their responsibility to look at the business from a long-range viewpoint. Such projections guide and support executives in making decisions that will affect the company plans and operations well into the future.

This chapter has provided you with a rough sketch of the environment, tasks, and uses of information systems. The duties of the information systems manager are similar to those of other functional managers. As you have seen, however, the services provided by this department are technical and complex in nature, giving rise to unique challenges and problems that are not always easy to manage or solve.

Select Terms to Know

application software	end-users	input-output (I/O) devices
central processing unit (CPU)	expert system	project team
computer program	hardware	software
data communication	information center	systems software
documentation	information system	

Review Questions

1. What are the components of a system?

2. How does data become information for the manager?

3. What is the main responsibility of the information manager?

4. How is the information center distinguished from the MIS department?

5. Why is planning an especially difficult task for the information systems manager?

6. What are the two main resources that in-hibit the activities of the information resources manager?

7. How does the project team concept assist the information manager in carrying out his or her duties?

8. List the major elements of an information system and describe each.

9. What is the difference between systems software and application software?

10. How are data used to produce information for the three levels of management?

Thought and Discussion Questions

1. Information systems development is back-logged three to five years. What implications does this have on the end-users?

2. Do you feel that for a company to stay competitive they must computerize and/or automate their major functions? Defend your answer.

3. Do you think it would be inappropriate for a company to give tests to job applicants to de-termine their aptitude for working with computers?

4. Do you believe that computers will eventually have as large an impact on our home lives as they currently do on our work life? Or does the impact already exist?

5. What are some suggestions you could offer to managers who are attempting to "weed out" irrelevant data from their information system?

Projects

1. Identify five information systems you come into contact with every day. For each system discuss the following:

a. Where does the data come from?
b. What process takes place to convert it into information for your use?

c. What use do you make of the information in your own decision making?

d. What technology is used, if any, to get the information to you?

2. John Raymond Stone, an attorney, uses a computer system in his office. The system consists of a microcomputer, a printer, and a telephone which is linked to a database in Memphis. His legal briefs are typed by using a word processing program. He also has a billing system. Several weeks ago he purchased the technology to link the computer on his desk to his secretary's computer. He stores his floppy disks for the computer in a cabinet on his desk.

a. What hardware does Mr. Stone use? Software?

b. What storage device does Mr. Stone use?

c. Does Mr. Stone have a communication system? What evidence do you find?

3. Select an information systems component (people, hardware, or software) for further investigation. Examples may be information center activities, software applications used by business firms, typical computer use by a business end-user, types of storage devices used by business, communication system components, use of expert systems, and duties of systems analysts or programmers.

a. Gather data for your study through personal interviews, library research, on-site visits, or textbooks.

b. Prepare a list of terms you have found to be associated with your topic.

c. Report your findings to the class or develop a bulletin board that highlights your findings.

4. Assume a company is installing its first computer system. Naturally they would like to computerize all the systems in every functional area, but they lack the two key ingredients—time and money. Review the major systems listed in Table 19-1 and select the two you feel should be implemented first. Why have you selected these systems? How would their implementation affect the firm?

5. Identify five areas that you think should be computerized but which presently are not. How would the change improve the systems you select? How would it change the lives of the people within the system and the people who would be the beneficiaries of the system?

Case Study: Computer Systems in the Medical Profession—Is It Healthy?

At the beginning of the chapter you read about the City Central Clinic which was maintaining records of its 100 staff members and 3000 outpatients who made 35,000 visits per year. They felt they were just beginning to use their computer system, and they added many more services.

The computerized data management program can generate work schedules for entire groups of employees. The office information system is designed to track progress toward major work objectives.

The patient files are arranged to contain such records as weight, age, surgical history, and spe-cial risk factors. These and other data may be accessed in just a few seconds to prepare reports or studies. For example, if all patients with a certain health condition were to be studied, the database program would provide a list.

Another benefit is the ability of the computer to store and calculate the data necessary to generate important reports for the government. These data are also incorporated into reports and feedback on clinic activities for use by the clinic's funders.

However, it is possible to be concerned about the use of computer systems in the medical profession. There are two potential problems. First, there is concern regarding a patient's right to privacy. What would happen, for example, if a patient with a certain health problem did not want that information released? Second, there is concern about what will happen in the future as doctors and nurses become more and more dependent on the computer system. Will they be able to function well if the computers are broken or if there is an emergency?

Sources: Richard Ensman, Jr., "Use Your Computer for More Productive Management," *Administrative Management,* January 1986; and H. Garrett DeYoung, "Hospital Keeps Patient Records Orderly," *High Technology,* November 1985.

1. Give some reasons why it could be very important for a health clinic, hospital, or doctor's office to maintain good patient records. How can a computer system help a clinic, doctor's office, or hospital in keeping these records?

2. If you had some type of disease, would you be concerned that a clinic, hospital, or doctor's office could release that information without your knowledge?

3. On the other hand, if you were suffering from an illness and a governmental agency was gathering information about those who had the illness (looking for a cure for the illness), would you support the government's efforts?

4. In the future it could be possible for health care professionals to come to depend too much on a computer system. How could this be prevented?

CHAPTER 20

Careers in an Information Economy

Crushed Job Hopes

Eager to keep climbing up the career ladder, one woman quit the good job she already had when offered a better one. In applying for a new position with another firm, she was promised a vice president's job. Instead, she was assigned to administrative support duties.

She quit because, it seemed to her, she was a victim of a job bait-and-switch (getting someone interested in a particular job and then changing the rules). Crushed hopes can lead to dismay and a stalled career for job applicants. And for the firms that hire people under false or very misleading pretenses, crushed hopes can lead to high employee turnover.

Learn more about how some job seekers have suffered the effects of job bait-and-switch in the end-of-chapter case study, "Victims of Misleading Job Interviews."

Study the contents of this chapter to learn more about career opportunities and job search techniques and to help you answer the questions in the end-of-chapter.

With the United States losing its share of the world market in manufacturing, mining, and agriculture, what is the job outlook for the labor force through the end of the century? To answer this question, the U.S. Department of Labor commissioned the Hudson Institute to conduct a study. The study's findings were released in 1988. Hudson's most striking conclusion was that blue-collar and unskilled jobs are decreasing and skilled information and service jobs are increasing.

To give you some ideas about careers in the information economy and how to get them, this chapter addresses topics that identify:

- Career opportunities
- Career paths and goals, with self-assessment

- The traits that business is looking for among job applicants
- How to prepare job search documents and perform well in the job interview.

CAREER OPPORTUNITIES

From shopping malls to corporate computer centers, from fast-food restaurants to high-tech plants, a common plea is popping up all across the United States: HELP WANTED. The worker deficit has come about in part because of the low birthrate ("baby bust") of the 1960s and early 1970s. Because of the baby bust, fewer young Americans are available to enter the job market. Moreover, the trend is likely to continue until the twenty-first century.

With the decline in manufacturing and agricultural jobs, more people are needed in the information and service sectors. Besides women and minorities, businesses are also looking among immigrants and older people to find workers to fill these many jobs.

The Information Sector

People in the information sector process, manage, and create information. Thus the information sector needs operators, people handlers, supervisors, managers, and a wide range of technical and professional workers.

Information Operators and People Handlers. Operators deal directly with the processing of information, using computers and other electronic equipment. People-handling workers process information in face-to-face situations and over the telephone.

Supervisors and Managers. Supervisors work directly with operators and other information workers. Some managers work with technical operations—with machines and the development of efficient working systems. Other managers work with people—with the supervisors and with other workers who report to these managers.

Technical and Professional Workers. Technical workers design equipment and systems and deal with changes and trends to meet information needs. In this category are professionals who deal with accounting, economics, finance, market-

---

Career Brief 20-1

Computer Whiz Kid

Jonathan Rotenberg is the president of the Boston Computer Society (BCS). According to a Lotus Development Corp. marketing manager, BCS is "probably the most influential (computer) users' group in the country." BCS market tests public acceptance of new personal computers and software.

How did BCS come into existence? It all started when Jonathan wanted to buy a personal computer (PC) and couldn't get much data from computer stores. Rotenberg was only 15 years old and a student at Commonwealth School. "I still had braces, and my voice hadn't changed," he said. This computer whiz kid has proven, yet again, that successful ideas and a successful career are not the exclusive preserve of any one age group.

Source: Alex Beam, *Business Week,* March 9, 1987, pp. 97–98.

ing, and the like. Also included are consultants, trainers, and teachers. Figure 20-1 shows what jobs are on the increase in the information economy.

The Service Sector

Another fast-growing field is the service sector, where many young people find their first jobs. Both basic and people skills are essential, such as the ability to use the language (read, write, speak), to do math (make change, etc.), and to operate cash registers and the telephone.

Since these skills are so essential, few high school dropouts can meet the needed qualifications. Yet college-educated applicants don't want this kind of work. A study by the National Restaurant Association says that its members "could experience a shortfall of 1 million workers by 1995." Adds a report by the

Figure 20-1. Where the Jobs Will Be, 1990–2000. (*Source:* U.S. Bureau of Labor Statistics.)

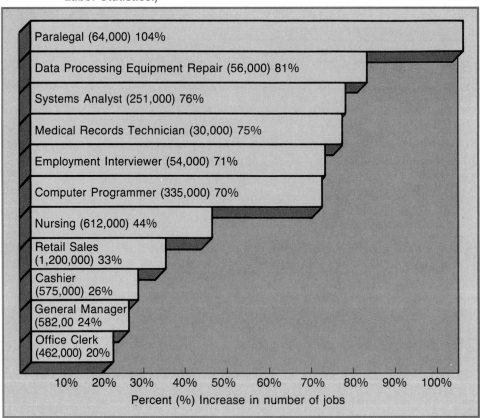

Paralegal (64,000) 104%
Data Processing Equipment Repair (56,000) 81%
Systems Analyst (251,000) 76%
Medical Records Technician (30,000) 75%
Employment Interviewer (54,000) 71%
Computer Programmer (335,000) 70%
Nursing (612,000) 44%
Retail Sales (1,200,000) 33%
Cashier (575,000) 26%
General Manager (582,00 24%
Office Clerk (462,000) 20%

10% 20% 30% 40% 50% 60% 70% 80% 90% 100%
Percent (%) Increase in number of jobs

National Retail Merchants Association: "Youth shortages impact the retail business more than many other industries."

College educated students typically seek higher paying managerial and professional positions within the service industry. The fields of most promise in the 1990s are expected to be in accounting, advertising, banking, finance, consulting, communications, information handling (see above), health care, insurance, law, shipping, tourism, transportation, and public service. Service jobs in international trade and marketing also offer promise as more and more services will be sold across national borders.

CAREER PATHS AND GOALS, WITH SELF-ASSESSMENT

Maybe your goal will be to get your foot in the door of a firm in an industry that appeals to you. You might prefer advancement, or moving laterally—into some position quite different from where you get hired. Thus a technical or managerial position could appeal to you. Or perhaps you'll be interested in getting a variety of business experiences so that you can become a company trainer, a business teacher, a management consultant, or an entrepreneur.

Staying Put Versus Following a Career Ladder or Lattice

Many people are not interested in moving up or over. Once they get a job, even an entry-level job, they're happy to stay put. They have fewer needs and wants than others and are satisfied with a lower standard of living.

Other people, however, develop short- and long-range goals. These objectives are designed to take them upward on a career ladder or sideways on a career lattice. Both these career paths usually call for specialized training, often college degrees.

Career Ladders. With only a high school diploma and limited work experience, many workers start their work lives as an entry-level clerk or an industrial worker. With experience and top-notch performance ratings, they can usually move up, at least a few steps. People with technical training, taken from community colleges and/or trade schools, can sometimes get jobs at the midlevel without having to start at the bottom. (See Figure 20-2.) But even for people with some postsecondary

Career Brief
20-2

Former Football Coach Hammers Home a New Gospel

Arthur Williams, former renowned high school football coach in Columbus, Georgia, is building a nationwide reputation for racking up fantastic scores once more. Now employed in the $820 billion-a-year insurance industry, he concentrates on a single product: inexpensive term insurance.

Williams hammers home the gospel of term insurance through a door-to-door sales force of 140,000 part-timers spread across 49 states and Canada. The sellers are linked by a $5 million private satellite TV network over which the stocky, balding Williams delivers daily pep talks.

Source: Gordon M. Henry, *Time,* July 21, 1986, p. 53.

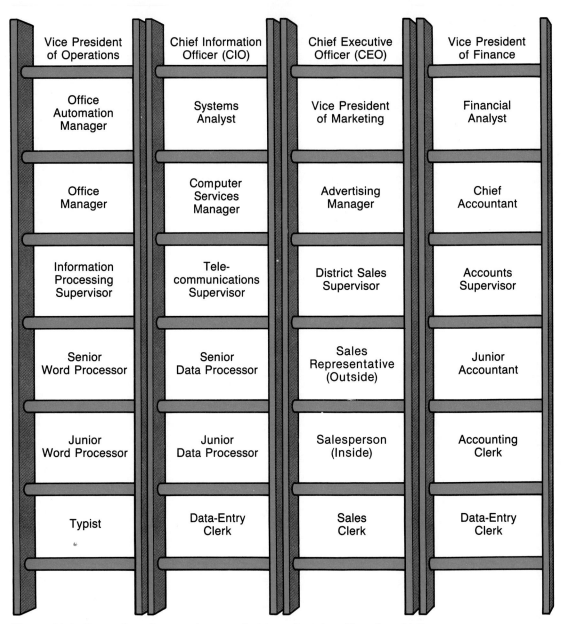

Vice President of Operations	Chief Information Officer (CIO)	Chief Executive Officer (CEO)	Vice President of Finance
Office Automation Manager	Systems Analyst	Vice President of Marketing	Financial Analyst
Office Manager	Computer Services Manager	Advertising Manager	Chief Accountant
Information Processing Supervisor	Tele-communications Supervisor	District Sales Supervisor	Accounts Supervisor
Senior Word Processor	Senior Data Processor	Sales Representative (Outside)	Junior Accountant
Junior Word Processor	Junior Data Processor	Salesperson (Inside)	Accounting Clerk
Typist	Data-Entry Clerk	Sales Clerk	Data-Entry Clerk

Figure 20-2. Examples of several career ladders. People with only a high school diploma, provided they have taken preparatory classes, are hired for the lower-level jobs on these career ladders. The mid-level jobs go to people with experience, a fine reputation, and good performance evaluation ratings. With community college or special training, some people can jump onto the ladder at one of the mid-points. But even for people with some postsecondary education and lots of experience, the mid-point on any of these ladders is usually as high as they can go, until and unless they get a four-year degree in business. The Masters of Business Administration (MBA) is the more common background these days, however, for people who aspire to go all the way to the top.

education and lots of experience, the midpoint of a career ladder is usually as high as they can go until and unless they get a four-year degree, often in a business field.

What about going all the way to the top of the ladder, for example, becoming a vice president or chief executive officer (CEO) of a company? For people who aspire to go all the way to the top of the ladder, a master of business administration (MBA) is a common requirement these days. In other words, the person who aspires to the highest-level positions usually must successfully complete postgraduate courses in business.

Career Lattices. A career lattice differs from a ladder in that you can move sideways, even downward, on another line. The purpose is to get experience in that line or field before starting to climb again. One means of traveling the career lattice route is by getting assigned to participate in unique projects. Such experiences can help you identify aptitudes. Another means of identifying likes and dislikes, attributes and aptitudes is to conduct a self-assessment.

Knowing Yourself Through Self-Assessment

When you "know yourself," you have developed the ability to decide what type(s) of work tasks and work environments are more likely to bring you job satisfaction. Assessing your needs and preferences before committing yourself to take a job can help you match yourself to the job—get the best type of job for yourself. The goal is to avoid becoming a square peg in a round hole.

Identifying Aptitude Needs. Knowing yourself includes identifying what type of tasks you prefer. Ponder your likes and dislikes regarding classes, hobbies, and work experiences (paid or unpaid). Identify for yourself which work duties are most and least likely to appeal to you from the following options:

• Working with machines such as computers and software programs

• Working with detail-oriented tasks such as records management

• Working with the language—talking, negotiating; writing letters, reports, or advertising copy

- Dealing with people especially important in a selling or public relations or personnel type of job or in team relationships where you contribute to the group to meet team objectives

- Generating ideas and creating things—vital in developing marketing campaigns, new systems and designs, and similar creative tasks

- Collecting and interpreting data—used to gather and prepare research data to produce information

- Analyzing and using information and statistics such as analyzing financial statements and accounting procedures

- Solving problems and making decisions on your own—and getting the credit when things go well but taking the blame when they don't

- Supervising a work unit to get work done through others

Identifying Psychological and Social Needs. Personal satisfaction comes from finding those things that match your psychological and social needs. Ponder your likes and dislikes on the bases of experiences with your family and friends and situations that have happened in your neighborhood and school. Ask yourself which environment(s) you might prefer from the following options:

- Working in a small firm versus a medium-size or large firm

- Working in a small town versus a city or suburb

- Working alone or with a small team versus with many people

- Desiring or needing a top-paying job that requires a college degree or other long-term specialized training and experience

- Desiring status, prestige, power over others

- Staying put versus seeking transfers and promotions

WHAT BUSINESS IS LOOKING FOR—"KASH"

Business looks for knowledge, attributes, skills, and habits (**KASH**). Job applicants who can demonstrate a somewhat equal balance of all four have a better chance of getting hired. See Figure 20-3 and the descriptions that follow. Then continue to assess yourself regarding how much KASH you already have and which items it might be wise to obtain.

Knowledge Needed in Business

The broad knowledge base needed on the mid- to upper steps of the career ladder (see Figure 20-1) can be categorized by academic business discipline. Quality schools or departments of business (in colleges and universities) are accredited by the American Assembly of Schools and Colleges of Business (AASCB). Such colleges offer these programs of study: accounting, economics, finance, management, management of information systems (MIS), marketing, production/operations management, personnel/human resources management, and sometimes business technology. Other types of postsecondary schools offer business programs that cover some or all of these subject areas as well.

Attributes Needed in Business

An **attribute** is defined as "to regard, assign, or ascribe to; belonging to or resulting from someone or something. A quality or characteristic belonging to a person or thing; a distinctive feature." Numerous studies have confirmed that the attributes shown in Table 20-1 are what employers look for in job applicants for business positions.

Skills Needed in Business

Needed in business are skills covering the abilities to facilitate, manage or lead, articulate, solve problems creatively, and make decisions.

The ability to facilitate means to see that things run smoothly. Effective facilitators manage information, materials, methods,

TABLE 20-1 Attributes Employers Look For in Job Applicants

Work Attributes	Social or Interpersonal Attributes
Accurate	Career-oriented
Analytical	Clean, neat
Articulate (effective with oral and written language)	Cooperative
	Conscientious
Businesslike	Considerate
Concise	Courteous
Dependable	Creative
Diligent	Diplomatic
Effective	Honest
Efficient	Innovative
Flexible	Intelligent
Money conscious	Knowledgeable (about the company, its products, etc.)
Organized	
Needs little supervision	Loyal
Persuasive	Motivated, self-starter
Profit conscious	Poised
Prompt	Sensitive to the needs of others
Responsible	
Time conscious	Tactful
Trainable	Works well under pressure

machines, and personnel so that all components fit together and all tasks get done accurately and when needed.

The ability to manage (or lead) includes being able to delegate work to others and to get productive work done through others. Leadership is the ability to motivate subordinates and others to volunteer and willingly follow the manager's assignments and suggestions.

The ability to articulate includes effective use of language and word choice. Practice until you can use the English language correctly as appropriate in a business setting.

The ability to solve problems and make decisions covers math problems, and much more. This skill also means looking at things in new ways to come up with logical and creative changes to improve operations. Since the human mind is never at rest, try using yours to analyze things you've never thought about before. Mentally, or even on paper, re-create or modify TV commercials. When you're annoyed with poor service or products that don't do what you expect, think how you would improve them if you were in charge.

Habits Needed in Business

Habits are behaviors. If you're dependable, you'll get to work every day and on time. If you're honest, you'll never steal money or even pencils. You won't steal the company's time, either, by wasting it to visit or fool around. See the list of attributes in Table 20-1 to think of other examples of habits. Start replacing poor habits with good ones.

PREPARING JOB SEARCH PAPERS

Successful job applicants prepare these job search papers: application letters, inquiry letters, résumé, and follow-up letters. These documents speak for you until you get an interview. Let's describe these documents, assuming their preparation for a mid-level job requiring more than a high school diploma.

The Application Letter

The **application letter** briefly introduces you and is mailed to firms that are advertising existing job openings. The objective is to make your letter eye-catching and therefore make you stand out from the crowd of other applicants. Getting a positive response to your letter means the personnel director is interested in seeing you and hearing more about you. Getting action means getting a personal interview.

To get a positive response, make sure the letter is perfect in appearance and also in grammar, punctuation, word choice, sentence structure, and spelling. Type or word process the letter. Proofread and make corrections. Revise the letter at the computer terminal or, if necessary, retype the letter until it represents you at your best.

In the first paragraph, refer to the specific job advertised. Then say something nice about the firm. Be sincere. That won't be hard if you've gathered data and studied the company. The second paragraph refers the reader to the résumé you've prepared and enclosed. Describe, very briefly, why hiring you can benefit the firm. If you use the same attributes the employer listed in the job vacancy notice, you'll stand a better chance of getting your application letter noticed.

The third and last paragraph asks for a personal interview. Make sure the employer or personnel director knows where to reach you and when. You probably can't plan to sit at the phone all day for the next two weeks. (See Figure 20-4.)

Career Brief
20-4

From Secretary to President

Jamaican-born Melba J. Duncan, a former secretary, has now reached the top of her career ladder. She's president of a recruiting firm for executive secretaries. Tapping into the vast network she developed while working for top executives, Duncan seeks job applicants who are intelligent, highly skilled, and come with top attributes. Those who survive 1½ hours of testing and interviews meet with job-hiring clients who also have been thoroughly interviewed. Job applicants pay fees of 30 percent of their first year's salary, which can range from $30,000 to $50,000.

Source: Susan Ochshorn, *Venture,* May 1986, p. 13.

Date

(Inside address)
Specific person's name and title
Name of firm
Address of firm

Dear Mr./Mrs./Ms. (last name of addressee):

From (the source), I understand that you have a management
trainee's position available that requires (skills and attributes). I am keenly interested in (name of firm), because of
the reputation your organization has attained, not only in the
marketplace, but also with the public for its integrity and
progressive views. I believe that with my background, my
association with your firm could prove mutually beneficial.

As you will see from the enclosed resume, I meet both your
required and preferred qualifications. I received my (educa-
tion/training) at (institution). My (degree or certification
name) program included: (a few of the most relevant courses).
Some attributes former employers have used in describing my
abilities include: (no more than five of the attributes
you've identified that best describe you, that most closely
match the firm's stated needs). I am competent with (a maximum of five top skills or abilities the company is specifically asking for; see the resume for examples). I have
also had a variety of paid and unpaid work experiences that
should prove helpful in my fulfilling the position you have
advertised.

I would like the opportunity to meet with you (addressee's
last name), to exchange information about (name of firm) and
my qualifications in respect to the position advertised-- or
any other similar position. I can be reached at (___) ___-
____ any weekday between 10 a.m. and 2 p.m. during the next
two weeks. Or you may write to me at the above address.

Sincerely yours,

(Your signature)

(Your typed name)

Enclosure (resume)

Figure 20-4. Sample master inquiry letter that you might prepare in the
future when seeking a mid-level position on a career ladder.

The Inquiry Letter

Inquiry letters are addressed to firms you'd like to work for but where no jobs you want have been advertised. Your objective with the inquiry letter is to get your papers on file in case a job opens up soon. The objective is still to get your papers noticed.

The same procedures are used as outlined for the application letter. You may decide not to enclose a résumé. (See Figure 20-5.)

The Résumé

The **résumé** is another name for a personal data sheet (see Figure 20-6). The résumé should also be perfect in grammar and appearance. The best résumé is concise, while exceptional or unique. The objective, like the application or inquiry letter, is to attract attention and elicit a positive response.

The work history begins with the most recent job and work period (beginning and ending dates) and proceeds to the first or earlier jobs held. Notice from Figure 20-6 how positive attributes are incorporated in every description of prior work experiences. Notice, too, that the specific type of industry or firm is cited as part of the work history.

The reason for stating the type of firms where you've worked is to show prospective employers that you're familiar with the industry. In fact, many job listings say something like this: "Experience in finance (or real estate or law, etc.) preferred."

The education history is also reported in reverse chronological order, with the most recent listed first. Notice, in Figure 20-6, that classes and special seminars are included, even though no diploma or degree resulted.

For *references,* it's permissible to merely state: "References available upon request." Don't list references, however, unless you've first contacted the people you want to speak on your behalf. Get their permission to use their names. When making personal contacts, be ready to share with these people the top attributes that describe you in a positive way. Ask your references if they agree and, if so, will they please mention these attributes in their letters of reference.

The Application Form

Unlike the typed résumé, the application form is often filled out by hand. Good penmanship and the ability to follow in-

Date

(Inside address)
Specific person's name and title
Name of firm
Address of firm

Dear Mr./Mrs./Ms. (last name of addressee):

Are you looking for someone who is productive, organized,
articulate, logical, and creative? Do you need someone who
can take initiative and follow through in a responsible and
analytical fashion to get things done? If so, the attributes
and skills I can bring to your firm might be just what you
are looking for.

I am keenly interested in (name of firm), because of the
reputation your organization has attained, not only in the
marketplace but also with the public for its integrity and
progressive views. I believe, (addressee's last name), that
with my background, my association with your firm could prove
mutually beneficial.

I am seeking a position as an administrative assistant in the
finance, marketing, or human resources department. Hired to
assist with finance, marketing, or human resources, I would
expect to learn a great deal in and on behalf of (name of
firm). In any of these or related positions, I would work
well in team relationships that call for, among other things:
facilitating teleconferences, meetings, and special projects;
supervising and motivating subordinates; gathering and analyzing data; and making recommendations leading to the improvement of productivity, systems, and morale.

My communication, information processing, and accounting skills
are highly developed. Moreover, people that I have worked for
and with say I can be counted on to produce, that I have high
standards, and that I'm easy to get along with. To verify my
skills, knowledge, and attributes, you may check with my references, which are available upon request. If you are interested
in what you have heard so far, (addressee's last name), please
call me for an appointment so that we can discuss my proposed
contributions to (name of firm). I can be reached at (___)
___-____ after 2 p.m. until (three weeks from the current date),
or you can write to me at the above address.

Sincerely yours,

(Your signature)

(Your typed name)

Enclosure (resume)

Figure 20-5. Sample master application letter that you could prepare in the future when seeking a mid-level job.

```
                            (YOUR NAME)
                (Address where you can be reached)
        (Telephone number where you can be reached during the job search)


EMPLOYMENT OBJECTIVE:  (Individualize, according to job applied for, or
                       position desired in selected organizations where you'll inquire.)

Examples:   Supervision or management of information functions or departments.
            Human resources training and development.
            Administrative assistant (in a preferred department).


WORK EXPERIENCE

1989-       Purchasing Agent, JKL, Inc., a manufacturing firm in the apparel
            industry.  Collect and analyze vendor data and make purchasing
            recommendations; meet with vendors, work with in-house personnel;
            establish and maintain database; participate with other managers
            on numerous projects.  Last performance rating: "organized,
            responsible, cooperative, money-and-time oriented, innovative,
            flexible."  (Note use of attributes.)

1986-'89    Telecommunications Supervisor, Exxell Corp., a mining and petroleum
            firm.  Supervised the retrieval, processing, and transmittal of
            information via computer and telecommunications.  Familiarity with
            information retrieval, word processing, spreadsheet, computer-
            billing, desktop publishing programs, and management functions.
            Performance-rating: "dependable, analytical, self-starter, crea-
            tive, good at motivating and managing staff."

1984-'86    Receiving Secretary-Bookkeeper, Real Estate Investments, a fin-
            ancial-service firm.  Handled calls and visitors; prepared escrow
            and related legal and real estate papers; kept accounts and
            records; filed; took dictation and transcribed.  Real estate
            broker's evaluation comments:  "conscientious, businesslike,
            poised, tactful, honest and loyal."

1982-'84    Instructor's Aide, Riverton Community College.  Provided tutorial
            assistance to students enrolled in business and office administra-
            tion programs; assisted instructors with curriculum development,
            media preparation, training and supervision, verifying accuracy
            of student papers; maintained files, equipment, and facilities.
            Instructors' recommendation:  "Get into training, teaching, or
            management--you have an aptitude for working with people, while
            at the same time you have a flare for maintaining records and
            systems."


EDUCATION

1987-'89    Refresher courses and seminars in office automation, accounting,
            management, purchasing, and human resource development.

1984        Associate of Arts (AA), Riverton Community College.  Dean's Honor
            Roll, four semesters (GPA, 3.6).

1982        High school diploma, Plainview, Texas.  Grade point average, 3.2.
            Among others, excelled in these classes:  accounting, business
            law, economics, information processing, and marketing.

REFERENCES:  Available upon request
```

Figure 20-6. Sample résumé that you might prepare in the future if seeking
a mid-level job requiring more than a high school diploma.

structions completely and accurately tell the people who make hiring decisions something about you. Like the résumé, this form contains personal data about your education and work history. Take your résumé with you when you apply in person to use as a guide.

Follow-Up Letter

Another job search document is the follow-up or thank-you letter. Besides demonstrating your courtesy, it's used to help ensure that you are not forgotten. Address the letter to the name of the person who interviewed you. (Get the full, correctly spelled name of this person during the interview.)

In the letter, repeat the date and time of the interview and the job for which you interviewed. Thank the interviewer for his or her time and effort in conducting the interview. Close the letter with a brief statement that reinforces your continuing desire to work for the firm and the benefits the company can derive from hiring you. (See Figure 20-7.)

FACING THE JOB INTERVIEW

If your application and/or inquiry documents pass the firm's screening procedures, you'll be invited to interview for the position. Thus one of your objectives is *selling*. Sell the interviewer on the idea that you are the employee he or she needs, that you can do the job, and that you'll bring to the job the skills and attributes the firm is looking for.

The Job Interview

When you get invited for a face-to-face interview, be aware of the factors interviewers are watching for. Interviewers generally make fast first impressions and judgments. They make these judgments on the bases of appearance, nonverbal *and* verbal communications, attitude, and behavior. Use the following questions and recommendations to ensure that you'll make a good impression:

- How will I look? Dress appropriately according to the type of job for which you're applying. For example, wear business dress for a business job—suit, shirt or blouse, polished shoes—and have clean hair and nails.

Date

(Inside address)
Specific person's name and title
Name of firm
Address of firm

Dear Mr./Mrs./Ms. (last name of addressee):

It was very nice of you to see me on (such-and-so date) in the middle of such a full schedule. I appreciated your comments about (name of firm) and (specific job title interviewed for). I hope I will be seriously considered as a candidate for the position we discussed, because I believe I have the necessary experience, incentive, and drive to do a great job for (name of firm).

The atmosphere in your offices, your firm's widespread reputation for quality (specific names of major products or services, if appropriate), and the obvious dedication of everyone I met there make me even more enthusiastic at the prospect of joining (name of firm and/or specific department).

Although I have had several other job offers (if true), and will be interviewing with (no.) more firms, your position is very important to me. I enjoyed our meeting and look forward to hearing from you in the near future. I can be reached until (one week from today), between 2 and 5 p.m., at (___) ___-___.

Very cordially yours,

(Your signature)

(Your typed name)

Figure 20-7. Sample "thank you" follow-up letter to a job interview.

Computerized Job Matching

Some personnel agencies offer a new wrinkle in a trend called computerized job matching. Job seekers in fields like management, education, and engineering have their résumés, salary, and other needs assembled in large computer banks. Then employers have instant access to lists of qualified job applicants.

Many corporations have automated personnel records. Still others are keeping computerized records on job candidates. One company, for instance, uses a computer to process the records of potential employees, or job applicants. They use the system to keep track of the job moves, achievements, and related data supplied by thousands and thousands of applicants that the firm has on file.

One firm even plans to track outstanding teenagers. This firm hopes to use its system to track teens who are recommended by their high school teachers as potential future employees.

Critics of the computerized job matching system, however, say you can't treat job applicants like pieces of inventory. They claim that computers can never provide the subtle nuances of experience and personality. The latter are what personnel managers look for when they interview job applicants in person.

Yet computerized processing can look for, record, and screen hard data as found on application forms and job applicants' typed résumés. The largest user of computers in employment is the government. In many states, job seekers who use public employment agencies are offered computerized job listings. Federal agencies also use computers to screen job applicants.

Source: Thomas J. Lueck, "Computerized Job Matching," *The New York Times,* August 5, 1982, p. D2.

- How will I speak? Rehearse, get someone to listen to you, to ensure that you use the language correctly and avoid slang.
- What attitudes will I exhibit? Avoid criticizing or blaming a former employer, supervisor, or colleagues. Demonstrate pleasantness, cooperation, and tact.
- How will I act? Can I portray confidence, maturity, responsibility, intelligence? Smile and make eye contact. Sit up straight and lean forward to show earnestness and sincerity. Respond to questions with complete and straightforward answers, without wandering all over or around the topic. Ask meaningful questions about the firm, the job, and your duties.

The Dual Purpose of the Job Interview

Has it occurred to you that the job interview is a two-way street? The employer or personnel director will of course be looking you over. But this conversational exchange also gives you, the job applicant, a chance to look over the company. As a result of the interview, and what you learn about the company and the working environment, you could decide that you'd never ever want to work there.

Incidentally, understanding that you're buying as well as selling should help you overcome some of the nervousness you'll otherwise feel. Look at the interview as a means not only of having someone else look you over but as a means of your looking over the firm. If you approach it with the right attitude, the interview is a two-way street.

Select Terms to Know

application letter	KASH	résumé
attributes	knowledge	skills
inquiry letter		

Review Questions

1. Why is conducting a self-assessment important before developing even a tentative career goal plan?

2. How does a career ladder differ from a career lattice?

3. Describe each of the job search papers successful job applicants usually prepare.

4. Describe job interview behaviors to elicit a positive response.

Thought and Discussion Questions

1. Express your opinion about why manufacturing and agricultural jobs are decreasing and information and service jobs are increasing.

2. Discuss careers that are increasing from now to the year 2000 (see Figure 20-1).

3. From what you know about yourself now, which career goal plan appeals most, the career ladder or the career lattice (see Figure 20-2)?

4. How can you bypass some of the lower rungs of the career ladder (of your choice) to jump onto the rungs at the midpoint? Discuss the relationship of education to various steps on the career ladder and what business is looking for (KASH). (See Figures 20-1 to 20-3.)

Projects

1. Conduct a self-assessment by responding to the items at the beginning of the chapter. Interpret the findings from this task by trying to match your own likes, dislikes, aptitudes, and attributes to the type of jobs that appear in Figures 20-1 and 20-3. Then record three to five jobs you think you might like to get. Explain why.

2. Collect a minimum of 10 classified help-wanted ads that match your job needs (as defined in project 1 above or in some other way). Besides the data found in each ad, get other data about the firms, using the yellow pages, prior knowledge, talking to parents and friend, etc. From all sources, look for and record data such as:

- The names and addresses of the firms advertising the jobs
- A contact person for each firm, such as a personnel director
- The telephone numbers for the contact people
- The reputation of the firm's major products or services, if known
- The qualifications required or preferred regarding skills and attributes

To record the above data, create a manual recording form or establish an electronic file. If you have access to a computer and a database software program, and know how to use them, open a document entitled DATABASE JBS (JBS stands for jobs). Write or format column headings with the above categories and more, as identified from group discussion and personal interest.

3. From the list of attributes (see Table 20-1), select only 5 work and 5 social/interpersonal attributes, a total of 10, that best describe you now. Then prioritize each list. (You can also use these descriptors when you prepare the job search documents in the activities that follow.)

4. Prepare one sample each of the application letter, the inquiry letter, the follow-up or thank-you letter, and a résumé. From project 2, select the firm (and the job it offers) which is the most appealing and address your letters to the contact person.

Incorporate the 5 to 10 attributes that best describe you (see project 3 above). Also use some of these 10 attributes, if possible and true, in describing your education and work history for the résumé.

For the résumé, make whatever *realistic* assumptions you like. That is, consider the job experience and education you will have completed at the time you're ready to initiate a formal job search. Enter this information on the résumé.

When you have completed the "sample" job search papers, print and share them with your classmates. Compare, discuss, analyze, and revise according to your classmates' reactions to your papers.

5. Participate in one or more mock job interviews. Play the roles of both interviewer and interviewee. To make the interview as realistic as possible, exchange the job search papers you prepared in Project 4 with your role-play partner.

As the interviewer, take the role of the contact person (addressee) listed on the interviewee's papers. As the interviewer, you represent the employing firm. (Ask your teacher for the list of questions interviewers often ask job applicants.) Follow the recommendations of the teacher for interviewing a job applicant.

As the interviewee, study the questions that job interviewers often ask (your teacher may be able to provide such a list). Be prepared to answer these questions as honestly and completely as possible while still being brief.

Case Study: Victims of Misleading Job Interviews

Incident 1: An advertising saleswoman says she was hired as sales manager for a new magazine. During the interview, she says she was promised the job of national advertising director. But before she started—and after she'd quit her previous job—she discovered that the company had also hired another person for the very same job. It seemed to the woman that she was expected to compete for the job with the other new hire.

Incident 2: Shortly after Ian Dowie, a former marketing vice president, began work, his company reorganized its office-products unit and placed another manager above Dowie. He was also passed over for other important jobs. Two years later he was fired.

In some incidents, like Dowie's, employees whose hopes have been crushed claim they were misled during the job interview.

A more common problem, say personnel specialists, is for applicants to skip over job descriptions. When this occurs it's *not* a question of the interviewer misleading the job applicant, but rather the applicant not knowing what to ask in order to clarify the nature of the job. As a result, the job applicant may leave the interview with a blurry, ill-defined, and idealistic rather than realistic picture of the job. By failing to ask the right questions, the applicant in a certain sense misleads himself or herself. "It's amazing," said one Connecticut management consultant, "how

much applicants take for granted and don't ask questions." Studies have shown, in fact, that job interviewees are more likely to ask about coffee breaks and sick leave time than asking: "What's this job about?"

Source: Larry Reibstein, *The Wall Street Journal,* June 10, 1987, p. 27.

1.   How can you avoid incidents like the above and still get the information you need to make a decision about a job and firm?

2.   How can you get the facts when the interviewer explains the job in a sketchy or confusing way?

3.   Especially when you're under pressure (to get a job), how can you ensure that you're looking at any job and firm realistically instead of idealistically?

4.   If you know you want to move up the career ladder (or over, as on a career lattice), how can you let the interviewer know you're ambitious without seeming to be too pushy?

Self-Insuring Your Career

The following article was written by Robert Half, a nationally recognized expert on career and job placement and chairman of Robert Half International Inc. Read the article and then respond to the discussion questions.

Young men and women forging careers in business have a great deal to think about. The future is unknown, the present chaotic. There are difficult choices to be made. It's nothing new; . . . jumping feet first into the world of business has always been as anxiety-provoking as it is exhilarating.

Naturally, I've thought a great deal about this during my almost 40 years in the employment field, but a new thought struck me not long ago. It has to do with "insuring" one's career.

It occurred to me that we pay a great deal of attention to insuring everything else in our lives—our homes, our automobiles, our health and lives—but we don't realize that we can—and should—insure our careers.

"Insure a career? Whom do I call, John Hancock, Metropolitan Life, Equitable, Prudential?"

No. They don't offer the sort of insurance I'm suggesting. The person to call is yourself. You become your own self-insurer.

From the moment a person enters the workplace, a process evolves in which that individual's daily actions and attitudes toward a career will determine future success. Success doesn't happen by chance. It comes to those who not only do a good job but also think about their business lives as a career. Once that thought takes hold, the "career insurance policy" has been written and coverage commences.

How do we insure a career? . . . .

First, look beyond whatever job you are currently doing (or plan to do). You're involved in a career, not just a job.

Be nice. That might sound simplistic, but it isn't. It's hard to hire people who aren't nice. It's hard to fire a nice person. Adopt the attitude that if you're going to bother getting up in the morning, you might as well make your life, and the lives of people around you, pleasant and productive.

Adopt a positive view of that old-fashioned and too often maligned concept of loyalty. It wasn't too long ago that loyalty to an employer, like patriotism to a country, was sneered at. . . . Fortunately, that's changing. Being loyal to an employer doesn't mean never seeking to better yourself elsewhere. It does mean giving your best effort as long as you're being paid by your company. It means not bad-mouthing your employer, and not abusing company facilities, and using company time to pursue activities unrelated to your job. . . .

Begin building your own personal "personnel file." Get in the habit of making notes of your business accomplishments. This should start when you're preparing your first résumé. . . .

Start your résumé early in your career, and update it continuously. This pays big dividends when seeking a raise, or when looking for a new and better job. It's an excellent form of self-insurance.

Sharpen your communication skills. Studies prove conclusively that there is a definite correlation between success and the ability to effectively communicate ideas to superiors, other employees, customers, and clients. . . .

Maintain an ongoing network of business contacts who can provide insurance for you when, and if, you need it. Establish a file-card system in which you note each new contact—name, address, phone number, and pertinent details. Be active in professional organizations. . . .

Keep contact with your network. . . . Make sure, however, that you don't turn it into a one-way street by calling and writing your contacts only when you need something. Reach out to do things for the people in your network. It's incredible how fast situations come full circle. . . .

Be visible. Volunteer. Write articles for your company's internal publications and for trade journals in your industry. Offer to speak to community and professional groups. Here is where sharpening your communications skills holds you in good stead. By being visible your network grows and you become known outside the confines of your daily employment.

Insure your current job (or the one you plan to get) by becoming almost indispensable. Be the person in your department or firm who knows the most about company operations. Prove yourself to be a prime problem-solver, even if it takes extra hours and effort. Your superiors will respect you more—and be less likely to fire you, even during times when your industry is in a downswing. . . .

DISCUSSION QUESTIONS

1. What do you think are the three most important ways to "insure" one's career?

2. Do you share the author's views about the importance of loyalty to an employer? Explain your answer.

3. Do you think that KASH (See Chapter 20, page 432) is a factor in self-insuring one's career success? Why or why not?

4. How can you begin almost immediately to write your own "career insurance policy"?

Source: Excerpted from Robert Half, "How to Insure the Success of Your Career," *Business Week Careers,* February 1987, pp. 36–38.

Glossary/Index

Absolute advantage when one nation or region can produce a good or service less expensively than another, 97–98

Accounting a system of principles and concepts used to record, classify, process, summarize, and interpret financial data, 189
financial, 198
managerial, 198

Accounting elements, 193–196
assets, 194–195
liabilities, 195
owner's equity, 195–196

Accounting equation assets = liabilities + owner's equity, 196

Accounting information, 20

Accounting period a specific time period (a month, quarter, or a year) during which transactions are recorded and then summarized, 197–198

Accounting system, 196–198
input of data into, 196–197
output of data from, 198
processing data through, 197–198

Accounts payable amount owed for goods and services bought on credit, 195

Accounts receivable money owed the business by customers, 194

Activity ratios show how often a business is turning its assets into cash, 207–208

Administrative law part of our legal system dealing with government control and/or regulation of businesses and individuals, 155–158
industry regulation, 155–157
social regulation, 157–158

Adobe company, 40–41

Advertising any paid form of nonpersonal presentation and promotion of ideas, goods, or services by an identified sponsor, 301
by direct mail, 311
in newspapers, magazines, and other print media, 310–311
on outdoor media, 311
on television and radio, 310
timing of, 309–310
in the yellow pages, 311

Advertising budget expenditures on media, promotions, and operating expenses, 306–307

Affirmative action plans positive steps to increase the hiring and promotion of minorities and other groups, such as females, 344

AFL-CIO (American Federation of Labor-Congress of Industrial Organizations), 32, 376

Agent (legal) a person or company authorized by a company to carry out business and enter into agreements on their behalf, 149

Agents (intermediaries) salespeople who represent a number of different companies that produce similar, but noncompeting, products, 324

Agricultural economy when the majority of the income in a society is earned from goods that come from the land, 24, 25
change to an industrial economy from, 30
first American entrepreneurs, 27
legislation concerning, 27–28
rapid expansion of, 28

Airline industry, 392

Aldus company, 40–41

Alhadeff, Victor, 16

American economy, growth of, 24–45
four eras of, 25–26
process of gradual change, 26–27
(*See also* Agricultural economy; Industrial economy; Information economy; Service economy)

Annual report, 199

Annuity investment income that is payable to a person at regular intervals over a period of time, 253

Antitrust anticompetitive business practice which abuses economic power, 154
laws regulating, 154–155

Apple Computers, 40

Application for employment a preprinted form which is completed by all persons interested in working for an organization, 349

Application form, job, 437, 440

Application letter briefly introduces you and is mailed to firms that are advertising existing job openings, 435
example of, 436

Application programs computer programs written for a particular situation, 416

Apprenticeship training new employees work as assistants to skilled workers for a specified period of time and complete supplementary classes related to the job, 354–355

Arbitration occurs when union and management

strikes and, 377–378
types of, 376
union representation, 376–377
Language as a barrier to trade, 108
Layoffs temporary separations of employees from an organization, 357–358
Leadership, 369–371
personal traits of, 369–370
situations and, 370–371
Lease gives temporary, partial control of real property, 148
Legal information, 20
Lever Brothers, 273
Leverage the use of borrowed money to purchase assets which in turn are used to make more money, 191
Levi Strauss, 286
Lewis, Reginald, 19
Liabilities economic resources obtained through borrowing, 194
current, 195
long-term, 195
Liability:
limited, 123
strict, 146–147
unlimited, 121, 122, 125
Liability risks financial losses that a firm might suffer if it is held responsible for property damages or injuries suffered by others, 241
insurance against, 250–252
for business premises, 250
costs of, 251–252
for goods and services, 250–251
malpractice, 251
Licensing, 99–100
Lichty Mfg., 400
Life cycle of a product the phases of introduction, growth, maturity, and decline, 270
declining phase, 271
growth phase, 270
introduction phase, 270
mature phase, 271
Life insurance pays a set amount to survivors in the event of death, 252
Likert, Rensis, 368–369
Limited liability, 123
Limited partner does not usually play a direct role in the management of the partnership and has a limited liability, 123
Line-and-staff organization adds specialists to a line organization, 176, 177
Line authority delegation of authority from top levels of management to middle managers to lower-level managers, 176
Line of credit a specific sum that a lender earmarks for a firm that may be drawn on as needed over a specified period of time, 228

Liquidity the measure of how quickly assets can be converted into cash, 192
Liquidity ratios used to tell the investor or financial manager the ability of the business to pay debts when they are due, 207
Lobbying any effort by a group to influence legislators and government administrators to pass laws and interpret them to the advantage of the group, 378
Lockheed Corporation, 153–154
Lockout occurs when management refuses to allow workers into a plant to work, 378
Logo (logotype) a distinctive design that depicts a firm's name, brand name, or a trademark, 283, 303
Long-term liabilities debts which will be paid over a number of years, 195
Long-term planning (*see* Strategic planning)
Loss the accidental decrease or total disappearance of value, 240
chance of (*see* Risk)

McDonald's, 34–35
McGregor, Douglas, 368
Mail-order promotions, 304
Maintenance any type of activity designed to keep an organization's resources in working condition or to put them back in such condition, 399
Making economic choices, 55–58
opportunity costs and, 55, 57
trade-offs and, 57–58
Malpractice insurance covers losses due to damages or injuries caused by the insured while performing professional services for clients, 251
Management the process of achieving organizational goals by working with people and other resources, 163–181
autocratic, 370–371
functions of (*see* Management functions)
levels of, 168–172
common features of, 170–172
first-line, 170
middle, 169–170
top, 169
lure of, 164
participative, 370–371
roles played by, 165–168
decision making, 167–168, 178–181
informational, 166–167
interpersonal, 165–166
style, 179
technology, change, and, 181
workstyle, 178
Management functions what managers do, 172–178
controlling, 177–178
directing, 176–177